The Law
and
Its Fulfillment

The Law
and
Its Fulfillment

A Pauline Theology of Law

Thomas R. Schreiner

Baker Books

A Division of Baker Book House Co
Grand Rapids, Michigan 49516

Published by Baker Books
a division of Baker Book House Company
P.O. Box 6287, Grand Rapids, Michigan 49516-6287

Printed in the United States of America

Library of Congress Cataloging-in-Publication Data

Schreiner, Thomas R.
    The law and its fulfillment : A Pauline theology of law / Thomas R. Schreiner
       p. cm.
    Includes bibliographical references and indexes.
    ISBN 0-8010-8353-2
    1. Law (Theology)—Biblical teaching. 2. Bible N.T. Epistles of Paul—
Theology. I. Title.
BS2655.L35S374 1993
241′.2′09015—dc20   93-3968

To my father (deceased 1982) and mother,
who have taught me so much about love

Contents

Abbreviations

1QM	Milḥāmāh (War Scroll)
2 Apoc. Bar.	Syriac *Apocalypse of Baruch*
ʾAboth	Mishnah Tractate ʾAboth
AJT	*American Journal of Theology*
ATR	*Anglican Theological Review*
AusBR	*Australian Biblical Review*
BBR	*Bulletin for Biblical Research*
BDF	F. Blass, A. Debrunner, and R. W. Funk. *A Greek Grammar of the NT*
Bib	*Biblica*
BJRL	*Bulletin of the John Rylands University Library of Manchester*
BR	*Biblical Research*
BSac	*Bibliotheca Sacra*
BZ	*Biblische Zeitschrift*
CBQ	*Catholic Biblical Quarterly*
CD	Cairo Genizah text of the *Damascus Document*, Qumran texts
CT	*Christianity Today*
EBC	Frank E. Gaebelein, gen. ed. *Expositor's Bible Commentary* (12 vols.)
ETL	*Ephemerides théologicae lovanienses*
EvQ	*Evangelical Quarterly*
EvT	*Evangelische Theologie*
ExpT	*Expository Times*
HeyJ	*Heythrop Journal*
HBT	*Horizons in Biblical Theology*
HR	*History of Religions*
HTR	*Harvard Theological Review*
Int	*Interpretation*
ITQ	*Irish Theological Quarterly*
JAAR	*Journal of the American Academy of Religion*
JBL	*Journal of Biblical Literature*
JEH	*Journal of Ecclesiastical History*
JETS	*Journal of the Evangelical Theological Society*
JSJ	*Journal for the Study of Judaism in the Persian, Hellenistic and Roman Period*
JSNT	*Journal for the Study of the New Testament*
JSOT	*Journal for the Study of the Old Testament*
J Th So Africa	*Journal of Theology for Southern Africa*
JTS	*Journal of Theological Studies*

Jub.	*Jubilees*
Judaica	*Judaica: Beiträge zum Verständnis*
KJV	King James Version of the Bible
LS	Louvain Studies
LW	J. Pelikan, ed. *Luther's Works* (1957)
LXX	Septuagint
Macc.	Maccabees (1–4)
MT	Masoretic Text
MTZ	*Münchener theologische Zeitschrift*
NIV	New International Version of the Bible
NovT	*Novum Testamentum*
NRSV	New Revised Standard Version of the Bible
NT	New Testament
NTS	*New Testament Studies*
OT	Old Testament
Pss. Sol.	Psalms of Solomon
RB	*Revue biblique*
ResQ	*Restoration Quarterly*
SBLSP	*Society of Biblical Literature Seminar Papers*
SE	Studia Evangelica I, II, III (= TU 73 [1959], 87 [1964], 88 [1964], etc.)
SEÅ	*Svensk exegetisk årsbok*
Sib. Or.	Sibylline Oracles
Sir.	Sirach
SJT	*Scottish Journal of Theology*
SR	*Studies in Religion/Sciences religieuses*
ST	*Studia theologica*
StudBib	Studia Biblica
T. Dan	Testament of Dan
T. Naph.	Testament of Naphtali
TBl	*Theologische Blätter*
TDNT	G. Kittel and G. Friedrich, eds. *Theological Dictionary of the New Testament*
TLZ	*Theologische Literaturzeitung*
TP	*Theologische und Philosophie*
TrinJ	*Trinity Journal*
TynBul	*Tyndale Bulletin*
TZ	*Theologische Zeitschrift*
VD	*Verbum domini*
WTJ	*Westminster Theological Journal*
Wisd. Sol.	Wisdom of Solomon
ZAW	*Zeitschrift für die alttestamentliche Wissenschaft*
ZNW	*Zeitschrift für die neutestamentliche Wissenschaft*
ZTK	*Zeitschrift für Theologie und Kirche*

Preface

I have been working on the issue of the Pauline theology of the law for more than ten years, and I never dreamed when I began that I would write a book on the subject. Now that I have finished it is difficult to release the book to the wider public. It is tempting to keep revising and revising until I am fully satisfied with the work. On the other hand, the day when I will perfectly grasp Paul's theology will not come in this world, and thus I will never "master" the subject. My understanding of the law in Paul has been deepened by interacting with other scholars, even (I should say especially) those with whom I disagree. I am still convinced that the Reformers understood Paul better than those who are espousing new approaches. Some may be tempted to discard my work upon reading this. I only ask that such readers would carefully consider my exegetical case for this conclusion without dismissing it out of hand.

I am grateful to my teaching assistants Jerry Wall and Ken Schonberg, who were of significant help in the writing of this work. Jerry Wall read the manuscript carefully and made numerous helpful suggestions that improved the work substantially. Ken Schonberg was of immense help in that he checked every biblical reference and the footnotes and compiled the bibliography. In addition, he spotted a number of errors in the manuscript that needed correction. Jim Weaver of Baker Book House was a constant encouragement, and I am thankful to Matthew Maloley for producing a clear and accurate manuscript. Of course, any errors that remain are my responsibility.

I would like to extend my thanks to Bethel Theological Seminary, which provided a sabbatical that made the completion of this work possible. My wife, Diane, has encouraged me in my work and reminded me that there is more to life than the writing of books. I have dedicated this work to my mother and father, who have taught me so much about love and have had such an immeasurable influence on my life.

Some of the material here has appeared previously in scholarly journals. In almost every case I have revised substantially what I wrote earlier, or I have referred the reader to those articles for a more detailed discussion. In some places I have used the exact wording from my previous articles, but no article appears here precisely as it did in the journals. I am grateful that the editors of the journals listed below granted me permission to include in this work some of the material I had written previously. The articles which I draw upon are as follows: "Is Perfect Obedience to the Law Possible? A Re-examination of Galatians 3:10," *The Journal of the Evangelical Theological Society* 27 (1984): 151–60; "Paul and Perfect Obedience to the Law: An Evaluation of the View of E. P. Sanders," *Westminster Theological Journal* 47 (1985): 245–78; "The Abolition and Fulfillment of the Law in Paul," *Journal for the Study of the New Testament* 35 (1989): 47–74; "'Works of Law' in Paul," *Novum Testamentum* 33 (1991): 214–44; "Israel's Failure to Attain Righteousness in Romans 9:30–10:3," *Trinity Journal* 12 (1991): 209–20; "Paul's View of the Law in Romans 10:4–5," forthcoming in *Westminster Theological Journal*; "Does Paul Teach Justification by Works? Another Look at Romans 2," forthcoming from the *Bulletin for Biblical Research*. The translations of the biblical text are my own.

Introduction

The Background to the Debate

Articles and books on Paul's view of the law continue to appear at an astonishing pace, and doubtless some would like to call a temporary halt so that we can catch our breath.[1] Nevertheless, the vast amount of effort being expended is defensible since Paul's theology of the law constitutes an essential part of his gospel, for we cannot grasp Pauline theology without explaining his understanding of the law and justification. If we want to understand Paul we cannot suspend judgment on his view of the law and leave it as a perpetual question mark in our thinking. Grasping Paul's theology in this area is essential for understanding his soteriology, the death of Jesus, Christian ethics, the relationship between Jews and Gentiles in the new community, and the continuity and discontinuity between the Testaments.

The flood of literature about the law in Paul bespeaks the complexity and difficulty of the topic, lending itself to a great diversity of interpretations. Hans Joachim Schoeps says the Pauline understanding of the law is "the most intricate doctrinal issue in his theology."[2] W. D. Davies correctly observes that one can fall into numerous pitfalls when reconstructing Paul's theology of law.[3] Paul's various statements concerning

---

1. For a survey of older literature see Otto Kuss, "Nomos bei Paulus," *MTZ* 17 (1966): 177–210. More recent literature is surveyed by Douglas J. Moo ("Paul and the Law in the Last Ten Years," *SJT* 40 [1987]: 287–307) and Dieter Zeller ("Zur neueren Diskussion über das Gesetz bei Paulus," *TP* 62 [1987] : 497–99); see also F. F. Bruce, "Paul and the Law in Recent Research," *Law and Religion* ed. Barnabas Lindars (Cambridge: James Clarke, 1988), 115–25. For a survey of law in OT scholarship see Stephen Westerholm, "Whence '*The* Torah' of Second Temple Judaism," *Law in Religious Communities in the Roman Period*, ed. Peter R. Richardson and Stephen Westerholm; Waterloo, Iowa: Wilfrid Laurier University Press, 1991), 19–43; Christopher J. H. Wright, "The Ethical Authority of the Old Testament: A Survey of Approaches," parts 1, 2, *TynBul* 43 (1992): 101–20, 203–31.

2. Hans Joachim Schoeps, *Paul: The Theology of the Apostle in the Light of Jewish Religious History* (Philadelphia: Westminster, 1959), 168.

3. "Paul and the Law: Reflections on Pitfalls in Interpretation," *Jewish and Pauline Studies* (Philadelphia: Fortress, 1984), 91–122.

the law have led scholars to suggest radically different interpretations of his theology of law. Indeed, some scholars have argued that Paul contradicted himself, concluding that any attempt to reconcile the various statements produces forced harmonization.

Not only is the Pauline theology of the law notoriously difficult to systematize, but recent scholarship has increasingly questioned the view of Paul's theology that has been mediated to us through Reformers, such as Martin Luther and John Calvin. This "new perspective" in Pauline studies has inevitably resulted in fresh analyses of Paul's theology which, if accepted, will revolutionize our understanding of Paul.[4]

In this book I want to ascertain Paul's view of the law by exploring the Pauline letters afresh. The influence of the new perspective has pushed this question to the forefront of New Testament scholarship. I do not intend, however, to provide an in-depth exposition of this new look in Pauline studies, but rather to reexamine some central Pauline texts and themes on the law. Our goal is to uncover the meaning of these texts, dialoguing along the way with alternative views. I will not limit my presentation of other views to those of the new perspective, although recent changes in Pauline studies illustrate the need for a reexamination of Paul's view of the law. I should emphasize again, though, that this book fundamentally aims to explain Paul's view of the law by investigating the meaning of the biblical text.[5]

In this introduction some of the significant contributions in recent scholarship will be touched on in order to sketch in the background. The summary should acquaint the reader with the current issues as we begin to explore the biblical text.

Luther and Calvin

The most profound interpreter of Paul's theology of grace in the early church[6] was undoubtedly Augustine, who explicated his understand-

---

4. The phrase *new perspective* is taken from an article by James D. G. Dunn. See note 28.

5. The most important texts for Paul's understanding of the law are contained in the letters that are accepted as authentic by virtually all scholars (Romans, 1 Corinthians, 2 Corinthians, Galatians, Philippians, 1 Thessalonians, and Philemon). I will occasionally refer to the other Pauline letters since I am persuaded that they are authentic as well. Nevertheless, since the bulk of the discussion on law is found in the undisputed letters, the issue of authenticity is not a crucial one in constructing Paul's theology of law.

6. For a brief survey on the place of the law in the early church see Richard N. Longenecker, "Three Ways of Understanding Relations between the Testaments: Historically and Today," in Gerald F. Hawthorne and Otto Betz, eds. *Tradition and Interpretation in the New Testament: Essays in Honor of E. Earle Ellis* (Grand Rapids: Eerdmans, 1987), 22–28; see also Wright, "Ethical Authority," 101–5.

ing in the debate with Pelagius.[7] For our purposes the Reformers' under-standing of Paul's theology of law is particularly significant, since the Reformers' conception of Paul has had a massive influence on biblical scholarship, and the new look in Pauline studies is, at heart, a counter to the Reformational view.

I will focus briefly on Luther and Calvin since they were the two most influential Reformers.[8] They agreed that no one can be justified by the works of the law, for no one keeps perfectly the law's demands.[9] Only flawless obedience justifies, and since all people sin, justification can-not be obtained through obeying the law. They also insisted that the "works of the law" are not limited to the ceremonial law.[10] When Paul asserted that no one stands justified by the "works of the law" he was speaking of the law as a whole, insisting that no one can be right in God's sight through obedience to the law.

Luther and Calvin agreed that legalism posed a great problem, both in Paul's day among the Jews and in their day among Roman Catho-lics.[11] They defined legalism as the belief that one could merit favor with God by doing good works, so that sufficient goodness would earn eternal life. Such a stance, according to both Luther and Calvin, was ultimately due to idolatry that prized the ability and goodness of human beings. Legalism has its origin in self-worship. If people are justified through their obedience to the law, then they merit praise, honor, and glory. Legalism, in other words, means that the glory goes to people rather than God.

The true gospel, however, teaches that all human beings are funda-mentally flawed by sin, and thus salvation is only available by relying on and trusting in God, who has sent Jesus Christ to atone for sins. God receives the glory and praise in this gospel because in his mercy he saves helpless sinners through the work of Christ on the cross. Even though no one can be justified by the law, it still has a role in God's plan. It has a convicting function in that it points out that we have fallen

---

7. See *Saint Augustine: Anti-Pelagian Writings* in *Nicene and Post-Nicene Fathers of the Christian Church*, vol. 5, edited by P. Schaff; repr. (Grand Rapids: Eerdmans, 1987).

8. See D. F. Wright, "The Ethical Use of the Old Testament in Luther and Calvin: A Compar-ison," *SJT* 36 (1983): 463–85; Wright, "Ethical Authority," 105–14. For a lucid historical survey of the role of law and gospel from Aquinas until the contemporary period see Donald G. Bloesch, *Freedom for Obedience: Evangelical Ethics in Contemporary Times* (San Francisco: Harper and Row, 1987), 106–25.

9. "Treatise on Christian Liberty," *LW* 2:317; *Institutes*, 2.7.3–5.

10. *LW* 26:122–23, 126–27, 131, 139–40, 253–60, 268; 27:219, 223–25, 256–57; *Calvin's Commentaries*, edited by D. W. Torrance and T. F. Torrance (Grand Rapids: Eerdmans, 1961), 8:78–79; 11:53–55.

11. *Institutes*, 3.14.1–17 and 3.15.1–7; *LW* 26:33, 124–27, 135–36, 140, 176, 266, 396, *passim*; 27:223–25.

short of God's standards.[12] It also has a prophetic function in that it points to the salvation of God provided in Jesus Christ. But any attempt to gain salvation by obeying the law compromises grace and introduces legalism.

A significant difference between Luther and Calvin lay in their understanding of the "third use of the law," that is, whether the moral law of the Old Testament is in force for the Christian today.[13] Luther's comments on the topic were somewhat ambiguous, but on the whole one receives the impression that the believer is freed entirely from the law of Moses, even the moral law.[14] The Old Testament law is binding only insofar as it agrees with the New Testament and mirrors natural law. Calvin maintained that the moral laws of the Old Testament are obligatory for the believer and asserted that this is the "principal use" of the law.[15] Thus, Calvin and Luther differed dramatically on the relevance of the Old Testament law for the life of the Christian. In Calvin's eyes the necessity of keeping the moral law does not compromise the message of grace, for keeping the moral law does not *earn* salvation but is a *response* to the grace received in Christ. In fact, Calvin believed that such obedience is one sign that a person is truly a Christian, for he believed that the grace given by God not only provides forgiveness of sins but also gives a new power to live a godly life.

The Continuing Influence of the Reformation

The theology of the law hammered out by the Reformers maintained its dominance in Protestant circles until the twentieth century, and it is still a common way of understanding Paul. The continuity between the Reformers and the present century is illustrated in the work of Rudolf Bultmann. Bultmann did not change the fundamental teaching of Luther on the law but reapplied that teaching to the contemporary situ-

---

12. "Treatise on Christian Liberty," *LW* 2:317; *Institutes*, 2.7.7,9.

13. The idea that the moral law is still binding for the church is probably present in Tertullian and definitely in Origen. See Longenecker, "Understanding Relations," 24, 26, 31n.

14. "How Christians Should Regard Moses," *LW* 35:161–74. See also W. Joest, *Gesetz und Freiheit. Das Problem des "Tertius usus Legis" bei Luther und die neutestamentliche Paränese,* 3d ed. (Göttingen: Vandenhoeck and Ruprecht, 1961), 133; Heinrich Bornkamm, *Luther and the Old Testament* (Philadelphia: Fortress, 1969), 124–49; Gerhard Ebeling, "On the Doctrine of the *Triplex usus Legis* in the Theology of the Reformers," *Word and Faith* (Philadelphia: Fortress, 1963), 62–63; P. D. L. Avis, "Moses and the Magistrate: A Study in the Rise of Protestant Legalism," *JEH* 26 (1975): 154–55. For a modern Lutheran analysis of the distinction between law and gospel in which the traditional Lutheran separation between the two is defended see W. Elert, *Law and Gospel* (Philadelphia: Fortress, 1967). Paul Althaus (*The Divine Command* [Philadelphia: Fortress, 1966]) is actually quite close to Calvin's understanding of the role of the law, but he prefers to use the word *command* rather than *law.*

15. *Institutes*, 2.7.12; see Avis, "Moses and the Magistrate," 163.

ation by means of existential philosophy.[16] According to Bultmann, the attempt to be justified by doing the law signifies the human striving to gain security through self-effort. The desire to obey the law, though it appears commendable, is actually an insidious way to try to gain recognition before God. This explains why, according to Bultmann, the very attempt to obey the law is sinful. The human desire to fulfil God's law stems from a motivation that longs for approval from people instead of God. The Pauline gospel declares that human security is only available through faith in Jesus Christ; self-striving and self-effort are ultimately false paths.

Bultmann, obviously, was not a carbon copy of Luther, but his own theology did not call into question the essence of Luther's teaching on justification. Indeed, it seemed to affirm it. Another stream of thought had entered the scholarly arena earlier in the twentieth century in the work of William Wrede and Albert Schweitzer. Wrede affirmed that justification by faith was not the central teaching in Paul's theology, but a polemical response to the Judaism of his day.[17] He supported such a view by pointing out that apart from letters in which Paul struggled with Jewish opponents (Romans, Galatians, and Philippians) the doctrine hardly appears. The real fulcrum of Paul's theology was his eschatological teaching on redemption, in which human beings are liberated from the evil powers of this age. Schweitzer's view was remarkably similar to Wrede's. Justification by faith was simply a "subsidiary crater" in Paul's theology, and eschatological redemption was the vital element in his thought.[18]

The work of Wrede, Schweitzer, and others revealed that the Reformational understanding of Paul's view of the law was beginning to be questioned, but most New Testament scholars continued to describe Paul's view of the law in a way that basically would have been acceptable to Luther and Calvin. Indeed, if Bultmann substantially articulated the view of Luther, then Charles E. B. Cranfield repristinated the work of Calvin. In 1964 Cranfield wrote a ground-breaking article on Paul's view of the law, and in his magisterial two-volume commentary on Romans he further dissects Paul's theology of law.[19] Cranfield's greatest

16. For Rudolf Bultmann's view of the law the following contributions are the most important: *Theology of the New Testament* (New York: Scribner's, 1951), 1:259–69; "Romans 7 and the Anthropology of Paul," *Existence and Faith* (New York: Meridian, 1960), 147–57; "Christ the End of the Law," *Essays Philosophical and Theological* (London: SCM, 1955), 36–60.

17. William Wrede, *Paulus,* 2d ed. (Tübingen: J. C. B. Mohr, 1907).

18. Albert Schweitzer, *The Mysticism of Paul the Apostle* (1931; repr., New York: Seabury, 1968).

19. Charles E. B. Cranfield, "St. Paul and the Law," *SJT* 17 (1964): 42–68, and *A Critical and Exegetical Commentary on the Epistle to the Romans,* 2 vols. (Edinburgh: T. and T. Clark, 1975, 1979), especially 845–62.

concern was that an unduly negative view of the law's role in the Christian life may result from misreading certain texts—especially in Galatians—on the law. Paul never taught, says Cranfield, that the law has been abolished with the coming of Christ. Of course, believers do not obey the ceremonial laws since their purpose has been fulfilled with the coming of Jesus Christ. Nevertheless, believers should still obey the moral law. Keeping the law does not signify living in the old era, but is the proper outcome of life in the Spirit. Paul's negative comments on the law do not signal the abolition of the law, according to Cranfield. What Paul has in mind when he speaks negatively of the law is not the law itself, but the legalism that distorts and perverts the law. Paul believes the law itself is good, and keeping the law is praiseworthy. He simply attacks the legalistic teaching that people can earn salvation by the law, a legalism which is contrary to the gospel Paul proclaims. Living without any law can easily lead to a vague sentimentality that may permit almost any course of action.

The Consensus Collapses

E. P. Sanders

The influence of Schweitzer and Wrede came to fruition in the monumental work *Paul and Palestinian Judaism,* published by E. P. Sanders in 1977.[20] The impact of Sanders' work has led to the collapse of the Reformational consensus regarding the Pauline view of the law. Sanders agrees with Schweitzer that justification by faith cannot be accepted as the center of Paul's theology. Participation in Christ is a better metaphor for describing Pauline theology, although Sanders hesitates to use the word *center* in analyzing Pauline theology. Such terms as *reconciliation*, *redemption*, *sanctification*, and *justification* were simply alternate ways to describe the believers' union with Christ. To exalt any of these terms as the center of Pauline theology confuses a part for the whole.

The distinctive contribution of Sanders in *Paul and Palestinian Judaism*, however, lies not in his view of Paul but in his explanation of Palestinian Judaism. He contends that the long-entrenched conception of Palestinian Judaism as a legalistic religion is mistaken. The idea that the Judaism of Paul's day taught that one could earn salvation by keeping the law, says Sanders, simply cannot be defended from the Jewish literature of the Second Temple Period. The Judaism of Paul's day is more

20. E. P. Sanders, *Paul and Palestinian Judaism: A Comparison of Patterns of Religion* (Philadelphia: Fortress, 1977).

aptly described as a form of "covenantal nomism." One did not enter into the covenant by performing good works but by God's grace. When God entered into covenant with his people, he mercifully forgave all their sins. He did not demand a certain level of attainment before entering into relationship with them.

Nor is it true, Sanders asserts, that one had to obey the law perfectly in order to be saved. The covenantal arrangement God had instituted provided a means of forgiveness via the sacrificial system for those who sinned. One's relationship with God would be severed only if one committed apostasy by abandoning the God of Israel altogether. Thus, the idea that one had to obey the law 51 percent of the time in order to be saved in Judaism is a myth. The Jews did not weigh their good works, calculating that salvation would be gained if the good works outweighed the bad. Palestinian Judaism was a gracious religion in which forgiveness of sins was available.

What then was the place of the law in Judaism? The law was obeyed as a *response* to God's gracious and redeeming work. People maintained their position in the covenant by obeying the law, but such obedience was never a way of earning or meriting salvation. God graciously saved his people, and they should respond to his grace in grateful and humble obedience. The subsuming of law under the covenant explains why Sanders selects the term *covenantal nomism*. Christian scholars have often made the mistake, Sanders claims, of separating or abstracting the law from the covenant in Judaism and then proclaiming that Judaism was legalistic. But, Sanders says, we need to understand that the detailed regulations found in the Mishnah all assume a covenantal context. It is not legalistic to specify precisely what would please God in particular situations. It would only be legalistic if obedience to these regulations were necessary to merit salvation, but the Rabbis never taught this. Obedience to detailed regulations was a way of showing thanks to the God who had graciously included them in his covenantal mercies.

When the Rabbis tried to explain why God elected Israel they gave three answers: (1) for God's own name's sake; (2) because of the merit of the fathers, and (3) because Israel chose to obey Torah and the other nations refused to submit to it. One might read a merit theology into these answers, but Sanders cautions against doing so because Jewish thinkers were not interested in formulating a systematic theology. They were unconcerned about statements that would appear contradictory. Moreover, the Rabbis attempted to answer the question of why God elected Israel because they did not want God to appear arbitrary. They were not smuggling in a merit theology in these discussions, but were trying to show that God was not capricious.

Sanders' analysis of Judaism has had a massive impact on Pauline studies, to which we shall return shortly. His work, as he freely acknowledges, was anticipated by earlier scholars such as George Foote Moore,[21] Claude Montefiore,[22] and Hans Joachim Schoeps.[23] These previous works were not ignored altogether by scholarship, but they did not have the same impact as Sanders'. Both Montefiore and Schoeps, for example, argued that Paul failed to understand the importance of covenant in Jewish thinking because he had been influenced by Hellenistic rather than Palestinian Judaism.[24] Sanders agrees with them in viewing Judaism as a religion of grace and in seeing the centrality of the covenant. But Sanders does not make their mistake of rigidly separating Palestinian from Hellenistic Judaism. Martin Hengel's massive work on Hellenistic Judaism has demonstrated that a neat distinction between the two cannot be maintained since Hellenism also penetrated and affected Palestinian Judaism in significant ways.[25]

How did Sanders' reevaluation of Judaism affect his understanding of Paul's view of the law? In his second book, *Paul, the Law, and the Jewish People*, he amplifies, supplements, and corrects some of his initial observations in *Paul and Palestinian Judaism*.[26] He does not, however, retract his views on Palestinian Judaism. He continues to assert that it was not legalistic. Sanders maintains that Paul did not present a unified and systematic explanation of the law in his letters. This lack of unity is due to the individual situations Paul confronted in his letters, causing him to respond to the various situations in different ways. Nevertheless, basic convictions underlie Paul's statements on the law. Paul did not reject the law, according to Sanders, because no one could obey it perfectly, or because devotion to the law led to legalism. Paul rejected the law because he believed that salvation was now available only through Christ. And since people could only be saved through Christ, it follows that the law should not be made the entrance requirement for salvation. Thus, Paul did not reject the law because it had any intrinsic defect. He rejected the law because he believed that salvation only comes through

21. George Foote Moore, "Christian Writers on Judaism," *HTR* 14 (1921): 197–254.

22. Claude G. Montefiore, *Judaism and St. Paul* (London: Max Goschen, 1914).

23. Schoeps, *Paul*. See note 2.

24. For an excellent survey of Jewish scholarship on Paul see Donald A. Hagner, "Paul in Modern Jewish Thought," in Donald A. Hagner and M. J. Harris, eds., *Pauline Studies: Essays presented to Professor F. F. Bruce on His Seventieth Birthday* (Grand Rapids: Eerdmans, 1980), 143–65.

25. Martin Hengel, *Judaism and Hellenism: Studies in Their Encounter in Palestine during the Early Hellenistic Period*, 2 vols. (Philadelphia: Fortress, 1974).

26. E. P. Sanders, *Paul, the Law, and the Jewish People* (Philadelphia: Fortress, 1983).

Christ. Sanders represents Paul as arguing from "solution to plight." Paul first came to believe that redemption is through Christ alone; then he reflexively concluded that the law is not the way of salvation. Paul did not begin, in other words, by seeing a great problem with the law due to human disobedience or legalism and then find Christ to be the answer to the human dilemma. He began by presupposing that Christ offers the only way to be saved and reasoned back that, therefore, the law cannot be the way to salvation.

The idea that the law was not an entrance requirement for salvation was appealing to Paul because this facilitated the inclusion of the Gentiles into the people of God. Gentiles became part of the people of God without being required to observe the elements of the Jewish law that divided Jews from Gentiles, such as circumcision, food laws, and observance of the sabbath. Nevertheless, after the Gentiles were within the new community, says Sanders, Paul required that they observe the law. The law he wanted them to keep does not include such cultural practices as circumcision and food laws. Indeed, the law Paul wanted Gentile converts to keep seems remarkably close to what traditionally has been called the *moral law*. Nonetheless, Sanders claims that such a distinction cannot be defended, for Paul did not reflect in a systematic way what he had in mind when he enjoined his converts to observe the law.

The lack of consistency is particularly evident, according to Sanders, in the ultimate purpose of the law. Sometimes Paul argued that the purpose of the law is to *lead* to sin, while in Romans 7 he concluded that sin subverted God's purpose for the law by effecting a result God did not want. The inconsistency in Paul's thought here, says Sanders, should not blind us to the conviction that undergirded his discussion of the purpose of the law. Paul maintained that people could not be saved by the law, but only through faith in Christ.

Heikki Räisänen

Heikki Räisänen's book *Paul and the Law* is significantly influenced by Sanders' paradigm for understanding Judaism.[27] Räisänen agrees that Judaism was not legalistic and that Christian scholarship that proceeds on such an assumption is seriously mistaken. But Räisänen takes a step beyond Sanders by arguing that Paul's view of the law is plagued throughout by inconsistencies and contradictions.

What are some of these contradictions?

27. Heikki Räisänen, *Paul and the Law* (Philadelphia: Fortress, 1983).

First, Paul does not use the word *law* (νόμος, *nomos*) consistently. In some places it refers to the entire law, while in others it is limited to the moral law. Such a divergence in usage paved the way for inconsistency in the Pauline theology of the law.

Second, in some texts Paul claims that the law is abolished and no longer has any function in the life of Christians (Rom. 7:1–6; 2 Cor. 3; Gal. 3), so that Christians are free from the prescriptions of the law. Yet in other texts he establishes the law and urges Christians to fulfil and obey it (Rom. 8:4; 13:8–10; 1 Cor. 7:19; Gal. 5:14)! It is logically fallacious, says Räisänen, for Paul to assert that the law is no longer binding on Christians and then say elsewhere that Christians should obey its commandments.

Third, Paul argues in a number of texts that no one can obey the law perfectly (for example, Rom. 1:18–3:20; Gal. 3:10), that all fall short of doing what the law commands. And yet he maintains in other places that even non-Christian Gentiles have the ability to obey the law (Rom. 2:14–15, 26–27). It is contradictory to say no one can fulfil the law (Rom. 7), and then turn around and say that even some non-Christians keep it. Moreover, Paul also affirms that Christians actually keep the law (Rom. 8:4; 13:8–10; Gal. 5:14), but even though he says this, such letters as 1 Corinthians demonstrate that his congregations did not do a very good job of obeying the law. Paul seems to be guilty of the most blatant kind of partisanship here, for he accuses his Jewish opponents of failure to obey the law and claims that Christians actually keep the commandments. However, no evidence implies that Christians observed the law any better than Paul's Jewish adversaries.

Fourth, Paul's explanations of the origin of the law and its relationship to sin are full of problems. He usually says that the law came from God, but in one emotional passage he even denies this (Gal. 3:19) and claims that the law actually originated with angels. Paul also could not decide why God gave the law. In one place he says God's intention in giving the law was to lead to life (Rom. 7:10), but then in other passages he argues that God's actual intention was to bring about sin (Rom. 5:20; Gal. 3:19). If God intended to bring about life through the law, one wonders why he was not wise enough to foresee the problem with giving a law for an unattainable end. And if God gave the law to produce more sin, he seems to be rather cynical. Moreover, Romans 7:7–11 suggests that the law causes people to sin, whereas Romans 5:20 implies that sin existed before there was a law. Obviously both of these statements cannot be true, says Räisänen. Did the law cause sin to exist in the first place, or did it provoke more sinning?

Räisänen also thinks that Paul did not consistently explain whether the law makes sin known, defines sin, or causes sin. In Romans 3:20 it seems that the law makes sin known, while in Romans 4:15 and 5:13 the law defines sin. Even more surprising, in Romans 5:20; 7:5, 7–11; 1 Corinthians 15:56, and Galatians 3:19 the law is said to produce sin. Räisänen sees a remarkable lack of clarity here regarding the precise relationship between the law and sin. Indeed, in Romans 5:13 Paul says that if there is no law, then people are not held accountable for sin since "sin is not taken into account when there is no law." But this is baldly contradicted by Romans 2:12, where Paul says that "all who sin apart from the law will also perish apart from the law." If people who sin without the law perish because of sin, then it follows that they are *held accountable for sins committed even though there was no law*. But this contradicts Romans 5:13, which says that sin is not charged to a person if there is no law. Apparently, Paul forgot what he wrote in Romans 2:12 by the time he wrote Romans 5:13.

Fifth, Paul distorts Jewish soteriology by describing it as legalistic, while he portrays his own theology as gracious. Christians of subsequent generations have followed Paul in drawing this same unfortunate conclusion.

Räisänen speculates that Paul's problem with the law was due to a desire to uphold the divine authority of the law, while at the same time he did not want all of the law imposed upon Gentiles. The problem, says Räisänen, is that it is impossible to assert that the law is divinely inspired and then proceed to argue that Gentiles do not have to keep it. Räisänen believes we can applaud Paul's motivation, which was to include the Gentiles in the people of God without requiring them to obey the Old Testament law. Nevertheless, we must jettison the tortuous and logically flawed reasoning Paul used to support the inclusion of the Gentiles. As modern people we can easily accept, says Räisänen, that many of the Old Testament laws were not divinely inspired. Paul, because of his Jewish background and place in history, could not rid himself of the idea that the Old Testament law was given by God.

Räisänen also suspects that Paul's own reaction to the law was due to the psychological crisis that led to his conversion. He concedes that any theory about Paul's psychological state is tentative but suggests that Paul probably viewed his life under the law as a form of slavery, contrasting it with the freedom and joy that became his upon conversion. Paul's theological reflection upon the law is a form of rationalization for his own conversion and the inclusion of Gentiles into the people of God apart from the law.

James D. G. Dunn

The work of Sanders and Räisänen has stimulated a number of responses, one of the most interesting from James D. G. Dunn.[28] Dunn believes that Sanders has demonstrated conclusively that the Judaism of Paul's day was not legalistic, but he protests that Sanders and Räisänen err in portraying Paul as arbitrary, idiosyncratic, and contradictory in his theology of law and justification. Dunn believes they have done a great service to scholarship by removing the blinders of the Reformation and the myth of Jewish legalism from our interpretation of Paul, but Sanders does not take advantage of his own conclusions and see clearly the real issues in Paul.

Dunn sets forth his own view in some major articles and has worked it out thoroughly in his excellent two-volume commentary on Romans. While he agrees with Sanders' thesis that Judaism was not legalistic, Dunn tries to demonstrate that Paul never assumed such, nor did he ever criticize it for being so. This does not mean Paul saw no problems with Judaism at all. Dunn rejects Sanders' claim that the main weakness of Judaism in Paul's eyes was that it was not Christianity, for it is precisely at this point that Sanders' view of Paul is too idiosyncratic and arbitrary.

The flaw in Judaism that stimulated Paul to criticize it was not legalism but nationalism. The Jews had limited the people of God so that only those who joined the Jewish people were members of the people of God. Gentiles could join God's people only if they submitted to circumcision, observed the sabbath, and practiced Jewish food and purity laws. Circumcision, purity laws, and sabbath observance were precisely what distinguished Jews from Gentiles in the Greco-Roman world. Jews, by insisting that Gentiles observe these laws, exalted Jewish nationalism and ethnicity above all else. Paul broke with the Jews because he disagreed with such an exclusive definition of the people of God. He wanted all who put their faith in Jesus as Messiah to be included in the people of God and did not make the observance of Jewish rituals a central issue. Paul dismissed circumcision and other practices not because they were *rituals*. After all, he imposed baptism and the Lord's Supper. Paul resisted the nationalistic and exclusive impulse that lay behind the imposition of these rituals.

Dunn, then, contends that Pauline theology should be reconceived as a result of Sanders' reinterpretation of Palestinian Judaism. The Reformation view of Paul should be discarded, for Paul criticized his Jewish

28. Note the following works by James D. G. Dunn: "The New Perspective on Paul," *BJRL* 65 (1983): 95–122; "Works of the Law and the Curse of the Law (Galatians 3.10–14)," *NTS* 31 (1985): 523–42; *Romans*, 2 vols. (Dallas: Word, 1988), and *Jesus, Paul, and the Law: Studies in Mark and Galatians* (Louisville: Westminster, 1990).

opponents for reasons other than their legalism; also, he did not claim that no one could keep the law. Paul directed his polemic against the exclusive spirit that infected Judaism, an exclusivity demanding that Gentiles adhere to Jewish nationalistic practices in order to become part of the people of God.

Lloyd Gaston and John G. Gager

The rethinking of Pauline theology as it relates to Judaism has been carried out most radically by Lloyd Gaston[29] and John G. Gager.[30] These two scholars substantially agree with one another, and Gager admits his dependence upon Gaston. They both deplore the anti-Semitism and anti-Judaism that have been so influential in Christian theology. But they hold a distinctive understanding of Paul's stance toward Judaism. The Pauline assertion that salvation does not come through the law relates to the Gentiles—not to the Jews. Gentiles were not in covenant with the God of Israel, and the law given to Israel could never save them. Indeed, the law only served to condemn, kill, and curse Gentiles, and thus it would be folly for them to attempt to be saved by the law.

On the other hand, Paul never says that Jews are under a curse because of the law, or that they must obey the law perfectly to be saved, or that they are plagued with legalism. After all, Paul knew that Judaism was a gracious religion of covenantal nomism in which transgressions of the law could be forgiven through the sacrificial cultus. Paul does not speak negatively of the relationship of the Jews to the law. Only Gentiles are "under the law" and enslaved to the elements of the world. Since the Jews were in covenant with God, the law did not kill but was a means of expressing their love for God. The negative statements Paul makes about the law apply only to Gentiles since they were not in a covenantal relationship with God. Therefore, the law provoked sin, produced death, and led to slavery.

This does not mean, say Gaston and Gager, that Paul had no criticisms for the Jews of his day. The Jews should recognize that Jesus has come specifically to liberate the Gentiles from the curse of the law. Gentiles, unlike the Jews, should not be required to live by all the standards contained in the Torah, and Paul faulted those Jews who wanted to impose the law on Gentiles. The central problem of some Jews in Paul's day, then, was exclusivism—an exclusivism that, in effect, demanded Gentiles to become Jews to be part of the people of God.

29. Lloyd Gaston, *Paul and the Torah* (Vancouver: University of British Columbia Press, 1987).
30. John G. Gager, *The Origins of Anti-Semitism: Attitudes Toward Judaism in Pagan and Christian Antiquity* (New York: Oxford University Press, 1983).

The Pauline soteriology explained that Jews and Gentiles were saved in different ways. Jews were saved by being faithful to their covenant and revelation, while Gentiles were saved through the faithfulness of Jesus Christ. Jews mistakenly insisted that Gentiles must keep the law, for Jesus came to save Gentiles from the law. Similarly, Paul did not believe that Jews must put their faith in Jesus as Messiah to be saved, for Jews were saved by the gracious covenant God had made with Israel. In other words, Paul held to a two-covenant approach in which Jews and Gentiles were saved according to different covenants.

If Gaston and Gager are right, Paul does not criticize Judaism for its legalism or failure to obey the law. Christian scholars have read these criticisms into Paul's letters because they have failed to see that Paul addressed his letters to Gentiles. Paul insisted that Gentiles do not need to submit to the law of Moses for salvation and that Jesus is the Messiah for the Gentiles. The recognition that Paul nowhere criticized Judaism for its adherence to the law or compelled Jews to believe in Jesus as the Messiah, according to Gaston and Gager, will liberate us from the flawed picture of Judaism transmitted through the centuries. Indeed, such a theology contributed to the holocaust, and thus clear thinking on this issue is of the utmost importance.[31]

Developmental View

A dramatically different way of conceiving of the Pauline theology of the law was proposed at the same time the shock waves from Sanders' thesis were hitting Pauline studies. Hans Hübner and John W. Drane advance a developmental schema for understanding Paul's diverse statements on the law.[32] First, I shall sketch Hübner's view. In reaction against the Judaizing opponents in Galatia, Paul jettisoned the law altogether. Indeed, he went so far as to say that the law was given by demons (Gal. 3:19–20) and contended that it played no role in a Christian's life. Even the apparently positive comment about fulfilling the law in Galatians 5:14 should be interpreted ironically. Later, according to Hübner, Paul discovered that James interpreted the substance of the Council of Jerusalem differently, and that James thought Paul's letter to the Galatians unsatisfactorily expressed the gospel of Christ. Paul desired to maintain good relations with James since he thought his work would be in vain without James' approval (Gal. 2:2), and accordingly he rethought

31. This book will not specifically respond to Gaston and Gager. For a convincing critique see Frank Thielman, *From Plight to Solution: A Jewish Framework for Understanding Paul's View of the Law in Galatians and Romans* (Leiden: Brill, 1989), 123–32.

32. Hans Hübner, *Law in Paul's Thought* (Edinburgh: T. and T. Clark, 1984); John W. Drane, *Paul, Libertine or Legalist? A Study of the Theology of the Major Pauline Epistles* (London: SPCK, 1975).

his theology of law in Romans. In Romans he no longer casts the law in the negative tones which dominated Galatians. The law is not completely abolished, and it even has a positive role in the life of believers (Rom. 13:8–10). Indeed, Paul can even say some positive things about circumcision (Rom. 3:1 and 4:9–12). Instead of arguing for the total abolition of the law, Paul says in Romans that the misuse of the law has been set aside with the coming of Christ.

John Drane's position parallels Hübner's, though he does not speculate about James' role in the process of Pauline development. Drane also thinks that Paul, in response to the legalists in Galatia, trumpeted in Galatians the believers' freedom from the law. The law, according to Paul, should play no role in Christian living, and the Holy Spirit alone suffices for Christian ethics. However, Paul's opponents in 1 Corinthians, according to Drane, stimulated him to rethink his position, for they took up the very theology of freedom Paul articulated in Galatians to defend their licentious lifestyles. Paul responded in 1 Corinthians, says Drane, by becoming a legalist. Here he circumscribes the Christian life with a number of rules and regulations. However, in 2 Corinthians Paul was on the road to a more balanced and mature view of the relationship between libertinism and legalism, and the mature statement of his views reached its conclusion in Romans. In Romans Paul retracted the legalism that would define the Christian life as life under the law, but he also sees a fulfillment of the law by those who live according to the Spirit. Drane's understanding of the law fits nicely into a Hegelian schema of thesis, antithesis, and synthesis. The thesis of complete Christian liberty was set forth in Galatians. The antithesis to such libertinism was crafted in 1 Corinthians in response to the excesses of the Corinthian church. Unfortunately, Paul overreacted in 1 Corinthians and had become a legalist. The balanced and mature position—the synthesis—between Galatians and 1 Corinthians was expressed in Romans. Here Paul avoided both the libertinism of Galatians and the legalism of 1 Corinthians. According to Romans, believers are not under the law and legalism is excluded, but this does not amount to the libertinism of Galatians, for believers are to obey the law by the power of the Holy Spirit.

Reactions to the New Perspective

The rethinking of the Pauline theology of the law has provoked some responses that find some validity in the older views of the Reformation. Stephen Westerholm, in a beautifully written work, argues that Luther was substantially correct.[33] Westerholm says that Paul regarded law and

33. Stephen Westerholm, *Israel's Law and the Church's Faith: Paul and His Recent Interpreters* (Grand Rapids: Eerdmans, 1988).

gospel as fundamentally opposed to one another. Salvation, Paul contended, could only come through faith in Christ, not by obeying the law. The reason that salvation cannot be obtained through the law is that no one is able to obey the law perfectly.[34] The law and the new covenant virtually present two different ways of salvation, and Paul insisted that salvation was only attainable through Christ, not observance of the law.

The rehabilitation of Luther shows up in Westerholm's view of the ongoing role of the law for the Christian. He stresses that the believer is liberated entirely from the Old Testament law. The Spirit plays a central role in Pauline ethics, and the Old Testament law is not binding for believers. Indeed, to construe Pauline ethics in terms of the Old Testament law distorts the fundamental character of the Pauline gospel, according to Westerholm, for the genius of Paul was displayed in his claim that the Christian life was free and Spirit directed. The influence of Luther is unmistakable in Westerholm's adamant rejection of the third use of the law.

Nevertheless, Westerholm departs from Luther on a very significant point. He has been affected by Sanders to the extent that he does not detect legalism in the Judaism to which Paul responds. It seems that Luther did, according to Westerholm, fall prey to the mistake of reading the legalism of Roman Catholicism into the theology of Paul's Jewish opponents. Westerholm stresses that Paul differed from the Judaism of his day in rejecting the law as a way of salvation. Christ's coming has set aside the way of law. The claim that Judaism was fundamentally a legalistic religion, however, can claim no solid basis in the Pauline text.

Brice Martin's dissertation also reaches back to the Reformation for an understanding of Paul.[35] Martin is probably closest to Calvin for he, unlike Westerholm, thinks that the moral commands of the Old Testament law are still normative. He agrees that the law cannot provide salvation because no one can obey it perfectly. And perhaps, most significantly, he is convinced, despite the work of Sanders, that Paul does oppose Jewish legalism. In other words, Martin concludes that the thesis of Sanders is neither proven nor persuasive.

Frank Thielman in his dissertation takes another course.[36] He sees no firm evidence that Paul opposes any kind of legalism and, therefore,

---

34. It should be noted that on this latter point Westerholm agrees with Andrea van Dülmen and Ulrich Wilckens. See van Dülmen, *Die Theologie des Gesetzes bei Paulus* (Stuttgart: Katholisches Bibelwerk, 1968), *passim*; Wilckens, "Was heisst bei Paulus: 'Aus Werken des Gesetzes wird kein Mensch gerecht'?" *Rechtfertigung als Freiheit: Paulusstudien* (Neukirchen: Neukirchener Verlag, 1974), 77–109.

35. Brice L. Martin, *Christ and the Law in Paul* (Leiden: Brill, 1989).

36. Thielman, *From Plight to Solution.*

seems to be influenced by Sanders. Nonetheless, the major thesis of his book contends that Sanders fundamentally errs in organizing Paul's reasoning from solution to plight. Thielman draws on the Old Testament, the Second Temple Period literature of Judaism, and the Pauline letters to find a clear pattern of plight to solution. Paul did not reason reflexively that Christ provides the solution to humanity's inability to obey the law. Rather, Jewish literature long before Paul revealed that human beings could not obey the law. If Thielman is correct, then Paul would quite naturally contend that the law could not save because no one could obey it. The plight that confronted Paul and his ancestors was human inability to carry out the commands of the law.

Thielman also sympathizes with Calvin's idea that the moral norms of the law still obligate Christians. His defense of this idea, however, is distinctive. He interprets Paul's negative statements on the law as saying that Christ is the end of the *curse* of the law. The coming of Christ does not abolish the law in every sense; Christ brings to an end the curse of the law, which hung over people because of their disobedience.

A work that reached me after I finished writing this discussion is by Timo Laato, titled *Paulus und das Judentum*.[37] He acknowledges that Sanders rightly censures the caricature of a grossly legalistic Judaism. The grace of God was a constituent part of Jewish soteriology. Nonetheless, he criticizes Sanders for failing to see that Paul differed from Judaism in his doctrine of anthropology. Second temple Judaism offered an optimistic estimate of human ability, believing that people could keep God's commandments by exercising their free will. This led, says Laato, to a synergistic conception of soteriology in Judaism. Salvation was by God's grace and the keeping of the law. Paul, says Laato, rejected the synergistic theology of Judaism. He believed people have no ability to keep the law, so the exclusive hope for salvation is God's grace. Even faith is a gift from God, not something produced through exercising free will. According to Laato, Paul identified Judaism as legalistic because of its synergism. In contrast, Paul was a monergist: Any human action that pleased God was produced by God's grace alone.

The Role of the Law in Theology

Most New Testament scholars do not attempt to explain the Pauline theology of law in its relationship to the rest of Scripture and to systematic theology, so two recent attempts to do just that should be noted. The

37. Timo Laato, *Paulus und das Judentum: Anthropologische Erwägungen* (Åbo: Åbo Academy Press, 1991).

work of Daniel P. Fuller and the arguments of Christian reconstructionists both challenge some convictions of those who attempt to explain
what all of Scripture says about the law. Fuller's understanding of the
relationship between the law and gospel in Paul corresponds in many
respects to Cranfield's.[38] Like Cranfield, he asserts that the law has not
passed away in Paul's theology. The law continues to function as the
will of God, and believers should keep the moral law through the power
of the Holy Spirit. Fuller is also persuaded that any statements in Paul
that appear to teach the abolition of the law need to be interpreted differently. For instance, the deprecatory statements about the law in Galatians refer to legalism, which distorts the true meaning of the law, while
in Romans 10:4 the sense of the text is that Christ is the *goal* of the law,
not that he ends the law.

Indeed, says Fuller, the relationship between gospel and law in both
Testaments has a far greater continuity than is recognized by either covenant theology or dispensationalism. The former teaches that the
Mosaic law had a different function in the divine economy as a covenant
of works, while the latter often teaches that the law has been abolished
entirely. Fuller sees a significant area of agreement between covenant
theologians and dispensationalists in their conviction that the Mosaic
covenant has a different nature from the covenant with Abraham and
the new covenant Paul proclaims. Fuller says both dispensational and
covenant theology understand the Mosaic covenant to be based, to some
extent, on earning merit by good works. But such an interpretation of the
Mosaic covenant destroys the unity of Scripture. One divine covenant
runs throughout Scripture. In this covenant salvation is always by grace,
but good works are also necessary for justification. An underlying continuity informs the whole of Scripture in its portrayal of gospel and law.
People cannot be saved by the good things they do for God. Legalists
make the mistake of thinking that they can impress and bribe God with
their good works. Those who have experienced grace, on the other hand,
do not attempt to work for God; they let God work for them. In this way
God gets the praise and glory because he does the good work. The good
works people do, then, flow out of God's own work in them, and genuine faith inevitably leads to obeying the moral norms of the law.

A controversial movement called Christian reconstructionism or theonomy has emerged in the United States from Reformed circles.[39] The

---

38. Daniel P. Fuller, *Gospel and Law: Contrast or Continuum?* (Grand Rapids: Eerdmans,
1980); see also his "Paul and 'The Works of the Law,'" *WTJ* 38 (1975): 28–42.

39. The two books that best represent this movement are by Greg L. Bahnsen (*Theonomy in
Christian Ethics* [Nutley, N.J.: Craig, 1977]) and Rousas J. Rushdoony (*Institutes of Biblical Law*
[Nutley, N.J.: Craig, 1973]).

influence of this new movement is spreading, although people outside the United States and American evangelicalism may not be familiar with it. The distinctive tenet of theonomy warrants that the "standing laws" of the Old Testament should be the basis of law in civil society. In other words, the civil law of the Old Testament should function as the authoritative law for modern governments today. Most theonomists do not claim that people should be circumcised or observe purity laws, for they are generally convinced that the ritual laws have been fulfilled in Christ and therefore have been abolished. But reconstructionists do assert that the law of God should function as the standard for the government in power, not merely as a moral norm for the life of the individual. Reformed theology has typically argued that the moral norms of the Old Testament are in force for the individual believer, but theonomists insist, often quite vociferously, that the law of God should also be the basis for civil society today. This means, for example, that homosexual acts not only would be civilly prosecuted, but also that the penalty specified in the Old Testament law—death—should be applied.

Conclusion

This sketch of contemporary debate has been all too brief, and it has touched upon only a few highlights. It should be apparent, however, that these issues are theologically crucial. Whether one casts a glance at Räisänen's view that Paul is logically inconsistent, or the theonomist's view that the law should be the basis of civil society, momentous conclusions and implications are drawn from the Pauline view of the law. I am not so naïve as to believe that all of the issues broached above will be happily resolved in this book, but it seems the only way to make progress in the current debate is to return to the biblical text, ascertaining anew what Paul intends to say.

1

The Meaning of the Term *Law* in Paul

Is the Presence or Absence of the Article Significant?

Before examining Paul's theology of the law, the specific meaning of the term *law* (νόμος, *nomos*) should be investigated.[1] Some scholars have said that the presence or absence of the definite article before the word νόμος is significant. Thus, some have argued that *the law* (ὁ νόμος, *ho nomos*) refers specifically to the Mosaic law, while νόμος without the article refers to law in a general sense.[2] The anarthrous use of the word *law*, according to this view, signifies that Paul refers to the concept of law and not specifically to the Mosaic law.

1. My work here has been significantly influenced by Douglas J. Moo's treatment of the word νόμος in Paul in "'Law,' 'Works of the Law,' and Legalism in Paul," *WTJ* 45 (1983): 73–100 . For conclusions that are quite similar to Moo's see Stephen Westerholm, *Israel's Law and the Church's Faith: Paul and His Recent Interpreters* (Grand Rapids: Eerdmans, 1988); idem, "Torah, *nomos*, and Law: A Question of 'Meaning,'" *SR* 15 (1986): 327–36. A. F. Segal in "Torah and *nomos* in Recent Scholarly Discussion," *SR* 13 (1984): 19–27, and Westerholm correctly conclude that some scholars have wrongly posited sharp distinctions between Torah and νόμος. This error is illustrated in the article by G. Wallis, "Torah und Nomos: Zur Frage nach Gesetz und Heil," *TLZ* 105 (1980): 321–32. See now the recent work by Michael Winger, *By What Law? The Meaning of Νόμος in the Letters of Paul* (Atlanta: Scholars, 1992).

2. See, for example, J. B. Lightfoot, *The Epistle of St. Paul to the Galatians* (1865; repr., Grand Rapids: Zondervan, 1957), 118; John F. Walvoord, "Law in the Epistle to the Romans," *BSac* 93 (1937): 15–30. A. W. Slaten in "The Qualitative Use of νόμος in the Pauline Epistles," *AJT* 23 (1919): 213–18, argues that the lack of the article indicates a qualitative emphasis on the word νόμος, with the result that Paul is speaking particularly of the legalistic nature of the law when the article is lacking.

It is almost universally agreed today, however, that the distinction drawn regarding the presence or absence of the article with νόμος cannot be sustained.[3] For example, in Romans 2:17–27 Paul uses the term law ten times. Five times the article is used (2:18, 20, 23 [second use], 26, 27 [first use]), and on five occasions the article is lacking (2:17, 23 [first use], 25 [twice], 27 [second use]). The presence or lack of the article is irrelevant to the meaning of νόμος in this text, for it is quite clear that Paul is speaking of the Mosaic law throughout. Therefore, it is arbitrary to see Paul as alternating between speaking of the law in general terms and the Mosaic law.

That such a distinction does not hold up could be pointed out in a number of other passages (Rom. 5:13–14; 7; 10:4–5; Gal. 3:10–13, 17–24; 5:3–4). In Romans 5:13 Paul uses νόμος anarthrously twice, but the specific context proves he has the Mosaic law in mind. In verse 13 he says "until the law sin was in the world." Verse 14 defines this time period as "from Adam until Moses." Thus, we can conclude that the law came into existence at the time of Moses, proving that, even though νόμος does not have the article, it refers here to the Mosaic law.

Other Uses of Law

The above evidence does not demand that *law* in Paul always refers to the Mosaic law, for in a few places the word may be used in another sense. For example, in Romans 3:27; 7:21, 23, 25, and 8:2 many scholars think that *law* means "principle," "order," or "rule."[4] On the other hand, others contend that, even in these passages, the Mosaic law is intended.[5] This issue is notoriously difficult, and it is not my purpose to discuss it in detail; however, I think the former interpretation for these passages is

3. See E. Grafe, *Die paulinische Lehre vom Gesetz nach vier Hauptbriefen* (Tübingen: J. C. B. Mohr, 1884), 5–8; Richard N. Longenecker, *Paul: Apostle of Liberty* (1964; repr., Grand Rapids: Baker, 1976), 118–19; Peter Bläser, *Das Gesetz bei Paulus* (Münster: Aschendorff, 1941), 1–23; Andrea van Dülmen, *Die Theologie des Gesetzes bei Paulus* (Stuttgart: Katholisches Bibelwerk, 1968), 131–32; Moo, "Law and Legalism in Paul," 75–77; George E. Howard, "Christ the End of the Law. The Meaning of Romans 10:4ff," *JBL* 88 (1969): 331, n. 2; Heikki Räisänen, *Paul and the Law* (Philadelphia: Fortress, 1983), 16–18; Brice L. Martin, *Christ and the Law in Paul* (Leiden: Brill, 1989), 21–22. W. Gutbrod ("νόμος," *TDNT* 4:1047) argues that such a distinction cannot be sustained in Jewish literature either.

4. For a thorough recent defense see Heikki Räisänen, "Das 'Gesetz des Glaubens' (Rom. 3:27) und das 'Gesetz des Geistes' (Rom. 8:2)," *NTS* 26 (1980): 101–17; see also Westerholm, *Israel's Law*, 123–26; Douglas J. Moo, *Romans 1–8* (Chicago: Moody, 1991), 251–53, 487–88, 490–92, and 504–7.

5. See, for example, Gerhard Friedrich, "Das Gesetz des Glaubens Röm 3,27," *TZ* 10 (1954): 401–17; Hans Hübner, *Law in Paul's Thought* (Edinburgh: T. and T. Clark, 1984), 137–40; Peter von der Osten-Sacken, *Römer 8 als Beispiel paulinischer Soteriologie* (Göttingen: Vandenhoeck and Ruprecht, 1975), 245–47; C. T. Rhyne, *Faith Establishes the Law* (Chico, Calif.: Scholars, 1981), 67–71; Martin, *Christ and the Law*, 26–31.

slightly stronger. Those who argue that the Mosaic law is in view have in their favor the fact that νόμος elsewhere in Paul usually refers to the Mosaic law. In addition, Romans 3 and 7–8 spotlight the Mosaic law. Those who prefer this interpretation also rightly emphasize that Paul can speak of the law in a negative and a *positive* manner.

But these arguments do not settle the question. The issue is whether Paul uses the word in a general manner in the midst of a discussion of the Mosaic law. Heikki Räisänen has demonstrated that a broader use of the word νόμος is well attested in Greek literature.[6]

A play on the word *law* seems to be the most natural way of constru-ing Romans 7:21 where Paul says, "I find then a law, that when I want to do good that evil is present in me."[7] It is hard to see here how *law* can refer in any meaningful sense to the law of Moses.[8] The translations "principle" or "rule" are more plausible. Romans 7:22 strengthens this interpretation. Paul specifically contrasts "the law of God" with "the other law" (7:23). The law designated as "the law of God" obviously refers to the Mosaic law, which is "holy" (Rom. 7:12). Since Paul distin-guishes "the law of God" from the "other law," it would seem to follow that the "other law" cannot be the Mosaic law.[9] In fact, verse 23 suggests that "the other law" is nothing other than the power of sin, for Paul describes it as "in my members" and as "waging war against the law of my mind and taking me captive to the law of sin that is in my members." The "law of my mind," then designates the "law of God" of verse 22, while "the law of sin that is in my members" describes "the other law."

The phrases "law of faith" (Rom. 3:27) and "the law of the Spirit" (Rom. 8:2) are also probably metaphorical, introducing in a creative way the contrast between the law and the new order received by faith and made possible by the power of the Spirit. Those who see *law* in these texts as referring to the Mosaic law correctly insist that the law also plays a positive role in Paul. Righteousness by faith is attested by the law and prophets (Rom. 3:21). Paul's gospel establishes the law (Rom. 3:31). And those who are in Christ fulfil the law (Rom. 8:4). But Paul, as

6. Heikki Räisänen, "Sprachliches zum Spiel des Paulus mit ΝΟΜΟΣ," in *Torah and Christ* (Helsinki: Finnish Exegetical Society, 1986), 119–47.

7. The accusative νόμον is a direct object; it is very unlikely that it is an accusative of respect. If it is a direct object, then it is hard to see how this verse could refer to the Mosaic law. On this grammatical point see Moo, *Romans 1–8*, 487. Charles E. B. Cranfield (*A Critical and Exegetical Commentary on the Epistle to the Romans* [Edinburgh: T. and T. Clark, 1975], 361–62) says that other interpretations proposed "are so forced as to be incredible."

8. Despite the recent criticism of Räisänen by Peter von der Osten-Sacken, *Die Heiligkeit der Tora: Studien zum Gesetz bei Paulus* (München: Kaiser, 1989), 13–32.

9. Moo (*Romans 1–8*, 491) rightly points out that ἕτερος (*heteros*) does not always refer to "another of a different kind" in distinction from ἄλλος (*allos*) but "it does always mean 'another,' distinguishing two separate entities."

we shall argue later, is careful to insist in both Romans 2–3 and Romans 7 that righteousness does not come through the law. One enters the people of God by faith alone, and possession of the law alone does not save people but kills them. Since these contexts stress entrance into the people of God by faith and through the work of Christ, and not through the law, Romans 3:27 and 8:2 likely do not refer positively to the Mosaic law. More likely, Paul uses *law* here metaphorically. One becomes righteous on the "principle" of faith alone (3:27), and the "power" of the Spirit grants new life (8:2). The priority for Paul rests on faith and the power of the Holy Spirit, although he does also insist that such faith and the work of the Spirit result in obedience to the law.

Therefore, *law* in Paul does not always signify the Mosaic law but can refer metaphorically to "principle," "order," "rule," or "power."

Some say that the law the Gentiles obey (Rom. 2:14–15, 26–27) cannot be limited to the Mosaic law since the text informs us that these Gentiles do not possess the Mosaic law.[10] But this point should not be pressed, for even though the Gentiles do not possess the whole of the written law, what is written on their hearts corresponds with the Mosaic law. The moral norms written on the hearts of Gentiles are not different from the Mosaic law, for when they keep those moral norms they "do the things of the law" (2:14) and "keep the ordinances of the law" (2:26).

The "law of Christ" in Galatians 6:2 (also 1 Cor. 9:21) cannot be limited to the Mosaic law since Paul explicitly designates it as *Christ's* law, rather than the law of Moses. What Paul means by the "law of Christ" has been the subject of some controversy, but it seems incontrovertible that it cannot be equivalent in every respect to the Mosaic law. Paul insists in Galatians that the churches should not submit to circumcision (Gal. 5:2–6), which the Mosaic law clearly commands, but he does command them to keep Christ's law (Gal. 6:2). Thus, there seems to be little doubt that "the law of Christ" is not coterminous with the law of Moses.

Paul also employs the word νόμος to designate the Scriptures as a whole. For instance, Paul appeals to the law in 1 Corinthians 14:21, but he quotes Isaiah 28:11–12, not the Pentateuch. And in Romans 3:19 Paul describes his citations from the Old Testament in verses 10–18 as "what the law says." The Old Testament texts are derived from the Psalms (5:9; 10:7; 14:1–3; 36:1; 53:1–3; 140:3), Proverbs (1:16), Isaiah (59:7–8), and perhaps Ecclesiastes (7:20), which demonstrates again that *law* cannot be restricted to the Pentateuch, but in some places refers to the entire Old Testament. In Romans 3:21 he describes the whole of Scripture as "the law and the prophets," though here the word *law* may be limited to

10. See Moo, "Law and Legalism in Paul," 80.

the Pentateuch, and the word *prophets* probably includes the rest of the Old Testament. Finally, Paul appeals to the *law* in 1 Corinthians 14:34, where women are prohibited from speaking in the assembly. It has been implausibly argued that Paul appeals to a rabbinic saying rather than the Mosaic law.[11] Nowhere else does Paul use *law* to refer to rabbinic sayings, and thus he probably cites the Old Testament law.[12] This text is difficult for a number of reasons, including the fact that there is no clear reference here to any specific Old Testament text. The best explanation is that Paul has in mind the general teaching of the Old Testament on the role relationship between men and women, especially the teaching from Genesis 1–2.[13]

Michael Winger contends that Paul does not distinguish the Old Testament law from oral traditions.[14] He assumes that the burden of proof is on those who want to distinguish the Old Testament law from rabbinic traditions in Paul. Winger's case here is astonishingly weak. No Pauline use of νόμος clearly refers to oral tradition, but there is abundant, detailed evidence that Paul uses νόμος to refer to the Old Testament. Winger wonders how a distinction between the Old Testament and oral traditions is relevant, since it would have been meaningless to Paul's Gentile readers. But he is incorrect on this point as well. The use of numerous Old Testament citations in Paul shows that he believed it was authoritative for the church. Apparently he did not expect Gentile churches to protest, for he nowhere defends the Old Testament as authoritative. He assumes it will be accepted as such. But he does not appeal to oral traditions as authoritative.

Winger argues as well that *law* in Paul usually refers to the *Jewish* law, and the Jewish law describes what Jews typically do. This gives νόμος a sociological cast. The reason Gentiles are not subject to the law is precisely because it is the *Jewish* law, and Gentiles are not Jews. The Jewish law was given for the Jews and was to be practiced by the Jews, but it would be inappropriate for Gentiles to practice this law precisely because they are Gentiles. The Jewish νόμος describes what Jews do, not what Gentiles should do. Paul insists that Gentiles should not observe the law because it is the law of the Jews, not the law of the Gentiles. Winger, of course, is correct that most of these references mean

---

11. Walter C. Kaiser, Jr., *Toward an Exegetical Theology* (Grand Rapids: Baker, 1981), 76–77, 111 believes this saying stems from Paul's opponents and is refuted by Paul in v. 36. Winger, *By What Law?*, 71–72, argues that the OT law is not in view here.

12. See D. A. Carson, *Exegetical Fallacies* (Grand Rapids: Baker, 1984), 38–40.

13. So Martin, *Christ and the Law*, 22; D. A. Carson, "'Silent in the Churches': On the Role of Women in 1 Corinthians 14:33b–36," in J. Piper and W. Grudem, eds., *Recovering Biblical Manhood and Womanhood* (Wheaton: Crossway, 1991), 152.

14. Winger, *By What Law?*, 100.

the Jewish law, but his thesis is seriously flawed because he restricts Paul to a sociological understanding of the law. In Paul's mind the law does more than describe what the Jews do; it is also the Word of God. The Old Testament Scriptures retain authority for the churches. Winger's view may explain why circumcision and food laws do not bind Gentiles. But his view does not explain how Paul can cite the Old Testament as authoritative for Gentile churches, nor does he adequately explain how Paul can enjoin obedience to Old Testament law on Gentile churches (Gal. 5:14; Rom. 8:4; 13:8–10). The resolution of the problems posed by Paul's use of the term *law* cannot be solved with such a one-dimensional solution.

Law of Moses

In Pauline literature νόμος usually refers to the Pentateuch and often more specifically to the law given to Moses. When Paul cites the law as Scripture the Old Testament text may derive from the Pentateuch (see 1 Cor. 9:8–9; 14:34; Gal. 4:21–31). In 1 Corinthians 9:8–9 Paul affirms that the law supports his contention that as an apostle he deserves financial support (v. 8). In verse 9 he makes it clear that the law he has in mind is the Mosaic law, citing Deuteronomy 25:4 as a proof text. The Mosaic commands permeate Paul's references to "law:"[15]

> The demands of these laws should be obeyed: Romans 2:13, 25–26; 8:4; 13:8–10; Galatians 5:14.
> Failure to obey them is sin: Romans 2:12, 23, 25, 27; 3:20–21, 28; 4:15; 5:20; 7:5, 7–9; 1 Corinthians 15:56; Galatians 2:16, 19; 3:10; 5:3.

Some specific examples illustrate this. Paul says, "the *doers* of the law will be justified" (Rom. 2:13). Gentiles can instinctively "*do* the things of the law" (Rom. 2:14). Circumcision only profits if one "*practices* the law" (Rom. 2:25). Gentiles can be described as "*observing*" (φυλάσσω, *phylassō*) and "*keeping*" (τελέω, *teleō*) the law (Rom. 2:26, 27). The righteousness of the law consists in "*doing* it" (Rom. 10:5). The fulfillment of the law through love can be described by the *fulfillment* of specific commandments (Rom. 13:8–10; Gal. 5:14), and believers by the power of the Spirit will *fulfil* "the ordinance of the law" (Rom. 8:4). Galatians 3:10 makes the point in a way that is emphatic, if awkward. The law commands people to "*abide* by all things being written in the

15. W. D. Davies, "Paul and the Law: Reflections on Pitfalls in Interpretation," *Jewish and Pauline Studies* (Philadelphia: Fortress, 1984), 92–94, correctly says that νόμος refers to more than the commands of the law, but it should be emphasized that νόμος does focus on the commands.

book of the law *to do them*." One is obligated "*to do* the whole law" (Gal. 5:3). Ephesians 2:15 sums up the commanding focus of the law as "the law of the commandments consisting in decrees" (τὸν νόμον τῶν ἐντολ- ῶν ἐν δόγμασιν, *ton nomon tōn entolōn en dogmasin*). Paul specifically defines the law in terms of its requirements. To underline this point he describes the "law of the commandments" as consisting of decrees.[16] Whether one sees Ephesians as Pauline, the close connection between law and commandments in Paul is borne out by Romans 7, where he slides easily between law and commandment (ἐντολή, *entolē*), showing that the latter is the focus of the former (7:7–13).

Paul's focus on the commands and demands of the law is also clear when we note that most of the uses of *law* appear in sections in which he discusses sin. He speaks of those who "*sinned* in the realm of law" (Rom. 2:12), of "the *transgression* of law" (Rom. 2:23, 25, 27), and that "knowledge of *sin* comes through the law" (Rom. 3:20). The "law pro- duces wrath" because of *transgression* (Rom. 4:15). "*Sin* is not reckoned where there is no law" (Rom. 5:13). God gave the law "that the *transgres- sion* might increase" (Rom. 5:20). "The passions of *sin* were aroused through the law" (Rom. 7:5). *Sin* is not known apart from the law (Rom. 7:7). In fact, "*sin* is dead without the law" (Rom. 7:8). The law was "added for the sake of *transgressions*" (Gal. 3:19). Those "who receive circumcision *do not keep* the law" (Gal. 6:13). The sin of people reveals that they have failed to obey the specific requirements of the law. We can conclude, then, that Paul normally uses the word *law* to refer to the commands of the Mosaic law.[17]

Even though the commands of the Mosaic law are central in Paul's description of the law, the law is also bound to a particular era of salva- tion-history, when the Mosaic covenant was in force. The era of law was enacted 430 years after the covenant with Abraham (Gal. 3:17); hence, it was given at a certain point in history (Rom. 5:13, 20; Gal. 3:21). Paul describes the law as a child attendant that held sway over people until the coming of Christ (Gal. 3:24). But now that Christ has come, believers are not under the child attendant (Rom. 6:14–15; Gal. 3:25), which was designed for the period of infancy until Jesus Christ came and liberated those under the law (Gal. 4:1–7). Second Corinthians 3:14 describes the Mosaic law as "the old covenant" and contrasts it with the new cove- nant in Christ. Paul's uses of νόμος often link with a certain period of

---

16. Ἐν δόγμασιν here is probably appositional.

17. J. A. Sanders, "Torah and Christ," *Int* 29 (1975): 372–90, is incorrect, then, in thinking that Paul uses νόμος to refer to *haggadah* (story); rather, Paul, like the Rabbis, typically uses the word to designate *halakah* (specific commands of the law). See Moo, "Law and Legalism in Paul," 82–83, n. 38, for this criticism of Sanders.

redemptive history when the law was given to Moses.ᵻ Certainly the commands and requirements of the law are still in the forefront, but they are closely linked to the specific historical epoch under Moses.

The Law and Legalism

Some have argued that in some texts Paul conveys the idea of legalism when using the word.[18] We shall examine this interpretation in more detail later, but at this point it should be noted that such a meaning is not apparent from the use of νόμος itself.[19] *Law* usually focuses on the commands and requirements of the Mosaic law, and it cannot be demonstrated that the word bears the idea of legalism. It is very difficult to see in Galatians 3, for example, how Paul can be speaking of the Mosaic law in some verses (vv. 17, 19, 21), and then suddenly shift the meaning to legalism in an adjacent verse (v. 18).[20] Surely the most natural way of interpreting this text is to ascribe to *law* the same meaning throughout the passage. This does not prove that the Pauline letters contain no polemic against legalism, but only that the evidence fails to suggest that the word *law* in itself holds this meaning.

Ceremonial and Moral Law

Another question that arises is whether Paul speaks of the law as an indivisible entity. That is, does he distinguish between the so-called ceremonial and moral law? The use of νόμος does not indicate that he does. Indeed, texts like Galatians 5:3 show that Paul considered the law to be a unity, and as we saw above, Paul speaks in a number of texts of the Mosaic law as a body of laws that came into existence at a certain point in history. This does not prove, however, that Paul made no distinctions within the law. It only proves that, again, such distinctions cannot be gleaned from the use of the word νόμος.

18. Ernest DeW. Burton, *A Critical and Exegetical Commentary on the Epistle to the Galatians* (Edinburgh: T. and T. Clark, 1921), 458; C. F. D. Moule, "Obligation in the Ethic of Paul," in W. R. Farmer, C. F. D. Moule, and Reinhold R. Niebuhr, eds., *Christian History and Interpretation: Studies Presented to John Knox* (Cambridge: Cambridge University Press, 1967), 392–93; Daniel P. Fuller, *Gospel and Law: Contrast or Continuum?* (Grand Rapids: Eerdmans, 1980), 97–99.

19. See Westerholm, *Israel's Law*, 130–34; Moo, "Law and Legalism," 85–88.

20. Contrary to Fuller, *Gospel and Law*, 199–204.

2

Why the Works of the Law
Cannot Save

One of the most controversial issues in Pauline studies today is why Paul says that righteousness cannot be attained through the law. It is incontrovertible that he rejects righteousness by law. He proclaims in Galatians 2:16 that righteousness comes through faith in Jesus Christ and states three times that it is not available by works of law. Similarly, Romans 3:20 and 3:28 affirm that righteousness cannot be gained by works of law but only through faith (see Rom. 3:21). Galatians 3:2 and 3:5 indicate that the Spirit was received and supplied by "hearing with faith" not by works of law, while Galatians 3:10 says that "those who are of works of law are under a curse."

Some Pauline texts simply say that righteousness does not come via the law. In these texts the word *law* is probably synonymous with the phrase *works of law*. For instance, Galatians 3:11 says "Now that no one is justified by the law in God's sight is evident." *Law* here is probably shorthand for *works of law*, which Paul uses in the previous verse.[1] In Romans 3:21 Paul says "the righteousness of God has been manifested apart from the law," which probably means that righteousness is obtained apart from the works of the law, for Paul in the previous verse

1. So Hans Dieter Betz, *Galatians* (Philadelphia: Fortress, 1979), 126.

had explicitly rejected works of law as leading to righteousness.[2] Finally, Galatians 2:21 declares that Christ died for no purpose "if righteousness is through the law." In the larger context of 2:15–21, the rejection of righteousness by law is merely another way of saying that salvation cannot be obtained by works of law. Paul clearly rejects righteousness by works of law. The question, however, is why he rejects righteousness by works of law.

Survey of Solutions

Before I offer my understanding of this issue, I will briefly survey three popular solutions.

Rudolf Bultmann and his followers contend that Paul ruled out *in principle* justification through works of the law. This means that even if one were to obey the law perfectly, one would still be cursed, since salvation cannot be obtained through the law. The Bultmann school does not say that anyone can obey the law perfectly, but their distinctive slant on this issue is that the ability to obey the law is, in the last analysis, irrelevant. Bultmann says in a famous statement, *"Man's effort to achieve salvation by keeping the Law only leads him into sin, indeed this effort itself in the end is already sin."*[3] The last clause of this sentence is the crucial one. The very desire and effort to keep the law are sinful, because, according to Bultmann, those who attempt to keep the law are trying to establish their own righteousness and merit God's favor.

Hans Hübner espouses a view similar to Bultmann's. He says, "Even complete righteousness on the basis of works within the framework of the Torah does not mean righteousness in the sight of God."[4] And, *"Even the perfect man*—once again were there such, but there is not such!—is a sinner."[5] Günter Klein says, "The works of the law *generally*, independent of the question of their accomplishment, provide no possible ground for justification."[6] The fundamental problem with human beings, then, is not inability to obey the law. The root problem is the

---

2. See Charles E. B. Cranfield, *A Critical and Exegetical Commentary on the Epistle to the Romans*, 2 vols. (Edinburgh: T. and T. Clark, 1975, 1979), 201.

3. Rudolf Bultmann, *Theology of the New Testament*, 2 vols. (New York: Scribner's, 1951), 1:264. Emphasis Bultmann's. See also his "Christ the End of the Law" in *Essays Philosophical and Theological* (London: SCM, 1955), 52–53.

4. Hans Hübner, *Law in Paul's Thought* (Edinburgh: T. and T. Clark, 1984), 119. Emphasis Hübner's.

5. Ibid., 120.

6. Günter Klein, "Sündenverständnis und theologia crucis bei Paulus," *Theologia Crucis—Signum Crucis. Festschrift für Erich Dinkler*, edited by C. Andersen and Günter Klein (Tübingen: J. C. B. Mohr, 1979), 260; see also 268–70, 272, 275–76.

desire to obey it in order to gain salvation, for such a desire reveals human idolatry and an attempt to gain security and salvation through self-effort.

A very different answer to the question as to why salvation cannot be obtained through the law has been given by E. P. Sanders.[7] Sanders argues that Paul's rejection of the law as a way of salvation was not because of human inability to obey it perfectly, nor was the problem that devotion to the law led to legalism and boasting. The root of Paul's rejection of the law was located in his Christology. Paul, says Sanders, came to believe that salvation and righteousness were only available through Christ. But if the only way to salvation is through Christ, then the law must be excluded as a way of salvation. Here we find Sanders' well known conception of "solution to plight." After Paul decided that the solution to humanity's problems is found in Christ, he reasoned that life under the law could not provide salvation. Sanders suggests that Paul saw no problem with the law *before* he came to believe in Christ, but only after his conversion did he deny that the covenant with the Jews was effective. Paul's real problem with Judaism was that it was not Christianity.

James D. G. Dunn acknowledges his debt to Sanders but is troubled by the arbitrariness of the Paul that Sanders describes.[8] Dunn suggests there is more to why Paul rejected Judaism than that it was not Christianity. He concurs with Sanders' conviction that the Pauline attack against the law was not due to legalism, nor to human inability to keep it. Dunn says Paul's polemic was not against "activism" but "nationalism." Paul attacked any Jewish notion of privilege because of their covenantal status. The Jews wrongly boasted in their national privilege as God's elect people, but they did not boast in their good works. So when Paul spoke of "those who are of the works of the law" in Galatians 3:10, he referred to "those who have understood the scope of God's covenant as Israel *per se*, as that people who are defined by the law and marked out by its distinctive requirements."[9] The curse of the law lies not on those who disobey the law, but on those who restrict the promise on

---

7. E. P. Sanders, *Paul and Palestinian Judaism: A Comparison of Patterns of Religion* (Philadelphia: Fortress, 1977), 442–47, 474–511; idem, *Paul, the Law, and the Jewish People* (Philadelphia: Fortress, 1983), 17–91.

8. For his view see James D. G. Dunn, "The New Perspective on Paul," *BJRL* 65 (1983): 95–122; "Works of the Law and the Curse of the Law (Galatians 3.10–14)," *NTS* 31 (1985): 523–42; *Romans*, 2 vols. (Dallas: Word, 1988); *Jesus, Paul, and the Law: Studies in Mark and Galatians* (Louisville: Westminster, 1990); "Yet Once More—'The Works of the Law': A Response," *JSNT* 46 (1992): 99–117. See also Hendrikus Boers, "'We Who Are by Inheritance Jews; Not from the Gentile Sinners,'" *JBL* 111 (1992): 273, 275–76; Elmer A. Martens, "Embracing the Law: A Biblical Theological Perspective," *BBR* 2 (1992): 14–17.

9. Dunn, "Works of the Law," 534.

nationalistic terms to the Jews. The law must be repudiated as a way of salvation because it created a social barrier between Jews and Gentiles, limiting salvation to a certain ethnic group.

I would like to argue, however, that all of the answers suggested above are unpersuasive, or only partially true. Paul rejected the law as a way of salvation because of human inability to obey it. No one can be justified by the works of the law because no one can obey the law perfectly. If one could do all that the law requires, then one would be counted as righteous in God's sight. But since everyone falls short of obeying the law, therefore, righteousness cannot be obtained through the law. In addition, the law was rejected for salvation-historical reasons. A salvation-historical shift has occurred now that Messiah has come. Old Testament sacrifices no longer atone since Jesus has provided definitive atonement on the cross. In fact, his atoning work casts light back on Old Testament sacrifices, showing that they were defective, because they could not provide effective and final forgiveness.

Human Inability in Galatians

Galatians 3:10 and Works of Law

My support arises from both Galatians and Romans, since these two letters focus on this theme. Paul asserts three times in Galatians 2:16 that righteousness cannot be obtained by the works of the law but only through faith in Christ Jesus. He does not in this context, however, explain systematically why justification is not by works of law, although the difficult verses in Galatians 2:17–18 suggest that the fatal problem is human sin.[10]

Nonetheless, Galatians 3:10 is a clear statement as to why righteousness is not through works of law: "For as many as are of the works of the law are under a curse, because it is written, 'Cursed is everyone who does not abide by all things written in the book of the law to do them.'" What Paul is saying can be expressed in a syllogism:

Those who do not keep everything written in the law are cursed (3:10b).
No one keeps everything written in the law (implicit premise).
Therefore, those who rely on the works of the law for salvation are cursed (3:10a).

---

10. See Ronald Y. K. Fung, *The Epistle to the Galatians* (Grand Rapids: Eerdmans, 1988), 120–22; F. F. Bruce, *The Epistle to the Galatians* (Grand Rapids: Eerdmans, 1982), 141–42.

The explicit reason given (γάρ, *gar*) for the curse is failure to do every-thing (οὐκ ἐμμένει πᾶσιν, *ouk emmenei pasin*) that the law commands. The word "all" (πᾶσιν, *pasin*) is not found in the Hebrew Masoretic text (MT) of Deuteronomy 27:26 but is taken from the Septuagint (LXX). Its inclusion indicates that *perfect* obedience is necessary to escape the curse. In the concluding words of the verse Paul identifies the problem as a failure "to do" (ποιῆσαι, *poiēsai*) what the law commands. In con-text it is evident that Paul maintains, as he assumes his readers do, that no one can "do" the whole law.

Galatians 3:10 is an extremely important verse for understanding Paul's theology of the law. Scholarly debate on the meaning of the verse has been extensive. It is not surprising, therefore, to discover that not all agree with the interpretation I have presented above. For example, Sanders says that Paul's main purpose in Galatians 3 is to prove that Gentiles are righteous by faith.[11] Thus, Paul selects certain Old Testa-ment passages to sustain his view that Gentiles are heirs of Abraham by faith. In Galatians 3:10, then, Paul selects Deuteronomy 27:26, not because it implies that the law must be obeyed in its totality, but because it is the only passage in the Old Testament where the term *law* is con-nected with *curse*. Paul simply intends to prove that living by the law leads to a curse. He does not explain why living under the law results in a curse, according to Sanders.

Sanders claims the hermeneutical key to understanding the use of the Old Testament proof texts is to be found in the Pauline explanation of the Old Testament citation, not in the wording of the citation itself.[12] The citation of Deuteronomy 27:26 in Galatians 3:10b adds nothing to the flow of the argument in Galatians 3. What Paul means by the proof text is found solely in Galatians 3:10a, where he says that those who accept the law are cursed.

We need to remember, says Sanders, that the only purpose in Gala-tians 3:8–14 is to argue for the inclusion of the Gentiles into the people of God.[13] Verses 10–13 play a subsidiary function in the context, while Paul highlights the participation of Gentiles in the Abrahamic bless-ing.[14] Thus, Sanders thinks it is wrong-headed to see Paul as giving rea-sons why the law does not save. Paul merely uses arguments from the Old Testament to support his thesis.[15] According to Sanders, Paul

---

11. Sanders, *Paul, The Law*, 19–21.

12. Ibid., 22.

13. Despite the comments of Timo Laato *Paulus und das Judentum: Anthropoligische Erwä-gungen* (Åbo: Åbo Academy Press, 1991), 220–21, Sanders correctly understands that the issue in Galatians is entrance into the people of God.

14. Sanders, *Paul, The Law*, 19–21.

15. Ibid., 26–27.

excludes people from salvation, not because they cannot obey the law, but simply because salvation comes only through Christ, not the law.

We shall see when we come to Galatians 3:13 that Sanders correctly detects a salvation-historical shift in Paul's thinking. Paul is convinced that salvation now comes only through Christ. But Sanders' interpretation does not explain sufficiently why salvation is only through Christ. The striking element in his argument on the use of the Old Testament in Galatians 3:10 is that he offers assertions rather than proof.[16] He claims Paul selects Deuteronomy 27:26 because it contains the words *law* and *curse*, and the real meaning of the verse is to be found in Paul's own words and not the Old Testament citation, but he does not provide any significant evidence to support his claim. Contrary to Sanders, the citation of Deuteronomy 27:26 does provide a reason why the works of law lead to a curse. Paul clearly gives a reason when he quotes Deuteronomy 27:26, since the two halves of the verse are connected by "for" (γάρ, *gar*). The "for" shows that Paul is explaining *why* those who are of the works of law are under a curse—*because* all are cursed who do not obey the entire law. Sanders' distinction between reasons and arguments is also specious. It is hard to see how Paul could have hoped to convince the Galatians that the Judaizers were wrong if he simply provided arguments from Old Testament citations to support his own dogmatic position but failed to give any reasons for his position.

Even though Sanders is correct about the central point of this passage (the inclusion of the Gentiles), he wrongly sunders the subsidiary arguments used in the text from the main conclusion. It makes more sense if the subsidiary arguments Paul uses function as reasons for the main point he wants to make. Most intelligent people argue in this manner. They at least try to ensure that the conclusion follows from the premises. But if one follows Sanders' interpretation, Paul never divulges why the law is to be excluded as a way of salvation. He simply asserts that since salvation is through Christ, it cannot be through the law. I do not see how such an argument would have convinced the Galatians, for the argument of the Judaizers was that salvation was attained through Christ *and the law*. Paul likely would have needed reasons to counterattack successfully the Judaizers. Sanders' interpretation amounts to Paul insisting that his view is true simply because he said so. Sometimes debates are won by sheer emotion, force of personality, or verbal trickery. Nonetheless, the preservation of the letter to the Galatians is better explained by the hypothesis that accepts it as a logical argument for

16. For a more detailed evaluation of Sanders' interpretation see Thomas R. Schreiner, "Paul and Perfect Obedience to the Law: An Evaluation of the View of E. P. Sanders," *WTJ* 47 (1985): 245–78.

Paul's position. Most scholars have seen Galatians as a carefully composed and structured letter, which contains reasons for the rejection of the law as a way of salvation.

That the central problem was failure to keep the law is supported by the Old Testament. In Galatians 3:10 Paul cites Deuteronomy 27:26, where, in its larger context of Deuteronomy 27–30 God threatens Israel with covenantal curses for failing to observe the law. The climax of the curses involved subjugation to a foreign power (28:49–52), and exile from the land (28:64–68; 29:24–28; 30:1). Such curses would come because Israel was "not careful to observe all the words of this law that are written in this book" (Deut. 28:58). Leviticus 26 exhibits the same theme: Failure to obey the law will bring down the curses of the covenant. The climax of the curses parallels those in Deuteronomy. Israel will be destroyed by a foreign power and scattered among the nations; those left in the land will live in a pitiful state (Lev. 26:27–39). The reason for the curse is set forth in 26:14: failure to obey *all* the commandments. The author of Deuteronomy makes it clear that Israel will inevitably disobey, and the curses of the covenant will come to pass (Deut. 30:1; 31:16–22). The Song of Moses (Deut. 32:1–43) was written as a witness against Israel so she would recognize that her punishment was the result of such disobedience.

Paul, as Thomas Wright has convincingly argued, would have seen the Israel of his day as under these covenantal curses.[17] She was under the dominion of Rome and thus subject to a foreign power. Israel was in exile, scattered among the nations, and not enjoying the blessings of freedom and prosperity described in Leviticus 26 and Deuteronomy 28. Paul understood that the exile and subsequent Roman domination testified that Israel had failed to obey the law and that the curse was operative. The blessings promised in the Pentateuch had not come to pass.

Indeed, when Paul read the Scriptures he was confronted again and again with the theme that exile and subjugation to a foreign power were due to the sin of God's people. Joshua warns the people that covenant unfaithfulness will lead to loss of the land (Josh. 23:14–16). The author of 2 Kings attributes the exile to the sin of Israel in forsaking the Lord and serving other gods (2 Kings 17:7–23). One of the major themes of the prophets was that God would punish Israel with exile for her disobedience. For example, Isaiah interprets Israel's defeat and despoliation at the hands of Babylon as due to sin. "Who gave Jacob up for spoil, and Israel to plunderers? Was it not the Yahweh, against whom we have sinned, and in whose ways they were not willing to walk, and whose

17. N. Thomas Wright, *The Climax of the Covenant: Christ and the Law in Pauline Theology* (Minneapolis: Fortress, 1991), 137–56.

law they did not obey?" (Isa. 42:24). Failure to obey the law engendered the curse upon Israel.[18]

We shall examine Romans 3, where Paul contends that all are under the power of sin. Interestingly, in Romans 3:15 Paul cites Isaiah 59:7, which attributes the collapse of Israel (before the Babylonian conquest) to Israel's sin. The curses of the covenant that Israel experienced so long ago were, according to Paul, still operative against Israel in his day, for she remained under the control of a foreign power.

Nearly all scholars agree that the Old Testament prophets threatened the people with the curses of the covenant for failure to obey the terms of the covenant, and the capitulations to Assyria in 722 B.C. and Babylon in 587 B.C. were the outcome of such disobedience. It is not necessary to document this theme in every prophetic book, but two texts are especially helpful for the interpretation of Galatians 3:10—Jeremiah 11 and Daniel 9.

Jeremiah 11 thematically parallels Deuteronomy 27:15–26. Jeremiah refers to the curses that are enacted when people fail to obey the covenant. What Israel failed to obey was surely the law since the text speaks of "the words of this covenant that I commanded your forefathers in the day that I brought them out of the land of Egypt" (Jer. 11:3–4). The link between Jeremiah 11 and Galatians 3:10 is also striking, for God threatens to curse those who fail to practice the words of the covenant. The adjective *cursed* (ἐπικατάρατος, *epikataratos* in the LXX of Deut. 27:26 and Jer. 11:3) is the same word Paul uses in Galatians 3:10.[19] We have already noted that Paul stresses that one must do *all* that the law enjoins. The same emphasis on doing all the law is found in Jeremiah 11, for the people, according to the LXX, are commanded to "do all things that I command you" (ποιήσατε πάντα, ὅσα ἐὰν ἐντείλωμαι ὑμῖν, *poiēsate panta, hosa ean enteilōmai hymin*, 11:4). They face judgment because they did not do the law (11:8). Paul's words in Galatians 3:10 indicate that he saw the same curse that was present in Jeremiah's day.

Daniel 9 constitutes a conceptually parallel passage. Daniel confesses the sin of his people, acknowledging that God has righteously inflicted on them the curses of the covenant. The curse he particularly has in mind is the exile. What precipitated his prayer was the promise in Jeremiah 25:11–12 and 29:10 that Yahweh would restore Israel to the land after seventy years of captivity. Daniel prays that the Lord will have

---

18. That the failure to keep God's law leads to exile is also found in CD 3:4–12; 4 Ezra 3:25–27.

19. See also Ps. 118:21 in the LXX which proclaims a curse upon those who shun God's commandments. Once again the curse is connected with failure to keep God's law, for even though the word νόμος is not used, the concept is surely present in the word ἐντολή.

compassion on his people despite their sin and restore them to the land. The crucial verse for our purposes is Daniel 9:11: "All Israel has transgressed your law and turned aside, not obeying your voice. Thus, the curse has been inflicted on us, and the oath that is written in the law of Moses the servant of God, for we have sinned against him." In the LXX the "curse" (κατάρα, *katara*) has come because Israel "transgressed" (παρέβησαν, *parebēsan*) the law, and "sinned" (ἡμάρτομεν, *hēmartomen*) against God.

Thus, even a cursory reading of the Old Testament shows that one of its manifest themes was that Israel did not experience the blessing of the covenant because of disobedience. Paul probably read the history of Israel's remarkable failure to obey and concluded that Israel (and, therefore, all people) *could not obey* the law. The only hope was the circumcision of the heart by God himself (Deut. 30:6–8), the writing of the law upon the heart (Jer. 31:31–34), and the giving of a new heart and spirit so people could keep the law (Ezek. 36:26–27).

Despite my agreement with Wright's exegesis in terms of the punishment of exile, he wrongly claims that Galatians 3:10–14 relates to Israel and Gentiles corporately, not individually. He defends this corporate emphasis by noting that Paul claimed to be blameless with regard to the law (Phil. 3:6), and thus presumably other individual Israelites could reach this level as well. In any case, atonement was offered under the Old Testament cultus for those who did sin. Thus, Galatians 3:10–14 must be referring to national and corporate sin which could not be covered through Old Testament sacrifices, according to Wright.

I shall explain later why it is mistaken to read "blameless" (Phil. 3:6) to mean "sinless" and why the sacrifices of the Old Testament cultus were no longer sufficient. A rigid distinction between corporate groups and individuals is quite popular in New Testament studies today, but the distinction is a flawed one. What Paul says about the group in question also applies to individuals. Individuals and a group are not mutually exclusive. In Galatians 3 Paul has in mind the Gentiles or Galatians as a corporate group. But does this mean, as Wright maintains, that the sin and curse in view in Galatians 3:10 are only corporate? Was the reception of the Spirit in Galatians 3:2 and 3:5 corporate or individual? Certainly the Galatians corporately possessed the Spirit, but it is also true that they individually expressed faith and then received the Spirit. Would anyone say that the exercise of faith in Galatians is only corporate? Neither does it seem sensible to me to claim that the sin of Galatians 3:10 refers only to corporate sin. Indeed, Paul uses third singular forms in Galatians 3:12. Of course, he also uses plural designations in

Galatians 3:7, 8, 9, 10, 13, and 14. This would seem to support the interpretation that the corporate and individual are not mutually exclusive.

If my argument in the above paragraph is on target, then the curse
does fall on individuals who do not keep the law perfectly. "Cursed is
every one (πᾶς ὅς, *pas hos*) who does not abide by all things written in
the book of the law" (Gal. 3:10). This curse would apply to corporate
entities as well, but the corporate groups would be comprised of individuals who failed to keep the law. The upshot of this discussion is that
the Reformational way of reading this verse is not an imposition of Western categories onto Paul. Those who restrict the meaning of the text only
to corporate realities fail to interpret the verse as accurately as Luther
and Calvin.

Finally, Sanders' idea that Paul argues only from solution to plight
has been effectively refuted by Frank Thielman.[20] Thielman demonstrates that the Old Testament, Jewish literature of the Second Temple
Period, and the Pauline writings contained a consistent admission that
people (even God's people) were sinners, and that the eschatological
intervention of God was needed to rescue them from the power of sin.[21]
The Old Testament background to Galatians 3:10, therefore, powerfully
supports Paul's assertion that the curse falls on those who do not obey
the law perfectly.

Another way to explain Galatians 3:10 has been provided by the Bultmann school. For instance, Heinrich Schlier thinks Galatians 3:10 is
saying that the person is cursed *who does* or *attempts to do what the law
commands.*[22] Günter Klein's exegesis is similar, and he says that Galatians 3:10a shows that existence under the law by definition leads to the
curse, whether one obeys the law or not.[23]

But, contrary to Schlier, the curse is not threatened for those *who do
the law.* Galatians 3:10b clearly pronounces the curse on those *who fail
to do everything written in the law.* Klein wrongly isolates 3:10a from
3:10b. Verse 10a says that "those who are of the works of the law are
under a curse," but 10b should not be separated from 10a because it
gives the reason why those who are of the works of law are under a
curse—they failed to do all that the law commands. Paul does not

20. Frank Thielman, *From Plight to Solution: A Jewish Framework for Understanding Paul's View of the Law in Galatians and Romans* (Leiden: Brill, 1989).
21. Nonetheless, Sanders correctly sees a salvation-historical shift in Paul's thinking as well. Robert H. Gundry, in his critique of Sanders in "Grace, Works, and Staying Saved in Paul," *Bib* 66 (1985): 1–38, rightly observes that Paul argues both from the human plight and salvation-history.
22. Heinrich Schlier, *Der Brief an die Galater* (Göttingen: Vandenhoeck and Ruprecht, 1965), 132–33.
23. Klein, "Sündenverständnis," 270–72.

abstractly say that existing under any sort of law puts one under a curse. In the context and flow of the argument he supplies the specific reason why existence under the law results in a curse—disobedience.

Dunn says that the curse falls on those who restrict the promise on nationalistic terms to the Jews. And the curse takes effect on "those who have understood the scope of God's covenant people as Israel *per se*, as that people who are defined by the law and marked out by its distinctive requirements."[24] *Works of law* refers to the whole law but focuses on "identity markers," such as circumcision, food laws, and sabbath, which separate Jews from Gentiles.[25] Contrary to Reformation exegesis, Paul does not criticize self-achievement, legalism, or the doing of the law. What Paul has in mind when he speaks of works of law is the social function of the law insofar as it divides Jews and Gentiles, according to Dunn. The problem is with Jewish nationalism and particularism, not with legalism or activism. Those Jews who insist on Gentiles observing the works of law are requiring Gentiles to become Jews in order to enter the people of God, limiting the people of God on a racial and ethnic basis.

The term *works of law* (ἔργα νόμου, *erga nomou*) is crucial. Therefore, we must pause for a rather long discussion of the background to Dunn's understanding of the term, and then I will show why it is mistaken.

Two scholars in particular anticipated Dunn's conclusions. Ernest Lohmeyer claims that *works of law* does not refer primarily to the performance of the specific deeds commanded by the law.[26] Instead, the focus lies on the religious context of existence in which the law is kept. J. B. Tyson, depending upon the work of Lohmeyer, holds a similar view. The focus is not on law as the demand of God that must be fulfilled; instead, the emphasis is on the condition of life under Torah, particularly the demand to observe food laws and be circumcised.[27] Tyson describes such a way of life as "nomistic service" and "Jewish existence." Paul rejects works of law for salvation-historical reasons, with the coming of Jesus the era of separation between Jews and Gentiles has ended.

Even though Dunn concurs that *works of law* designates the whole law, his claim that it focuses on "identity markers" is not borne out in Romans. Some preparatory explanation on *works* (ἔργα, *erga*) is needed to support my thesis. Both Douglas Moo and Stephen Westerholm have

24. Dunn, "Works of the Law," 534.

25. Dunn makes it clear that *works of law* refers to the whole law, but focuses on identity markers. See Dunn, "Once More," 100–2; idem, *Jesus, Paul, and the Law*, 203–13, 237–41 .

26. Ernest Lohmeyer, "Probleme paulinischer Theologie. II. 'Gesetzeswerke,'" *ZNW* 28 (1929): 177–207.

27. J. B. Tyson, "'Works of Law' in Galatians," *JBL* 92 (1973): 423–31.

convincingly argued that *works* (ἔργα) in Paul refers to "deeds that are performed" and that *works of law* signifies the "deeds" or "actions" demanded by the Mosaic law.[28] Most Pauline scholars believe that *works* (ἔργα) refers generally to human deeds. Romans 9:11–12 seems to confirm this definition. In verse 12 Paul claims that "calling" is not "on the basis of works."[29] In verse 11 the electing work of God is "not based on anything done whether good or evil." The "electing purpose" of God (v. 11) is equivalent to "calling" in verse 12. So, too, the "doing of good and evil" in verse 11 is another way of describing "the works" of verse 12. Thus, *works* can be defined as the performance of deeds, both good and evil.

Other Pauline passages support this general understanding. God "will repay each one according to his works" (Rom. 2:6). All who perform these works are described subsequently as those "who do evil" (κατεργαζομένου τὸ κακόν, *katergazomenou to kakon*, 2:9), and those "who do good" (ἐργαζομένῳ τὸ ἀγαθόν, *ergazomenō to agathon*, 2:10). Apparently, *works* in Paul refers to the performance of actions in a general way, whether good or evil. The "end" of the false teachers in Corinth "shall be according to their works" (2 Cor. 11:15). If election is "by grace, then it is no longer by works" (Rom. 11:6). Believers are to "put off the works of darkness" (Rom. 13:12), and evil works are described as "works of the flesh" (Gal. 5:19).[30] It seems clear, then, that *works* refers generally to human deeds or actions, which are either good or evil.

The question is whether the word *works* in *works of law* is also a general term, referring to the whole law. On first glance *works of law* would seem to be a natural way of describing the whole law. At least nothing in the term itself focuses on certain parts of the law.[31] And when we examine the closest parallels in Second Temple Jewish literature, the theory that *works of law* refers generally to the whole law is strengthened. No exact parallel using ἔργα νόμου exists in the LXX. But in the

28. Douglas J. Moo, "'Law,' 'Works of the Law,' and Legalism in Paul," *WTJ* 45 (1983): 90–99; Stephen Westerholm, *Israel's Law and the Church's Faith: Paul and His Recent Interpreters* (Grand Rapids: Eerdmans, 1988), 106–21.

29. Many English versions follow the KJV in placing the word *works* in verse 11. But see the NIV and NRSV and the Greek text for the versification followed here.

30. If one accepts all the letters attributed to Paul as authentically Pauline, the evidence accumulates. Colossians refers to those "who are alienated and enemies in mind because of evil works" (1:21). In Ephesians salvation is "not of works" (2:9), believers are created for "good works" (2:10), and should "not participate in the unfruitful works of darkness" (5:11). See also 1 Tim. 2:10; 5:10, 25; 6:18; 2 Tim. 1:9; 4:14; Titus 1:16; 2:7, 14; 3:5, 8, 14.

31. Dunn's claim ("Once More," 103–4) that the Qumran literature supports a focused understanding of *works of law* is not persuasive. The evidence I present below suggests that the term does not focus on a particular part of the law.

Qumran literature (4QFlor 1:7) the Hebrew equivalent, מַעֲשֵׂי תוֹרָה (*maʿăśēy tôrâ*), probably refers to all the works commanded in the law since the context does not circumscribe the term. A similar phrase, "his works of law" (מַעֲשָׂיו בַּתוֹרָה, *maʿăśāyw battôrâ*), shows up in the Community Rule (1QS) of Qumran (5:21; 6:18). A careful reading of 1QS 5–7 shows that this passage describes general obedience to the law. Members pledge to "return to the law of Moses according to *all* that he commanded" (1QS 5:8, לָשׁוּב אֶל תוֹרַת מוֹשֶׁה כְּכוֹל אֲשֶׁר צִוָּה, *lāšûb ʾel tôrat môšeh kĕkôl ʾăšer ṣiwwâ*). The text enumerates many specific commands for members of the community which in no way can be limited to part of the law, nor is there an emphasis on laws which separate Jews from Gentiles.

The commands include matters such as avoidance of anger, impatience, hatred, lying, insulting elders, blasphemy, malice, foolish talk, and nakedness, etc. (see 1QS 5:25–26; 6:24–7:18).[32]

A similar expression in the Qumran literature is "works of righteousness" (1QH 1:26 מַעֲשֵׂי הַצְּדָקָה, *maʿăśēy haṣṣĕdāqâ*; 4:31 מַעֲשֵׂי צְדָקָה, *maʿăśēy ṣĕdāqâ*).[33] The Damascus Document 3:5–16 also supports the idea that there is no focus on part of the law. Instead, the Qumran community emphasizes obeying all commands. This call to obey the whole law is also found in the pseudepigraphical work *Testament of Judah* 26:1.[34] Indeed, there is no focus on that which distinguished Jews from Gentiles in the *Testaments of the XII Patriarchs*. Howard Clark Kee remarks that the law is used in "broad moral terms" in the *Testaments*.[35] Eckart Reinmuth demonstrates that, if anything, there was a special focus on moral infractions of the law in much of early Jewish literature.[36] This is not surprising since the Torah was the norm for all of life, not just ritual matters. Torah referred to the whole law in Judaism,

32. Karl-Wilhelm Niebuhr's careful study of early Jewish literature, *Gesetz und Paränese: Katechismusartige Weisungsreihen in der frühjüdischen Literatur*, is also illuminating. He shows that there was a focus on the moral norms of the law in this literature ([Tübingen: J. C. B. Mohr, 1987], esp. 7, 12–14, 26, 59, 61–64, 160, 162, 233–34). This may suggest that it is incorrect to see a focus on cultic law in the term *works of law*. There is no direct parallel, however, since the phrase is not found in the literature Niebuhr examines. The early Jewish literature investigated by Niebuhr contains no criticism or polemic against cultic law, nor does it suggest that only the moral norms of the law are still binding. The whole law is God's law. The focus is probably on the moral law because of contact with Hellenistic culture. Nonetheless, the whole law still remains God's law.

33. See also 2 *Apoc. Bar.* 57:2.

34. See also *T. Ben.* 10:11; *T. Naph.* 8:7.

35. Howard Clark Kee, "The Ethical Dimensions of the Testaments of the XII as a Clue to Provenance," *NTS* 24 (1977–78): 260.

36. Eckart Reinmuth, *Geist und Gesetz: Studien zu Voraussetzungen und Inhalt der paulinischen Paränese* (Berlin: Evangelische Verlagsanstalt, 1985), 22–41.

strengthening the idea that no distinctions are contemplated in the phrase "works of law." [37]

It is always possible, however, that Paul used *works of law* in a distinctive way to concentrate on the sections of the law distinguishing Jews from Gentiles. Paul's own usage should carry the most weight in discerning what *works of law* means. But an examination of *works of law* in Romans demonstrates, contrary to Dunn, that the phrase refers generally to the works demanded by the law of Moses.[38] *Works* (ἔργα, *erga*) and *works of law* (ἔργα νόμου, *erga nomou*) differ merely in that the former denotes all human works, while the latter denotes all works commanded by the Mosaic law. Therefore, no compelling evidence indicates that *works of law* focuses on certain portions of the Mosaic law.

The attempt to descry a particular emphasis in *works of law* founders on Romans 3:27–4:8, where *works of law* and *works* are parallel.[39] The example of Abraham (4:1–25) confirms what Paul said earlier, especially 3:27–31, where he affirms that justification is by faith, not by *works of law*. The phrase *works of law* in Romans 3:20, 28 directly connects with the conception of *works* developed in Romans 4:1–8.[40]

Works in Romans 4:1–6 does not focus on particular commandments dividing Jews and Gentiles. If Abraham was not justified by his "works" (v. 2) nor by "working" (vv. 4–5), he was not justified by what he did. We need not read Dunn's circumscribed definition of *works of law* into the term *works* here, for we already have seen that *works* in Paul refers generally to people's deeds. The illustration in verse 4 supports this interpretation. Those who work for a living think their wages are deserved, and they do not believe their wages are a gracious gift from their employer. The illustration shows that work deserves a reward.

---

37. That the law continued to function as a general norm of conduct in the Second Temple Period is also confirmed by Eckhard J. Schnabel, *Law and Wisdom from Ben Sira to Paul: A Tradition Historical Enquiry into the Relation of Law, Wisdom, and Ethics* (Tübingen: J. C. B. Mohr, 1985), 29–63, 97–99, 106–9, 113–16, 120–21, 126–27, 135–36, 143–47, 154–58, 169–90.

38. Charles E. B. Cranfield, "'The Works of the Law' in the Epistle to the Romans," *JSNT* 43 (1991): 89–101, sees no focus on "identity markers" in the term *works of law* in Romans. Dunn's response to Cranfield ("Once More," 99–117) identifies some oversights in Cranfield's study. Nonetheless, Cranfield correctly argues that there is no emphasis on "identity markers" in the term *works of law* in Romans.

39. Compare *works of law* in 3:28 with *works* in 3:27; 4:2, 6. Verbal forms of ἐργάζομαι (*ergazomai*) are used in 4:4, 5. The only qualification I would add is that ἔργα refers to all human works in general, while ἔργα νόμου refers to all the works commanded in the Mosaic law.

40. Dunn's attempt to posit a distinction between *works* and *works of law* ("Once More," 113) is unpersuasive, for the discussion on *works* in Rom. 4:1–8 parallels what is said about *works of law* in Rom. 3:27–31. Boers also fails to see that Rom. 4:2–8 damages the theory that Paul refers only to exclusivism. See Boers, "We Who Are," 267.

Again, nothing indicates that Paul refers only to the kinds of works that separate Jews from Gentiles.

Paul's argument from the life of David in Romans 4:6–8 also confirms this interpretation of *works*.[41] David was circumcised, kept the sabbath, and observed purity laws. It follows, then, that if David was "reckoned righteous apart from works" (4:6) the works he lacked could not refer to any laws dividing Jews from Gentiles. David was a Jew, and he kept all of those laws. Paul likely thinks "lawless deeds" and "sins" (4:7) of David refer to his adultery with Bathsheba and his murder of Uriah. Paul does not focus on that part of the law dividing Jews and Gentiles in Romans 3:27–4:8. W*orks* and *works of law* denote, respectively, human works in general and all the works demanded by the Mosaic law.[42]

Neither does the attempt to confine *works of law* to a segment of the law account for the context of Romans 3:20. The failure to be justified by works of law in Romans 3:20 arises from the Jewish failure to obey the *moral claims of the law*— not Jewish adherence to the ritual law for nationalistic reasons. In Romans 2:17–29 Paul rebukes the Jews specifically for stealing, adultery, and robbing temples (2:21–22). These infractions clearly come from the moral realm, not the ritual law. Moreover, Paul contrasts the failure of the Jews to obey the law even though they are circumcised (2:25, 27) with the keeping of the law by Gentiles, who are uncircumcised (2:26–27).[43]

The contrast between circumcised Jews who do not obey and uncircumcised Gentiles who do, raises two arguments against Dunn's interpretation. First, Paul does not condemn the Jews for imposing circumcision on Gentiles but for failing to keep other parts of the law. Of course the Jews observed sabbath, purity laws, and circumcision, but they failed morally (Rom. 2:21–22).[44] Contrary to Dunn, the Jews are not condemned for excluding Gentiles from the promise, but for failing to keep the law themselves. Second, the fact that Gentiles can keep the law without being circumcised verifies this interpretation. Gentiles keep the moral portion of the law, but do not observe the part of the law separating Jews from Gentiles. The Gentiles here function as a foil to the Jews.

41. It could be objected that the words of Rom. 4:6–8 do not necessarily refer to David since the pronouncement of blessing is in the 3d-person plural. But Ps. 32:3–5 indicates that David was thinking of his own experience of denying and then later admitting his sin, which led him to pronounce as blessed all those who confess sin. Gundry ("Grace," 15) remarks that it is irrelevant whether the psalm was really about David; for Paul obviously thought it was about David.

42. Cranfield ("Works of the Law," 95) suggests also that Paul would have constructed his argument differently in Rom. 14:1–15:13 if Dunn's view of *works of law* were correct. Paul probably would have spoken much more harshly of Jewish distinctives with respect to the observance of days and abstention from certain foods.

43. The identity of the Gentiles who keep the law will be explored in chapter 7.

44. See also Cranfield, "Works of the Law," 94–95.

This contrast must have in view the moral code. Gentiles clearly do not observe the ritual law—they are uncircumcised—but they do keep the moral law. At this point Paul does not criticize the Jews for imposing circumcision on Gentiles. He condemns them for cherishing the delusion that somehow circumcision will protect them from God's wrath.

Dunn's response[45] to my observations on his thesis with respect to Romans 2[46] clarifies where we agree and disagree. I believe Dunn is correct in saying that Paul condemns the Jews both for their disobedience and their attitude. Paul faults the Jews for relying on circumcision to protect them from God's judgment. Dunn's remarks have convinced me that I overstated my position in saying that "nothing is said here about a wrong attitude."[47]

We still disagree in identifying the specific attitude for which the Jews are condemned. In Romans chapters 2 and 3 Jews are not condemned for imposing circumcision on Gentiles, for excluding Gentiles from the promise, nor for nationalistically excluding Gentiles from membership in the people of God. The Jews are indicted for thinking that their election, possession of the law, and circumcision guarantees protection from God's wrath against law-breakers. Paul *fundamentally* charges that the Jews do not obey God's law. Paul does not suggest anything is wrong with *possessing* the law or circumcision (Rom. 3:1). These are gifts of God which the Jews should celebrate. But obedience to the law is necessary for eternal life. That Paul disagrees with imposing circumcision upon Gentile converts is clearly implied in Romans 2:25–29. But that is not the same as finding the Jews guilty of imposing "identity markers" upon Gentile converts.

Dunn's latest article[48] indicates a significant shift in his emphasis. His earlier work on *works of law* stresses that the attitudes for which the Jews are condemned are their imposing the law on Gentiles and their exclusivism. He still thinks this is true.[49] But his actual explanation of the attitude of the Jews in Romans 2 more closely aligns with my exegesis.

In Romans 3:9–18 Paul indicts both Jews and Gentiles for unrighteousness, lack of understanding, failure to seek God and do good, poisonous and destructive speech, wreaking violence and misery on others, a lack of peace, and, most significantly, a failure to fear God.

The root cause why Jews fail to keep what the law itself says, is that their hearts lack a proper fear of God (3:18). When Paul concludes in

---

45. "Once More," 106–9.
46. "'Works of Law' in Paul," *NovT* 33 (1991): 225–31.
47. Ibid., 228.
48. "Once More."
49. Ibid., 102, 110–11.

Romans 3:20a that "no flesh can be justified by works of law," it follows from the preceding context that no one can be justified by obeying all requirements of the law of Moses.[50] In 3:20b he confirms this interpretation by providing a reason (γάρ) why righteousness is not obtained through works of law—"through the law comes knowledge of sin." The verse illustrates why righteousness is not gained through works of law; law reveals sin, and no one stands innocent. *Works of law*, then, refers to the law as a whole, and Paul indicts both Jews and Gentiles for failing to practice it.

In Galatians a better case can be made for placing the laws dividing Jews from Gentiles under *works of law*. But even here the distinction falls. First, it seems unlikely that Paul would apply the term in a different sense from its use in Romans, since he again discusses how one obtains righteousness. Second, there is concrete evidence in Galatians that *works of law* refers to the entire law. Galatians 3:10 describes *works of law* as "everything written in the book of the law." The word *everything* (πᾶσιν, *pasin*) denotes the whole law. The defect in returning to the law is that "I will demonstrate myself to be a transgressor" (Gal. 2:18). Paul says this after affirming three times that righteousness is not available by "works of law" (Gal. 2:16). The problem with rebuilding the law, according to verse 18, is that a return to the law reveals that one cannot keep it. Surely the inability to keep the law cannot be restricted to laws that separate Jews from Gentiles, for a scrupulous person such as Paul would take pains to observe sabbath and purity laws.

In addition, those who receive circumcision are obligated to keep the whole law (Gal. 5:3) and even the opponents who have submitted to circumcision do not obey the law (Gal. 6:13). I conclude that one cannot sustain the thesis that *works of law* focuses upon Jewish ethnic laws in Galatians.

After this excursus on the phrase *works of law*, we return to Galatians 3:10 to draw a conclusion regarding Dunn's interpretation of this verse. He says that Israel is cursed in Galatians 3:10 for a wrong attitude towards Gentiles, and a nationalistic spirit.[51] But nothing in this verse speaks to an exclusive attitude or nationalism. Nor is it evident that Paul focuses on only the Jewish part of the law. Indeed, the specific wording indicates the whole law since he says all are cursed "who do not abide by *all things written in the book of the law*." And the connection between Galatians 3:10a and 3:10b, as we have seen, shows that the curse is pronounced for *failure to do the law*. I do not deny that Paul was concerned about the inclusion of the Gentiles into the Abrahamic promise. It does

---

50. Rightly Cranfield, "Works of the Law," 93–94.
51. See pp. 43–44.

not follow from this concern, however, that Jews stand condemned in Galatians 3 *because* they excluded Gentiles.[52]

Another interesting interpretation of Galatians 3:10 has been suggested by Daniel P. Fuller. He thinks it a "highly arbitrary procedure" to insert in this verse the proposition that no one is able to keep the law.[53] The verse simply says that "those who are of the works of the law are under a curse." But what does it mean to be "of the works of the law"? Fuller argues that the phrase refers to the misinterpretation of the law by Judaizers who were attempting to bribe God by their good works and thereby earn his favor. The citation of Deuteronomy 27:26 is interpreted similarly. Fuller says that Deuteronomy 27:26, in the context of Deuteronomy 27, refers to "the legalistic frame of mind, which seeks to earn God's favor . . . since it involves trying to bribe God to impart blessing on the basis of good works that one does."[54]

I do not doubt, as I shall demonstrate in a later chapter, that legalism was present in the Galatian churches. But it is quite unlikely that this is what Paul means by *works of law*. The most natural way to understand this phrase, as we saw above in discussing Dunn's view, is to see Paul as describing the works commanded by the law. *Works of law* itself merely refers to what the law commands, and is not shorthand for legalism.

The key to Fuller's exegesis lies in Deuteronomy 27. He errs by not realizing that neither Deuteronomy 27 as a whole nor 27:26 in particular denounces the sin of legalism. The curses fall, not because someone legalistically observes the law, but rather the curses fall upon one who does not observe some part of the law. A glance at a few of the verses shows the author had this in mind. People are liable to the curse if they

---

52. See Christopher D. Stanley, "'Under a Curse': A Fresh Reading of Galatians 3:10–14," *NTS* 36 (1990): 481–511, see especially 500–1; J. P. Braswell, "'The Blessing of Abraham' Versus 'The Curse of the Law': Another Look at Gal. 3:10–13," *WTJ* 53 (1991): 76, 78, and Wright, *The Climax of the Covenant*, 145, contend that Gal. 3:10 refers to the "possibility" or "risk" of being cursed. They argue that the point of verse 10 is not that no one is able to obey the law, and so all are cursed. Rather, Paul *threatens* those who would submit to the law with the curse *if* they fail to obey the law perfectly. Paul does not think it is impossible to obey the law, but there is the potential that one will disobey it, and thus one should not abandon Christ for the law because in Christ there is certain blessing, while those who submit to the law may find themselves disobeying it and thereby end up being cursed. This interpretation is quite similar to my own, but it fails to read the connection between the verses carefully enough. Gal. 3:10a does not say "that those who are of the works of the law are *threatened with the curse*, or *that they may potentially be cursed*." The verse says "that those who are of the works of the law *are* under a curse." The reason for the curse is given in 3:10b: All those who fail to obey the law perfectly *are* under a curse. Paul says this because he thinks it is impossible for anyone under the law to escape the curse. Paul is not only threatening those under the law; he is actually condemning them.

53. Daniel P. Fuller, "Paul and 'The Works of the Law,'" *WTJ* 38 (1975): 33.

54. Ibid., 32–33.

make an idol (v. 15), or dishonor father and mother (v. 16), or lie with their father's wife (v. 20), or slay their neighbor in secret (v. 24). Fuller thinks the author condemns those who violate the integrity of the law, not those who disobey certain requirements of the law.[55] But this is a distinction without a difference, for Deuteronomy 27:15–25 makes it clear that the "integrity of the law" is violated when one disobeys it. Verse 26 differs from the previous verses because no particular infraction of the law is mentioned. The verse contains a generalizing summary: "Cursed be he who does not confirm the words of this law by doing them." There is no indication here that the author of Deuteronomy condemns any kind of legalism.[56] He censures failure to practice all that the law commands.

It seems unlikely, then, that Paul cited Deuteronomy 27:26 in Galatians 3:10 to condemn the sin of legalism. A more natural way of reading the citation sees Paul as condemning the failure to keep all that the law commands. This is strengthened by Paul's use of a text (similar to that of the LXX) that pronounces a curse on one who does not abide by "all" that is found in the book of the law.[57]

Galatians 3:11–14

Galatians 3:11–14 is informed by the thesis of verse 10 that no one can keep the whole law. Verse 11 says, "And that no one is justified by the law in God's sight is evident, because the just shall live by faith." This verse should not be interpreted as contradicting verse 10. Paul does not suggest here that, even if one keeps the law perfectly, justification still does not come through the law but only through faith.[58] Instead, Paul assumes and builds on verse 10 where he asserts that no one can be righteous by works of law, since all sin.[59] Verse 10 should be understood as the foundational sentence. Verse 11 shows the way

55. Daniel P. Fuller, *Gospel and Law: Contrast or Continuum?* (Grand Rapids: Eerdmans, 1980), 92.

56. Compare Bruce, *Galatians*, 158.

57. Fuller's complaint that my view wrongly adds an implied proposition to the text is not a compelling objection ("Works of Law," 33). Implied propositions are a common feature of human language, and they are not surprising in Paul since he did not write in formal syllogisms. The real question is whether the context supports reading an implied proposition into this verse, and for reasons already given I believe supplying an implied proposition is the most satisfying way to construe the text.

58. Contra Stanley, "Under a Curse," 502.

59. So Jan Lambrecht, "Gesetzesverständnis bei Paulus," in K. Kertelge, ed., *Das Gesetz im Neuen Testament* (Freiburg: Herder, 1986), 112–20; Ulrich Wilckens, *Der Brief an die Römer*, 3 vols. (Neukirchen: Neukirchener Verlag, 1978, 1980, 1982), 1.175. Charles H. Cosgrove sees Gal. 3:11 as a paraphrase of 3:10, but he glides over 10b without giving it adequate treatment. See C. H. Cosgrove, *The Cross and the Spirit: A Study in the Argument and Theology of Galatians* (Macon: Mercer, 1988), 52–58.

one can be righteous—not by doing the law (since all sin) but by exercising faith. Verse 11 complements verse 10, not only restating that justification cannot come through the law, but by clearly showing that justification is available through faith.

Verse 12 at first blush posits an absolute dichotomy between law and gospel. Here Paul says that "the law is not of faith, but the one who does them shall live by them." Klein sees here the fundamental reason why Paul rejects the law, arguing that law and faith are fundamentally antithetical.[60] We need to be careful, however, that we do not read into this verse an entire systematic theology on the relationship between law and gospel, as if by using *law* here Paul has in mind the entire Old Testament and concludes that salvation in the Old Testament was not by faith. Such an interpretation would be mistaken since Paul has just claimed that Abraham was justified by faith (Gal. 3:6–9).

The meaning of "the law" in verse 12 should also be sought from its context. In verse 11 Paul probably refers to the works of the law when he uses the phrase *by law* (ἐν νόμῳ, *en nomō*), since verse 11a restates and elaborates on verse 10. "The law" in verse 12, therefore, also probably refers to works of law. If so, we can paraphrase verse 12 as follows: "Salvation by works of the law is contrary to faith, for salvation by works of law means that the one who does the law will live by his obedience." Paul has already established in verse 10 that no one can escape the curse through the works of the law, since all are sinners. What he said in verse 10 informs verse 12, for verse 10 is the topic sentence for this paragraph. Thus, Paul does *not* say in verse 12 that, even if one does what the law says, one will be cursed anyway. His point is that salvation by law and by faith are fundamentally different because the former is based on "doing" the commandments (ποιήσας, *poiēsas*, v. 12), while the latter is based on "believing." Paul's fundamental objection, though, is not with doing *per se*, but with inability to "do" perfectly.

The major problem with reading verse 12 to say that life under the law leads to a curse, even if one obeys the law perfectly, is that such an interpretation does not fit the specific wording of the verse. The verse does not say that even if one obeys the law, one will die anyway. The text says, "the one who *does* the commandments will live by them." Paul promises life to the one who obeys the law, not death. But if he promises life to the one who obeys the law, then why is righteousness available only through faith? Here the foundational character of verse 10 reappears, for that verse implies that no one can do perfectly what the law commands. Thus, the way of the law will always lead to a curse.

60. Klein, "Sündenverständnis," 270–72.

Galatians 3:21–22 supports this interpretation of verse 12. Paul asks, "Then is the law contrary to the promises of God? Of course not. For if a law was given that was able to give life, then righteousness would have actually been by the law. But Scripture has shut up all people under sin, in order that the promise by faith in Christ Jesus might be given to those who believe." Paul does not polarize gospel and law as the Bultmann school does. For if the law could provide life, then people would be righteous through the law. The implication seems to be that if people had the ability to put the law into practice, then righteousness would be realized through the law. The sad fact is, however, that the law is not the source of life.[61] It provides no power. Indeed, the law simply documents that all people are enclosed under the power of sin. Since no one keeps the law, the way of righteousness is only through faith in Jesus Christ.

The interpretation of Leviticus 18:5 in Ezekiel 20 and Nehemiah 9 also supports this understanding of Galatians 3:12. Ezekiel alludes three times to Leviticus 18:5, which affirms that a person who keeps God's commands and judgments will live (Ezek. 20:11, 13, 21). Ezekiel does not reprimand Israel for the attempt to obey the commands of the law. Israel's judgment was due to failure to obey the law. "They rejected my ordinances, and as for my statutes, they did not walk in them" (Ezek. 20:16; see also 20:13, 21, 24). The judgment anticipated Israel's dispersion among the nations (20:23).[62]

Nehemiah 9 consists of a prayer that records the history of God's dealings with Israel. Nehemiah praises God for choosing, redeeming, and saving Israel. He contrasts God's mercy with the unfaithfulness of the Jews, who continually strayed and disobeyed his law. Because of Israel's disobedience God handed them over to oppressors (v. 27), and their persistent disobedience finally resulted in exile (v. 30). God has been just in meting out punishment because Israel failed to observe the law (vv. 33–34). Thus, God's people are enslaved by a foreign power (vv. 36–37). Once again we see that Israel's subjugation is rooted in its failure to observe the covenant. Verse 29 alludes to Leviticus 18:5: "Yet they acted arrogantly and did not listen to your commandments but sinned against your ordinances, by which a person who observes them will live." The message of Nehemiah parallels Ezekiel's. Those who keep the law will

---

61. For this interpretation of Gal. 3:21 see Moisés Silva, "Is the Law Against the Promises? The Significance of Galatians 3:21 for Covenant Continuity," in William S. Barker and W. R. Godfrey, eds., *Theonomy: A Reformed Critique* (Grand Rapids: Zondervan, 1990), 157–66.

62. One of the themes of Ezekiel 20 is that the Lord has been gracious to Israel, even though their sin was sufficient to warrant complete destruction. Nevertheless, the Lord for the sake of his name and holiness had not completely destroyed them (20:9–10, 14, 17, 22), and he would restore Israel from exile once again (20:33–44).

live. Israel has suffered punishment and exile because of its disobedience and failure to keep the law. Israel is not condemned for desiring to keep the law but for failing to keep it. Paul's knowledge of the Old Testament strengthens the assumption that he would not have understood Leviticus 18:5 differently than would Ezekiel and Nehemiah, who would have agreed that the obstacle to blessing was not the law itself but failure to do it.

In Galatians 3:14 Paul concludes that the blessing of Abraham and the promise of the Spirit can be obtained only through faith. The promises made to Abraham were not fulfilled until the death and resurrection of Jesus Christ. The promise of Genesis 12:3 that "all families shall be blessed" in Abraham was fulfilled in the proclamation of the gospel (Gal. 3:8). Gentiles are "sons of Abraham" (Gal. 3:7) and "blessed with the faithful Abraham" (Gal. 3:9) by believing God as did Abraham (Gal. 3:6). The inclusion of Gentiles into the church shows that the promise to Abraham of a worldwide family was now coming to fruition. The main concern of Galatians 3:10–14 is to prove that one cannot inherit the blessing of Abraham through the law. Christ bore the curse so that Gentiles could obtain "the blessing of Abraham" (3:14) and receive the promised Holy Spirit.[63]

Christ removed the curse from those who could not obey the law (v. 10) by taking the curse of the law upon himself by hanging upon the cross (v. 13). Paul sees in the death of Jesus the reception and localization of the curse of sin. Since Jesus has absorbed the curse, blessing can flow to all, both Jews and Gentiles, who become part of Abraham's family by faith.[64]

Verse 13 reveals the weakness of those who say that Paul could never have demanded perfect obedience to the whole law in verse 10. The objection is that all Jews agreed that atonement was available through sacrifice in the temple.[65] Such a view fails to understand the genius of

---

63. The "we" in the verb λάβωμεν (*labōmen*, 3:14) most likely includes Gentiles, and does not focus on the Jews, contra Wright, *The Climax of the Covenant*, 154. The reception of the Spirit by the Gentiles in 3:14 recalls Gal. 3:1–5 where Paul drives home that the Galatians must be part of the new community since they have experienced the empowering Spirit. In fact, Paul's argument depends on the idea that all those who have received the gift of the Spirit have obtained "the blessing of Abraham." Thus, to see the reception of the Spirit as focusing only on the Jews in verse 14 is to miss the genius of Paul's argument. The fact that Paul places both Jews and Gentiles under the "elements" (στοιχεῖα, *stoicheia*, 4:3, 9) also shows that the distinction between "we" and "they" should not be pressed in Galatians. Thus, T. L. Donaldson, in "The 'Curse of the Law' and the Inclusion of the Gentiles: Galatians 3.13–14," *NTS* 32 (1986): 94–112, claims that ἡμᾶς (*hēmas*) in verse 13 refers particularly to Jewish Christians is unpersuasive. See on this latter point Fung, *Galatians*, 148–49.

64. Compare Wright, *The Climax of the Covenant*, 151.

65. George Howard, *Paul: Crisis in Galatia. A Study in Early Christian Theology* (Cambridge: Cambridge University Press, 1979), 53; see also Fuller, *Gospel and Law*, 91–92.

Paul's argument. Paul now rules out what Judaism still maintains. In other words, for Paul the only atonement for sins is now found in the death of Christ on the cross. The animal sacrifices of the Old Testament are no longer considered to be adequate for the removal of sins. Thus, Paul can threaten those who return to the law with the curse, not because he does not believe in the forgiveness of Yahweh, but because he believes that, now that Messiah has come, atonement can only be obtained through his death. The sacrifices of the old covenant once were sufficient—probably in Paul's mind only provisionally since they pointed to Christ's death—but to return to them now rules out the importance of the death of the Messiah. If Old Testament sacrifices do atone, then "Christ died needlessly" (Gal. 2:21). The fact that Old Testament sacrifices no longer atone reveals the salvation-historical shift in Paul's thinking. What the Old Testament sacrifices anticipated and pointed to has arrived, and now that the fulfillment has come that which predicted the fulfillment is set aside.

In fact, Paul's sustained polemic against the law only makes sense if there is a shift in salvation history. Otherwise, forgiveness could be obtained through the Old Testament cultus. Sanders correctly maintains that the Pauline polemic against the law is rooted in a salvation-historical shift. Paul was convinced that salvation was only available through Jesus Christ. But the argument from redemptive history is wedded to the reality of human ability. The inadequacy of the Mosaic covenant was apparent because it did not produce the obedience God required.

Galatians 5:3

The inability of human beings to fulfil the law is also the most probable interpretation of Galatians 5:3. "I testify again to every man being circumcised that he is a debtor to do the whole law." It is doubtful Paul merely reminds Galatians attracted to circumcision of something they already knew—that submission to circumcision also entailed obedience to the rest of the law.[66] In any case, if Paul were merely revealing to the Galatians the full import of receiving circumcision, they could have replied, "All right, then we will obey the rest of the law as well."

The content of 5:3 corresponds remarkably to 3:10, and thus it seems likely that the word *again* (πάλιν, *palin*) refers to the former verse.[67] The crucial word in 5:3 is *debtor* (ὀφειλέτης, *opheiletēs*). Paul stresses the obligation incumbent upon anyone receiving circumcision to keep the rest of the law, since he specifically stresses that one must keep "the

---

66. Against Walter Schmithals, *Paul and the Gnostics* (Nashville: Abingdon, 1972), 33.
67. So Betz, *Galatians*, 260–61.

whole law" (ὅλον τὸν νόμον, *holon ton nomon*).[68] Paul links acceptance of circumcision in this context to justification, as 5:4 makes clear. They receive circumcision because they "are trying to be justified by law." It seems fair to conclude, given the content of 5:4 and its proximity to verse 3, that Paul suggests in 5:3 that anyone who submits to circumcision must also keep the rest of the law in order to be justified. The fact that Paul says that one must keep the whole law *in order to be justified* shows how radically he has departed from the Jewish view that would include the possibility of atonement through animal sacrifices. He insists that, if one submits to circumcision, the rest of the law must be kept perfectly in order to be justified.

This explanation of 5:3–4 would explain why Paul says in 5:2 that "if you receive circumcision, Christ will not profit you at all." Either one relies upon observing the law for salvation, or one trusts in Christ and his atoning work to remove the curse (Gal. 3:13). The thematic connection between Galatians 5:2 and 2:21 is apparent, for in the latter text Paul says that "if righteousness is through the law, then Christ died for nothing."

Thus, Galatians 5:3 implies that no one can keep the law perfectly. Three reasons support this view: First, I have already said that *again* probably refers to Galatians 3:10, which implies that the curse is due to human inability to keep the law. Second, the emphasis on "the whole law" and "debtor" in 5:3 shows that, if the Galatians submit to circumcision, they must carry out every command of the law for justification. Third, Paul sees the threat in 5:3 as so ominous because he thought the law unfulfillable. Indeed, Paul does not depart from Jewish tradition when he says that the law cannot be obeyed.[69] Thus, the claim that all people are sinners would not be controversial in Paul's day. Paul differs from many Jews of the Second Temple Period in no longer thinking forgiveness is available through the Old Testament cultus. One must believe in Jesus to be forgiven, and to accept circumcision was, for Paul, to renounce Jesus and the benefits of his sacrifice. Thus, Paul can say that those who try to be justified by receiving circumcision "have been cut off from Christ"(Gal. 5:4).

Galatians 6:13

Galatians 6:13 also seems to indicate that no one could keep the law perfectly. "For neither do those who accept circumcision keep the law,

68. For a similar view see Donald Guthrie, *Galatians* (Grand Rapids: Eerdmans, 1973), 129. Bruce (*Galatians*, 231) thinks Paul is only saying that life under the law was one of bondage, but this latter view does not explain adequately the emphasis on "the whole law" in 5:3.

69. See 1 Kings 8:46; 2 Chron. 6:36; Job 4:17; Pss. 130:3 and 143:2; Prov. 20:9, and Eccl. 7:20. It should be noted that these texts stem from narrative, hymnic, and wisdom literature.

but they want you to be circumcised, in order that they might boast in your flesh." It is quite unlikely that Paul accuses the opponents of failing to observe any part of the law at all. After all, circumcision *was* part of the law, and obviously the adversaries were law-observant in at least this regard. Paul simply points out at the end of this letter, after establishing the necessity of keeping the whole law to obtain justification, that the adversaries themselves fail to keep every part of it. The opponents face the same peril as those who submit to circumcision since they too fail to obey the whole law.

I conclude, then, that in Galatians the reason righteousness cannot be obtained through the law is that human beings cannot keep it perfectly. Such perfect obedience is indispensable since Old Testament sacrifices do not atone for sins. Given the impossibility of perfect obedience, the cross of Christ, therefore, provides the only means of forgiveness.

Human Inability in Romans

Romans 3:9–26

We have already seen in Romans 3:9–20 that *works of law* refers to the whole law. Here we need to show in more detail that the reason justification cannot be attained through works of law is human inability to keep the whole law. In Paul's summary statement in Romans 3:19–20 he says, "Now we know that whatever the law says it says to those who are in the realm of the law, in order that every mouth might be closed and all the world might be accountable to God. Because by the works of law no flesh shall be justified before him, for through the law there is knowledge of sin." If we work backward in these verses we see that the law makes people aware of their sin, and, therefore, justification is not available through the law. There is a debate over verse 20 concerning whether Paul speaks of the law *revealing* sin, *defining* sin, or *causing* sin. In this context Paul probably denotes the cognitive dimension of sin, which means that he stresses that the law *reveals* people to be sinners.[70] He reasons that justification cannot be obtained through the law; the law merely documents that all are sinners. The "for" (γάρ, *gar*) connecting Romans 3:20a to 3:20b reveals that the presence of sin in all people prohibits them from being justified through the law. The logical relationship between verses 19 and 20 also confirms the futility of seeking justification through the law. The law causes every mouth to be shut and renders the whole world accountable to God. But how does the law shut

---

70. See Heikki Räisänen, *Paul and the Law* (Philadelphia: Fortress, 1983), 141, 145; Jeffrey A. D. Weima, "The Function of the Law in Relation to Sin: An Evaluation of the View of H. Räisänen," *NovT* 32 (1990): 223–24.

every person's mouth? The "because" (διότι, *dioti*) in verse 20 provides the answer. Every mouth is shut because all sin, which makes righteousness unobtainable. And 3:19 makes it clear that there are no exceptions: "*Every* mouth is shut and *all the world* is accountable to God."

Human inability to obey the law is also established by the Old Testament catena in 3:10–18. Paul opens 3:9 by saying that "we have charged both Jews and Greeks to be under sin." The inclusion of both Jews and Greeks indicates that he brands the whole human race as sinners. Subsequent verses confirm this exegesis: "There is none righteous, no not even one" (3:10); "All have turned aside" (3:12); "There is no one who does good; there is not even one" (3:12). In 3:20 Paul infers that no one can be right before God through the works of the law. This deduction is hardly surprising since the catena in 3:10–18 prepares the reader for the conclusion articulated in 3:20.[71]

Romans 3:21–26, like Galatians 3:13, stresses that the only means of forgiveness is the cross of Christ. Righteousness with God does not come through obeying the law, for no one obeys it perfectly. Instead, people become righteous before God through faith in Jesus Christ's atoning death, which liberated God's people from sin's bondage and satisfied God's righteousness.

Romans 1:18–2:29

Romans 1:18–2:29 also expresses the theme of universal human sinfulness. For example, in the indictment of the Gentile world in 1:18–32 Paul does not allow for Gentiles who have responded positively to the revelation given through nature. Paul refers only to people "who suppress the truth in unrighteousness" and receive God's wrath (1:18). They "are without excuse" (1:20) because God has revealed himself through his creation. The root human sin is a failure to delight in God as God (1:21). After casting aside the one true God, people indulged in speculation as to the nature of God, worshiping images of animals and human beings (1:23). Failure to worship, love, and delight in God resulted in the

---

71. Neil Elliott says Rom. 1:18–3:20 only proves that all are accountable, not that all are guilty (*The Rhetoric of Romans: Argumentative Constraint and the Strategy of Paul's Dialogue with Judaism* [Sheffield: JSOT, 1990], 105–46). He says (p. 106) that in a parenetic letter the rhetorical pattern demands that the writer lead the reader along to his conclusion, but in Rom. 1:18–3:20 the latter verses only show that all are under sin, and there is no evidence that this was Paul's intention from the beginning. Elliott concludes, then, that Paul's purpose in this section is not to prove that all are sinners. Elliott's approach is a classic example of imposing a rhetorical form on a letter and then demanding that the letter follow that form! He even admits (p. 99) that the parenetic form is not discussed in rhetorical handbooks, and then insists that Paul must follow the pattern of rhetoricians in the way he constructs his argument. I do not doubt that Romans has a parenetic function ultimately. The weakness of Elliott's scheme is that he imposes too rigidly a form upon Paul that cannot even be found in the handbooks.

worship of people, in the exaltation of the creature rather than the blessed Creator (1:25).

The main burden of Romans 2 is to show the Jews that possession of the law does not mean the wrath of God will be averted. They will be spared God's judgment only if they practice the law. God impartially judges all people by their works (2:6). Those who practice evil will be judged on the last day (2:5, 8–9). God's present patience is designed to lead people to repentance (2:4). Since God is an impartial judge, the Jew who sins with the law will be judged on the basis of that law, just as the Gentile will be judged by obedience to the law written upon the heart (2:12–15).

Paul does not deny that the law (2:17–20) and circumcision (2:25; 3:1) are great advantages to the Jew. But they nullify these advantages by not keeping the very law that they treasure and teach (2:21–25). And circumcision is no better than uncircumcision if the Jews fail to obey the law (2:25).

Paul does not explicitly say in 1:18–2:29 that all Jews and Gentiles are sinners and without excuse. Nonetheless, such a thesis seems to be implied, and the context leads us to the conclusion that all, without exception, are sinners. We already have seen that when Paul comes to the conclusion of his argument in 3:9–20 he thinks he has established that all—both Jews and Gentiles—are sinners. Thus, in 3:9 he says that "we have charged both Jews and Greeks all to be under sin." Paul also indicts all people in 3:19. In fact, the flow of argument in 3:19 is illustrated in the following paraphrase: "We know that whatever the law says it says particularly to the Jews, who are in the realm of the law, and since even the Jews who have received the law fall short, then it follows that the purpose of the law is to stop every mouth and make the whole world accountable to God."

Further, Romans 2:1 also indicates that Paul considers all people sinners. There Paul says that "you are without excuse, O man, every one who judges, for in that you judge another, you condemn yourself, for you, the one who judges, do the same things." In this verse Paul addresses the person who because of moral standards condemns the behavior described in 1:18–32. The problem with such a person is not that he or she passes judgment on the behavior of others. Paul has clearly disapproved of the behavior of those depicted in 1:18–32 as well, and yet he himself does not expect to face eternal judgment. The defect Paul finds in people who judge is that they "do the same things" which they condemn in others. Note that Paul says that this is true of "everyone who judges" (πᾶς ὁ κρίνων, *pas ho krinōn*). What is startling here is that Paul should say that *all* who judge others are condemned because they also practice evil. The only conclusion we can draw is that there is not a single person in the world who condemns the evil behavior in others but is himself free from sin.[72]

Some Objections Regarding Romans

Several objections have been raised regarding the idea that in Romans 1:18–3:20 Paul is saying all (without exception) are sinners. First, Paul cannot be condemning all as sinners in Romans 2, when in the same context he teaches that some will be righteous by works (see Rom. 2:6–7, 10, 13–15, 26–29).[73] I will explain in chapter 7 what Paul has in mind when he says some will be justified by works. I will attempt to show why it does not contradict his assertion in 3:20 that no one can be justified by works of law.

Second, Klyne Snodgrass sees divine righteousness rather than human sin as the theme of 1:18–3:20.[74] The polarity Snodgrass draws here is misleading since the burden of this section expresses that God reveals his righteousness in his judgment of sinners. Snodgrass points out that Paul does not use the word *sin* (ἁμαρτία, *hamartia*) before 3:9, showing that human sin was not a central issue. This is a red herring. The *concept* of sin permeates the text even if the *word* is not used before 3:9. To demand the use of this word hearkens back to a word study approach that should be laid to rest.

Third, the accusations made against the Jews in 2:17–24 refer to gross transgressions that could not accurately reflect the life of all Jews.[75] All Jews were not thieves, adulterers, and robbers of temples. However, Paul does not charge every Jew with committing the specific sins of 2:21–22. Instead, he employs colorful specific examples to support the general principle that the Jews do not practice what they preach. Paul establishes the principle that "you dishonor God through your transgression of the law" (2:23). All Jews, according to Paul, transgress the law; the examples of 2:21–22 are merely specific cases used to establish a larger truth.

Fourth, Sanders thinks Paul borrows a synagogue sermon in 1:18–2:29, and Paul's exaggerated statements here do not harmonize with

72. The reason Paul will escape judgment himself, therefore, is not because he did not "do the same things" (Rom. 2:1). Paul was as guilty as every other person in the world, but he was counted righteous by trusting in the death of Jesus Christ (Rom. 3:21–26).

73. See Räisänen, *Paul and the Law*, 97–109; Sanders, *Paul, The Law*, 78, 123–35; Klyne R. Snodgrass, "Justification by Grace—To the Doers: An Analysis of the Place of Romans 2 in the Theology of Paul," *NTS* 32 (1986): 76.

74. Snodgrass, "To the Doers," 76.

75. Räisänen, *Paul and the Law*, 98–101; Sanders, *Paul, The Law*, 124–25; Snodgrass, "To the Doers," 76.

what he said about the law elsewhere.[76] If Paul borrowed this material (and this part of Sanders' thesis is itself a hypothesis), it is a priori unlikely that he would cite material that contradicted what he had written elsewhere. When I make this point, of course, my own presuppositions about Pauline consistency surface. But the burden of proof should be on the scholar who asserts that a writer contradicts himself or herself. When I examine the issue of justification by works I will attempt to show that Paul's thought is not contradictory in Romans 2.

Finally, Glenn Davies contends that Romans 3:9–20 should not be used to say that all people without exception are sinners.[77] Davies argues that 3:9–18 only proves that *the wicked* among Jews and Gentiles are sinners and stand under God's condemnation.[78] He stresses that not all people are wicked, for Romans 2 has already made it clear that there are righteous Jews and Gentiles. Moreover, the Old Testament catena of verses 10–18 does not show that all are sinners without exception, says Davies. A distinction exists between the righteous and the wicked in the Old Testament texts that Paul cites, and Davies thinks Paul did not violate the Old Testament contexts in using this material. Moreover, he claims 3:19–20 constitutes a transition in the argument of Romans. Paul shifts from addressing the wicked and now addresses the righteous Jews.

Davies' exegesis of this section, though stimulating, is not convincing. First, either Paul speaks hypothetically about obeying the law in Romans 2, or he refers to Christians who have been transformed by the Holy Spirit. If it is the former, then the problem vanishes. If it is the latter, then those who are *now* righteous *were formerly wicked*, and thus Davies' objection remains unpersuasive.[79] Second, Dunn and Moo rightly point out that Paul's use of the Old Testament is more subtle in verses 10–18 than Davies allows.[80] Paul uses the same texts that described the wicked in the Old Testament, and applies them to self-righteous Jews of his day. His purpose in doing so is to show that all are sinners without exception, even those who believe they are exempt from God's judgment because of their ethnic heritage. Third, the Old Testament catena needs to be interpreted in its context in Romans. Here Paul stresses that "no one is righteous" (v. 10), "not even one." He labors to prove that there are no exceptions to his indictment. Fourth, Davies'

76. Sanders, *Paul, The Law*, 123, 129–32.

77. Glenn N. Davies, *Faith and Obedience in Romans: A Study of Romans 1–4* (Sheffield, England: JSOT, 1990), 80–104.

78. So also Hermann Lichtenberger, "Paulus und das Gesetz," in M. Hengel and U. Heckel, eds., *Paulus und das antike Judentum* (Tübingen: J. C. B. Mohr, 1991), 371.

79. See chapter 7 for support of this argument.

80. Dunn, *Romans*, 1:150–51; Douglas J. Moo, *Romans 1–8* (Chicago: Moody, 1991), 205.

assertion that Romans 3:19–20 applies to righteous Jews and represents a shift in the context is highly improbable. The theme is remarkably similar to 3:9–18 (all are sinners), and the obvious break in the text comes in 3:21 ("But now apart from the law the righteousness of God has been manifested, being witnessed by the law and the prophets"). And even if 3:19–20 is addressed to the Jews, the conclusion drawn relates to all people—"*every* mouth should be closed" and "*all* the world is accountable before God," and "*no flesh* will be justified by the works of the law."[81]

Philippians 3:6

Some use Philippians 3:6 as an objection to Paul's contention in Romans that all are sinners. Here Paul says that according to the righteousness that is by law he was "blameless" (ἄμεμπτος, *amemptos*). This is firm evidence, says Sanders, that Paul sees human sinlessness as a possibility, even though it contradicts what he says elsewhere.[82] This objection seems even stronger considering that elsewhere Paul speaks of believers being blameless at the parousia (1 Thess. 3:13; 5:23; see also 1 Cor. 1:8), suggesting that the word refers to sinlessness. In the context of Philippians 3:6, however, Paul probably does not mean "sinlessness" when he uses the word *blameless*. Paul provides a preconversion perspective of his life here, and his purpose is to say that his obedience to the law was extraordinary compared to his contemporaries (see Gal. 1:13–14).[83] Obviously, Paul would no longer salute his persecution of the church as laudable. In fact, elsewhere he suggests that his persecution of the church unveils the gravity of his sin, and thus he was particularly conscious of his unworthiness to receive divine grace (1 Cor. 15:9). As a Christian Paul considers his former persecution of the church to be sin, not a mark of his righteousness. I am not disputing that Paul's obedience to the law before his conversion was remarkable, but extraordinary obedience would never be confused with sinlessness in the Jewish view.[84] Zechariah and Elizabeth are called "blameless" by Luke (Luke 1:6), but there is little doubt that they were still sinners, for

81. Lichtenberger ("Paulus und das Gesetz," 371, 376) says that Paul argues that the law *is not* fulfilled, not that it *cannot be* fulfilled. For God could not hold people guilty if he gave them a law they could not keep. The latter argument fails, for in Pauline anthropology human beings cannot (Rom. 8:7) keep the law since the fall of Adam. Human beings could keep the law before the fall, but have since lost that ability. Lichtenberger's argument, then, introduces a false dichotomy. The law which *is not* kept *cannot be* kept.

82. Sanders, *Paul, the Law*, 23–24; see also Räisänen, *Paul and the Law*, 106.

83. So Cranfield, *Romans*, 847.

84. So John M. Espy, "Paul's 'Robust Conscience' Re-examined," *NTS* 31 (1985): 165; Peter T. O'Brien, *The Epistle to the Philippians* (Grand Rapids: Eerdmans, 1991), 380.

Zechariah is rebuked by the angel for his unbelief (1:18–20). Indeed, as Thielman says, it was common for law-abiding Israelites to speak of themselves as righteous compared to those who blatantly broke the law (for example, Pss. 7:8–9; 17:3–5; 18:20–29; 26:9–12).[85] And Gundry is probably correct in saying that Philippians 3 focuses on outward obedience. Therefore, Paul's devotion to the law, however remarkable, would not imply sinlessness.[86] Finally, it is not surprising that a person could be blameless at the *parousia* since it culminates God's saving work.

Conclusion

Paul says righteousness cannot be obtained by works of law or through the law. This is so because perfect obedience is required for right-standing with God, and such obedience is impossible. Old Testament sacrifices no longer atone; only Christ's death on the cross provides forgiveness. The focus on human inability to obey the law is substantiated in a number of texts in Romans and Galatians, and chapter 3 will expand this conclusion, showing that the law did not restrain sin but exacerbated it.

---

85. Thielman, *From Plight to Solution*, 110.

86. Robert H. Gundry, "The Moral Frustration of Paul Before His Conversion: Sexual Lust in Romans 7:7–25," in D. A. Hagner and M. J. Harris, eds., *Pauline Studies: Essays Presented to Professor F. F. Bruce on His Seventieth Birthday* (Grand Rapids: Eerdmans, 1980), 234. See also J. A. Ziesler, "The Role of the Tenth Commandment in Romans 7," *JSNT* 33 (1988): 51.

3

The Purpose of the Law

I argued in the previous chapter that righteousness could be attained through the law if it is kept perfectly. Since no one obeys the entire law, the only way of salvation is through believing in Christ, who atoned for sin by his death on the cross.

Paul takes a step further, however, in his theology of the law. Most Jews of his day believed that a greater understanding of the contents of the law would curb the sinful impulse and prevent sin from dominating a person's life.[1] Paul turns this theology on its head by saying that the law does not restrain sin but *stimulates* and *provokes* it. The Jews would have been shocked by a theology claiming that the law, a gift from God, led people to sin more. This, however, was precisely Paul's contention. The law, instead of dousing the sinful impulse, actually kindled it.

Romans 5:20

The idea that the law provokes sin is found in Romans 5:20. "The law entered in so that the transgression might increase." Contrary to the normal Jewish view, the purpose of the law was not to limit sin. God intended that sin would increase through the law. What does Paul mean

1. See especially Timo Laato, *Paulus und das Judentum: Anthropologische Erwägungen* (Åbo: Åbo Academy Press, 1991), 83–94; Hans Dieter Betz, *Galatians* (Philadelphia: Fortress, 1979), 165; Hans Joachim Schoeps, *Paul: The Theology of the Apostle in the Light of Jewish Religious History* (Philadelphia: Westminster, 1959), 194–95.

here when he says that the intention was for "transgression" to "increase"? Is he saying that the law *makes known, defines, or causes* sin? In this verse it is probably the latter; the incursion of the law *increased* the power of sin.[2]

The cognitive interpretation of this verse claims that sin is *made known* through the law. The law brings a greater subjective awareness of human unrighteousness, so that through the law sin is *recognized* as sin in human experience. The cognitive interpretation fails, however, because the corresponding increase in grace in 5:20 is not merely an increase in the subjective awareness of grace but an increase in the power of grace.[3] Romans 6 confirms that the power of grace is in view. Paul argues that those who have experienced grace and died with Christ will sin less because the power of sin has been decisively broken in their lives. Those crucified with Christ do not receive merely a greater mental awareness of God's grace but a new power in their lives, which brings significant victory over sin.

The definitional interpretation of Romans 5:20 can also be excluded, for Paul speaks of the increase of sin, not the nature of it.[4] It is hard to see how the verb multiply (πλεονάζω, *pleonazō*) defines the essence of sin. The law was given to increase the power of sin, states 5:20, so the law led people to sin more, not less. The continuation of Paul's argument in Romans 6 indicates that the power of sin is in view, for there he declares that those who have died to sin should not let sin dominate their lives. Romans 5:20 is crucial for Pauline anthropology. Instruction and dissemination of moral norms are not necessarily a boon to morality since people without the Holy Spirit will actually do more evil once they become aware of what is good.

Galatians 3:19

"The law was added for the sake of transgressions" (τῶν παραβάσεων χάριν, *tōn parabaseōn charin*), observes Galatians 3:19. It is unlikely, given the negative view of the law which informs the context of Galatians 2–4, that Paul speaks positively of the law *restricting* transgressions.[5] He may merely be saying that the law *defines* sin, and if this is the case, then his point would be quite similar to Romans 4:15, which

2. So Jeffrey A. D. Weima, "The Function of the Law in Relation to Sin: An Evaluation of the View of H. Räisänen," *NovT* 32 (1990): 232; Heikki Räisänen, *Paul and the Law* (Philadelphia: Fortress, 1983), 143–44.

3. Räisänen, *Paul and the Law*, 144.

4. The alteration from παράπτωμα (*paraptōma*, "transgression") to ἁμαρτία (*hamartia*, "sin") shows that these words are basically synonymous in Rom. 5:20.

5. Contra David J. Lull, "'The Law Was Our Pedagogue': A Study of Galatians 3:19–25," *JBL* 105 (1986): 481–98.

says "Where there is no law, neither is there transgression." In other words, the law provides a standard by which sin can be technically defined. To say transgression is absent without the law does not imply that there is no sin whatsoever without the law, for Romans 5:13 notes that "sin was in the world until the law." Thus, Paul's point in Romans 4:15 and perhaps Galatians 3:19 is that the standard of the law identifies sin in a technical and legal sense. He does not doubt that sin exists without the law. It seems more likely, though, that the intent of Galatians 3:19 is not to declare that the law defines sin. Both the context of Galatians and the parallel with Romans 5:20 suggest that Paul teaches that the law was given *to cause* sin.[6]

First of all, the near context of Galatians 3 confirms that salvation cannot be attained through the law. Paul says in 3:21 that if the law could give life, then righteousness would be through the law. The problem, of course, is that the law is not a source of life and provides no power for obedience. Galatians 3:22 confirms the point of Galatians 3:21 that people do not have the power to obey the law by saying, "Scripture has shut up all under sin." The "but" (ἀλλά, *alla*) linking verse 21 to 22 demonstrates that verse 22 contrasts verse 21. Verse 21 says the law does not give life, and verse 22 affirms that all are confined under the power of sin. The shift from "law" to "Scripture" should not be pressed unduly, for even though the terms are not univocal, neither are they polar.[7] The Mosaic law comprises a subset of Scripture. Scripture itself documents that one purpose of the law was to confine all people under the power of sin.[8]

6. Weima opts for the definitional or cognitive view, maintaining that it is difficult to see why God would want to increase sin until the time that Christ came. See Jeffrey A. D. Weima, "Function of the Law," 226–27. The idea that the law simply defines sin is certainly possible, though I incline to the causative view. As to Weima's objection, it is also hard to see why the law would only define sin until Christ came. Presumably some standard by which sin could be identified would still be needed after Christ's coming. God willed that sin would increase through the law in order to show all people that the law has no power to restrain sin. Sin can only be conquered through the coming of the Messiah.

7. E. P. Sanders, in *Paul, the Law, and the Jewish People* (Philadelphia: Fortress, 1983), 87, n. 6, contends that the terms are synonymous.

8. Lull ("The Law," 485–86) thinks "the law" and "Scripture" are not coterminus since Scripture is an "active agent," and the law is not described as an active agent in these verses. I agree that the terms are not univocal, but Lull overinterprets the metaphor of scripture shutting up all under sin. Paul is not suggesting here that Scripture is the active agent which produces sin. His point is that Scripture *documents* that all are under sin. Linda L. Belleville also stresses the discontinuity between "law" and "Scripture," but her conclusion is based on the idea that the role of the law in Gal. 3:21–4:11 is basically neutral. See Belleville, "'Under Law': Structural Analysis and the Pauline Concept of Law in Galatians 3.21–4.11," *JSNT* 26 (1986): 56–58, 70–71. God intended it to function as a temporary code until the time of Christ in order to restrain sin. Such a neutral view of the law is off the mark in Gal. 3:21–4:11. Paul stresses that it provides no power for righteousness (3:21), and in a parallel text in Gal. 4:3 he says that "we were enslaved under the elements of the world." Thus, the redemption which Christ accomplished (Gal. 4:5) was redemption from the power of sin which reigned during the era of the Mosaic covenant.

I have argued previously (pp. 44–59) that Galatians 3:10 says that those who are under the law are cursed because they cannot keep it. In 3:10 Paul stresses human inability to keep the law and maintains that the law cannot make people righteous because it contains no life-giving power. Since the law confines all under the power of sin (3:21–22), it is very unlikely that Paul suggests that the law restrains people from sinning in 3:19. Nowhere else in Galatians does Paul intimate that the law somehow prevents people from sinning. In fact, he consistently says it reveals sin or enslaves people.[9] Furthermore, to admit that the law restrains sin would be a very odd argument for Paul to use in Galatians since he is trying to discourage the Galatians from accepting circumcision and the Mosaic law. The position that the law actually restrains sin would fit nicely with the Judaizers' stance, not Paul's. Thus, 3:19 argues that the law actually stimulates people to sin more.[10]

Second, the close parallel between Galatians 3:19 and Romans 5:20 strengthens the case for understanding Galatians 3:19 to say that the law escalates transgressions. David Lull protests that the parallel texts in Romans are not decisive because the context of Galatians should receive primary consideration.[11] In addition, he thinks the parallel texts in Romans 4:15, 5:13–14, and 5:15–18 are either incoherent, or reflect an inconsistent use of the words παράβασις (*parabasis*) and παράπτωμα (*paraptōma*) for "transgression." Lull correctly states that the Galatian context should be primary, but that very context supports my interpretation. He also correctly observes that Paul does not use παράβασις and παράπτωμα as technical terms in every instance in Romans 4–5. But such an admission does not mean that Paul contradicts himself. It simply means Paul does not intend these words to function as technical terms that bear the same meaning every time they are used. Context must determine meaning. Lull demands that Paul use these terms technically, and because Paul does not use them that way he is accused of contradiction.

It would be methodologically suspect to impose Romans upon Galatians. But New Testament scholars have exercised too much care to hermetically seal off each Pauline letter from on another. Such an approach is artificial. When Paul speaks on the same subject (for example, the law) in a similar context, one letter can shed light on another. When I read other writers, I understand them more profoundly as I read more of their works. Wider reading casts light on what they have said elsewhere. This

---

9. I shall prove this claim further when I examine the meaning of the phrase *under sin*.

10. Of course, this raises the question as to whether the law plays any positive role in the life of a Christian. This issue will be examined in chapter 6.

11. Lull, "The Law," 481, 483–85.

interpretive approach should not be jettisoned when we are trying to understand Paul. Some scholars think that to interpret each letter without any consideration of the others will yield more objective results, but it is more probable that it will simply yield more interpretive hypotheses, with little agreement on the meaning of each text.

I conclude that both Romans 5:20 and Galatians 3:19 communicate the same message: The law did not restrain sin, but rather it provoked more sinning.

To Be "Under Law" Is to Be "Under Sin"

The close relationship between "under law" (ὑπὸ νόμον, *hypo nomon*) and "under sin" (ὑπὸ ἁμαρτίαν, *hypo hamartian*) in Paul also denotes the role of the law in arousing sin. Romans 6:14 identifies plainly the linkage between the two: "For sin shall not rule over you, since you are not under law but under grace." Verse 14a contains a promise that "sin shall not rule over you." The reason for the promise is "because" or "since" (γάρ, *gar*) "you are not under law but under grace." Verse 14 implies that if people are under the law, sin rules over them. If they are under grace, rather than the law, sin will have no dominion in their lives.[12] To be under the Mosaic law, says Paul, is to be under the power, authority, and dominion of sin, but to be under grace (see also Rom. 6:15–23) means liberation from the tyranny of sin.

Galatians also suggests that to be under law is to be under sin. In Galatians the following phrases are closely related: "to be under a curse" (3:10), "under sin" (3:22), "under law" (3:23; 4:4–5; 5:18), "under a pedagogue" (3:25), "under guardians and managers" (4:2), and "under the elements of the world" (4:3). Some interpreters doubt that Paul in Galatians sees the law as inciting sin. The debate centers on the precise significance of the terms παιδαγωγός (*paidagōgos*, pedagogue or tutor, Gal. 3:24–25), ἐπίτροπος (*epitropos*, "guardian," 4:2), and οἰκονόμος (*oikonomos*, "manager").[13] Historically, παιδαγωγός has often been understood as having an educational purpose, in the sense that the law functioned as a teacher to bring people to Christ.[14] Similarly, some modern inter-

12. First Cor. 9:20 does not directly say that life "under the law" is life under the domination of sin, but what Paul says there accords with my understanding of the phrase. He says that he lived "under the law" when ministering to those "under the law," but he is careful to point out that he himself is not "under the law."

13. For helpful surveys on the meaning and cultural background of these terms see Richard N. Longenecker, "The Pedagogical Nature of the Law in Galatians 3:19–4:7," *JETS* 25 (1982): 53–61; Lull, "The Law," 489–96; Belleville, "'Under Law,'" 59–63; Norman H. Young, "*PAIDAGOGOS*: The Social Setting of a Pauline Metaphor," *NovT* 29 (1987): 150–76.

14. See Georg Bertram, "Παιδαγωγός," *TDNT*, 5:620–21.

preters understand Paul to be referring positively or neutrally to the law as a bridle or restraint upon sin since the pedagogue of a child was hired to deter the child from misbehavior, and guardians and managers had the function of encouraging acceptable behavior in children.[15] Richard N. Longenecker thinks the emphasis lies on the supervisory nature of the law for a certain period in salvation history,[16] while T. David Gordon argues that the main purpose was to underscore the law's role in guarding and protecting Israel from intermixing with the Gentiles until the coming of Christ.[17] Similar in some respects is Norman Young's view in which he argues that the purpose of the metaphor is to underline the restrictive nature of the law for a certain period of salvation history, focusing on practices separating Jews and Gentiles.[18]

Many of the interpretations listed above depend upon finding the specific nuance of the word παιδαγωγός. The problem with interpreting παιδαγωγός is that virtually all of the above suggestions are possible given the usage of the word in Greco-Roman literature. What must be discerned, however, is the precise significance of the term in the context of Galatians 3–4. The force of the metaphor must not be imported from its use elsewhere in Greek literature, since it is employed in a variety of ways. Paul does not employ παιδαγωγός to say the law is a teacher, or that it restrains sin, or even that it preserves distinctions between Jews and Gentiles. Galatians 3–4 do not highlight the "instructional" function of the law. And if Paul were referring to the law as a "teacher," it seems unlikely the law would no longer have this role now that Christ has come (see Gal. 3:25; 5:14). Nor do chapters 3–4 provide evidence that the law restrains sin; rather 3:10 and 3:21–22 suggest the contrary. Finally, it is unconvincing to say the word παιδαγωγός stresses the law's role in preventing the contamination of the Jews by the Gentiles. This latter point was probably one of the reasons the law was given, but Paul does not specifically draw this conclusion in Galatians 3–4. The context (Gal. 3:15–4:7) does not refer to practices separating Jews from Gentiles.

Paul employs the words *pedagogue, guardians,* and *managers* because all these words stress that one is still a child, needing adult supervision. The terms all describe a time period before one reaches maturity. Paul uses them to illustrate that the law was designed to be in force for only a certain period of salvation history, and now that Messiah has come the era of law is over. The temporal force of the words

15. Lull, "The Law," 486–96; Belleville, "'Under Law,'" 55–69.
16. Longenecker, "Pedagogical Nature," 53–61.
17. T. David Gordon, "A Note on ΠΑΙΔΑΓΩΓΟΣ in Galatians 3.24–25," *NTS* 35 (1989): 150–54.
18. Young, "*Paidagogos,*" 150–76.

guardians and *managers* is apparent in Galatians 4:1–7. While the heir is a "minor" (νήπιος, *nēpios*), he is no different from a slave (v. 1). Submission to "guardians and managers" is a temporary expedient "until the appointed time of the father" (v. 2)—that is, until the child reaches adulthood. Paul applies this illustration to life under the law. Those who live under the law are "minors" (νήπιοι, *nēpioi*, v. 3) who are "enslaved" (δεδουλωμένοι, *dedoulōmenoi*, v. 3) and need "redemption" (ἐξαγοράσῃ, *exagorasē*, v. 5) from the law. The time of adulthood is obtained through the death of Christ who liberates people from slavery (vv. 4–5). Those who are so redeemed are no longer "minors" but "sons" (υἱοί, *huioi*). The words *sons* (v. 6) and *son* (v. 7) signify adulthood in Galatians 4:1–7, in contrast with the words *minors* and *slaves*. Thus, the period under "guardians and managers" contrasts the time of infancy with time of adulthood now attained by believers through the coming of Christ. The context of 4:1–7 says nothing about guardians and managers restraining sin, preventing contamination from Gentiles, nor about their role in instruction. The point Paul makes is that they function in this role only for a certain period of time.[19]

So too, the word *pedagogue* is used for temporal reasons in Galatians 3:23–25. One who was still "under a pedagogue" had not yet grown up. Paul's intention here is to make a salvation-historical point. Now that Christ has come the pedagogue is no longer needed. Once again temporal words dominate the context. Galatians 3:17 indicates that the law was established 430 years after the covenant with Abraham. The law was intended to be in force "until" (ἄχρις, *achris*) the seed arrives. People were guarded under the law "before faith came" (πρὸ τοῦ ἐλθεῖν τὴν πίστιν, *pro tou elthein tēn pistin*, v. 23a), and were shut up "to the faith which was going to be revealed" (εἰς τὴν μέλλουσαν πίστιν ἀποκαλυφθῆναι, *eis tēn mellousan pistin apokalyphthēnai*). The law functioned like a pedagogue "until the time of Christ" (εἰς Χριστόν, *eis Christon*).[20] The arrival of faith means that people are "no longer" (οὐκέτι, *ouketi*) under the pedagogue. The connection between verses 25 and 26 confirms that Paul used the word *pedagogue* to make a temporal point. Verse 25 asserts that believers are no longer under the pedagogue, and verse 26 explains why: Believers are "sons of God through faith in Christ Jesus." We have already seen in 4:1–7 that the word *son* contrasts adulthood with the time of infancy. The same contrast is in view in

---

19. The number of phrases and terms in this text with an explicit temporal sense is striking. Ἐφ᾽ ὅσον χρόνον, νήπιος (v. 1); ἄχρι τῆς προθεσμίας τοῦ πατρός (v. 2); ὅτε ἦμεν νήπιοι, ἤμεθα (v. 3); ὅτε δὲ ἦλθεν τὸ πλήρωμα τοῦ χρόνου (v. 4); οὐκέτι (v. 7).

20. The temporal indicators in Gal. 3:25 suggest that εἰς is temporal in 3:24.

3:25–26. Believers are no longer children who need a pedagogue, but have reached adulthood and are full-fledged sons of God.

Pedagogues, guardians, and managers, therefore, are appropriate illustrations since they contrast childhood with adulthood. Paul does not try to communicate the nature of the law or its specific function with these terms. He uses these words to stress that the law was not intended to be in force forever. It has a temporal limit in salvation history. By reading more specific meanings into these words, interpreters squeeze more from them than Paul intended.

This excursus on *pedagogue, guardians,* and *managers* was necessary since these terms are often appealed to as proof that the law was given to restrain sin. I have argued that the evidence for this interpretation is unpersuasive, and thus I can proceed with the thesis that the law actually stimulates sin.

Four pieces of evidence suggest a close identification between being *under law* and being *under sin.* First, Galatians 3:21–22 suggests that those under law are controlled by sin. Second, Galatians 4:3 says, "When we were children, we were enslaved under the elements of the world." A significant debate continues over the meaning of "elements of the world" (τὰ στοιχεῖα τοῦ κόσμου, *ta stoicheia tou kosmou*).[21] All that needs to be established here, however, is that Paul forges a connection between "the elements of the world" and life under the law. In 4:9–10 Paul charges that the Galatians were returning to "the weak and poor elements" (ἀσθενῆ καὶ πτωχὰ στοιχεῖα, *asthenē kai ptōcha stoicheia*) by submitting to the law. The link between the elements of the world and the law is also suggested by the under phrases noted above (p. 77). Since all these phrases refer to life under the law, "under the elements of the world" likely does as well. Galatians 4:3 says "we were enslaved (ἤμεθα δεδουλωμένοι, *ēmetha dedoulōmenoi*) under the elements of the world" (see also 4:9). Life "under the law" does not restrain one from sin, nor does it instruct one in righteous living. What Paul says is that it "enslaved" people in a life of sin. This is forceful evidence that life "under the law" spells life under the tyranny of sin.

Third, Galatians 4:4–5 says God sent his Son to "redeem those under the law." If those who are under the law need redemption, then the implication is that life under the law is one of slavery and captivity. To be under the law is to be under the dominion of sin, and Jesus' death liberated those under the law from such captivity. Someone might object that 4:4 states that Jesus "was born under the law," and he was not sinful; therefore life under the law is not inherently controlled by sin. Jesus,

21. For a summary of positions and the relevant literature see Belleville, "'Under Law,'" 64–69.

however, is the exception that proves the rule. He was unique in that he lived in the era of the law and never sinned; he was born "in the likeness of sinful flesh" (Rom. 8:3) in order to break the power of sin.

Fourth, Galatians 5:18 provides further proof that Paul uses the phrase *under law* to describe life under the power of sin. "But if you are led by the Spirit, you are not under the law." We could rephrase this: "If you are *not* led by the Spirit, then you *are* under the law." Anyone who is not led by the Spirit is under the control of sin. It follows, then, that life under the law is life under the authority of sin. The parallel between 5:16 and 5:18 bears this out. The former says, "Walk by the Spirit, and you will not fulfil the desire of the flesh." "Walking in the Spirit" in verse 16 corresponds to "being led by the Spirit" in verse 18. And the "desire of the flesh" in verse 16 parallels being "under the law" in verse 18. This implies that those who are under the law are captive to the desires of the flesh. Verse 18 is a devastating blow against those who contend that the Galatians need to submit to the law in order to conquer sin. Paul counters by saying that life "under the law" steals the power of the Spirit and plunges one into sin.

2 Corinthians 3

The law's role in stimulating sin is also evident in 2 Corinthians 3.[22] Verse 6 says, "the letter kills, but the Spirit gives life." The word "letter" (γράμμα, *gramma*)[23] clearly refers to the Mosaic law for six reasons:[24]

First, verse 3 contrasts a letter written with ink to one written by the Spirit, and one written on "stony tablets" to one written on human hearts. "Stony tablets" obviously refer to the Mosaic law (Exod. 31:18;

22. Second Corinthians 3 is notoriously complex. Only a separate book on this chapter would be sufficient. For two recent works see Linda L. Belleville, *Reflections of Glory: Paul's Polemical Use of the Moses-Doxa Tradition in 2 Corinthians 3.1–18* (Sheffield: JSOT, 1991); Carol K. Stockhausen, *Moses' Veil and the Glory of the New Covenant: The Exegetical Substructure of II Cor. 3,1–4,6* (Rome: Pontifical Biblical Institute, 1989). See especially the forthcoming work on 2 Cor. 3:4–18 by Scott J. Hafemann, tentatively titled *Paul and Moses, The Letter\Spirit Contrast and Argument from Scripture in 2 Cor 3* (Tübingen: J. C. B. Mohr); see also Otfried Hofius, "Gesetz und Evangelium nach 2. Korinther 3," *Paulusstudien* (Tübingen: J. C. B. Mohr, 1989), 75–120.

23. In the history of interpretation γράμμα has often been understood as referring to a particular way of interpreting the OT. For a survey of interpretation and an argument against the hermeneutical understanding of the "letter-spirit" contrast see Bernard Schneider, "The Meaning of St Paul's Antithesis 'The Letter and the Spirit,'" *CBQ* 15 (1953): 163–207.

24. For the OT antecedents and a discussion of Paul's use of that tradition see Stockhausen, *Moses' Veil*, 42–86, 97–109, and 135–50. Belleville, *Reflections of Glory*, 24–79, examines the multiple traditions that inform Paul's use of the Moses tradition in 2 Corinthians 3. The contribution of the various traditions seems less significant to me than Belleville suggests. The question of the use of traditions, however, warrants more discussion than is possible here.

32:15), whereas the work of the Spirit and "hearts of flesh" relate to the covenantal promises of Ezekiel (Ezek. 11:19; 36:26–27).

Second, the reference to the "new covenant" in verse 6 alludes to Jeremiah 31:31–34, where Jeremiah says a new covenant will be made that is "not like the covenant I made with their fathers in the day I took them by the hand to bring them out of the land of Egypt" (Jer. 31:32). The covenant made when Israel left Egypt is obviously the Mosaic covenant ratified on Mount Sinai.

Third, as we have seen, "ink" and "stony tablets" in verse 3 contrast with "the Spirit" and "hearts of flesh." This corresponds to the contrast between "the letter" and "the Spirit" in verse 6, demonstrating that the use of the word *letter* is another way of describing the ink and stony tablets of verse 3.

Fourth, the "ministry of death" describes the effect of the Mosaic law, which "was engraved in *letters* on stones" (v. 7). "Letters on stones" shows that Paul continues to refer to the Mosaic law. The last part of verse 7 confirms this when it links the glory of "the ministry of the death" with the face of Moses.

Fifth, verse 13 refers to Moses, again demonstrating that the Mosaic covenant is in view.

Sixth, verse 14 explicitly mentions "reading the old covenant," which is synonymous in verse 15 with "reading Moses." This seals the case for a reference to the Mosaic covenant in this text.

Therefore, when Paul says in verse 6 that "the letter kills," he refers to the law of the Mosaic covenant. The law does not produce life, and apart from the Holy Spirit it only kills because people are powerless to obey its commands.[25]

Paul does not critique the content of the Mosaic law here, but notes its inability to effect righteousness. The Spirit is given, not to abolish the law, but so that the law can be kept. Therefore, the law (even "the letter") is good. Nonetheless, the law itself does not furnish the power to put it into practice. The law apart from the work of the Spirit only kills. Thus, Paul describes the Mosaic covenant as a "ministry of death" (2 Cor. 3:7) and a "ministry of condemnation" (2 Cor. 3:9).

---

25. Rightly Hofius, "2. Korinther 3," 82; Richard B. Hays, *Echoes of Scripture in the Letters of Paul* (New Haven: Yale University Press, 1989), 131. Thomas E. Provence says that γράμμα refers to the perversion of the law. See Provence, "'Who Is Sufficient for These Things?' An Exegesis of 2 Corinthians ii 15–iii 18," *NovT* 24 (1982): 62–68. There is a sense in which this is true, since human failure to obey the law is a perversion of its immanent intention. Provence is also correct in asserting that there is no critique here of the content of the law. Nonetheless, the word γράμμα still refers to the law. Paul's purpose is to explain that the law cannot be kept apart from the work of the Holy Spirit.

Since the Spirit was lacking in the law, Paul designates the Mosaic covenant as a "ministry of death," while calling the new one "the ministry of the Spirit." Even Moses recognized that the giving of the law was not accompanied by power to keep it: "Yahweh has not given to you a heart to know, or eyes to see, or ears to hear to this day" (Deut. 29:4 MT; see also 31:14–29).[26] The curses of the covenant described in Deuteronomy 27–30 will fall on the nation. The only hope is that in future days God will circumcise the hearts of his people (Deut. 30:6). Paul saw this promise fulfilled in the gift of the Spirit. The Mosaic covenant was a glorious one (2 Cor. 3:7, 10), but Paul's use of Jeremiah 31 shows that the defect he sees in the law is the same one Jeremiah saw—Human beings "broke" the covenant (Jer 31:32). The law does not need to be changed, but it needs to be written upon the heart so it can be obeyed (Jer. 31:33). Paul also appropriates the promise of Ezekiel, which says that God's statutes and ordinances will be obeyed when a "new spirit" is given (11:19–20; 36:26–27). The law alone, then, does not produce righteousness or life, but kills and condemns. This is consistent with Pauline theology elsewhere; the law apart from the Spirit does not prevent sin but exacerbates it.

1 Corinthians 15:56

Paul also comments on the law's inability to grant life in a revealing statement found in 1 Corinthians 15:56: "The power of sin is the law." The law does not provide the ability or strength to keep the commandments of God. Instead of restraining sin the law provokes it. Sin's tyranny holds sway through the law and is maximized through the law. Romans 5:13 says "until the law sin was in the world," showing that sin existed before the law. First Corinthians 15:56 indicates that sin takes on greater strength through the law. The power of sin would be decreased if the law did not exist. This statement in 1 Corinthians stands out since the context does not prepare us for a reference to the law, since 1 Corinthians displays no evidence of nomistic difficulties.[27] Thus, Paul's statement here reflects one of his axioms on the role of the law—the law itself provides no power for resisting sin, and sin's dominion expands through the law.

26. Hofius, "2. Korinther 3," 105–6, argues that Deut. 29:4 (29:3 LXX) is in Paul's mind in 2 Cor. 3:14a.

27. See Gordon D. Fee, *The First Epistle to the Corinthians* (Grand Rapids: Eerdmans, 1987), 806. Thomas Söding qualifies this point by pointing out some connections with this statement and 1 Cor. 15:20–28; 15:41–49. See Söding, "'Die Kraft der Sünde ist das Gesetz' (1 Kor 15,56): Anmerkungen zum Hintergrund und zur Pointe einer gesetzeskritischen Sentenz des Apostels Paulus," *ZNW* 83 (1992): 74–84. Söding reads too much into this text, however, when he sees it as teaching the abrogation of the law.

Romans 7

Romans 7 undoubtedly serves as the best commentary on 1 Corinthians 15:56. Romans 7:5 denotes the law's function in provoking and inciting sin: "For when we were in the flesh, the passions of sin were aroused through the law in our members, in order to bear fruit for death." I have noted the debate regarding Romans 3:20; 5:20, and Galatians 3:19 as to whether the law reveals, defines, or causes sin. In 7:5, however, Paul undoubtedly sees the law as causing or provoking sin because he says, "the passions of sin were *aroused through the law*" (τὰ παθήματα τῶν ἁμαρτιῶν τὰ διὰ τοῦ νόμου ἐνηργεῖτο, *ta pathēmata tōn hamartiōn ta dia tou nomou enērgeito*). Nevertheless, it would be wrong to conclude that the law itself is sinful (7:7). "The law is holy and the commandment is holy and righteous and good" (7:12). Sin has used the law as its instrument in order to provoke more sin (7:7).

The many complex issues in Romans 7 cannot be examined in detail here,[28] but it seems fair to conclude that Paul suggests that sin uses the law to incite the formerly latent desire to sin. He says in verse 8 that "without the law sin is dead." This does not mean that before the law sin was nonexistent, for Romans 5:13 says "until the law sin was in the world," but it was "dead" in comparison to its effect after the law. Verse 8 explains how the law fomented sin. The prohibition against coveting stimulated in Paul "every kind of coveting."[29] The point seems to be that the prohibition increases the desire to engage in the activity.[30] W. D.

---

28. For example, Rudolf Bultmann argued that the sin of Romans 7 is the very desire to keep the law. See Bultmann, "Romans 7 and the Anthropology of Paul" in *Existence and Faith* (New York: Meridian, 1960), 147–57. Robert H. Gundry understands ἐπιθυμία to refer to sexual lust which began to afflict Paul when he entered his teenage years ("The Moral Frustration of Paul Before His Conversion: Sexual Lust in Romans 7:7–25," in Donald A. Hagner and M. J. Harris, *Pauline Studies: Essays Presented to Professor F. F. Bruce on His Seventieth Birthday* [Grand Rapids: Eerdmans, 1980], 228–45). J. A. Ziesler, in "The Role of the Tenth Commandment in Romans 7," *JSNT* 33 (1988): 41–56, shows the inadequacies in the interpretations of Bultmann and Gundry. Contrary to Bultmann, Romans 7 does not speak against the desire to obey the law but failure to keep it. Gundry's contention that ἐπιθυμία refers only to sexual lust is too specific. Paul has coveting of every kind in mind in accord with the tenth commandment.

29. Ziesler ("Tenth Commandment," 41–56) confirms that the selection of the tenth commandment strengthens Paul's thesis that no one can obey the law. Unfortunately, he fails to grasp the implications of his own study, concluding that "in this chapter Paul is not at his clearest" (51). Instead, his own study helps us see why Paul focused on the tenth commandment. Even if people can successfully abstain from adultery and murder, the presence of sin is still revealed in covetous desires in the heart. It illustrates that people are helpless to obey the whole law perfectly, even if they successfully keep the other commandments.

30. A good example of this was reflected in the actress who played Thérèse Raquin in Émile Zola's novel as it was portrayed on "Masterpiece Theater." She said that she found particular delight in the sexual scenes because it appealed to her to do something that was corrupt and forbidden.

Davies also rightly observes that the desire to sin goes deeper than this. It is rooted in "the rejection of God's rightful claims, the refusal to recognize dependence upon him."[31]

Paul carefully insists that the ultimate problem lies not with the law. That sin can pervert something as beautiful and holy as the law only shows the horrible nature of sin (7:13). Romans 7 dramatically depicts the plight of the person who longs to keep the law but cannot. The law is prized as "spiritual" (7:14) and "good" (7:16). The inner person desires to put it into practice (7:22), but the power of sin is stronger than the law, and it actually uses the law to effect more sin (7:13). Even the person who loves the law cannot obey it. Such people end up doing what they hate (7:15), because they find a power in them stronger than their desire to keep the law, and this power compels them to sin (7:17, 20). The tyranny of sin holds them in bondage (7:14) and makes them feel wretched (7:24). Romans 7 describes in personal terms what we have found throughout this chapter, namely, that the law actually provokes people to sin more, and therefore, righteousness cannot be obtained through the law.[32]

The Pauline view of human inability differs sharply from that of first-century Judaism. Timo Laato has shown that Second-Temple Judaism taught that human beings, by exercising their free will, could obey the law (Sir. 15:11–22; *Pss. Sol.* 9:4–5; *2 Apoc. Bar.* 54:15, 19; 85:7; ʾAboth, 3:16).[33] Paul, on the other hand, argued that human beings are born slaves to sin (Rom. 5:12–19; 6:15–22; 8:5–8) and cannot obey the law. Unregenerate people do not have the ability to do what is good. Judaism taught that people only needed to choose to put the law into practice. Paul's pessimistic estimate said that people are *free* to choose what they wish, but as descendants of Adam they always will choose to sin. Paul rejects the synergism of Second-Temple Judaism. For him all good works are the result of the Spirit's work in the heart.

Is Paul's View of the Function of the Law Contradictory?

One might conclude that the claim that the law actually stimulates sin is not only directed against Jewish legalists but is also contrary to the Old

---

31. W. D. Davies, "Law in the New Testament (NT)," *Jewish and Pauline Studies* (Philadelphia: Fortress, 1984), 236.

32. Robert B. Sloan rightly emphasizes that the law cannot save because of the power of sin, although he exaggerates the role of evil powers and understates the role of human disobedience. See "Paul and the Law: Why the Law Cannot Save," *NovT* 33 (1991): 35–60.

33. Laato, *Paulus und das Judentum*, esp. 83–97. James D. G. Dunn ("The Justice of God: A Renewed Perspective on Justification by Faith," *JTS* 43 [1992]: 8), misses this point when he says Judaism is really comparable to the Reformation view of Paul.

Testament. Paul thinks the law provokes sin, but the psalmist says that it "restores the soul" (Ps. 19:7). Paul says that the law produces death in Romans 7, but Psalm 119:93 says, "I will never forget your precepts, for by them you have revived me." Is Paul's view of the law fundamentally contrary to Old Testament piety, the delight in the law found in Psalm 19, and the conviction that the law brings restoration and revival? No. When Paul says the law incites and stimulates sin, he is not suggesting this is the only function of the law. We shall see in chapter 6 that Paul affirms a positive role for the law in the life of a Christian.

The assertion that the law provokes sin refers to the function of the law in the unregenerate. "*When we were in the flesh* the passions of sin were aroused through the law in our members, and bore fruit for death" (Rom. 7:5). Paul does not argue that the only role of the law is to produce death. The argument is that when unregenerate people are confronted with the law, the law does not quench sin but inflames it.[34] This also accords with 2 Corinthians 3. The letter of the law kills when it functions apart from the Holy Spirit. I shall argue in chapter 6 (pp. 149–52), however, that the law is not a burden for those who are indwelt by the Holy Spirit. The author of Psalm 119 was also aware that the law *alone* is not sufficient to produce obedience. He implores God to "turn my heart to your testimonies" (119:36). The appeal to God to incline the heart shows that mere possession of the law is not enough. The psalmist recognizes, in accord with Paul's belief, that he needs an internal work of God so that he desires to obey the law. Paul would agree with the Psalmist that the law with the Spirit is joyous and plays a positive role in the life of the believer.

Paul insists on a number of occasions that the law provokes sin in unbelievers. First Timothy 1:8–11, however, seems to point in another direction.[35] Here Paul affirms that the law is good (see also Romans 7:12, 16) but argues that the law is not appointed for the "righteous." Instead, its function relates to the unrighteous and ungodly, to those who kill their parents, murder, commit sexual sin, kidnap others, and commit perjury. The theme seems to be that the law *restrains* sin.[36] This seems

---

34. If Rom. 7:14–25 describes Christian experience, this statement still stands. The extent to which believers cannot keep the law reveals the extent to which they lack the power of the Spirit.

35. Of course, many scholars maintain that the Pastorals were not written by Paul. A good defense of Pauline authorship is found in Gordon D. Fee, *1 and 2 Timothy, Titus* (Peabody: Hendrickson, 1988), 23–26 (see also 1–23); Donald Guthrie, *New Testament Introduction*, rev. ed.; (Downers Grove, Ill.: InterVarsity, 1990), 607–49; D. A. Carson, Douglas J. Moo, and Leon Morris, *An Introduction to the New Testament* (Grand Rapids: Zondervan, 1992), 359–71.

36. That the point being made here is that the law restrains sin is argued by Martin Dibelius and Hans Conzelmann, *A Commentary on the Pastoral Epistles* (Philadelphia: Fortress, 1972), 22; Donald Guthrie, *The Pastoral Epistles* (Grand Rapids: Eerdmans, 1957), 60; Fee, *1 and 2 Timothy*, 45.

to contradict palpably the Pauline assertion that the law *provokes* and *increases* sin. The alleged contradiction is more apparent than real. Paul's statement about the law's restraining function in 1 Timothy corresponds to Romans 13:1–7, where the state punishes evildoers.[37] Where there is law and swift punishment for lawbreakers, the law restrains people from carrying out the evil that is in their hearts. When Paul says the law provokes sin, he is not considering immediate and severe punishment for law breaking. In Romans 7 he focuses on an internal desire—coveting, which was not extinguished through the law. The prohibition against coveting actually arouses the desire to covet. There is no swift and immediate penalty against coveting, and thus the law would not function as a restraint in this case. Further, even when there is immediate punishment, the law does not effectually remove the desire for the forbidden activity. The fear of consequences restrains a person from doing what he or she wishes. The texts that speak of the law *arousing* sin and *restraining* sin, therefore, have different things in view. In the latter, Paul refers to the law's function of immediately penalizing a violator. In the former, Paul asks whether the law assists in removing the desire for sin from the heart.

Both Sanders and Räisänen contend that Paul's explanations of the purpose of the law are contradictory. For example, according to Sanders, Paul says three different things about the purpose of the law that do not harmonize.[38] First, God gave the law in order to increase sin with the intention of sending his Son to rescue those under the power of sin (Gal. 3:22, 24). Thus, Romans 5:20 says that the "the law was given so that the transgression might increase." But this did not frustrate God's plan, for "where sin increased, grace abounded all the more." God apparently intended all along that sin would be conquered by the grace given through the death of his Son.

Second, in Romans 7:7–13 Paul now says that the law was given so that it might be obeyed and that people would find life through the law. Verse 10 says that "the commandment that was intended for life resulted in death." Sin thwarted God's purpose, however, by using the law to bring about transgression and death. So now, contrary to point one above, sin is no longer the will of God. A rather unflattering picture of God also emerges. He enacted a plan to save people through the law, and since this plan did not work he resorted to sending his Son to rescue people. Lastly, in Romans 7:14–8:4 Paul tries to cut the connection between the law and sin altogether. The law is not responsible for transgression, but the full weight of responsibility devolves on human sin.

---

37. On this point see Dibelius and Conzelmann, *Pastoral Epistles*, 22.
38. Sanders, *Paul, the Law*, 70–81.

Paul ends up describing human beings as so weak and incapable of obeying that one wonders, says Sanders, if God is good in creating people who are so incapable of doing what is right.

What Sanders sees as contradictory can also be explained from another perspective as complementary. The first point of Sanders suggests that even sin does not violate God's sovereignty. God had sovereignly planned from the beginning that salvation would not come through obedience to the law, but only through faith. Human sin did not take God by surprise, and he never intended that salvation would be obtained through obedience to the law. Human history develops under God's control, and this accords with Paul's belief that God sovereignly controls history. But to focus only on God's transcendent control of history may cause one to underestimate sin's power to frustrate God's will (Rom. 7:7–11). Paul can speak of sin as within the realm of God's sovereignty and as an enemy contrary to his will. In a sense sin does not accord with God's sovereign plan, but, ultimately, the existence of human sin fits into God's design. This does not lessen the evil of sin, nor does it minimize the fact that immanently sin contravenes God's will. The presence of sin is ultimately due to God's will, even though God himself is not morally responsible for sin. "God shut up all under disobedience, in order that he might have mercy on all" (Rom. 11:32). God ultimately willed that sin would occur, so that he might display his mercy in salvation. This tension between God's sovereignty and human responsibility is not unusual in Paul. He similarly asserts that salvation depends upon God's electing work (Rom. 9:6b–29; 11:1–32) without denying the role of human responsibility.

Sanders' third objection, from Romans 7:14–8:4, does not seem compelling. Romans 7:14–8:4 complements 7:7–13, for in verses 7–13 he labors to show that the law is good and lays the responsibility for disobedience on sin. Romans 7:14–8:4 intensifies this same point, stressing that death is ultimately due to human sin, not the law. So it is difficult to see how it contradicts 7:7–13. Interestingly, Sanders finds Paul's logic "torturous" in Romans 7, particularly because Paul depicts human ability to do God's will in such bleak terms. I would contend that such a depiction of human nature is not at all torturous or contradictory; instead, it fits with what I have argued in chapters 2 and 3. Human beings are unable to keep God's commandments; they are enslaved to sin, so justification cannot be attained through the law. I suspect Sanders finds Romans 7 contradictory because he imposes his own schema of "solution to plight" on the other Pauline texts we have examined. But if one acknowledges that human inability to obey the law is a common theme in Paul, then what Sanders sees as "torturous" seems compatible with what Paul says elsewhere.

Räisänen also lists a number of contradictions, three of which I shall examine. First, Romans 7:8 ("Sin taking opportunity through the commandment worked every kind of coveting in me") suggests that the law stimulated people to sin, but Romans 7:14 reports that people are already "sold under sin" before they encounter any commandments.[39] How can the law stimulate people to sin if they are already in bondage to sin? Second, Romans 7:7–11 says that sin came into existence through the law, whereas Romans 5:20 says the law causes the number of transgressions to increase. Thus, the latter verse shows that sin was already in existence before the law was established, while the former says the law brought sin into existence.[40] Third, Romans 5:13 says that "sin is not reckoned without the law." But Romans 2:12 says "those who sinned without the law perish without the law." Even though Romans 5:13 asserts that sin is not reckoned when there is no law, Paul obviously assumes in Romans 2:12 that sin is reckoned for those who do not possess the law. For in the latter verse those who sin without the law "perish." Romans 2:12–16 says that they perish without the law because they do not keep the law written on their hearts. Räisänen avers that Paul contradicts himself by saying that sin is *not reckoned* for those who do not have the law (5:13), whereas in 2:12 he apparently sees sin as *reckoned* to those who do not possess the law.[41]

Räisänen clarifies the issues by raising penetrating questions about the coherence of Paul's theology, but his objections are not convincing.[42] I will deal with his third objection first. Romans 5:13 does not contradict the assertion in Romans 2:12 that those who sin without the law perish without the law. When Paul says "sin is not reckoned without the law," it is illegitimate to infer that sin is unpunished where there is no law. Romans 5:14 shows that those who did not have the law died, proving that there was punishment[43] since death is a consequence of and punishment for sin (see Rom. 6:23). Paul does not assert that there is no punishment when there is no law, but simply distinguishes the sin of Adam from the sin of those who lived between Adam and Moses.

---

39. Räisänen, *Paul and the Law*, 142.

40. Ibid., 144.

41. Ibid., 145–47.

42. My response to Räisänen draws heavily on the fine article by Weima, "The Function of the Law in Relation to Sin," 219–35.

43. Of course, there is much debate over the meaning of these verses. I am unconvinced that Paul suggests in Rom. 5:13–14 that the people who died between Adam and Moses died only because of Adam's sin. For this view see John Murray, *The Imputation of Adam's Sin* (Grand Rapids: Eerdmans, 1959). Rather, people die because of their own sin (the most natural view of Rom. 5:12b), and the sin of Adam (Rom. 5:15–19).

Adam transgressed by disobeying a specific commandment revealed by God (5:14). Those who lived between Adam and Moses did not violate a specific commandment as Adam did, and in this technical sense they did not commit transgression. Nevertheless, in Romans 5:12–14 Paul stresses that they still sinned, and therefore they died, verifying that they sinned and deserved God's punishment. The point is that their sin was not quite as heinous as that of Adam, who disobeyed a commandment directly revealed by God. This is remarkably similar to Paul's argument in 2:12–16. Both Jews and Gentiles who sin will face judgment. In chapter 2 the responsibility of the Jews is exacerbated, however, because they were the privileged recipients of God's law. There is no contradiction, then, between 5:13 and 2:12. In both texts those who sin, even if the commandment has not been specifically revealed to them, face judgment and death. Neither does it follow that the description of sin as "transgression" (see Rom. 4:15) when there is law connotes a technical triviality.[44] Those who violate a revealed commandment of God are more blameworthy since this constitutes more overt rebellion. This does not lead to the conclusion, however, that those who sin apart from the law are without reproach.

What I said about Romans 5:13 leads naturally to a response to Räisänen's second objection. To say, "apart from the law sin is dead" (Rom. 7:8) does not mean that apart from the law sin does not exist. Romans 5:13 makes it plain that sin predated the law, but implies that it is not reckoned as transgression prior to the law. In fact, both 5:20 and 7:7–11 strike the same chord—Sin existed before the law came on the scene, but its power increased with the arrival of the law.

Räisänen's first objection is quite similar to the second. He errs by thinking that "bondage to sin" (Rom. 7:14) implies that people are therefore as sinful as they possibly can be. This must be his objection since he wonders how sin can be "dead" (7:8) if people are in bondage to it. But Paul's very objective in Romans 7 is to show that those who are in "bondage to sin" sin more when they encounter the law. Paul did not think that bondage to sin necessitates that one performs as many sinful actions as possible. Instead, the law exacerbates the problem of sin. The person who attempts to obey the law realizes how impotent and incapable of obedience he or she is. Thus, the law sharpens a person's sense of inadequacy and even stimulates sin.

44. Contra Räisänen, *Paul and the Law*, 146.

Conclusion

For Paul, God's transcendent purpose in giving the law was to increase sin, for the multiplication of transgressions would demonstrate that no one could be righteous through obeying the law. Salvation is only through Jesus Christ. Moreover, the power of God's grace shines brighter when conquering human sin. God's grace in Christ triumphs over sin, assuring believers that the hope of victory in Christ is certain.

4

Is Paul Opposing Jewish Legalism?

We saw in the introduction that a revolution in Pauline studies occurred when E. P. Sanders published his massive *Paul and Palestinian Judaism*.[1] Sanders argues strenuously that the Judaism of Paul's day was not legalistic, and that such claims cannot be supported by examining the textual evidence. We also noted that Sanders has persuaded many scholars that his thesis is true, and this has led to an attempt to reconstruct what Paul meant when he asserted that righteousness was not by law. I will attempt to prove in this chapter that Sanders' thesis cannot be supported in the Pauline literature, since significant evidence exists that Paul opposes a form of Jewish legalism.[2] I will examine four different strands of evidence to show that Paul did think the Judaism of his day, at least to some extent, was legalistic: (1) the contextual use of the phrase *works of law*; (2) Romans 3:27–4:8; (3) Romans 9:30–10:8, and (4) Philippians 3:2–11. Finally, the evidence Sanders presents from

---

1. E. P. Sanders, *Paul and Palestinian Judaism: A Comparison of Patterns of Religions* (Philadelphia: Fortress, 1977). For a survey of some contemporary New Testament scholarship on the issue of soteriology see Stephen Westerholm, "Law, Grace and the 'Soteriology' of Judaism" in Peter R. Richardson and Stephen Westerholm, eds., *Law in Religious Communities in the Roman Period* (Waterloo: Wilfrid Laurier University Press, 1991), 57–74.

2. I do not argue that legalism is present in the teaching of the Old Testament, for the covenant with Moses was not legalistic since it was given after God had graciously liberated his people from Egypt (Exod. 19:3–6; 20:2–17). My thesis is that the Jews of Paul's day had distorted the law and used it for legalistic purposes. See Brice L. Martin, *Christ and the Law in Paul* (Leiden: Brill, 1989), 93–96 and Robert H. Gundry, "Grace, Works, and Staying Saved in Paul," *Bib* 66 (1985): 1–38, for two recent analyses which support the thesis that Paul is opposing legalism.

Jewish literature can be interpreted to support the theory that Paul was opposing legalism.

When I say Paul opposed legalism it does not follow that there was no emphasis on God's grace in Judaism. Sanders rightly disputes the caricature that Judaism had no theology of grace and was consumed with earning merit. My thesis is that Paul detected legalism in Judaism because its soteriology was synergistic. Salvation was by God's grace and human works. Judaism believed human beings were endowed with free will so that they could cooperate with God. Paul believed human beings lacked the ability to choose what is good. Even faith is a gift of God.[3]

Works of Law and Legalism

Chapter 2 examined in some detail the Pauline claim that no one is able to obey the law perfectly; all people sin and fall short of the glory of God (Rom. 3:23); therefore, righteousness and the reception of the Spirit cannot be obtained by works of law. To sharpen the point, when Paul says that right-standing with God is not attained by works of law, he does not exclude works of law as a way of salvation because they are legalistic. Works of law are the deeds or actions demanded by the law.[4]

Now if the exclusion of righteousness by works of law (Rom. 3:20, 28; Gal. 2:16; 3:2, 5, 10) does not strictly speaking refer to legalism, then how does the term relate to legalism at all? Legalism is present when one believes that good works play a part in meriting or earning salvation. Although the term *works of law* does not denote legalism, Paul condemns legalism when he says righteousness is not by works of law. When Paul writes that no one can be righteous by works of law, these words are presumably directed against some people who thought they could be righteous by doing what the law commanded. Galatians makes evident that the letter is a response to adversaries who have made significant inroads into the Galatian community.[5] Even in Romans (3:20, 28), it is doubtful that Paul articulates a theological axiom unrelated to a problem he had faced. Paul did not write systematic treatises but letters intended to help churches in their new-found faith. Some apparently believed that righteousness could be attained in part by works of

3. See Timo Laato, *Paulus und das Judentum: Anthropologische Erwägungen* (Åbo: Åbo Academy Press, 1991), 83–97.

4. Contra Daniel P. Fuller, *Gospel and Law: Contrast or Continuum?* (Grand Rapids: Eerdmans, 1980), 93–99; rightly Stephen Westerholm, *Israel's Law and the Church's Faith: Paul and His Recent Interpreters* (Grand Rapids: Eerdmans, 1988), 117–21; Douglas J. Moo, "'Law,' 'Works of the Law,' and Legalism in Paul," *WTJ* 45 (1983): 90–99.

5. See, for example, F. F. Bruce, *The Epistle to the Galatians* (Grand Rapids: Eerdmans, 1982), 19–32.

law. Paul counters by insisting that, if this is true, they must obey the law perfectly. He believes this is impossible to do.

Those attempting to be righteous by works of law probably believed their obedience played a vital role in gaining righteousness. They probably did not think *perfect* obedience was necessary to be saved but they did argue that one must obey certain commandments (such as circumcision) to be righteous before God. In fact, circumcision was particularly crucial because it was deemed necessary for one to enter into a covenant relation with God.[6] Any notion that one must obey certain commandments to merit entrance into the people of God involves legalism, a trust in works rather than the atonement provided by God through Christ Jesus (Gal. 3:13). The motivation of those who thought they could be righteous by works of law involved legalism, even though they also would appeal to God's grace. They believed their obedience to the law would contribute to attaining eternal life. Paul argues that such a belief is delusive since God demands perfect obedience, which is impossible for fallen human beings. The only way to escape the curse of the law (Gal. 3:10–13) is by faith in Jesus Christ.

Romans 3:27–4:8[7]

Certain lines of evidence converge to indicate that Paul is opposing legalism in Romans 3:27–4:8.[8] First, the "therefore" (οὖν, *oun*) of 3:27 points back to 3:21–26. Here Paul affirms that "the righteousness of God is manifested apart from the law," and is realized through faith in Jesus Christ, whose atoning death spares believers from God's judgment. Paul in 3:27 excludes all boasting, because salvation is not attained because of what one does. Right-standing with God is "apart from the law" (3:21) and is obtained through believing in Jesus Christ.[9] Now, it fol-

---

6. See Thomas R. Schreiner, "Circumcision," in G. F. Hawthorne and Ralph P. Martin, eds., *Interpreting Paul and His Letters* (Downers Grove, Ill.: InterVarsity, forthcoming).

7. There is general agreement that Rom. 3:27–31 and 4:1–8 are closely related in theme. See Hans Hübner, *Law in Paul's Thought* (Edinburgh: T. and T. Clark, 1984), 118; Ernst Käsemann, *Commentary on Romans* (Grand Rapids: Eerdmans, 1980), 106; Charles E. B. Cranfield, *A Critical and Exegetical Commentary on the Epistle to the Romans*, 2 vols. (Edinburgh: T. and T. Clark, 1975, 1979), 224, 226; C. T. Rhyne, *Faith Establishes the Law* (Chico, Calif.: Scholars, 1981), 78, 158 n. 81.

8. That legalism is being opposed here is the view of many. See, for example, Käsemann, *Romans*, 102–3; Hübner, *Law in Paul's Thought*, 116, 119–20; Cranfield, *Romans*, 219, 228; Rhyne, *Faith Establishes the Law*, 67; Gundry, "Grace," 14–16.

9. The meaning of the phrase πίστις Ἰησοῦ Χριστοῦ in Paul is debated. For a full bibliography and a brief defense of the translation "the faithfulness of Jesus Christ" see Richard N. Longenecker, *Galatians* (Dallas: Word, 1990), 87–88. I am persuaded that the translation "faith in Jesus Christ" is still preferable. For this latter view see Moisés Silva, *Philippians* (Grand Rapids: Baker, 1992), 186–87.

lows logically that if one's works do not secure salvation, but it is a gift from another's hand, then one's works offer no ground for boasting. Conversely, boasting would be legitimate if salvation came partially through one's works. Here, then, we have immediate evidence that Paul is countering the temptation to boast in good works when he stresses that human works play no role in procuring righteousness.

Second, the line of thought in 3:27–28 supports the idea that Paul is excluding legalistic boasting in one's own works. He begins by saying that "boasting is shut out." In 3:27b he gives the reason: It is not excluded through "the law of works" but by "the law of faith."[10]

This apparently means that boasting would be legitimate if righteousness were on the basis of works, for presumably one would be entitled to boast if one's own efforts contributed to obtaining righteousness. Indeed, the polarization between "the law of works" and "the law of faith" suggests that boasting would have been appropriate if righteousness were attained by the former. Nevertheless, Paul rules out boasting since righteousness is based on faith instead of works. The word *for* (γάρ, *gar*) demonstrates that verse 28 supports the thesis of verse 27. "*For* we reckon a person to be justified by faith apart from the works of the law." The connection between verses 27 and 28 is that boasting is eliminated because righteousness comes by faith, not by works. He implies, though, that if righteousness were by works, then boasting would be legitimate because one would have gained righteousness by observing the law, by doing good works.

Third, Romans 4:2 says, "If Abraham was justified by works, he has a reason for boasting, but not before God." The similarity of the subject matter between 3:27–28 and 4:2 is remarkable. The ideas of boasting, works, and justification are found in both texts.[11] The meaning of verse 2 is not difficult. If Abraham became right with God because of the things he did, then it would be appropriate for him to brag about his own goodness. Here we see the essence of legalism, for if anyone becomes right with God because of works, he or she rightly deserves honor, praise, and glory. However, Paul insists that Abraham was not justified

---

10. Some scholars maintain that the "law of works" and "law of faith" here both refer to the Mosaic law. See Gerhard Friedrich, "Das Gesetz des Glaubens Röm 3,27," *TZ* 10 (1954): 401–17; Hübner, *Law in Paul's Thought*, 137–40; Peter von der Osten–Sacken, *Römer 8 als Beispiel paulinischer Soteriologie* (Göttingen: Vandenhoeck and Ruprecht, 1975), 245–47; Rhyne, *Faith Establishes the Law*, 67–71; Martin, *Christ and the Law*, 26–31. But others give strong (and I think persuasive) arguments for the interpretation "rule," "principle," or "order" of "works" and "faith." See Heikki Räisänen, "Das 'Gesetz des Glaubens' (Rom. 3:27) und das 'Gesetz des Geistes' (Rom. 8:2)," *NTS* 26 (1980): 101–17; also Westerholm, *Israel's Law*, 123–26; Douglas J. Moo, *Romans 1–8* (Chicago: Moody, 1991), 251–53.

11. On the possible distinction between the words καύχησις and καύχημα see Moo, *Romans 1–8*, 249, and Cranfield, *Romans*, 165.

before God on the basis of his works. Abraham could have boasted if he had performed the necessary works, but Paul shows that Abraham failed to do the requisite works when he says that Abraham could not boast before God.

When verse 2 states, "but not before God," it does not suggest that Abraham could boast in the presence of people but not in God's presence.[12] The first part of verse 2 makes it clear that the discussion relates to boasting in works in terms of *justification*.[13] Paul does not infer that Abraham performed all the good works, but God did not justify him anyway. Paul proposes that Abraham did not perform the requisite works. Indeed, if he had done the necessary works, then God would be failing to pay him a "debt" (ὀφείλημα, *opheilēma*). Verse 5 implies that Abraham did not do the necessary works. He is designated as ungodly. Abraham was justified the way all ungodly people are made righteous: not by working for God but by believing upon him. Verse 3 makes this clear, "For what does the Scripture say? 'Abraham believed God, and it was reckoned to him as righteousness.'" Abraham could have boasted if his works obtained justification, but his works were not sufficient, and he could only find right-standing with God by faith.

Fourth, Romans 4:4–5 argues against legalism: "Now to the one who works, wages are not reckoned as grace but as a debt. But to the one who does not work, but believes upon the one who justifies the ungodly, his faith is reckoned as righteousness." Verse 4, in fact, could be the legalist's credo. The employee does not consider payment to be a gift but something deserved. Even today employees may politely say thank you when the paycheck is handed out, but they view their wages as *deserved*. When they are *not* paid for their work, they rightly view it as an injustice. Paul relates this commonsense observation from everyday life to the issue of righteousness before God. If a person earns right-standing with God through works, then the conferring of righteousness would not be appreciated as a gift but expected as payment. Moreover, the one who has done the work would deserve praise and glory for a successful effort; hence, boasting would be legitimate. The doing of good works to earn righteousness is the heart of legalism.

Verse 5 makes it clear, however, that righteousness cannot be gained through the performance of works. Rather, it is obtained when ungodly people trust in God. We do not gain righteousness by working for God,

---

12. Contra Günter Klein, "Sündenverständnis und theologia crucis bei Paulus," in C. Andresen and G. Klein, eds., *Theologia Crucis—Signum Crucis: Festschrift für Erich Dinkler* (Tübingen: J. C. B. Mohr, 1979), 276–77.

13. So Moo, *Romans 1–8*, 264; see also Cranfield, *Romans*, 228, and Jan Lambrecht, "Why Is Boasting Excluded? A Note on Rom 3,27 and 4,2," *ETL* 61 (1985): 366–68.

but by letting him work for us. And if God is the one who does the justifying, then the praise and glory and honor go to him.

It should be said here that Paul does not exclude a priori human
boasting in works. That is, if people could actually perform the required
works, boasting would be legitimate and justified, not sinful. It is crucial
to see that Paul's discussion of boasting in works (Rom. 3:27–4:8) occurs
after he has established that all people are sinners (Rom. 1:18–3:20). The
problem with boasting in works is that such boasting has no basis
because no one can do the necessary works. Paul assumes that Abraham
was "ungodly" (4:5) and David was a sinner (4:7). There is nothing
intrinsically wrong with working to obtain righteousness if one could
perform the requisite works. According to Paul, no one can do the
required works, and thus any attempt to be justified by works inevitably
will fail. Thus, at the heart of legalism rests the delusion that human
beings are good, and that their works can be sufficient.

Answers to Objections

Recent exegesis has challenged vigorously the theory Paul is opposing legalism in Romans 3:27–4:8. First, E. P. Sanders sees no evidence
that Paul is counteracting legalism here.[14] He asserts that Paul does not
imply in Romans 4 that Abraham attempted to be righteous by works.
The text simply makes a factual argument to the effect that Abraham was
not justified by works and, therefore, could not boast. Paul does not
attack an Abraham who actually tried to be righteous by works. Romans
4:4 does exclude boasting in self-achievement, says Sanders, but nothing in the text indicates that the law kindles such boasting.

Sanders correctly assesses that Abraham did not attempt to be justified by works, but does Paul raise the issue of boasting in works merely
for theoretical reasons? Paul was not a writer who made theological
statements that were unrelated to the situations in his churches. His letters responded to problems in the churches over which he had apostolic
oversight.[15] Thus, he would not stress that righteousness could not
come by works if no one struggled with that problem. It seems hard to
escape the conclusion that some thought they could obtain salvation in
part by obeying the law. At the very least, this was Paul's perception of
his opponents. It is highly unlikely that Paul simply makes the hypothetical point that no one can obey the law for justification, while no one

14. E. P. Sanders, *Paul, The Law, and the Jewish People* (Philadelphia: Fortress, 1983), 33–35.
15. The purpose of Romans is a matter of significant controversy. More scholars today are
arguing that it was written to address a specific situation in Rome. See Karl P. Donfried, ed., *The
Romans Debate*, rev. ed. (Peabody, Mass.: Hendrickson, 1991).

(at least in Paul's view) was attempting to do so. He excludes salvation by "works of law" precisely because some thought salvation could come by such law obedience, even though their sinfulness precluded such a possibility. Some sinners live under the illusion that they can impress God with their works, even though they are ungodly and the works are actually lacking.[16]

Second, James D. G. Dunn also declares, contra Charles Cranfield,[17] that Paul's polemic is not against legalism.[18] Paul criticizes "privileged status as *attested* and *maintained* by obedience to the law."[19] These two positions are not necessarily contradictory, as Dunn acknowledges.[20] Paul condemns the attempts to enter the covenant community by human effort or to remain in the covenant via the flesh (Gal. 3:3). Nonetheless, Dunn's view that the issue is maintenance within the covenant is doubtful. Romans 3:21–4:12 is full of language about righteousness, indicating that entrance into the new covenant is in view. Paul has already shown that people are not made right with God through the law, for all sin (Rom. 1:18–3:20). Now he argues that people become right with God—members of the covenant people—through faith in Jesus Christ. The discussion on circumcision in Romans 4:9–12 strengthens this view. Jews typically considered circumcision mandatory for induction into the people of God. When Paul asks whether one must be circumcised in order to be righteous, he is asking if one must be circumcised to be part of the people of God. The specific issue in the context of 3:21–4:12 supports Cranfield's thesis that Paul is opposing the attempt to enter the people of God by works.

Dunn wonders how this analysis could be correct since Jews thought they were already within the covenant, and thus there was nothing to earn.[21] This objection misses the point, for if the Jews thought they were "in" because they were circumcised, then their entrance into the covenant was based on "doing" rather than "believing."[22]

---

16. Sanders' observation that the law is not explicitly mentioned in Rom. 4:4 is correct, but this is hardly a decisive point since there is a close connection in Rom. 3:27–4:8 between righteousness not being by "works" (Rom. 4:2, 4, 6) and righteousness "apart from the works of the law" (Rom. 3:28).

17. Charles E. B. Cranfield, "'The Works of the Law' in the Epistle to the Romans," *JSNT* 43 (1991): 96.

18. James D. G. Dunn, "Yet Once More—'The Works of the Law': A Response," *JSNT* 46 (1992): 111, 113.

19. Ibid., 113 (italics Dunn's).

20. Ibid.

21. Ibid.

22. Rom. 4:9–12 makes it clear that it is possible to enter the covenant through faith and circumcision. Circumcision is not essential, however. Gentiles enter by faith without circumcision.

Romans 4:4–5 is one of the most difficult texts for those who see no polemic against works-righteousness.[23] Dunn asserts that Paul uses the illustration of working for pay, not to oppose legalism[24] but only to explain that he is not using the word *reckon* (λογίζομαι, *logizomai*) with its typical commercial and business connotations when the relationship between God and people is in view. Even if Dunn is correct regarding the reason for the illustration, he hardly goes far enough. Why does Paul think it is necessary to explain that *reckon* is different in divine-human relations? This is not merely a point of scholarly interest to his readers. More likely he makes the point because some might mistakenly think that one's status with God is reckoned on a commercial basis, that is, on the basis of works. The comment regarding the pastoral thrust of this text applies to Dunn as well as to Sanders. The close parallel between verses 2 and 4, and verses 3 and 5 indicates that Paul opposes legalism here.[25]

Third, some scholars give other reasons why Paul is not responding to or criticizing Jewish legalism. For example, Richard Thompson says Paul criticizes Jewish boasting for two reasons:[26] All people fail to obey the law, and Paul's argument is salvation-historical, not existential.[27] Now that Christ has come, salvation is only through him and not via the law. The revelation of the Christ event has decisively excluded the law as a way of salvation. Similarly, Jan Lambrecht contends that "it would seem that the boasting terminology in 2:17; 2:23; 3:27, and 4:2 is rather neutral; by itself it does not point to a morally perverse 'Selbstruhm.'"[28] After all, Paul commends the Jewish zeal to perform the law (Rom. 10:2-3). The real objection Paul has with works of law is that no one could obey them sufficiently. Because of this inability, the law is not the way to salvation.

I do not deny that inability to obey the law and salvation history are two reasons Paul excludes salvation by works of law and works. I

23. For a confirmation of my interpretation of the text see Laato, *Paulus und das Judentum*, 241–48.

24. Dunn, "Once More," 112.

25. N. Thomas Wright suggests that the reference in Rom. 4:3–8 to earning merit is "secondary" in "Romans and the Theology of Paul," SBLSP 1992, edited by E. H. Lovering, Jr. (Atlanta: Scholars, 1992), 192. This is a tacit admission that the theme of merit is in the text. Even if it is secondary, which I think is doubtful, some explanation must be given to account for *why* Paul inserted it in the passage.

26. Richard W. Thompson, "Paul's Double Critique of Jewish Boasting: A Study of Rom 3:27 in Its Context," *Bib* 67 (1986): 520–31.

27. See Ulrich Wilckens, *Der Brief an die Römer* (Neukirchen: Neukirchener Verlag, 1978), 1.246–48; see also Heikki Räisänen, *Paul and the Law* (Philadelphia: Fortress, 1983), 170–71; Reinhold Liebers, *Das Gesetz als Evangelium: Untersuchungen zur Gesetzeskritik des Paulus* (Zürich: Theologischer Verlag, 1989), 31–54, 71–73.

28. Lambrecht, "Why is Boasting Excluded?" 366; see also 365–69.

argued for this very thesis in chapter 2. It is likely, however, that Paul also critiques legalism. The theory that Paul only makes a salvation-historical observation ignores the close connection between Romans 3:27–28. Paul contrasts faith and works fundamentally, not just as two periods of salvation history.[29] Moreover, the attempt to restrict the argument to salvation history is called into question by the appeal to Abraham and David in Romans 4:1–8.[30] Paul argues that they were saved by faith and not by works, precisely the way believers in his day are saved. Lambrecht is correct that "boasting" per se is not necessarily evil, but boasting is evil and foolish when sinners, who cannot obey the law, attempt to use their obedience to impress God. As I argued with regard to Sanders above, Paul's reference in Romans 3:27–4:8 to boasting in works suggests that some believers were falling prey to this very error.

Reinhold Liebers defends the salvation-historical view for 4:1–8 as well.[31] "Works" refers to "works of law," not meritorious works, according to Liebers. *Works, boasting, reward,* and *debt* are neutral concepts. All are positively described elsewhere in Scripture. Liebers finds that Paul opposes, not works-salvation, but Torah-salvation. His case suffers from three major flaws: First, he assumes ἔργα (*erga*) in 4:1–8 is equivalent to ἔργα τοῦ νόμου (*erga tou nomou*). He emphasizes the fundamental opposition in the text between Torah and belief in Christ. But the word *law* never appears in verses 1–8. Paul uses *works* instead of *works of law* to contrast faith and works fundamentally. Liebers, by importing *law* into the text actually reverses Paul's emphasis. Second, Liebers defines Abraham's "ungodliness" in terms of his uncircumcision.[32] He leaps over the paragraph break in doing this, for this idea is mined from verses 9–12. More seriously, he overlooks the significance of the appeal to David in verses 6–8. David's ungodliness consisted in his failure to do good works, not in his failure to be circumcised. Similarly, Abraham's ungodliness in verse 5 must be understood in moral terms. Lastly, Liebers rightly demonstrates that the words ἔργα (*erga,* "work"), ὀφείλημα (*opheilēma,* "debt"), μίσθος (*misthos,* "reward"), and καύχημα (*kauchēma,* "boasting") are neutral terms that are conceived of positively elsewhere. He fails to show, however, that they have a positive meaning in this context. The collocation of these terms together, set in contrast to believing, bespeaks a works-righteousness mindset.

29. See also Moo, *Romans 1–8,* 250.
30. So also Gundry, "Grace," 14.
31. Liebers, *Das Gesetz als Evangelium,* 31–40, 71–73.
32. Ibid., 32–33.

The third objection claims that Paul does not speak against boasting in meritorious achievement in this text but against the Jews' pride in their elect status and national privilege.[33] Paul's focus on the inclusion of Gentiles in Romans 3:29–30 and 4:9–12, 14 shows that the real target of his argument is not works-righteousness but a perception of special privilege for the Jews. Paul rejects "the attitude of the Jew who relies on a uniquely privileged position."[34]

This objection suffers from the same logical flaw as the previous one. Doubtless Paul was concerned about the exclusion of the Gentiles from blessing, but this does not disprove a polemic against legalism here. This theory also demands that the term *works of law* focuses on "boundary markers" that separate Jews and Gentiles. But we have already seen in chapter 2 that *works of law* refers to the law as a whole, and thus the evidence that only part of the law is in focus is lacking. Moreover, the close connection between "works of law" in 3:28 and "works" in general in 4:2, 6 (see also vv. 4–5) shows that Paul thinks of works in a principial way and does not limit them to "badges" that separate Jews and Gentiles.

This argument also fails to convince since Jewish nationalism and exclusivism cannot be neatly separated from Jewish obedience to the law. Jewish nationalism was intimately and inextricably tied up with devotion to Torah. The Qumran community considered itself to be the true Israel, in contrast to the rest of Israel, precisely because of its devotion to the law. It was not sufficient to be an ethnic Israelite; one also had to observe Torah. And that substantial and significant obedience to Torah was considered necessary by Jews has been convincingly argued by Thielman.[35] Israel in both the Old Testament and the Second Temple Period explained God's judgments on the nation as chastisements for sin. The Jews of the Second Temple Period did not expect God's blessings solely for ethnic reasons. A purified people devoted to the law would be the recipients of salvation.[36] Thus, heritage and possession of the law were not the only reasons Jews felt superior to Gentiles. Jews typically thought their obedience to the law was superior to that of the Gentiles. The Gentiles deserved God's punishment precisely because

33. James D. G. Dunn, *Romans*, 2 vols. (Dallas: Word, 1988), 1:185–88, 227; Sanders, *Paul, the Law*, 33–36; Räisänen, *Paul and the Law*, 170–72; J. A. Ziesler, *Paul's Letter to the Romans* (Philadelphia: Trinity Press International, 1989), 117, 123–25; Francis Watson, *Paul, Judaism and the Gentiles: A Sociological Approach* (Cambridge: Cambridge University Press, 1986), 133–35; Dieter Zeller, "Zur neueren Diskussion über das Gesetz bei Paulus," *TP* 62 (1987): 490.

34. Watson, *Sociological Approach*, 133.

35. Frank Thielman, *From Plight to Solution: A Jewish Framework for Understanding Paul's View of the Law in Galatians and Romans* (Leiden: Brill, 1989), 28–45.

36. See, for example, *Psalms of Solomon* 17–18.

they were not as morally righteous as Israel and did not keep God's law.[37] Thus, a typical designation for Gentiles was "sinners."[38] It is precisely this attitude that Paul attempts to puncture in Romans 2. The nationalism of the Jews simply cannot be separated from a feeling of moral superiority rooted in their adherence to the law. Thus, the attempt to separate Jewish exclusivism from the performance of the law cannot be successful. The two inevitably go together and are harmonized, therefore, in a number of Pauline texts (for example, Rom. 9:30–10:4; Phil. 3:2–11).

Francis Watson argues that Paul's rejection of works of law should be explained sociologically—that Paul rejects the Torah to legitimate the separation of his congregations from the Jewish synagogues.[39] Watson's provocative study is flawed because it too neatly separates theology from sociology.[40] It is too simplistic to conclude that social factors alone were decisive in Paul's viewpoint on the law and the Jew-Gentile issue. This is an example of reductionistic reasoning, for it seems more likely that both theological and social factors contributed to Paul's thinking.

Despite Watson's disclaimer that he is not eliminating Paul the theologian,[41] he relegates theology to insignificance. Pauline arguments for including Gentiles become rationalizations for what he wanted to prove in the first place, according to Watson.[42] If sociological analysis is applied too simplistically Watson's own thesis can be explained on the same basis. It is true that sociological reality is a factor in Paul's thinking, but the influence of sociology does not eliminate the theological dimensions of Paul's arguments. The inclusion of Gentiles into the people of God cannot be separated from Paul's claim that righteousness does not come by observing the law. The two issues cannot be separated without doing violence to Paul's writings.

---

37. Compare 4 Ezra (2 Esdras) 7:37; *Wisd. Sol.* 14:12–31; *2 Apoc. Bar.* 82:6; *T. Naph.* 3:3; *T. Dan.* 5:5; *Jub.* 3:31; 22:16–18; 25:1; 1QM 4:7. See the discussion in Eckart Reinmuth, *Geist und Gesetz: Studien zu Voraussetzungen und Inhalt der paulinischen Paränese* (Berlin: Evangelische Verlagsanstalt, 1985), 40–42.

38. See 1 Macc. 1:34; 2:48; *Jub.* 23:23–24.

39. Watson, *Sociological Approach*, 63–72, 132–42.

40. John M. G. Barclay, *Obeying the Truth: A Study of Paul's Ethics in Galatians* (Edinburgh: T. and T. Clark, 1988), 237–42; William S. Campbell, "Did Paul Advocate Separation from the Synagogue? A Reaction to Francis Watson, 'Paul, Judaism and the Gentiles: A Sociological Approach,'" *SJT* 42 (1989): 457–67.

41. Watson, *Sociological Approach*, 20

42. Ibid., 201 n. 110. This statement may have elements of truth in it, although N. Thomas Wright correctly observes that some rationalizations are valid arguments for conclusions "reached originally by a leap of imagination." See N. Thomas Wright, "Putting Paul Together Again: Towards a Synthesis of Pauline Theology," in J. M. Bassler, ed., *Pauline Theology*, Vol. 1 (Philadelphia: Fortress, 1991), 193–94.

Romans 9:30–10:8

I have written elsewhere of my understanding of the controversial text, Romans 9:30–10:13.[43] What needs to be explored here is whether Paul opposes a form of Jewish legalism.

Paul explains in Romans 9:30–10:8 why the Gentiles have obtained right-standing with God, while the Jews have fallen short of it. Verse 31 says that the Jews "pursued the law for righteousness," but "they did not attain" right-standing with God.[44] In verse 32 Paul asks why the Jews did not obtain right-standing with God. He answers, "they did not pursue the law from faith, but as from works."[45] Verse 32 demonstrates that pursuing the law was neither a mistake, nor evil. Paul faults the Jews only for the way they pursued the law—"as from works." If they had pursued the same law "from faith," they would have obtained right-standing with God. To view the actual pursuit of the law as misguided veers from the specific wording of this text and likely is due to a more negative view of the law than Paul shares. The law itself is good (Rom. 7:12), and the gospel of Jesus Christ is the fulfillment of the Old Testament Scriptures (Rom. 1:1–3). The Jews did not go astray by pursuing the law with ardor and vigor. It was the subjective attitude with which they pursued the law that led them astray. They viewed the law as a means to establish their own righteousness. We can probably assume from what Paul says in Romans 7 that such a wrong pursuit of the law is inevitable for those who are "in the flesh" (unbelievers), since sin uses the law to accomplish its own ends. There is no harsh critique of the law here, however. The problem lies with human beings who approach the law in the wrong way. If the law had been pursued in faith, the Jews would have seen that they could not keep the law and that the law pointed to Jesus the Messiah as the only way of salvation (Rom. 9:32b–33).

Stephen Westerholm fails to see that Paul advances no criticism of pursuing the law from faith here. Thus, his remarks seem to suggest that there are two different ways of salvation, one by law and one by grace. He says:

43. "Israel's Failure to Attain Righteousness in Romans 9:30–10:3," *TrinJ* 12 (1991): 209–20; "Paul's View of the Law in Romans 10:4–5," forthcoming in *Westminster Theological Journal*.

44. The meaning of "righteousness" (δικαιοσύνη) in Paul is hotly debated and cannot be adequately investigated here. The most satisfying explanation of the term in texts speaking of "the righteousness of God" has been given by Moo (*Romans 1–8*, 65–70, 75–86), who sees God's righteousness both as a saving activity and a divine gift in which people have right status before him. This means that God's saving activity of making people right is forensic and does not denote the moral transformation of human beings.

45. I am supplying the verb διώκω in verse 32. So also Cranfield, *Romans*, 509; Dunn, *Romans*, 582; Rhyne, *Faith Establishes the Law*, 167 n. 41.

He [Paul] has derived from texts such as Leviticus 18:5 the conviction that the age of the Law required deeds of those who would be counted righteous in God's sight. What he perceives as his *opponents' error is their clinging to this path which, though indeed announced by Moses,* has proven unable to lead to righteousness because of human sin (Rom. 3:20; 8:3); a path which, moreover, has now and forever been set aside (Rom. 10:4) by the manifestation of righteousness "apart from law" through faith in Jesus Christ (Rom. 3:21–22; cf. Gal. 3:23–26).[46]

He continues:

Since, to Paul's thinking, none of this was possible under the old dispensation, it cannot be said that Israel had already been granted salvation by divine grace and that the prescribed works provided only the means for maintaining what had been granted. On the contrary, in the age of anticipation *the prescribed works take on the character of preconditions for entering a salvation* yet to be revealed. Thus Paul not unnaturally depicts Israel pursuing a path which requires deeds for justification, while Christians are thought to enjoy already the salvation of the new age, a gift of divine grace received by faith.[47]

I agree with Westerholm that people could not obey the law perfectly, but his suggestion that the law and faith are virtually two different ways of salvation should be rejected. The law was given only after Yahweh had liberated his people from Egypt. It was a gracious gift from Yahweh and did not teach salvation by works.[48] Romans 9:31–32 and 10:2–3 (as we shall see) make it clear that Paul does not fault Israel for zealously pursuing the law but for not pursuing it as from faith. The only way appropriate response to the Mosaic law ever was to pursue it from faith.

The assertion that Israel pursued righteousness "as from works" and therefore did not obtain it needs to be probed more deeply. If Paul uses the word *works* in its usual broad sense, and there is no reason to doubt that he does, then he condemns Israel for trying to be righteous by works. Indeed, verse 32 contains a contrast between "doing" and "believing" and depicts the Jews as guilty of legalism.

The chapter division separating Romans 9 and 10 is unfortunate, for 9:30–10:13 is really one section. Clearly Paul treats the same issues throughout, the failure of many in Israel to obtain salvation, the role of faith and works in salvation, and the cruciality of faith in Christ. In 10:2

---

46. Westerholm, "Law, Grace," 69; emphasis Schreiner's.

47. Ibid., 71; emphasis Schreiner's.

48. For the view that the Mosaic covenant is gracious see John Murray, *Principles of Conduct: Aspects of Biblical Ethics* (Grand Rapids: Eerdmans, 1957), 195–201; Elmer A. Martens, "Embracing the Law: A Biblical Theological Perspective," *BBR* 2 (1992): 1–11.

Paul commends the Jews for their "zeal for God." The zeal of verse 2 parallels the pursuit of the law in 9:31. Both the pursuit of the law and zeal for God are praiseworthy. Unfortunately, though, this zeal lacks knowledge (10:2). In fact, the fault of the Jews described in Romans 10:3 is strikingly similar to the indictment of 9:32. The zeal is misdirected because of ignorance, specifically ignorance of God's righteousness. The Jews "did not subject themselves to the righteousness of God because they were ignorant of God's righteousness and sought to establish their own" (10:3). This makes the same basic point as 9:32: The Jews thought righteousness could be gained by their own achievement in obeying the law, so they did not accept the saving gift of righteousness from God's hand. "Seeking to establish one's own righteousness" (10:3) describes the pursuit of the law "as from works" (9:32). Romans 10:5 strengthens the case that the establishment of one's own righteousness consists in doing the law to gain salvation, which is legalism.

Many scholars disagree with my interpretation, claiming 10:3 does not exclude meritorious achievement, but rather the nationalistic righteousness of the Jews excludes Gentiles from blessing.[49] They interpret 9:32 similarly: The works criticized include circumcision, sabbath, and food laws—those that engender separation.

This latter interpretation is plagued by fatal weaknesses, some of which were explained in discussion of objections to my interpretation of Romans 3:27–4:8 (pp. 102–3), so they will only be noted here. First, there is no evidence that the "works" in view relate to circumcision, sabbath, and other laws dividing Jews from Gentiles. None of these laws is mentioned or even implied in the context. The term *works* should be understood in the broadest sense unless evidence compels restricting it.

Second, to distinguish the nationalistic righteousness of the Jews from their observance of the law creates a false dichotomy. The Jews felt superior to Gentiles, not only because of their birth, but also because of their obedience to the Torah. Third, Paul does stress the inclusion of the Gentiles into the people of God in Romans 9–11, but nowhere in these chapters does he blame the Jews for excluding them. In fact, the only explicit warning in this regard is directed to the Gentiles who were inclined to believe that God was finished with the Jews (Rom. 11:17–24). The Jews are not criticized for excluding the Gentiles; rather, Paul censures them for trying to be righteous by their own works instead of trusting and believing in Jesus as Messiah.

49. Dunn, *Romans*, 581–83, 587–88, 593–95; see Lloyd Gaston, "The Inclusion of Gentiles," *Paul and the Torah* (Vancouver: University of British Columbia Press, 1987), 128–30; Ziesler, *Romans*, 251–59; George E. Howard, "Christ the End of the Law: The Meaning of Romans 10:4ff," *JBL* 88 (1969): 333–37.

Fourth, "their own righteousness" (τὴν ἰδίαν δικαιοσύνην, *tēn idian dikaiosynēn*) in Romans 10:3 refers to works-righteousness in the broad sense. This is confirmed by the parallel text in Philippians 3:9 where Paul speaks of his conversion in terms of "not having my own righteousness [ἐμὴν δικαιοσύνην, *emēn dikaiosynēn*] which is from the law, but the righteousness through faith in Christ." I shall argue below that the Philippian text also speaks against legalism. It suffices for now to point out the similarity of expression between Romans 10 and Philippians 3, suggesting that both refer to the same issue.

Other reasons have been given in support of the idea that Romans 9:30–10:8 contains no polemic against legalism. It is said, for instance, that Paul only reproves the Jews for failing to perceive a salvation-historical shift with the coming of Christ; *now* the only way to salvation is through believing in Christ.[50]

Surely the text betrays a salvation-historical element, inasmuch as faith now is directed toward Jesus Christ, but the contrast between believing and doing is too fundamentally grounded in the text to be explained only by salvation-historical considerations. The polarity between believing and doing examined in 9:32 and 10:3 is also present in 10:5–13. The "righteousness of the law" focuses on "doing" (ποιήσας, *poiēsas*, v. 5), while "righteousness of faith" (v. 6) relies on the work of Jesus Christ (vv. 6–8), and thus salvation is obtained through "believing" (vv. 11–13).[51]

T. David Gordon says that Romans 9:32 argues against failure to obey the law, not a criticism of the Jews for the manner in which they pursued the law.[52] In verse 32 he believes the verb *pursue* (διώκω, *diōkō*) should not be supplied to fill in the ellipsis. Paul does not say Israel "pursued" the law in the wrong manner and so did not obtain righteousness. Rather, the copula should be understood here. Paul explains in verse 32 that Israel did not obtain righteousness because the law is characterized by works instead of faith. Gordon marshals three arguments to support his view. First, his reading of Romans 9:32 matches what Paul says about the law in Galatians 3:12: The law "is not of faith" (οὐκ ἐκ πίστεως, *ouk ek pisteōs*). The only difference is that the verse in Galatians has the copula, which must be supplied in Romans. Second, he finds that the focus on performing the righteousness of the law is strengthened by using the word "doing" (ποιήσας, *poiēsas*) in Romans 10:5 and Gala-

50. For example, Sanders, *Paul, the Law*, 36–42; Räisänen, *Paul and the Law*, 174–75.

51. Laato (*Paulus und das Judentum*, 251) dismisses Sanders' exegesis as "completely arbitrary."

52. T. David Gordon, "Why Israel Did Not Obtain Torah-Righteousness: A Translation Note on Rom. 9:32," *WTJ* 54 (1992): 163–66.

tians 3:12. Third, the issue in the text is not the manner in which Israel
pursued the law because the Gentiles obtain righteousness by faith without pursuing it at all. Gentiles receive righteousness solely on the basis
of God's mercy.

Gordon correctly sees a polarity between doing and believing in this
text. He also centers Paul's reasoning in the fact that salvation does not
come via the law because it cannot be obeyed. I am not so sure as he that
we should supply the copula in Romans 9:32 instead of the verb *pursue*.
The parallel between Romans 9:32 and Galatians 3:12 breaks down
because in the former he adds the phrase, *as from works* (ὡς ἐξ ἔργων,
hōs ex ergōn), which is not specifically found in Galatians 3:12. Paul
does use the phrase "of works" (ἐξ ἔργων, *ex ergōn*) in Galatians 3:10, but
the crucial word *as* (ὡς, *hōs*) is missing. Inclusion of the word *as* in
Romans 9:32 indicates that Paul is speaking of the way Israel pursued
the law.[53] They pursued it "as" from works, that is, in such a manner
that they tried to establish their righteousness by works. If Gordon were
correct, I suspect Paul would have omitted the word *as* altogether, for
then the idea of a wrong kind of pursuit would not be as likely.[54]

Romans 10:2–3 confirms that Paul is not only criticizing Israel for
failure to keep the law. He does not reproach Israel for being zealous.
The problem is that they expressed their zeal by trying to establish their
own righteousness.[55] In addition, the close parallels in thought between
9:31–32 and 10:2–3 indicate that the verses are mutually explanatory. In
both Romans 9:30–33 and 10:1–8 Israel's failure comes in keeping the
law and in its legalistic attitude.

Gordon maintains the point cannot be that Israel pursued the law in
the wrong way, for the contrast is not that Israel pursued righteousness
in the wrong manner, and Gentiles pursued it rightly, but that Israel pursued righteousness, and Gentiles did not pursue it at all. His argument
here misses the point of contrast. He understands that Paul wants to
highlight God's mercy. God's election accounts for the Gentiles' faith
(Rom. 9:30; see also 9:24–26), for even though they did not pursue faith,
they have received it. Paul's purpose here, however, is not to say that
Israel should not have pursued the law. Israel and the Gentiles differ in

53. See Fuller, *Gospel and Law*, 72, 77–78, 82, on the significance of ὡς in verse 32.
54. Moreover, verse 32b continues the running theme of the text when it speaks of "stumbling." Racing imagery pervades the text for Paul speaks of "pursuing" (διώκω, 9:30, 31), "attaining" with two different verbs (καταλαμβάνω, φθάνω, 9:30, 31), and "stumbling" (προσκόπτω,
9:32). The prominence of racing imagery suggests that the verb διώκω should be supplied in the
ellipsis in verse 32.
55. For reasons already given above I do not find convincing Gordon's claim in "Torah-
Righteousness," 166 n. 9, that Rom. 10:3 only relates to the corporate or national righteousness
of Israel.

that God gave the law as a gift to Israel. But, apart from God's grace, even those who received the gift of the law pursued it legalistically. Those who received the law perverted it by trying to be righteous by works. Gentiles, who had no revelation from God at all, attained righteousness because of mercy. What Paul shows is that, apart from God's grace, even possession and pursuit of the law go awry.

So the fact that Gentiles did not pursue the law at all does not prove Gordon's argument. Obviously, Gentiles could not pursue the law since they did not possess it. The surprising element is that Israel did not obtain righteousness even though they possessed revelation from God. This does not indicate that the pursuit of the law was misguided but simply that, apart from God's grace, Israel pursued the law in the wrong way.

On the other hand, some scholars would criticize my exegesis of Romans 10:5 ("For Moses writes of the righteousness that is from the law, that the one who does [what is written in the law] will live by them"), claiming that the verse describes positively the obedience of faith, so that there is no contrast between verse 5 and verses 6–8.[56] According to this latter interpretation, the doing of the law is essential for life, and Paul sees this as compatible with faith in Christ (vv. 6–13). These scholars insist that most English versions are incorrect in translating δέ (*de*) in verse 6 as "but." Instead, δέ should be translated as "and," indicating the continuity between doing the law and faith in Christ. They stress that faith and obedience are not opposed to each other. Those who put their faith in Christ will obey the law. In fact, faith in Christ inevitably leads to obedience of the law. Furthermore, they contend that the whole argument of 10:5–8 collapses on the traditional view that there is a contrast between the doing of the law (v. 5) and faith in Christ (vv. 6–8). The argument fails if Paul cites one part of the Old Testament in verses 6–8 to criticize another part of the Old Testament in verse 5. Paul would not use an argument pitting one part of the Pentateuch against another, and no Jew would accept an argument that assumed the Scriptures contradicted one another. These scholars find it much more satisfactory to view righteousness by law and by faith as complementary, rather than contradictory.

The theology of this position is unobjectionable. The question is whether such an interpretation can be sustained in these specific verses. The problems with this position are so serious that it should be aban-

56. For example, Fuller, *Gospel and Law*, 85–88; Howard, "Romans 10:4," 335–37; Gaston, "The Inclusion of Gentiles," 130; Glenn N. Davies, *Faith and Obedience in Romans: A Study of Romans 1–4* (Sheffield: JSOT, 1990), 189–200; Robert Badenas, *Christ the End of the Law: Romans 10:4 in Pauline Perspective* (Sheffield: JSOT, 1985), 118–25.

doned. First, Paul has condemned the Jews for pursuing the law according to works and attempting to establish their own righteousness (9:31–
32; 10:3). Now, in the same context, will he switch gears and describe a
positive use of the law for righteousness in 10:5? Such a sudden shift
would be too confusing for Paul's readers. Second, the antithesis
between doing and believing pervades this text from 9:30 through 10:13.
It would be awkward for Paul to switch suddenly to a positive description of doing the law when the focus of the text is that righteousness is
not obtained by doing but by believing (9:30, 32–33; 10:4, 6, 8, 9, 10, 11).
Indeed, as argued above, the doing of the law in verse 5 describes in
another way the attempt to establish one's own righteousness (10:3).

Third, the parallel between 10:5 ("righteousness that is from the law"
[τὴν δικαιοσύνην τὴν ἐκ νόμου, *tēn dikaiosynēn tēn ek nomou*]) and
Philippians 3:9 ("not having my own righteousness which is from the
law" [μὴ ἔχων ἐμὴν δικαιοσύνην τὴν ἐκ τοῦ νόμου, *mē echōn emēn
dikaiosynēn tēn ek tou nomou*]) is too close to be explained away. Paul
obviously uses Philippians 3:9 to portray righteousness from the law
negatively. Since the wording between these two texts is so close, it is
difficult to believe that Paul describes law-righteousness in a positive
way in Romans, but negatively in Philippians. In addition, since Paul
already has spoken of "works" (9:31–32) and "one's own righteousness"
(10:3), there is good reason to believe that he continues this theme in
10:5. Even though Paul does speak positively of obeying the law elsewhere (for example in Rom. 2:26–27; 8:4; 13:8–10; Gal. 5:14), nowhere
does he make a positive reference to "righteousness that comes from the
law." Paul insists that righteousness does not have its source from (ἐκ)
the law but comes only from Jesus Christ. We have already seen in chapter 2 that he continually insists that righteousness does not come
through works of law, but only through faith in Christ. It is highly
improbable that Paul would ever refer to "righteousness based on law"
positively.

Fourth, the Old Testament citation used in Romans 10:5 is from Leviticus 18:5, and almost all agree that Paul uses the same citation in a negative sense in Galatians 3:12. It is hard to believe that Paul uses the same
citation, in similar contexts and on a similar subject, so differently in
Galatians and Romans. Daniel P. Fuller's exegesis of Romans 10:5 fails
here, for he says Paul uses the Leviticus text in a negative way in Galatians but positively in Romans.[57] Surely, the burden of proof lies with
Fuller since both passages relate to righteousness, the law, and faith.

---

57. Fuller, *Gospel and Law*, 98–99.

The major objection to my view contends that such an interpretation means Paul uses Leviticus 18:5 ("So you shall keep my statutes and my judgments, by which a person will live if he does them; I am Yahweh") contrary to its intended meaning in the Old Testament, and such a mis-use by Paul would never convince those who revered the Old Testament Scriptures.[58] Moisés Silva has provided the best solution to this difficult problem.[59] What Silva says about the use of Leviticus 18:5 in Galatians 3:12 also applies to Romans 10:5. It is not convincing to conclude that Paul merely cites the legalistic misinterpretation of Judaizers in Romans 10:5. Nonetheless, the scriptural exegesis of his opponents influences his citation of the Old Testament text. Paul's opponents believed that the law itself could provide life. Paul's introduction of the Leviticus 18:5 quote in Romans 10:5 ("Moses writes of the righteousness which is from the law") supports the notion that he is countering the view that righteousness "comes from" the law. The phrase *from the law* reveals that Paul responds to the belief that righteousness stems from the law. Thus, they pursued the law *as from works*, expecting to secure righteousness through their obedience. Righteousness here refers to right-standing before God, and the opponents' mistake was to think that they could establish their own righteousness (salvation) by their obedience to the law (10:3). Paul explains in verse 4 that those who believe in Christ cease using the law as a means of establishing their own righteousness; they recognize that Christ, not the law, is the source of life. When Paul cites Leviticus 18:5 in Romans 10:5, he stresses that no one can attain righteousness or eternal life by obeying the law since no one can obey sufficiently what the law demands.

The attempt to gain right-standing with God via obedience to the law is, then, what Paul criticizes in Romans 10:5. Indeed, that is the entire context of Romans 9:30–10:8. He rejects the idea that the law provides life or righteousness, even though the perfect keeping of the law would bring such righteousness (compare Rom. 3:19–20; Gal. 3:10–12). Paul's citation of Leviticus 18:5 is influenced by his Jewish opponents, who put forward that same verse to argue that the law is the source of righteousness. Paul does not flatly refute their interpretation by explaining Leviticus 18:5 in context. Instead, he counters their interpretation by citing Deuteronomy 30:12–14 (10:6–8). Silva notes that New Testament writers rarely call into question the interpretation of opponents by set-

---

58. It should be pointed out that some who disagree with my interpretation in Rom. 10:5 face exactly the same question in the use of Lev. 18:5 in Gal. 3:12.

59. Moisés Silva, "Is the Law Against the Promises? The Significance of Galatians 3:21 for Covenant Continuity," in William S. Barker and W. R. Godfrey, eds., *Theonomy: A Reformed Critique* (Grand Rapids: Zondervan, 1990), 153–57, especially 163–66.

ting forth an opposing contextual argument of the text in question.[60] He goes on to say that "Jewish literature contemporary to the New Testament shows a similar hesitation to score points by refuting the opponent's use of Scripture. And the later rabbinic scholars, as a rule, refuted an argument based on Scripture by counteracting with a different passage, not by demonstrating faulty hermeneutics."[61] In other words, Paul cites the Old Testament in 10:6–8 to show that obeying the law is not the means of obtaining righteousness; rather, Christ has accomplished all that is needed for salvation. The appropriate human response accepts in humble faith what God has done in Christ.

The upshot of my interpretation does not deny that Paul could use Leviticus 18:5 in another context as the redeemed's way of describing life within the covenant.[62] What Paul objects to in Romans 9:30–10:8 is the use of the law as the source of righteousness or life. Such a use of the law betrays legalism.

Philippians 3:2–11

Philippians 3:2–11 have usually been understood as an attack on Jewish legalism, where Paul uses his own history in an exemplary way. Dunn, however, thinks that Paul reprimands the Jews for trying to establish their own covenantal righteousness, which excludes Gentiles from covenantal blessings.[63] Sanders believes there is no criticism of meritorious righteousness or boasting here, for Paul says that his life under the law was a "gain" (v. 7).[64] Paul rejects the law only because he now realizes that salvation is through Christ. A salvation-historical shift has replaced the law as the way of righteousness with Christ as the way of salvation.[65]

Once again, the personal and existential flavor of the text cannot be excised so easily. Paul's "own righteousness that comes from the law" (v. 9) is linked with "placing confidence in the flesh" (vv. 3–4). Relying on the law and the flesh means that one does not trust in Christ (v. 9) or boast in Christ Jesus (v. 3). The contrast between "boasting in Christ Jesus" and "putting confidence in the flesh" (3:3) suggests that confidence in the flesh involves trusting in and boasting in one's own effort. And Paul's own confidence in the flesh is not limited merely to inclusion in the covenant. He argues in verses 4–6 that he has reason to

---

60. Ibid., 165.
61. Ibid.
62. See, for example, the discussion in Martens, "Embracing the Law," 7–10.
63. Dunn, *Romans*, 588.
64. Sanders, *Paul, the Law*, 44–45; also Liebers, *Das Gesetz als Evangelium*, 58–60.
65. Sanders, *Paul, the Law*, 139–141.

boast more than other Jews because his devotion to the law was more rigorous.[66]

If Dunn were correct, the only distinction between Jews and Gentiles would be those signs of the covenant that particularly differentiated Jews from Gentiles. But Paul goes beyond the mere listing of boundary markers in Philippians 3:4–6.[67] After all, the Judaizers would have observed the boundary markers themselves. Paul contends that, as a Pharisee with respect to the law and a fervent persecutor of the church, he is superior to the "dogs;" he was blameless in law-righteousness. If Sanders and Dunn are correct, and the only issues troubling Paul are that some Jews fail to see that salvation is now through Christ or that the Jews possess no covenantal advantage, why does Paul confuse the issue by comparing himself to his adversaries, arguing that he was more devoted to practicing the law than they? He should say plainly that salvation through Christ is apart from the law. Instead, Paul inserts the idea of the depth of his devotion to law observance. Presumably he does this because his opponents thought they were right with God because of their own devotion to God, manifested in their observance of the law.

The existential language Paul uses confirms this point.[68] He speaks of "putting confidence in the flesh" (vv. 3–4) because the opponents were guilty of boasting in their own devotion to the law. Of course, he does say that his life under the law was a "gain" to him (v. 7). I would suggest, though, that the "gain" spoken of here is in terms of Paul's perception of himself before his conversion. In any case, it cannot be separated from the fact that he was "more righteous" and more rigorously devoted to the law than other Jews. But now that Paul has been found by Christ, he realizes that this "gain" was nothing more than confidence in the flesh, that it is actually a "loss" because it cuts one off from Christ (vv. 7–8), and indeed it is "garbage" (σκύβαλα, *skybala*, v. 8).

Sanders errs in asserting that Paul's rejection is only in terms of salvation history, not legalism.[69] The experiential language used in this passage suggests that Paul also counters those who think they can gain salvation through observing the law, and thereby are inclined to boast.

Boasting for Paul is not neutral. Boasting in one's obedience to the law is evil because people who boast give the glory and honor and praise to themselves instead of to God (see Rom. 3:27–28; 4:1–5; 1 Cor. 4:7; Gal. 6:13; Eph. 2:9; Phil. 3:2–6). God's election to salvation of the weak rather

---

66. The identity of the opponents in Philippians is the subject of some debate. The most common and satisfactory answer is to see them as Judaizers, as in Peter T. O'Brien, *The Epistle to the Philippians* (Grand Rapids: Eerdmans, 1991), 26–35.

67. So also Gundry, "Grace," 13; O'Brien, *Philippians*, 369.

68. Again see Gundry, "Grace," 14, on this point.

69. So Silva, *Philippians*, 186 n. 28; O'Brien, *Philippians*, 394–96.

than the strong is intended to rule out all human boasting, so that people will boast only in the Lord (1 Cor. 1:29, 31). Paul can speak positively of human beings boasting in certain things (see, for example, Rom. 5:2–3, 11; 2 Cor. 5:12; Gal. 6:4), but it is always understood that the boasting is based on what God has done in Christ for believers (see esp. 2 Cor. 10:7–18).[70] Those who are righteous by law do not assign praise and glory to God for their salvation but ascribe glory to themselves.

A final word should be said about legalism and salvation by works. Some New Testament scholars, as we have seen, claim that people are condemned for trying to be justified by works even if they obey the law perfectly. I am not surrendering my criticisms of that view in asserting that Paul was opposing legalism, for if the law could be kept perfectly, then people would deserve salvation and therefore could boast. However, since all people sin and fall short of the glory of God, it is a great delusion for sinners to think that they can earn merit before God by their works. Paul condemns boasting in works because no one can possibly do all the works God requires. Human beings, though, are naturally given to idolatry (Rom. 1:18–25), and thus they deceive themselves into believing that their obedience to the law somehow suffices to impress God and warrant salvation. Such folly stems from the failure to see how gloriously perfect God is, and how infinitely repugnant sin is to God.

Was Palestinian Judaism Legalistic?

Sanders' magnum opus, *Paul and Palestinian Judaism*, has convinced many scholars that the evidence does not support the view that Palestinian Judaism was legalistic. However, the very data Sanders presents can be interpreted to support the idea that Palestinian Judaism was legalistic, as I will show.[71] Nonetheless, Sanders' study has had a salutary effect even for those who still see legalism in Palestinian Judaism, cautioning against naïve analyses of Judaism. Palestinian Judaism has suffered from being caricatured; consequently it sometimes has been portrayed as if legalism were the only reality in Jewish communities.

---

70. For a helpful discussion on boasting in 2 Corinthians see Scott J. Hafemann, "'Self-Commendation' and Apostolic Legitimacy in 2 Corinthians: A Pauline Dialectic?" *NTS* 36 (1990): 74–87.

71. For more wide ranging analyses of Sanders' work see Laato, *Paulus und das Judentum*, 6–82; Jacob Neusner, "Comparing Judaisms: A Review of *Paul and Palestinian Judaism* by E. P. Sanders," *HR* 18 (1978): 177–91. Significantly, even though Neusner questions Sanders' methodology at a number of points, he accepts Sanders' thesis that Judaism was not legalistic. But see the seminal comments by Moisés Silva in "The Law and Christianity: Dunn's New Synthesis," *WTJ* 53 (1991): 347–52, that support the theory that Paul was resisting a form of Jewish legalism.

Sanders' conclusions refute a simplistic portrait of Judaism. He shows that it is not evident that rabbis weighed merits against demerits. He warns that, due to the nature of rabbinic literature, one needs to be careful about constructing the entire theology of Judaism from the extant corpus. It is misleading to pit grace against works, and then claim that the Rabbis were only interested in the latter. Indeed, the reading of Jewish literature from the Second Temple Period (for example, the Qumran literature) reveals the Jews had knowledge of a gracious God. Not every Jew was legalistic (see Luke 1:6). All that needs to be said is that some Jews lived in a legalistic manner, and that some of them became the opponents of Paul (and Jesus!).

Legalism also may exist in practice, even if grace is trumpeted in theory.[72] Religionists may easily proclaim the primacy of grace and actually live as if the determining factor was human effort. The history of the Christian church amply demonstrates that a theology of grace does not preclude legalism in practice. It would be surprising if Judaism did not suffer from the same problem. Legalism threatens even those who hold to a theology of grace since pride and self-boasting are deeply rooted in human nature. My colleague, Robert H. Stein has remarked that, if Judaism were not legalistic at all, it would be the only religion in history that escaped the human propensity for works-righteousness.

Although not all Jews were legalists, at least three elements in Sanders' own discussion indicate that legalism infected Tannaitic Judaism.[73]

First, the sheer number and detail of laws which are codified in the Mishnah betray the presence of legalism. Sanders responds that the Jews looked upon the law as a blessing from God, and not as an onerous duty.[74] Moreover, modern people are familiar with an even greater number of laws and regulations in our legal and governmental systems. The attempt to describe what one should do in every situation could be viewed as a sign of devotion to God and, therefore, laudable. These comments put the most sympathetic construction on the presence of numerous detailed laws in the Mishnah. Nonetheless, the vast quantity of laws

72. See Donald A. Hagner, "Paul and Judaism: The Jewish Matrix of Early Christianity: Issues in the Current Debate" (Paper presented at a symposium, Institute for Biblical Research, San Francisco, November 1992).

73. Of course, Tannaitic Judaism is generally after the New Testament era (approximately A.D. 70–200), and there were surely major changes in Judaism after the destruction of the Temple. On the other hand, solid evidence suggests that both Jesus (for example, Luke 18:9–14) and Paul are responding to Jewish legalism. In addition, there was some continuity between the Judaism that was pre-A.D. 70 and post-A.D. 70 When we put together the resistance to Jewish legalism in New Testament documents and the presence of legalism in post-A.D. 70 Jewish documents, there is presumptive evidence that Jewish thinking did not change radically on this score after A.D. 70.

74. Sanders, *Paul and Palestinian Judaism*, 110–11.

in the Mishnah and the minutiae contained therein enshrine legalism.[75] When people begin to stress complex and detailed prescriptions for obedience, then the primacy of grace is threatened, even if the specific laws are viewed as a divine gift. The analogy of modern society and our governmental system fails since the question concerns one's relationship with God, not conformity to any random set of laws. In addition, the need for lawyers to interpret and understand the laws is greater today than ever before, suggesting that the vast tangle of laws is so impenetrable that the ordinary citizen needs an expert to explain whether he or she is obeying the law. It has often been pointed out, of course, that some rabbis reduced the law to one central element or to several key teachings, but this would ameliorate legalism only if the rest of the law naturally flowed from these central principles, and it is hard to see how this is the case with the kind of detailed laws found in the Mishnah.

The second intimation of legalism is suggested by the lack of reference to the covenant in Tannaitic writings. Sanders says, "Very seldom is *God's* role in the covenant directly discussed. It is assumed so thoroughly that it need not be mentioned."[76] This explains, says Sanders, the emphasis in rabbinic literature on the fulfillment of commandments.[77] Sanders' thesis on why the covenant is unmentioned may be granted in one sense. Presumably the rabbis did assume that God's covenantal mercies were the basis of all their behavior, and one must recall the nature of the literature found in the Mishnah and Gemara. Nevertheless, when one combines the failure to mention the covenant with the emphasis on obeying the detailed prescriptions of the law, one has a recipe for legalism. Such theology may not be legalistic in theory; it can always appeal to the covenant as the basis of all behavior. Theology, however, is not measured only by formal statements but also by what it stresses.[78] Any theology that claims to stress God's grace but rarely mentions it and that elaborates human responsibility in detail inevitably becomes legalistic in practice, if not theory. This principle applies to

75. See G. B. Caird, "Review of E. P. Sanders. *Paul and Palestinian Judaism: A Comparison of Patterns of Religion,*" *JTS* 29 (1978): 538–43.

76. Sanders, *Paul and Palestinian Judaism*, 82.

77. Ibid.

78. N. Thomas Wright (*Christian Origins and the Question of God*. Vol. 1: *The New Testament and the People of God* [Minneapolis: Fortress, 1992], 189) dismisses the claim that the Pharisees were legalistic as anachronistic. But later he says (p. 222), "The Pharisees believed that their brand of fidelity to the traditions of the fathers was the divinely appointed programme of Torah intensification, and thus *the means* of Israel's rescue" (emphasis Schreiner's). Contra Wright one can easily see how legalism could creep into a theology that based its own fidelity to Torah as necessary for deliverance. A synergistic conception of soteriology also is apparent here. Deliverance would come when Israel cooperated sufficiently with God's grace.

rabbinic Judaism and to Christian churches. A church outwardly laud-
ing grace as primary and fundamental may practice the most virulent
legalism.

These comments on Tannaitic Judaism are not being proposed solely
from Paul's charges against the first-century Jews. The emphasis on
human obedience and the failure to emphasize the covenant in the
Mishnah are empirical realities, suggesting that legalism was a problem
in Judaism. Sanders' claim that the covenant was assumed is technically
correct, but he fails to see that a theology that does not *stress* the covenant is in danger of legalism. Granted, the Mishnah did not purpose to
give a full-orbed picture of Tannaitic theology, and one should consider
the genre of the work.[79] However, the claim that Tannaitic Judaism
stressed the covenant cannot be defended from documentary sources.
The Mishnah, Pauline writings, and the teaching of Jesus contain specific textual evidence that legalism existed in Judaism.[80]

The rabbinic explanation of election also manifests legalism. Sanders
points out that the rabbis gave three answers behind God's election of
Israel:[81] (1) The covenant was offered to all nations but only Israel
accepted it; (2) Israel was chosen because of the merit of the fathers or
the generation of the exodus, and (3) God chose Israel for his own
name's sake. The first two reasons betray a legalistic mindset.[82] To say
Israel was elect because it accepted the covenant, whereas the Gentiles
rejected it, implies that the Gentiles were morally blameworthy for
rejecting God's covenant, and Israel commendably accepted the covenant. The acceptance of the covenant by Israel was a righteous act that
distinguished Jews from Gentiles. The decisive issue in salvation, then,
was the decision of Israel to accept the covenant, and thus the Jews
could boast that they had the wisdom and virtue to embrace it.[83]

Explaining election on the basis of the fathers' merit also involves
legalism. Because of their virtue, not because of his mercy, God chose
Abraham and the other fathers. Their meritorious works accrue to help
later generations. Such a perspective does not necessarily involve trying

79. So E. P. Sanders, *Jewish Law from Jesus to the Mishnah* (Philadelphia: Trinity Press
International, 1990), 330. Sanders' claim that "what is central is what is taken for granted" is
unconvincing. If it is taken for granted, it ceases to be central.

80. But see E. P. Sanders' own interpretation of the evidence from the Gospels, *Jesus and
Judaism* (Philadelphia: Fortress, 1985). See the persuasive critique by Scot McKnight, "Review
of E. P. Sanders, *Jesus and Judaism*," *TrinJ* 6 (1985): 219–25.

81. Sanders, *Paul and Palestinian Judaism*, 87–88.

82. So also D. A. Carson, *Divine Sovereignty and Human Responsibility: Biblical Perspectives in Tension* (Atlanta: John Knox, 1981), 89–91. For further criticisms by Carson see also
92–95.

83. See also Laato, *Paulus und das Judentum*, 187–90.

to earn salvation by good works, but it assumes salvation because of the works of the fathers (see Matt. 3:7–10).

Sanders tries to defend these rabbinic interpretations of election by saying that they were attempting to prove that God was not "capricious nor arbitrary."[84] They wanted to give an answer as to why God acted as he did. They needed to give "a reason for the election."[85] In any case, the rabbis were not Lutherans, and thus they felt no qualms about saying that election was both by God's grace and earned by people.[86] The language about earning should not be pressed, for the rabbis were not systematic theologians, and thus their comments should be understood as "an explanatory device."[87]

Paul, however, would have rejected any attempt to give an answer in terms of human works, merit, or acceptance of the covenant to the question of why God elected some rather than others. He forges a connection between election and grace in Romans 11:5–6, arguing that grace rules out meritorious works altogether. "Thus therefore in the present time a remnant has come about according to gracious election. And if the election is by grace, then it is no longer by works, otherwise grace is no longer grace." The idea that election rules out works-righteousness was not an invention of Luther but is rooted in Pauline theology. Paul teaches that God's electing work occurred before people "were born or did anything good or evil" (Rom. 9:11), and it does not depend "upon the one who wills or runs" (Rom. 9:16).[88]

Paul rejects any human rationalization that grounds election in human acceptance of the covenant or merit, for these explanatory devices rob God of his sovereign freedom and cancel out the freedom of grace. Thus, any explanation that tries to lessen the "capriciousness of God" by appealing to human acceptance of the covenant or the merit of the fathers should be rejected since it grounds salvation on human works. Human beings naturally desire to reduce divine election to works, since the so-called arbitrariness of God is lessened, which opens the door for human boasting. Paul, however, does not provide a full answer as to how God could be righteous if he is absolutely sovereign (Rom. 9:19–20), and thus the relationship between human responsibility and divine sovereignty remains mysterious. Those who attempt such

---

84. Sanders, *Paul and Palestinian Judaism*, 87.
85. Ibid., 99.
86. Ibid., 100.
87. Ibid.
88. For a detailed defense of this interpretation see John Piper, *The Justification of God* (Grand Rapids: Baker, 1983); see also Thomas R. Schreiner, "Does Romans 9 Teach Individual Election Unto Salvation? Some Exegetical and Theological Reflections" (forthcoming in *JETS*).

an explanation compromise divine sovereignty and grace, and thus any "explanatory device" should be excluded.[89]

If Sanders and I can use the same evidence and come up with remarkably different conclusions, then we probably have a different perspective on what constitutes legalism. So, too, Paul and the Jews may have held the same kind of differing perspectives.[90] This perspectival difference also fueled the debate between Martin Luther and Roman Catholicism.[91] Responding particularly to the *via moderna*, Luther charged that the Catholic Church had a deficient understanding of grace and had fallen prey to works-righteousness. Luther's opponents could legitimately counter that no good work was accomplished apart from grace in their theology.[92] The *via moderna* against which Luther reacted differed from Palestinian Judaism in numerous ways, but both founded soteriology in the covenantal relations between people and God. One could research the Roman Catholic side in the debate thoroughly (as Sanders has examined Palestinian Judaism) and conclude that any idea of legalism or earning merit was foreign to Roman Catholicism. But such a study would exclude Luther's interpretation of the situation. What the *via moderna* described as grace Luther saw to be legalism. What Jews firmly described as grace, Paul saw to be a theology based on legalism. Thus, Sanders may quite accurately explain the Jewish perspective from the vantage point of their self-understanding, while Paul had a different perspective on the movement.

This difference in perspective may account for why Sanders and Heikki Räisänen see Paul as an inconsistent thinker. Once their reconstruction of the perspective of Judaism is accepted as accurate, Paul's evaluation of Judaism appears to be either misleading or misinterpreted. Räisänen's point is that Paul ended up distorting Judaism by suggesting that salvation could be obtained by works.[93] This is an important

89. Laato (*Paulus und das Judentum*, 190–94) correctly maintains that Paul sees faith as a gift from God.

90. Even Heikki Räisänen concedes that Paul "understood the logic of his opponents' position in a different way than they themselves did." See Räisänen, "Legalism and Salvation by Law," in S. Pedersen, ed., *The Pauline Literature and Theology* (Göttingen: Vandenhoeck and Ruprecht, 1980), 80.

91. See K. T. Cooper, "Paul and Rabbinic Soteriology: A Review Article," *WTJ* 44 (1982): 127–29. Cooper notes that there are parallels in many respects between medieval nominalism and Sanders' description of Jewish soteriology.

92. Alister E. McGrath shows that the *via moderna* understood grace in covenantal terms and did not conceive of people earning salvation apart from grace. Luther, however, had a profoundly different estimation of grace in the theology of the *via moderna*. See McGrath, *Iustitia Dei: A History of the Christian Doctrine of Justification*, 2 vols. (Cambridge: Cambridge University Press, 1986), 1:37–187; 2:1–97; also 1:76–78, 87–89, 112, 124–28, 166–72; 2:1–32).

93. Räisänen, *Paul and the Law*, 188, 268; idem, "Paul's Call Experience and His Later View of the Law," *The Torah and Christ* (Helsinki: Finnish Exegetical Society, 1986), 82–83, 86, 92.

thought, for he ultimately agrees with my view that Paul did oppose a theology of works-righteousness. However, Räisänen thinks Paul was contradictory and that his perspective on the law should be explained as a form of psychological rationalization.[94] Thomas Wright correctly points out weaknesses in Räisänen's claim that Paul was inconsistent.[95] Also, the fact that Paul's letters were preserved by the churches implies that his arguments were considered relevant to actual views in the religious world of his readers.

It is becoming increasingly common to label the construction argued for here as anti-Semitic.[96] But it should be remembered that Paul was a Jew. He viewed his own theology as a fulfillment of the Old Testament (Rom. 1:2). His critique of Judaism (and even his own past) was in line with that of the prophets (Gal. 1:13–14; Phil. 3:2–11). This is no attack from outside Judaism but an intra-Jewish debate on the meaning of the Scriptures. Further, what Paul attacks is not Judaism per se but a fundamentally human problem. Human beings, since they are sinners, are prone naturally to worship the creature rather than the Creator (Rom. 1:23). One dimension of human idolatry is a perverted desire to boast in one's works before God so that one can earn merit in his sight. The Bultmann school, in dependence upon Luther, has correctly identified this as a profound analysis by Paul of the human condition. If Paul's analysis is correct, then what he declares is not anti-Semitic, for what he assails is not a Jewish problem but a fundamental problem of human existence.[97] Paul directs his argument to the Jews because they represent, as God's elect people, the highest form of piety. If even the nation upon whom God has set his favor struggles with legalism, then it follows that the rest of humanity does as well.

A chapter such as this lays itself open to the charge of reading Paul through the eyes of the Reformation instead of interpreting Paul historically. To sound such an alarm is a valuable warning, since it provokes us to examine fundamental assumptions and conventional exegeses of texts. Nevertheless, I suggest that Luther was substantially correct in his exegesis of Paul. Our culture also reads the biblical text from a certain historical context. For instance, church history's terrible mistreatment

94. Räisänen, *Paul and the Law*, 201, 231–36, 268–69.

95. Wright, "Putting Paul Together Again," 186–90.

96. For example, Rosemary R. Ruether, *Faith and Fratricide: The Theological Roots of Anti-Semitism* (New York: Seabury, 1974). For a more recent admission of anti-Semitism in Pauline theology see J. Christiaan Beker, "Romans 9–11 in the Context of the Early Church," *Princeton Seminary Bulletin Supp* (1990): 40–55.

97. Rudolf Bultmann makes this point eloquently in "Christ the End of the Law," *Essays Philosophical and Theological* (London: SCM, 1955), 43–44, 47. Some might respond that the attempt to earn merit before God is not a fundamental problem of human existence. Here the issue of perspective reappears; I am prepared to argue that the problem is common.

of Jews and the horror of the holocaust rightly cause us to be more cautious when we make theological statements about Judaism.

But it is also possible that past excesses have blinded us to the real criticisms Paul made in his letters, whether we agree with him or not. In the modern world criticism of others on doctrinal grounds has come to strike us as intolerant and prejudiced. We are tempted, then, to interpret Scripture to fit our own philosophical and cultural biases. The criticism of reading texts through biased lenses cuts both ways. All interpreters come to the text with certain presuppositions. The goal is to understand Paul on his own terms.

5

The Temporary Nature
of the Mosaic Covenant

One of the most difficult issues in Pauline theology is the question of
the permanence of the law. Certain texts in Paul suggest that since the
coming of Christ the law is now abolished (Rom. 6:14; 7:1–6; 2 Cor. 3:4–
18; Gal. 3:15–4:7). On the other hand, Paul also speaks positively about
fulfilling the law (Rom. 2:25–27; 8:4; 13:8–10; 1 Cor. 7:19; Gal. 5:14),
implying that the law of Moses continues to function as a standard of
conduct for the believer. In this chapter I will focus on two texts (2 Cor.
3:4–18 and Gal. 3:15–4:7) to explain what Paul means in claiming the
Mosaic era has now ended for the believer.[1] I will sketch in my understanding of the texts which intimate that the Mosaic covenant is only in
force for a portion of salvation-history. After presenting my own brief
exposition of the central texts, some of the major competing interpretations will be presented and critiqued. In chapter 6 I will examine those
texts which enjoin believers to fulfil the law. One can only gain an adequate perspective of my view of this controversial and complex area
after reading chapters 5 and 6.

1. I focus on 2 Cor. 3:4–18 and Gal. 3:15–4:7 as the crucial texts on this issue. The texts in
Romans speak of no longer being "under law" and being "released" from the law. We saw in
chapter 3 that "under law" is closely connected with being under the power of sin. Does it follow
that believers are no longer under the sway of the Mosaic Law? Romans could be interpreted to
say that we are no longer under law—in the sense that believers are not under the tyranny of sin
now that Christ has come. Chapter 6 will address this question further.

Galatians 3:15–4:7

The letter to the Galatians derides agitators who desired to impose circumcision upon Gentile believers in the Galatian churches.[2] Thus, it is imperative that we take into account the specific situation of the letter when we construct Paul's theology of law from Galatians.[3] In Galatians 3:15–4:7 Paul probably wrote to counter the idea that the Mosaic covenant climaxed God's revelation to his people. He affirms that the law is from God, for the law is not contrary to God's promises (3:21). He denies, however, that the giving of the Mosaic law represents the apex of God's covenant with his people. The Mosaic covenant is not the culmination of God's revelation, but an interim covenant given before the promise is fulfilled.

Indeed, the law itself provides no power for obedience. Righteousness cannot be gained through works of law (2:16), since no one is able to do everything the law requires (3:10). Moreover, the reception of the Holy Spirit is not grounded on works of law but "hearing with faith" (3:2, 5). What the opponents hope to gain through the law the Galatian believers already have experienced through the power of the Holy Spirit.[4] Paul objects to the theology of the agitators because they think that the law provides life and power. Paul insists, on the other hand, that the law cannot impart life (3:21). The mighty work of the Spirit is experienced only by faith (3:1–5). To be under the law connotes being under the tyranny of sin (5:18), but those led by the Holy Spirit are freed from the dominion of sin and overcome the flesh (5:16). The reception of the Spirit in 3:1–5 is intimately linked with the blessing of Abraham (note "just as," καθώς, *kathōs*) in 3:6[5]), and in fact is the fulfillment of the promise given to Abraham (3:8). The Galatians have begun to experience the fulfillment of God's promises to Abraham by receiving the Spirit, and to turn back to the law regresses to an era in which the law functioned apart from the Spirit. Thus, even before 3:15–4:11, Paul highlights the superiority of the Abrahamic covenant versus the Mosaic. The granting of the Spirit fulfils the blessing promised to Abraham, while the prescriptions of the Mosaic covenant were not kept by God's people.

2. Different suggestions have been put forward as to the identity of the Galatian opponents. The traditional view that they were Judaizers remains the most persuasive. For a recent survey of scholarship and the conclusion that the opponents were Judaizers see Richard N. Longenecker, *Galatians* (Dallas: Word, 1990), lxxxviii–c.

3. See W. D. Davies, "Paul and the Law: Reflections on Pitfalls in Interpretation," *Jewish and Pauline Studies* (Philadelphia: Fortress, 1984), 99.

4. On the importance of the Holy Spirit in Galatians see Charles H. Cosgrove, *The Cross and the Spirit: A Study in the Argument and Theology of Galatians* (Macon: Mercer, 1988).

5. See Sam K. Williams, "Justification and the Spirit in Galatians," *JSNT* 29 (1987): 91–100.

The subsidiary nature of the Mosaic covenant is unfolded further in 3:15–4:11. The covenant with Abraham is the fundamental covenant that God enacted with his people, and any later additions to the covenant do not repeal the original one made with Abraham. The promissory character of the Abrahamic covenant is underscored three times in these verses (3:16–18). The blessings promised to Abraham and his seed would not be realized because of human obedience but would come to fruition through the divine promise.

In verse 17 Paul says the law that came into being 430 years after the covenant with Abraham cannot void its promissory character. And in verse 18 he states, "If the inheritance is by law, then it is no longer by promise. But God graciously gave it to Abraham through a promise." Given what I have said previously about Paul's theology of law in Galatians, it is likely that he portrays here a fundamental contrast between two ways of obtaining the promise. Under the law the inheritance is realized through "doing." It is dependent upon human works, and therefore it is conditioned upon sufficient obedience. The promise of Abraham, on the other hand, is not predicated on "doing" but "believing." Indeed, since it is a "promise," God will see to it that the necessary conditions are fulfilled. To rely on the law to gain the inheritance is a false path, for no one can sufficiently fulfill the requisite commands.

The polarization of the law and promise described in the above paragraph might suggest that the Mosaic and Abrahamic covenants prescribe two different ways of salvation, one based on works and the other on faith. But such an understanding of the gospel-law antithesis founders because Paul did not see the law as contrary to the promises of God (3:21). In addition, the Mosaic covenant was a gracious one. First God graciously entered into relationship with his people and redeemed them from Egypt, and then he gave them his law so they would respond in humble obedience to his redeeming work.[6] Doubtless, some contrast is present between the Mosaic and Abrahamic covenants. Otherwise, Paul's discussion in 3:15–4:11 is beside the point. The way the two diverge must be explored further, however. It is unpersuasive to conclude that they differ by presenting two different and incompatible ways of salvation, one by works and the other by grace.

To comprehend Paul's view of the relationship between the Abrahamic and Mosaic covenants, we must consider the specific context of Galatians 3:15–4:11. The Galatian opponents believed that the law was the crucial element in conquering sin, and that the Galatians had to submit to circumcision to obtain the blessing of Abraham. When Paul

---

6. So, for example, Davies, "Paul and the Law," 95.

responds to these opponents, he refers to the Mosaic covenant and law, but his comments are refracted through the particular situation he addresses. Thus, in verse 17 Paul responds to the Judaizing adversaries when he says the law, which came at a later period in salvation history, cannot annul the promissory character of the covenant with Abraham. Paul does not imply that the law contradicts the gracious nature of the Abrahamic covenant, but that it cannot revoke the original basis upon which the Abrahamic covenant was enacted. Paul counters the Judaizers who perceived the Mosaic covenant as supreme in God's dealings with his people, insisting instead that the Mosaic covenant should be interpreted in the light of the Abrahamic covenant's priority.

Verse 18 supports Paul's argument in verse 17 because the two verses are connected with a "for" (γάρ, *gar*). The key question here is how does verse 18 support verse 17? Verse 17 often has been interpreted to say that the Mosaic covenant is distinct in nature from the Abrahamic: the former teaches salvation through obeying the law while the latter indicates that salvation is only through God's gracious promise. But this interpretation goes astray if my exegesis of verse 17 is correct, and Paul is responding to the view of the Judaizers. Instead, the connection between verses 17 and 18 should be understood as follows. The Judaizers, through their exaltation of the law, effectively (although not intentionally) gave the priority to the Mosaic covenant rather than the Abrahamic one. Rather than interpreting the Mosaic covenant through the lenses of the Abrahamic, they interpreted the Abrahamic covenant through the lenses of the Mosaic. Paul argues in verse 17 that this is a mistake because their interpretation of the Mosaic covenant cancels out the promissory character of the Abrahamic covenant, and he has already pointed out in verse 15 that no one can fundamentally change a covenant after it is ratified. Now in verse 18 he explains why the Judaizers' understanding of the Mosaic covenant is flawed. If the Mosaic covenant is the primary one and should be handled the way the Judaizers say, then the inheritance is to be obtained through obeying the law, which means the inheritance is no longer obtained by God's gracious promise. Paul's intention in verse 18, then, is to show that the Judaizers' interpretation of the Mosaic covenant is fundamentally wrong because their interpretation implies contradiction between the two covenants. Paul is not teaching that the Mosaic law actually teaches a different way of salvation.

Neither is Paul suggesting that the Mosaic and Abrahamic covenants are the same in every respect. I have argued that the Judaizers saw the Mosaic covenant as the primary one between God and his people. Presumably they held the standard view that the law was given to restrain sin. In Galatians 3:19–4:11, however, Paul attacks this understanding of the Mosaic law, and asks in 3:19 why God gave the law at all. He needs to answer this question because he has suggested that the Abrahamic covenant was God's principal pact with humans. If so, why did he give a subsidiary covenant at all? Paul answers by reversing the standard Jewish view. The law was not given to restrain sin but multiply it. In verse 19 Paul continues to underscore the secondary importance of the Mosaic covenant. It was not given directly by God but was transmitted through a mediator to the people. Paul is probably thinking here of God revealing himself to Israel through Moses in the giving of the law.[7]

To say that the law was given to provoke sin and that it was inferior to the promise leads to the question of Galatians 3:21. "Then is the law contrary to the promises of God?" An emphatic "of course not" confirms that Paul's purpose in 3:15–18 was not to teach that the Mosaic and Abrahamic covenants set forth two different ways of salvation. The reality is that the law does not "make alive" (ζωοποιῆσαι, zōopoiēsai). The Judaizers mistakenly viewed the law as a source of life.[8] People could never attain righteousness by the law because they lack the power to keep it. Paul argues that the law was never supposed to bring life and power, for Scripture declares that all are enclosed under the power of sin (3:22). It seems, then, that Paul says the law, rightly interpreted, does not deny the promises given to Abraham by teaching a different way of salvation. It is inferior to the promise given to Abraham because it does not supply any power to obey. The fulfillment of the Abrahamic promise involves the gift of the Spirit and the dynamic work of the Spirit in the community (3:1–6; see also 3:14; 4:6, 29; 5:5, 16–18, 22, 25; 6:1, 8). Those who look to the Mosaic law for power are "enslaved under the elements of the world" (4:3). To return to the law involves slavery (4:9).

The inferiority of the law also is underscored in the temporal distinctions enunciated between the law and the promise. We have already seen in Galatians 3:17 that Paul notes that the law came into being 430 years after the promise to Abraham. This verse does not clearly say that the law was to be in force for a limited period of time. In verse 17 Paul's aim is to prove that it is ancillary to the promise given to Abraham. As the argument progresses, however, Paul begins to make it clear that the Mosaic covenant was not intended to be in force forever. He says the law "was added for the sake of transgressions *until* the seed should come"

7. N. Thomas Wright, "The Seed and the Mediator: Galatians 3:15–20," in *The Climax of the Covenant: Christ and the Law in Pauline Theology* (Minneapolis: Fortress, 1991), 157–74.

8. For a similar interpretation see Moisés Silva, "Is the Law Against the Promises? The Significance of Galatians 3:21 for Covenant Continuity," in William S. Barker and W. R. Godfrey, eds., *Theonomy: A Reformed Critique* (Grand Rapids: Zondervan, 1990), 157–67.

(3:19), so presumably, now that the seed has come, the law is no longer in force. The temporal expressions pile up in Galatians 3:23–25, "*Before* faith came we were confined under the law, being shut up to the faith *that was about to be* revealed. So then, the law has become our pedagogue *until the time of* Christ,[9] in order that we may be justified by faith. And *now* that faith has come we are *no longer* under the pedagogue." Paul reasons here that the Mosaic covenant was designed to be in force for a certain period of salvation history, as an interim measure until the promise given to Abraham was fulfilled. With the coming of Christ the fulfillment of salvation history has arrived, and therefore, the interim role of the Mosaic covenant has ceased. Believers are no longer under the pedagogue of the law.

I argued in chapter 3 that when Paul speaks of being "under the pedagogue," he uses this illustration to stress that one is only under the era of the law for a certain period of time.[10] The reference to the pedagogue—and "guardians and managers" for that matter—makes a salvation-historical point. People were intended to be under the sway of the law for a limited period of time. I also maintained in chapter 3 that "under law" and "under the pedagogue" are ways of saying that believers are under the power of sin. If this is correct, then we have another indication that the law does not supply the power to obey. Of course, Paul is not suggesting that people cannot sin now that Christ has come. He intends to make a salvation-historical point: Why are the Judaizers encouraging the Galatians to return to the law since the law does not diminish but increases sin? People can still choose to live under the bondage of the law even though Christ has come, but Paul strives to convince the Galatians that they should not do so.

The illustration of the guardians and managers in 4:1–7 nails down the same lesson given in 3:23–25. The law is analogous to guardians and managers in that it was intended to be in force for only a certain period of time ("until the appointed time of the father," 4:2). During this period of infancy "we were enslaved under the elements of the world," that is, people were in bondage to sin under the law. But now that the fulfillment of salvation history has come ("the fullness of time came"), God's Son has liberated those who lived under the power of sin. Now people can live as free adults in God's family rather than as slaves (4:7). The law is not, strictly speaking, contrary to God's promises, but it supplies no

9. The word εἰς here should be interpreted temporally as the parallel verse with its temporal expressions in verse 25 shows. So F. F. Bruce, *The Epistle to the Galatians* (Grand Rapids: Eerdmans, 1982), 183; Ronald Y. K. Fung, *The Epistle to the Galatians* (Grand Rapids: Eerdmans, 1988), 169 n. 11; Longenecker, *Galatians*, 149.

10. See pp. 77–80.

power to effect those promises. Thus, it is clearly subsidiary to the fundamental covenant given to Abraham, and it was never intended to be in force forever. It was an interim measure designed for the interval between the promise and the fulfillment, furnishing no power for obedience but frustrating people with its high standard. The Abrahamic covenant is fulfilled, Paul argues in Galatians, with the gift of the Spirit, for then people are empowered to do what God wills. The Mosaic covenant was never intended to last forever. It played a subsidiary and temporary role in salvation history, and with the coming of Christ the era of the Mosaic covenant has come to an end.

2 Corinthians 3:4–18

This text is full of exegetical difficulties and knotty problems, including the way the Old Testament is employed. Such controversies cannot be examined in detail here.[11] I am interested in gleaning what 2 Corinthians 3:4–18 says about the permanence of the law. My thesis is that the basic message of this passage is quite similar to what Paul has said in Galatians 3:15–4:11.

There is an inseparable connection between the law and the Mosaic covenant in 2 Corinthians 3.[12] The law is in view when Paul speaks of letters of "ink" "written on tablets of stone" (v. 3), of the "letter" that kills (v. 6), "letters engraved on stones" (v. 7), and the reading of Moses (v. 15). The law is clearly that given by Moses on Mount Sinai, and the reference to "letters engraved on stones" shows that the emphasis is on the Ten Commandments. But Paul can alternately describe the giving of the law in covenantal terms. The reference to the "new covenant" in verse 6, which is the work of the Spirit suggests that "the letter" of the law refers to the old covenant.[13] This is confirmed in the following verses. The covenant with Moses is described as "a ministry of death" (v. 7), "a ministry of condemnation" (v. 9), and "the old covenant" (v. 14). Undoubtedly Paul refers to the Mosaic covenant, and the law of that covenant figures most prominently in this text.

---

11. See Linda L. Belleville, *Reflections of Glory: Paul's Polemical Use of the Moses-Doxa Tradition in 2 Corinthians 3.1–18* (Sheffield: JSOT, 1991); Carol K. Stockhausen, *Moses' Veil and the Glory of the New Covenant: The Exegetical Substructure of II Cor. 3,1–4,6* (Rome: Pontifical Biblical Institute, 1989). Also see Scott J. Hafemann, *Paul and Moses, The Letter/Spirit Contrast and Argument from Scripture in 2 Corinthians 3.* (title tentative; Tübingen: J. C. B. Mohr, forthcoming); Otfried Hofius, "Gesetz und Evangelium nach 2. Korinther 3," *Paulusstudien* (Tübingen: J. C. B. Mohr, 1989), 75–120; Richard B. Hays, *Echoes of Scripture in the Letters of Paul* (New Haven: Yale University Press, 1989), 122–53.

12. So Hofius, "2. Korinther 3," 76–77.

13. Thomas E. Provence ("'Who is Sufficient for These Things?' An Exegesis of 2 Corinthians ii 15–iii 18," *NovT* 24 [1982]: 64–65) is wrong to separate the "letter" from the OT law.

The Mosaic covenant or law is not itself disparaged. In verses 7–11 Paul stresses that it came in glory and was a glorious covenant. As in Galatians 3–4 the defect in the law is due to human inability to perform it.[14] The law provides no power to obey so that "the letter kills" (v. 6), and it results in "death" (v. 7), and "condemnation" (v. 9). The new covenant ministry of the Spirit is superior because the Spirit writes the law on the heart (v. 3), and "gives life" (v. 6). Moreover, the new covenant is superior because its glory lasts (vv. 8, 11), and it provides righteousness (v. 9). When Paul speaks of the law as a "letter" (γράμμα, *gramma*), the emphasis is on the inability of the law to transform people. It does not, strictly speaking, refer to legalism,[15] though the law apart from the Spirit may be used for legalistic purposes. The *letter* of the law refers to what is written in the law—its commands, statutes, and prescriptions.[16] The law was a glorious revelation from God, and its commandments are good (Rom. 7:12). The issue is not with the content of the law, nor with what the letter of the law says. The problem with the law is that it produces no power to obey, for in the time of Moses the Spirit was generally withheld from God's people, and the law without the Spirit produced death. The law without the Spirit is a dead letter which does not and cannot generate life.

In verse 14 Paul confirms that the problem was not with the law itself but with the people. He says that "their minds were hardened, for until this day the same veil remains when the old covenant is read."[17] Verse 15 adds, "Whenever Moses is read, a veil lies upon their heart."[18] No criticism of the law's content is found here. Paul does not suggest that they refrain from reading Moses. They failed to understand Moses properly because their minds were hardened and a veil lay over their understanding. Exodus 32–34 functions as the background to this passage.

14. Hofius ("2. Korinther 3," 80, 84, 113) is correct on this point as far as he goes, although he also seems to construct too rigidly a law-gospel antithesis (see, for example, 119–20).

15. Contra Charles E. B. Cranfield, *A Critical and Exegetical Commentary on the Epistle to the Romans*, 2 vols. (Edinburgh: T. and T. Clark, 1975, 1979), 2.854; rightly Bernard Schneider, "The Meaning of St. Paul's Antithesis: 'The Letter and the Spirit,'" *CBQ* 15 (1953): 164. Peter R. Richardson ("Spirit and Letter: A Foundation for Hermeneutics," *EvQ* 45 [1973]: 208–18) incorrectly perceives the letter-spirit contrast in hermeneutical terms. For criticism of this latter view see Provence, "Who Is Sufficient?," 63–64.

16. So Hofius, "2. Korinther 3," 82.

17. Paul's use of Exod. 34:29–35 has generated a great deal of discussion. Many interpreters have simply concluded that he appropriated the OT text for his own ends. A more promising explanation of Paul's use of the OT text is suggested by Hafemann in his forthcoming work. I have only seen part of Hafemann's work, but the strength of his study lies in its convincing explanation of Exodus 32–34 in its historical setting. See also Scott J. Hafemann, "The Glory and Veil of Moses in 2 Cor. 3:7–14: An Example of Paul's Contextual Exegesis of the OT—A Proposal," *HBT* 14 (1992): 31–49.

18. On the parallelism of "mind" and "heart" see Belleville, *Reflections of Glory*, 239–40.

Israel received the law (Exod. 20–23), entered into covenant with Yahweh (Exod. 24:1–8), and pledged themselves to obey all that the law demanded (Exod. 24:7). But when Moses went up on the mountain to receive the covenantal stipulations, Israel committed idolatry by fashioning and worshiping the golden calf. The author identifies the people's obstinacy and corruption as the problem (32:7–9; 33:3, 5; 34:9). Nevertheless, the Lord graciously renews the covenant with them, promises them his presence, and reiterates covenantal obligations (33:12–34:27). The Old Testament text confirms this interpretation of what Paul communicates in 2 Corinthians 3. The people were stiff-necked and obstinate, so they disobeyed the law. The law reveal's God's character and, by their response to it, shows Israel to be rebellious.

Paul's statement that "their minds were hardened" (2 Cor. 3:14) may allude to Deuteronomy 29:4.[19] In Deuteronomy 29 Moses rehearses the saving acts of God in delivering his people from Egypt and exhorts the people to obey his law so as to escape the curses of the covenant. In verse 4 he says, "Yahweh has not given you a heart to know, nor eyes to see, nor ears to hear to this day." Indeed, the words *to this day* in Deut 29:4 (ἕως τῆς ἡμέρας ταύτης, *heōs tēs hēmeras tautēs*, Deut. 29:3 LXX) probably are alluded to by Paul in 2 Corinthians 3:14 ("until this very day," ἄχρι γάρ τῆς σήμερον ἡμέρας, *achri gar tēs sēmeron hēmeras*). The people should obey the law in order to escape the curse, and yet Moses recognizes that God has not given them the ability or heart to do so. He knows they will not obey given the state of their hearts (Deut. 29:22–28; 30:1). Paul is probably reflecting on this state of affairs when he says, "their minds were hardened" (2 Cor. 3:14); that is, their minds were hardened by God so that they did not observe the law. Interestingly, biblical writers can speak of people being hardened by God and at the same time see them as responsible for sin.

Saying that the mind of Israel was hardened means they did not have the Spirit. Verses 17–18 suggest that such unveiling occurs through the powerful work of the Spirit. "Where the Spirit of the Lord is, there is freedom."[20] The transformation "from glory to glory" takes place by the agency of the Spirit (v. 18). Those who read the law, if illumined by the Spirit, see that it directs them to faith in Christ. Deuteronomy 30:6–8 indicates that people will love the Lord and obey his law when he circumcises their hearts. Interestingly, in Romans 2:28–29 Paul uses the same contrast of letter-spirit found in 2 Corinthians 3:6. The Romans

---

19. For this observation see Hofius, "2. Korinther 3," 105–6; see also Belleville, *Reflections of Glory*, 221, 226–27.

20. For a survey of research on verse 17 see Belleville, *Reflections of Glory*, 256–72.

passage refers to the circumcision of the heart, which the Spirit effects. By circumcising the heart, the Spirit enables people to keep the law.

Paul clearly teaches in 2 Corinthians 3 that the Mosaic covenant was not intended to be in force forever. Three contrasts between the ministry of Moses and Paul are listed in verses 7–11. The last contrast points to the temporary nature of the Mosaic covenant: "For if that which passes away came with glory, much more that which remains is in glory" (v. 11). Paul contrasts the two covenants here, asserting that one is "passing away" while the other is permanent. The word for "passing away" (καταργούμενου, *katargoumenou*) must refer to the temporary nature of the Mosaic covenant, in comparison with the new covenant "which remains" (μένον, *menon*). Paul evidently has constructed an antithesis in which one covenant is said to remain forever, while the other (the Mosaic) is coming to an end. The cessation of the Mosaic covenant is also suggested by the contrast between the "new covenant" (v. 6) and the "old covenant" (v. 14). The implication appears to be that the new covenant has replaced the old. Of course, the nature of that replacement is not explicated here, but the fact of replacement seems to be present in the use of the words *new* and *old*.

Charles E. B. Cranfield argues that Paul is not referring to the end of the Mosaic covenant or the law but "to the ministry of Moses at the giving of the law."[21] The text, however, does not permit establishing distinctions among Moses' ministry, the glory on his face, the Mosaic covenant, and the law.[22] For Paul the glory on Moses' face that was "passing away" (καταργούμενου, *katargoumenou*, v. 7) was a parable of the "passing away" of the old covenant.[23] The glory on Moses' face was due to the reception of the law on Mount Sinai, and thus the particular "ministry" of Moses was intertwined inextricably with the reception of the law. It also seems that Paul specifically establishes a link between the glory coming to an end on Moses' face and the covenant with Moses coming to an end. He uses the verb "pass away" (καταργέω, *katargeō*) with both (2 Cor. 3:7, 11, 13). Indeed, verse 13 employs the temporal idea more forcefully, referring to the cessation of glory on Moses' face as "the end of what was passing away" (τὸ τέλος τοῦ καταργούμενου, *to telos tou katargoumenou*).

---

21. Cranfield, *Romans*, 855.

22. See Heikki Räisänen, *Paul and the Law* (Philadelphia: Fortress, 1983), 45; Hofius, "2. Korinther 3," 102.

23. Belleville (*Reflections of Glory*, 204–5) argues that καταργέω means "fading." But support for this definition is not strong. The evidence points to καταργέω meaning "to bring to an end," "nullify," and "abrogate." See Hays, *Echoes of Scripture*, 134–35; Hofius, "2. Korinther 3," 96–99; Hafemann, "The Veil of Moses," 36–40.

The word τέλος (*telos*) may mean *goal* instead of *end* in verse 13. To interpret τέλος as goal, however, probably reads too much into the word in this context. Linguistically, it is preferable to see redundancy at work here. Paul uses the redundant expression "the end of what is passing away" to drive home his point.[24] In the New Testament literature, contrary to Robert Badenas,[25] the word τέλος usually means "end" or "outcome," and rarely "goal."[26] What is particularly instructive is that in every other passage in the New Testament where a preposition occurs before τέλος, it never means "goal" or "outcome" or "result." In fact, in seven of these thirteen texts the temporal meaning is clearly present.[27] The temporal meaning is quite possibly present in four other texts with a prepositional phrase,[28] and once again the meaning "goal" or "outcome" is not possible in these texts. The prepositional phrase εἰς τὸ τέλος (*eis to telos*) in 2 Corinthians 3:13, therefore, probably means "to the end." And even if τέλος does mean "goal," the idea of the cessation of the law is still found in the verb *pass away*.

So 2 Corinthians 3 coheres with Galatians 3–4 in teaching that the Mosaic covenant is no longer in force for believers. Galatians 3–4 drives this thesis home in a more sustained way, but a similar conclusion is apparent in 2 Corinthians 3. In addition, in both Galatians and 2 Corinthians Paul argues that the law is God's law. Nevertheless, the law apart from the Spirit does not produce obedience. The law apart from the Spirit does not save but kills.

24. For some helpful comments on redundancy see Moisés Silva, *Biblical Words and Their Meaning: An Introduction to Lexical Semantics* (Grand Rapids: Zondervan, 1983), 153–56.

25. Robert Badenas, *Christ the End of the Law: Romans 10:4 in Pauline Perspective* (Sheffield: JSOT, 1985), especially 38–80.

26. Rightly Hofius, "2. Korinther 3," 102–3, and especially 110–11, and Belleville, *Reflections of Glory*, 201–2. First, we shall summarize the Pauline literature. The only clear example of τέλος meaning "goal" is in 1 Tim. 1:5. A temporal meaning "end" is evident in two texts (1 Cor. 1:8; 15:24). First Thess. 2:16 and 2 Cor. 1:13 either have a temporal meaning or the prepositional phrase means "fully" or "utterly." A temporal meaning is probable in Rom. 10:4 (although this text is hotly disputed) and in 1 Cor. 10:11. The latter passage may have a teleological sense as well, but it should be noted that the word is plural in this verse. The meaning "outcome" or "result" is found in four passages (Rom. 6:21, 22; 2 Cor. 11:15; Phil. 3:19). In Rom. 13:7 the word is used twice to refer to the paying of taxes. In addition, the temporal meaning clearly predominates in the rest of the NT (Matt. 10:22; 24:6, 13, 14; 26:58; Mark 3:26; 13:7, 13; Luke 1:33; 21:9; Heb. 3:14; 6:11; 7:3; 1 Peter 4:7; Rev. 2:26; 21:6; 22:13). In two cases either "to the end" or "utterly" fit, although the temporal meaning still seems to be present (Luke 18:5; John 13:1). Compare also 1 Peter 3:8 which probably means "finally." The meaning "outcome" or "result" is likely in three texts (Heb. 6:8; James 5:11; 1 Peter 4:17), while the meaning "fulfillment" is present in Luke 22:37. The word may mean "goal" in 1 Peter 1:9. A reference to paying taxes is found in Matt. 17:25. The lexical evidence, then, is weighted toward "end" in a temporal sense outside of Paul as well.

27. Matt. 10:22; 24:13; Mark 13:13; 1 Cor. 1:8; Heb. 3:14; 6:11; Rev. 2:26.

28. Luke 18:5; John 13:1; 2 Cor. 1:13; 1 Thess. 2:16.

An Excursus on Romans 10:4

The statement that "Christ is the end of the law" in Romans 10:4 seems to harmonize with the idea that the Mosaic covenant was not intended to be in force forever. Elsewhere I have chronicled the never-ending debate that rages on this verse.[29] One significant objection to the above interpretation is that τέλος means "goal" rather than "end." But this objection, as I pointed out above, is improbable on lexical grounds. The word τέλος often contains temporal meaning, while only one New Testament passage (1 Tim. 1:5) uses τέλος in the indisputable sense of "goal." Probably, then, that Paul means "Christ is the *end* of the law."

Nonetheless, the verse does not provide fodder for those who think that the law has come to an end either. Thus, I titled this section an excursus because it does not really advance the argument that the Mosaic covenant has in some sense come to an end. The verse, however, could not be bypassed at this juncture since many cite it to prove the law has come to an end, and it is one of the most discussed verses regarding Paul's view of the law.

Scholars have typically approached Romans 10:4 seeking to defend a particular theological understanding as to how the gospel and law relate. The verse has been used to support radical discontinuity—Christ is the end of the law. But it has also been cited to defend the theory that a significant harmony and continuity exist between the Testaments; Christ is the goal to which the law points. Both interpretations are flawed since the purpose of Romans 10:4 is not to provide a global theological statement on the relationship between gospel and law. Instead, verse 4 should be interpreted in relationship to verse 3, inasmuch as the two are joined by "for" (γάρ).

Romans 10:3 says that Israel "did not subject themselves to God's righteousness because they are ignorant of God's righteousness and seek to establish their own." I argued in chapter 4 that verse 3 portrays Israel as legalistically attempting to secure their own righteousness by works. They did not subject themselves to God's saving gift of righteousness because they were ignorant that righteousness is a divine gift. This ignorance led them to the vain pursuit of trying to establish their own righteousness—a righteousness based on "doing" (Rom. 9:32; 10:5) instead of believing (9:32–33; 10:6–13). Here Paul counters a form of works-righteousness by which the Jews thought they could attain right standing with God. This is surely the most natural way of understanding the statement that "they were seeking to establish their own righteousness."

29. "Paul's View of the Law in Romans 10:4–5," forthcoming in *WTJ*.

A parallel verse in the near context, (9:32) informs the reader that Israel failed to attain righteousness via the law because they sought to attain righteousness "as from works" instead of by faith. Since "works" (ἔργα, *erga*) in Paul refers to "works" in a general sense and cannot be limited to only part of the law, and since there is no mention of matters like circumcision, food laws, or sabbath in the context, it is fair to conclude that Paul says that some Jews thought they could obtain righteousness by doing what the law says.

What is the connection, then, when Paul says in verse 4, "For Christ is the end of the law with reference to righteousness for everyone who believes"? Sam Williams observes that an implied proposition links verses 3 and 4 that the Jews were wrong in not subjecting themselves to God's righteousness.[30] Or the implied proposition is that those who believe in Christ have submitted to God's righteousness. In either case the context suggests that the Jews should have submitted to God's righteousness by believing in Christ. Verse 4 then provides the reason why the Jews should have subjected themselves to God's righteousness— that Christ brings to an end the attempt to establish one's own righteousness. The close connection between verses 3 and 4 demonstrates that in verse 4 Paul does not make some overarching theological statement on the relationship between gospel and law. He responds to the specific problem raised in verse 3 of people wrongly using the law to establish their own righteousness. In verse 4 Paul points out that those who believe in Christ cease using the law as a means of establishing their own righteousness.[31] Verse 4 makes an experiential statement regarding the use of the law, which I paraphrase: "Christ is the end of using the law to establish one's own righteousness for those who believe."[32]

The words "to every one who believes" support the idea that in verse 4 Paul does not make a global statement on the relationship between

30. Sam K. Williams, "The Righteousness of God in Romans," *JBL* 99 (1980): 283–84.am

31. Such an interpretation understands εἰς as an adverbial preposition of general reference (so Richard N. Longenecker, *Paul: Apostle of Liberty* [1964; repr., Grand Rapids: Baker, 1976], 152–53), not as introducing a result or purpose clause. Mark A. Seifrid's ("Paul's Approach to the Old Testament in Romans 10:6–8," *TrinJ* 6 [1985]: 9 n. 29) grammatical analysis shows that εἰς in such constructions often signifies result, but even his study shows that there are exceptions, and thus the key issue here is the existing context. The whole focus of the context is on Jews who wrongly use the law to establish their own righteousness.

32. Some lodge a complaint against this exegesis on the grounds that εἰς δικαιοσύνην is closer to Χριστός than it is to τέλος γὰρ νόμου (Cranfield, *Romans*, 519–20; E. P. Sanders, *Paul, the Law and the Jewish People* [Philadelphia: Fortress, 1983], 61 n. 114; Badenas, *Christ the End*, 116; Räisänen, *Paul and the Law*, 55 n. 59). But the latter phrase has been moved up front for emphasis, and Seifrid ("Romans 10:6–8," 9 n. 30) argues that εἰς δικαιοσύνην is not related to all that precedes but only to the predicate nominative τέλος νόμου.

gospel and law. Christ is not the end of using the law for righteousness for all people. Verse 3 demonstrates that some Jews wrongly try to use the law for their own righteousness. Thus, verse 4 claims that only those who believe, who trust in Christ for their righteousness, cease trying to use the law to establish their own righteousness.

Alternate Views on the Permanence of the Law

Paul's Teaching as Contradictory

Heikki Räisänen maintains that Paul's teaching on the permanence of the law is contradictory.[33] Paul sets aside and abolishes the law in some contexts, but in others he commands believers to fulfil and obey the law. Scholars have had difficulty, according to Räisänen, in harmonizing these two themes precisely because they cannot be harmonized; the problem lies in Paul's own incoherency and logical inconsistency.

One can understand why Räisänen would come to this conclusion, for Paul's teaching on this issue is difficult, but there is evidence in his letters that he was aware of the tension between his "abolition" and "fulfillment" statements. First Corinthians 7:19 says, "Circumcision is nothing and uncircumcision is nothing, what is important is keeping the commandments of God." In parallel statements in Galatians 5:6 and 6:15 Paul relativizes circumcision and exalts "faith working through love" and a "new creation." Räisänen thinks 1 Corinthians 7:19 "differs markedly . . . in content" from Galatians 5:6 and 6:15.[34] The assertion smacks of Paul's "conservative" and "almost legalistic" stance in 1 Corinthians, and thus Räisänen concludes that 1 Corinthians 7:19 is "very much Jewish" and has "very little specifically Christian" content.[35] Räisänen is entirely right to point out some differences between 1 Corinthians 7:19 and Galatians 5:6 and 6:15, and he is also right to suggest that the different emphasis is due to the particular situation to which Paul is responding. However, his contention that 1 Corinthians 7:19 is more Jewish than Christian completely misleads. It would have been unthinkable for most Jews, including those of the diaspora, to exclude circumcision from the divine commandments.[36] C. K. Barrett asserts that this is one of the most radical statements Paul makes about the law, for now he speaks of obeying God's commandments without

33. Räisänen, *Paul and the Law*, 42–83.
34. Ibid., 68.
35. Ibid.
36. See John Nolland, "Uncircumcised Proselytes?" *JSJ* 12 (1981): 173–94; contra Neil J. McEleney, "Conversion, Circumcision and the Law," *NTS* 20 (1974): 319–41.

including circumcision among them![37] In *one* verse Paul displays the very tension that Räisänen labels contradictory. He speaks negatively of circumcision and excludes it from the commandments of God, and yet he speaks positively of obeying the commandments. It is highly improbable that Paul would be unaware of this tension, especially when it occurs within a single sentence.

The same point could be made regarding Galatians 5:14.[38] It is unlikely that when Paul speaks of fulfilling the law by loving a neighbor he has forgotten his emphasis on liberation from law in the rest of the letter. In particular Paul certainly would not have regarded the statement in Galatians 5:3, which threatens those who desire to obey the whole law, as in conflict with his admonition to fulfil the whole law in 5:14, especially since the two exhortations are separated by only a few sentences. Galatians 5:3, as I have shown, warns those who are inclined to submit to circumcision. Paul alerts the Galatians that submission to circumcision would require perfect obedience to the law for justification. Galatians 5:14, on the other hand, guards against overreacting to the theme that believers are no longer under the law. How Paul can affirm freedom from the law and enjoin obedience to the law will be explored in the next chapter.

Developmental View

Other scholars also have seen contradictions or tensions in Pauline statements on the law, but their opinions can be distinguished from the previous position, since they claim these contradictions are not discernible in the same letter. Rather, the contradictions or tensions are detected when one compares Paul's letters, suggesting that Paul's understanding of the law developed over time. Those who espouse such a position invariably see the mature Pauline statement in Romans.[39] For instance, Hans Hübner thinks that in Galatians the law is excluded altogether as having any role in the life of the believer. Paul even attributes its origin to demonic powers in Galatians 3:19. By the time he writes Romans, however, Paul has moderated his stance on the

37. C. K. Barrett, *A Commentary on the First Epistle to the Corinthians* (New York: Harper and Row, 1968), 169; see Gordon D. Fee, *The First Epistle to the Corinthians* (Grand Rapids: Eerdmans, 1987), 312–14.

38. See Stephen Westerholm's critique of Räisänen on this verse "On Fulfilling the Whole Law (Gal. 5:14)," *SEÅ* 51–52 (1986–87): 229–37.

39. So Hans Hübner, *Law in Paul's Thought* (Edinburgh: T. and T. Clark, 1984); John W. Drane, *Paul, Libertine or Legalist? A Study of the Theology of the Major Pauline Epistles* (London: SPCK, 1975); Ulrich Wilckens, "Zur Entwicklung des paulinischen Gesetzesverständnisses," *NTS* 28 (1982): 154–90. See also Davies, "Paul and the Law," 103–8.

law. The law is no longer rejected completely but is abolished insofar as it is misused and abused. Similarly, John Drane sees Paul in response to the Judaizing heresy as teaching in Galatians the complete abolition of the Old Testament law. In 1 Corinthians, according to Drane, he reverses his position by espousing a legalism to counter the libertines in Corinth. By the time he writes Romans he has found the balance between being a libertine (Galatians) and legalist (1 Corinthians); therefore, Romans reflects his mature and seasoned perspective on the question of the law.

Appealing to development in Pauline thought to explain his view on the law is not a convincing solution for at least four reasons.[40] First, a suitable period for significant evolution in Paul's thinking about the law is lacking. This is the case even if one subscribes to an early date for Galatians,[41] but it is especially true if Galatians was written later.[42] One should not forget that Paul had been involved in missionary work a number of years before any of his letters were written, and thus he had probably already hammered out the essence of his theology. Second, Räisänen points out that the developmental view does not really solve the problem, for problematical statements on the law are found *within* the same letters.[43] Third, while there are noticeable differences between, say, Galatians and Romans, these should not be ascribed to a development in Paul. The varied nature of the response was conditioned by the specific circumstances Paul addressed. His statements on the law are more negative in Galatians than Romans because of the Judaizing opposition, which was such a severe threat to the Galatian churches. Fourth, the particular solutions of both Hübner and Drane are not convincing as other scholars have pointed out.[44]

Critique of Legalism

Others claim that Paul's negative statements on the law refer not to the law itself but to a legalistic interpretation of the law. This interpretation has received its major impetus from the magisterial commentary on Romans by Charles Cranfield and an earlier article which he wrote

40. J. Lowe is still helpful in analyzing the notion of development in Pauline theology ("An Examination of Attempts to Detect Developments in St. Paul's Theology," *JTS* 42 [1941]: 129–42). See also Räisänen, *Paul and the Law*, 7–10.

41. So Drane, *Paul*, 140–43.

42. This criticism applies particularly to Hübner (*Law in Paul's Thought*, 63) who says there was a significant period of time between Galatians and Romans.

43. Räisänen, *Paul and the Law*, 9.

44. For a critique of Hübner see Jerome Hall, "Paul, the Lawyer, on the Law," *Journal of Law and Religion* 3 (1985): 370–76; Daniel B. Wallace, "Galatians 3:19–20: A *Crux Interpretum* for Paul's View of the Law," *WTJ* 52 (1990): 235–42.

on the Pauline theology of law.[45] Cranfield concedes that Paul speaks in a deprecatory way about the law in Galatians 3. This depreciation, says Cranfield, is due to the situation in Galatia where Judaizing opponents were exalting the law above the promise. Most important, according to Cranfield, is to see that Paul's negative statements on the law are not a criticism or abolition of the law per se; the problem being addressed is the law apart from Christ, or legalism. Galatians 3 is misunderstood if it is employed to teach the abolition of law; it simply counters legalism, which is contrary to the true purpose of the law.

Despite the reservations of some scholars, Paul probably does wage a polemic against legalism in Galatians and Romans.[46] Nonetheless, the view that in Galatians 3 Paul only speaks against legalism, held by Cranfield and others, has problems. First, if Paul merely chides the Galatians for legalism, then why does he insist that circumcision is no longer required for Gentiles? Why not say that the Galatians should stop submitting to circumcision with a legalistic motive to earn favor with God, but circumcision should be practiced as the fruit and evidence of faith? After all, Paul does not teach the abolition of the law, according to Cranfield, but merely laments its misuse. It follows that circumcision itself would not be abolished, only a wrong understanding of circumcision. Of course, Cranfield realizes the ceremonial law is now abolished since Christ fulfilled it, and he believes that Galatians invalidates circumcision. Cranfield's view does not explain, however, why Paul thinks circumcision is no longer required. One could argue that Galatians implies that Old Testament sacrifices are passé now that Christ has been sacrificed on the cross. But how has the coming of Christ fulfilled the command to be circumcised? Those who see Paul only as disparaging legalism in Galatians have a hard time explaining why he nullifies the command to be circumcised.

An illustration from baptism may clarify. If someone said that you must be baptized to earn salvation, I would view this as a legalistic understanding of the sacrament. However, I would not argue that no one should be baptized and that baptism is now abolished. My goal would

45. Cranfield, *Romans*, especially 853, 857–61; idem, "St. Paul and the Law," *SJT* 17 (1964): 55, 60–66; see C. F. D. Moule, "Obligation in the Ethic of Paul," in W. R. Farmer, C. F. D. Moule, and Reinhold R. Niebuhr, eds., *Christian History and Interpretation: Studies Presented to John Knox* (Cambridge: Cambridge University Press, 1967), 391–92; Charles H. Cosgrove, "The Mosaic Law Preaches Faith: A Study in Galatians 3," *WTJ* 41 (1978): 146–64; Daniel P. Fuller, *Gospel and Law: Contrast or Continuum?* (Grand Rapids: Eerdmans, 1980), 65–120, 199–204. C. F. D. Moule ("Jesus, Judaism, and Paul," in G. F. Hawthorne and O. Betz, eds., *Tradition and Interpretation in the New Testament: Essays in Honor of E. Earle Ellis* [Grand Rapids: Eerdmans, 1987], 48), it should be noted, has now abandoned this position.

46. For a critique of Cranfield see Räisänen, *Paul and the Law*, 42–50; Douglas J. Moo, "'Law,' 'Works of the Law,' and Legalism in Paul," *WTJ* 45 (1983): 85–88.

be to instill a correct understanding of baptism, not to abrogate the rite altogether. In the case of circumcision, though, Paul does not merely correct the wrong understanding of circumcision but he also maintains that it is no longer valid. If Paul is only disparaging legalism, it is hard to see why circumcision is now annulled. But if a salvation-historical shift has rendered the Mosaic covenant obsolete, as I argued above from Galatians 3, then Paul provides a reason in Galatians why circumcision is abolished. Believers no longer should live under the authority of the Mosaic covenant now that Christ has come.

Second, Paul's use of the word *law* in Galatians 3:15–25 also shows that he does not exclusively attack legalism, for Paul does not restrict his comments solely to the misuse of the law. Verses 17 and 19 speak specifically of the Mosaic law, given on Mount Sinai 430 years after the promise to Abraham. The word *law* in verse 19 must also refer to the Mosaic law and not legalism, for Paul certainly does not ask, "Why, then, legalism?" And in 3:21 *law* again must refer to the Mosaic law since Paul says that the law is not contrary to the promises of God, something he would never say about legalism, which perverts the promises of God. I do not doubt that the Galatians were misusing the law in a legalistic way, but when Paul says "we are no longer under the pedagogue" (v. 25), he does not mean that we are no longer under *legalism*. Lexically, *law* refers to the law given by Moses.[47] Paul argues that believers are not bound by the covenant enacted with Moses.

Frank Thielman, on the other hand, argues that the law is not revoked absolutely, but only insofar as it encloses people under sin.[48] Although the parallels are not exact, he finds some precedence in Jewish literature for the removal of ceremonial rites like circumcision, food laws, and the observance of days.[49] Thielman should emphasize, however, the difference between Paul and his contemporaries on ceremonial rites. Some Jewish writers downplayed their distinctive rituals because they wanted to mesh with Hellenistic culture. Paul was profoundly different in that he argued from a theological conviction for the dissolving of these practices. The radical nature of Paul's position enraged some contemporary Jews of his day.

The claim that only the law's function of enclosing people under sin has ended is also questionable. Thielman rightly sees that the inauguration of the new covenant involves an ability to fulfil the law, which was

47. That the word *pedagogue* refers to the law in Gal. 3:25 is proved by the connection between the two in Gal. 3:24.

48. Frank Thielman, *From Plight to Solution: A Jewish Framework for Understanding Paul's View of the Law in Galatians and Romans* (Leiden: Brill, 1989), 76, 79.

49. Ibid., 54–59.

not given under the Mosaic covenant. Nonetheless, he (like those who see Paul as only abolishing legalism) does not answer why Paul abolishes circumcision and food laws. Presumably, the church, having received the Spirit, could now fulfil these laws more profoundly. Claiming that the law is abolished only insofar as it encloses people under sin scarcely explains why certain commandments are dissolved. The view that the Mosaic covenant has come to an end provides a more satisfactory solution.

An Excursus on Christian Reconstructionism

The Christian reconstruction movement, which is diverse and complex in thought, cannot be examined fully here.[50] As noted earlier, this movement believes that the civil government of nations today should be regulated by the "standing laws" of the Mosaic covenant.[51] The ceremonial law has passed away, but the laws that regulated Israel as a nation should be enforced today.[52] Not only should the standing laws of the Mosaic law be enforced but the penalties as well. For example, Greg Bahnsen argues that homosexuals, adulterers, rapists, and kidnappers should be executed for their sin.[53]

When modern Christians become aware of this movement for the first time, they are usually shocked by such a prescription for society's ills. Reconstructionists, however, defend themselves by pointing out that laws and penalties that originate with God cannot be evil. They see the ills of society as partly arising from a secular and humanistic framework, which invents its own laws. The major problem with Christian reconstructionism is a failure to see the salvation-historical shift from the Mosaic covenant to the new covenant.[54] Paul argues in 2 Corin-

50. For an examination of the movement see William S. Barker and W. R. Godfrey, eds., *Theonomy: A Reformed Critique* (Grand Rapids: Zondervan, 1990). See also Christopher J. W. Wright, "The Ethical of the Old Testament: A Survey of Approaches. Part II," *TynBul* 43 (1992): 213–20.

51. "Standing laws" refers to those laws that were not given to a particular individual or group for a particular occasion (such as the command for holy war), but laws which are applicable to all people for all time.

52. For a historical perspective on the issue of the normativity of the civil law see P. D. L. Avis, "Moses and the Magistrate: A Study in the Rise of Protestant Legalism," *JEH* 26 (1975): 149–72; Mark W. Karlberg, "Reformation Politics: The Relevance of OT Ethics in Calvinist Political Theory," *JETS* 29 (1986): 179–91. There are also three articles on this question in Barker and Godfrey, eds., *Theonomy*: W. R. Godfrey, "Calvin and Theonomy," 299–312; Sinclair B. Ferguson, "An Assembly of Theonomists? The Teaching of the Westminster Divines on the Law of God," 315–49, and Samuel T. Logan, Jr., "New England Puritans and the State," 353–84.

53. Greg L. Bahnsen, *Theonomy in Christian Ethics* (Nutley, N. J.: Craig, 1977), 445.

54. See Tremper Longman III, "God's Law and Mosaic Punishments Today," in Barker and Godfrey, eds., *Theonomy*, 41–54.

thians 3 and Galatians 3 that the covenant with Moses is no longer in force. The cessation of that covenant would apply to both the civil law and its respective penalties.

Here the insights of what James D. G. Dunn calls "the new perspective on Paul" are illuminating.[55] The commandments Paul specifically eliminates include circumcision (1 Cor. 7:19; Rom. 2:25–29; 4:9–12; Gal. 2:3–5; 5:2–6; 6:15; Phil. 3:3), food laws (Rom. 14–15; 1 Cor. 8–10; Gal. 2:11–14) and the observance of certain days (Rom. 14:5–6; Gal. 4:10; Col. 2:16–17).[56] These were the practices that separated Jews from Gentiles in the Greco-Roman world. These particular Jewish laws were the object of derision and curiosity.[57] Their special relevance is this: One reason the Mosaic covenant was abolished is that it was a covenant which God made specifically with the Jews. Practices such as circumcision and food laws were abolished once the new covenant arrived because they erected barriers between Jews and Gentiles. The new covenant, however, constituted the fulfillment of God's covenant with Abraham, which was designed to bless all nations (Gen. 12:3). The days of separation between Jews and Gentiles were over (see Eph. 2:11–3:13), so culturally divisive practices were also outmoded.

Many reconstructionists would agree that circumcision and food laws are not normative today since they belong to the ceremonial law, but they would insist that the standing laws of the Old Testament still apply to civil states today. Such a stance, however, fails to see why such practices as circumcision and food laws are abolished. One could argue from Galatians and Colossians that circumcision, for instance, is fulfilled in the cross of Christ.[58] Certain laws were given to Israel as God's elect nation to distinguish her from the surrounding nations. The scorn poured on certain Jewish practices by Gentiles in the New Testament period confirms that these customs did effectively separate Jews from Gentiles.

Christian reconstructionism falters at this very point. It fails to perceive Israel's uniqueness as a covenantal nation. We cannot simply import the civil laws from the Mosaic covenant, which were intended for ancient Israel, into contemporary nation states. The nation of Israel

---

55. James D. G. Dunn, "The New Perspective on Paul," *BJRL* 65 (1983): 95–122.

56. See Dunn, "New Perspective," 107–10, 114–15; Sanders, *Paul, the Law*, 100–3.

57. See Menahem Stern, *Greek and Latin Authors on Jews and Judaism*, 2 vols. (Jerusalem: Israel Academy of Sciences and Humanities, 1976, 1980), sections 195, 258, 281, 301.

58. See Peder Borgen's two essays, "Observations on the Theme 'Paul and Philo': Paul's Preaching of Circumcision in Galatia (Gal. 5:11) and Debates on Circumcision in Philo," in S. Pederson, ed., *The Pauline Literature and Theology* (Göttingen: Vandenhoeck and Ruprecht, 1980), 85–102; "Paul Preaches Circumcision and Pleases Men," in M. D. Hooker and S. G. Wilson, eds., *Paul and Paulinism: Essays in Honour of C. K. Barrett* (London: SPCK, 1982), 37–46.

was a unique entity as a covenant people. Today no nation has the unique privilege of a state and a religion ordained by God. This does not mean that the Old Testament law should not be consulted by nations today, nor does it deny that the nations are held responsible for failing to observe God's laws (Lev. 18:26–28; Deut. 2:10–23; Amos 1–2).[59] Moral principles found in the law are normative for all states in all places. But the standing laws of the Old Testament should not necessarily be accepted as normative for modern states simply because they hail from the Old Testament.[60]

Even if the moral principles of the Old Testament law are accepted as normative, that does not mean the penalties attached to the law are still in force. The penalties were probably stricter for Israel because she was supposed to be a holy nation, unique in all the earth. The church constitutes the people of God in the midst of many nations. None of these nations, though, intrinsically comprises God's special and peculiar people. The law commanded that those who commit incest be put to death (Lev. 18:6–18, 29). Paul in 1 Corinthians 5 still finds such a practice to be evil, but he does not suggest that the offender be put to death. Instead, the offender is to be put out of the church until he repents.[61]

59. For a more careful attempt to apply the OT law to modern states see Vern S. Poythress, *The Shadow of Christ in the Law of Moses* (Brentwood, Tenn.: Wolgemuth and Hyatt, 1991), 139–249. I am not endorsing all of Poythress' conclusions, but his analysis of the problem is more satisfying because he takes into account the covenantal shift between the Testaments.

60. See Karlberg, "Reformation Politics," 187–88, 190.

61. See Walter C. Kaiser, Jr., "God's Promise Plan and His Gracious Law," *JETS* 33 (1990): 292.

6

The Fulfillment of the Law by Christians

We saw in chapter 5 that the Mosaic covenant was a temporary covenant, designed to last until the coming of the Messiah. The atoning work of Christ and the descent of the Spirit indicated the end of the Mosaic covenant and signaled the fulfillment of the Abrahamic covenant. If the Mosaic covenant has ended, then it would seem to follow that the law has been completely abolished, and the Old Testament law would no longer play a role in the life of Christians. In this chapter I will explore inductively the issue of the continuing validity of the law, and determine what Paul himself taught on this question.

The Law and Pauline Commands

After examining the texts that stress the interim nature of the Mosaic law, it is surprising to discover a number of texts that exhort believers to fulfil the law. In Galatians 5:14, for example, Paul affirms that the whole Old Testament law is fulfilled in the commandment to love one's neighbor as oneself. The injunction to neighbor love is itself from the Old Testament law (Lev. 19:18), and thus Paul sees at least one Old Testament command as still in force for Christians. Romans 13:8–10 is conceptually parallel to Galatians 5:14, but it expands upon it, giving us more insight into what fulfilling the law involves. As in Galatians, Paul asserts that love for neighbor fulfils the law. "The one who loves another has fulfilled the law" (13:8). He also affirms that the entire law is summed up in the Old Testament command to love one's neighbor as oneself (Lev. 19:18 in Rom. 13:9), and concludes that "love is the fulfillment of the law" since it "does no wrong to the neighbor." It should be emphasized here that love is the heart of Paul's ethic. The centrality of love in Paul is evident throughout his writings. The true test of faith is that it works itself out in love (Gal. 5:6), love is the first and supreme fruit of the Spirit (Gal. 5:22), and heads up the parenesis in Romans 12:9. When Paul thanks God for the virtues manifested by believers, love is often mentioned, along with faith and hope (Eph. 1:15; Col. 1:4; 1 Thess. 1:3; 2 Thess. 1:3; Philem. 5), whereas other virtues usually are not mentioned in the thanksgiving. Colossians 3:14 describes love as "the bond of perfection," and in 1 Timothy 1:5 Paul calls love the "goal of his instruction."

First Corinthians 13 displays the centrality of love. It is superior to any spiritual gift, and even virtuous actions like giving all one's possessions to the poor and even sacrificing one's life profit nothing without love (1 Cor. 13:3). Verse 3 shows that love cannot merely be defined by certain external actions. It is possible to give up all of one's possessions for the poor and even sacrifice one's life and not have love.[1] Paul implies that love involves the affections and motives of the heart.[2] Love is the ultimate fulfillment of the law because one who lives in love has been transformed at such a deep level that love flows from the heart. In Pauline theology this kind of radical transformation cannot be accomplished apart from faith and the work of the Holy Spirit (Gal. 5:6). Only those who trust God's promises and provision and are empowered by the Holy Spirit are able to love. Love does not merely involve the keeping of certain external commandments, but, as a result of grace, is a renewing of the affections of the heart.

The priority of love explains why Paul does not have a casuistic ethic. Those who live by love do good to their neighbor in every situation (Rom. 13:10), and no law can exhaust the possible opportunities. Thus, Paul prays for greater love in his converts, which is informed by knowledge and discernment, so that believers can determine the best plan of action in each particular situation (Phil. 1:9–10). Paul does not provide

1. There is a textual dispute here inasmuch as the external evidence favors καυχήσωμαι. Nonetheless, contextual reasons suggest that the superior reading is probably καυθήσωμαι. So J. K. Elliott, "In Favour of καυθήσωμαι at 1 Cor. 13:3," *ZNW* 62 (1971): 297–98. For a contrary view see Gordon D. Fee, *The First Epistle to the Corinthians* (Grand Rapids: Eerdmans, 1987), 629 n. 18; 633–35.

2. See especially the helpful discussion in John Murray, *Principles of Conduct: Aspects of Biblical Ethics* (Grand Rapids: Eerdmans, 1957), 21–23. Murray's entire analysis of love and law (18–26) is valuable.

detailed ethical advice to treat every possible ethical dilemma that might arise. The loving response is not always immediately evident, so wisdom and discernment are needed to chart the best course. The animating principle of love is more important than providing detailed advice for every situation.

Even though Paul offers no casuistic ethic, he does not allow love to float free at the ethical center without any articulation of definite requirements. I have said that there is no attempt to provide an answer to every possible ethical situation. But although Paul did not legislate for *every* contingency, that does not mean one cannot apply Pauline moral norms or commands to *any* situation. Romans 13:8–10 illustrates this. Love is certainly the capstone of the exhortation. But love is a plastic word that can be twisted to fit almost anything. In verse 9 Paul nails down how love expresses itself by citing commandments of the Old Testament law prohibiting adultery, murder, stealing, and coveting. The injunction to obey specific commandments does not violate, hinder, or squelch love. Specific commandments and exhortations describe how love expresses itself in the concrete situations of life. Of course, Paul does not exhaustively describe how love manifests itself, but he does provide parameters for the expression of love, so believers will not deceive themselves into thinking that they are acting in love while they violate ethical absolutes.

Do Concrete Commands Squelch Love and the Holy Spirit?

Some scholars have described the ethical statements of Paul in misleading terms. They trumpet love as the center of the Pauline ethic, and suggest that any focus on ethical norms or law somehow diminishes love or squelches spontaneous dependence upon the Spirit.[3] In support they assert that believers are not bound by the law (Rom. 6:14; 1 Cor. 9:20), circumcision (Rom. 4:9–12; Gal. 5:2–6), food laws (Rom. 14:14, 20; Gal. 2:11–14), or the sabbath (Rom. 14:5; Gal. 4:10; Col. 2:16). They also point to the assertion that "all things are lawful" (1 Cor. 6:12; 10:23). I would argue that at every point they commit crucial errors in interpretation. When Paul declares that believers are not under law he does not intend that no ethical norms or absolutes are needed for Christian living.

---

3. So, for example, Stephen Westerholm in "Letter and Spirit: The Foundation of Pauline Ethics," *NTS* 30 (1984): 229–48; "The Law and the 'Just Man' (1 Tim. 1, 3–11)," *ST* 36 (1982): 79–95; "On Fulfilling the Whole Law (Gal. 5:14)," *SEÅ* 51–52 (1986–1987): 229–37, and Westerholm's book, *Israel's Law and the Church's Faith: Paul and His Recent Interpreters* (Grand Rapids: Eerdmans, 1988), 198–218. See also F. F. Bruce, "Paul and the Law of Moses," *BJRL* 57 (1975): 259–79, and Linda L. Belleville, "'Under Law': Structural Analysis and the Pauline Concept of Law in Galatians 3.21–4.11," *JSNT* 26 (1986): 70–71.

Certainly circumcision, food laws, and the observance of certain days are no longer required, but this does not prove that the law is set aside in every respect for believers. A number of texts in Paul indicate that some commandments are still in force. "All things are lawful" probably quotes the opponents. That statement evidently is a legitimate description of his position, but he reinterprets it. But this saying should not be used as a comprehensive exposition of the Pauline stance on the continuing validity of the law. This saying occurs in specific contexts that refer to *adiaphora*, for the context of 1 Corinthians 10:23–11:1 relates to eating food sold in the meat market, a matter in which Christian love and wisdom are needed since there is no ethical absolute.[4] The previous verses (10:19–22) show that there are some absolutes, for Paul forbids eating in idol temples as amounting to idolatry. The prohibition against idolatry is rooted in the first two commandments, and evidently Paul still sees these commands as normative. Strictly speaking, all things are not lawful, as in 1 Corinthians 6:12–20 where Paul makes it plain that "sexual immorality" (πορνεία, *porneia*) is intolerable.

Moreover, those who stress that love and the Spirit are a sufficient ethic for Paul do not adequately account for the detailed parenesis found in his letters (for example, Rom. 12:1–15:13; Gal. 5:13–6:10; Col. 3:1–4:6; 1 Thess. 4:1–5:22).[5] Paul never descends into casuistry, but in broad strokes he describes how love expresses itself. Apparently, he does not consider it sufficient to tell congregations to love one another—even the churches of Galatia that are being seduced by the law. Paul explains that freedom should not be used for license and in broad strokes describes life in the Spirit (Gal. 5:22–23) in contrast to the "works of the flesh" (Gal. 5:19–21). He mentions such specific matters as envy (Gal. 5:26) and the need to pay teachers (Gal. 6:6), presumably to remind the Galatians how love would express itself in particular circumstances.

Paul does not hesitate to condemn incest (1 Cor. 5:1–13), lawsuits (1 Cor. 6:1–8), and divorce (1 Cor. 7:10–11), probably because love is violated in these situations. In 1 Thessalonians 4:1–8 he specifically forbids sexual immorality, while in Romans 13:1–7 he enjoins subjection to governing authorities. The exhortation to obey specific commandments is not contrary to love. Neither do the commandments quench life in the Spirit, for the Spirit uses the commandments to inform believers about what is required. Paul believed that giving specific commands would strengthen believers to live in a more loving manner. In any case, there is

---

4. See Fee, *First Corinthians*, 252; W. Schrage, *Die konkreten Einzelgebote in paulinischen Paränese* (Gütersloh: Gerd Mohn, 1961), 57–58.

5. This point is powerfully argued by Schrage, *Die konkreten Einzelgebote*; Thomas J. Deidun, *New Covenant Morality in Paul* (Rome: Biblical Institute Press, 1981), 188–217.

no suggestion of people obeying the commands in their own strength. The indicative always undergirds the imperative, and obedience to the law is only possible through reliance upon the Holy Spirit. Since Paul employs parenesis so much, he apparently did not think such exhortations would diminish dependence upon the Spirit or squelch true love, for the same Paul highlights the power of the Spirit and the priority of love.

The Call to Fulfil the Law

What Paul says about parenesis in general applies in principle to law. That some Old Testament laws remain normative does not contradict Paul's theology of the Spirit or the preeminence of love. If Pauline theology contains moral norms at all—and the parenesis shows it does—then the normative character of some of the Old Testament law does not violate the Pauline gospel, unless one insists that the presence of any parenesis at all is a denial of the genuine Pauline gospel. Those who see the presence of any parenesis as a liability fall into the error of being more Pauline than was Paul.

The question remains, however, as to whether any of the Old Testament law is normative for Paul. This whole discussion on parenesis and love was prompted by our examination of Romans 13:8–10. We have seen already from Galatians 5:14 that at least one command of the Old Testament is still in force for Paul—the injunction to love one's neighbor. Paul reiterates this command in Romans 13:9 by expanding upon what he said in Galatians. Paul specifically cites certain commands from the law (the prohibitions against adultery, murder, stealing, and coveting), and he expects believers to fulfil these commands. In other words, these specific commandments help the community understand how love concretely expresses itself.[6] These are obviously not the only aspects of love, but no one can claim to be practicing love and living in adultery. In addition, other commands of the law could have been added to the list, for after itemizing the four named above he adds the words "and if there is any other commandment" (13:9). The point is that love is summed up not only in the commandments specifically named but also in other commands from the law. The tension between love and commandments must be maintained. Love must remain the

---

6. This point is not sufficiently appreciated by Victor Paul Furnish (*Theology and Ethics in Paul* [Nashville: Abingdon, 1968], 199–200) and Andreas Lindemann ("Die biblischen Toragebote und die paulinische Ethik," in W. Schrage, ed., *Studien zum Text und zur Ethik des Neuen Testaments* [Berlin: de Gruyter, 1986], 242–43, 263 n. 108). Herman Ridderbos (*Paul: An Outline of His Theology* [Grand Rapids: Eerdmans, 1975], 282) goes to the other extreme when he says, "The Law does not find its criterion in love, but just the reverse, the requirement of love is so imperative because in it lies the summary of the law."

priority so that obedience to commandments does not degenerate into external fulfillment without the transformation of the heart by the Holy Spirit. Nevertheless, specific commandments are necessary. People tend to be sentimental so that love is shaped to fit whatever lifestyle they prefer.[7]

Romans 13:9 also indicates that some commandments of the Old Testament law are still normative for believers. Paul can affirm the cessation of the Mosaic covenant and also enjoin believers to keep some of the commands in the Mosaic law. Shortly I will explore whether Paul contradicts himself in these dual affirmations. It should be noted that the commandments in Romans 13:8–10 that still apply to believers hail from the decalogue.

That the law should be obeyed by Christians is also the most probable meaning of Romans 8:4 where Paul says that God sent Jesus to die "in order that the ordinance of the law might be fulfilled in us who do not walk according to the flesh but according to the Spirit." The meaning of this verse continues to be debated. Some think that the passive verb (πληρωθῇ, plērōthē, "be fulfilled"), and the stress on what is accomplished "in us" (ἐν ἡμῖν, en hēmin) along with the focus on what God has accomplished in the cross of Christ suggest that Paul is speaking of what has been objectively accomplished in the cross of Christ, not in the obedience of Christians.[8] In this view "the ordinance of the law" refers to what God has done in Christ, not to believers concretely doing what the law demands. This view is certainly a possibility, although for the following reasons I think Paul is speaking of concrete obedience of the law by believers. First, the passive verb *be fulfilled* probably does not indicate that Paul speaks only of the objective fulfillment by Christ of the law's requirement. Instead, Paul uses the passive to stress that the believer's obedience has its basis in Christ's work on the cross and in the liberating power of the Spirit, which frees one from the power of sin and death (Romans 8:2).[9] The passive verb indicates that the fulfillment of

7. Charles E. B. Cranfield ("St. Paul and the Law," *SJT* 17 [1964]: 67) perceptively says that we "need the particular commandments into which the law breaks down the general obligation to save us from the sentimentality and self-deception to which we all are prone." See also Schrage, *Die konkreten Einzelgebote*, 267–71. Deidun (*New Covenant*, 171) rightly says that love cannot be limited "to the fulfillment of calculated ethical demands." He goes on to say, "But if love goes *beyond* calculable obligation, it does not go *around*."

8. Ernst Käsemann, *Commentary on Romans* (Grand Rapids: Eerdmans, 1980), 218; Leander E. Keck, "The Law and 'The Law of Sin and Death' (Rom. 8:1–4): Reflections on the Spirit and Ethics in Paul," in J. L. Crenshaw and S. Sandmel; eds., *The Divine Helmsman: Studies on God's Control of Human Events, Presented to Lou H. Silberman* (New York: Ktav, 1980), 51–53; Douglas J. Moo, *Romans 1–8* (Chicago: Moody, 1990), 514–17.

9. Rightly Eckart Reinmuth, *Geist und Gesetz: Studien zu Voraussetzungen und Inhalt der paulinischen Paränese* (Berlin: Evangelische Verlagsanstalt, 1985), 70.

the law by the believer is actually due to God's work.[10] Paul's use of the verb *fulfil* (πληρόω, *plēroō*) elsewhere shows that the passive use involves human activity (see 2 Cor. 10:6; Eph. 5:18; Phil. 1:11; Col. 1:9).[11] So, for example, believers are commanded "to be filled with the Spirit" (Eph. 5:18). The passive *be filled* (πληροῦσθε, *plērousthe*) signifies that it is God who does the filling. Nonetheless, human activity is also involved since it is a command addressed to the church.

Second, Paul refers in Romans 8:3 to the death of Christ on behalf of believers, whereby he took upon himself condemnation in order to pay the penalty demanded by the law. The question here, though, is whether the appeal solely to God's work exhausts the meaning of Romans 8:3–4. It seems probable in this context that Paul goes beyond what he said previously in Romans 3:21–26, where he explained that the death of Jesus paid the penalty for sin. Romans 6–8 as a whole sets forth the new life believers live since they are in Christ, and thus the connection between 8:3–4 probably reveals that the work of Jesus on the cross is the basis and ground for believers fulfilling the law.

The immediate context of Romans 7–8 strengthens this point. Chapter 7 emphasizes that the law provides no power for obedience. Indeed, the law does not liberate people from sin, but sin uses the law to promote and generate more sin. Paul wants to prove in chapter 8 that life in the Spirit does not incite people to sin more. Instead, the work of the Spirit (8:2) and the work of Christ on the cross (8:3) enable believers to obey the law (8:4). Such an argument destroys the view of Jews who claim that the law is the crucial means for holiness. The law itself provides no power for holiness and righteousness, while those who have the Holy Spirit fulfil it.

The last clause in Romans 8:4 also indicates that Paul speaks of the fulfilling of the law by Christians. The phrase "to those who do not walk according to the flesh but according to the Spirit" may be descriptive rather than instrumental, but in either case the use of the verb *walk* shows that the activity of believers is in view. If Paul had merely wanted to describe those who are in Christ, he could have written "to those who are not in the flesh but in the Spirit." The reference to walking shows that Paul describes the active obedience of believers.

Other verses in the near context also support this interpretation. When Romans 8:2 says that "the law of the Spirit of life in Christ Jesus has set you free from the law of sin and death," surely Paul refers to the

10. See Peter von der Osten-Sacken, *Die Heiligkeit der Tora: Studien zum Gesetz bei Paulus* (München: Kaiser, 1989), 44–45.
11. It should be said, though, that none of the parallel passages has the exact same construction as Rom. 8:4.

forensic work of Christ (8:1, 3). But it is hard to believe that this is all that Paul means. He has just said in 7:23 that "another law" makes one captive to the law of sin, and the captivity described there is enslavement to sin. Romans 7:14 speaks similarly of being "sold under sin." The liberation from sin in 8:2 answers Romans 7. To be liberated from the law of sin and death means that believers are now set free from the bondage to sin. The work of Christ on the cross, then, provides for the transforming work of the Spirit, which affects the moral life of believers.

Romans 8:5–15 also suggests that Paul describes the transforming work of the Holy Spirit. Those of the flesh are not subject to the law of God, nor are they able to be (8:7). Given Paul's contrast between the flesh and Spirit here, he probably suggests that, while unbelievers cannot obey God's law, believers are able to keep it. That life in the Spirit involves obedience is spelled out in Romans 8:13–15. Those who live according to the flesh will experience death, but those who live by the Spirit "put to death the deeds of the body" (v. 13). Being led by the Spirit (v. 14) should be understood in terms of the mortification of the deeds of the body in verse 13 since the two verses are connected by "for" (γάρ). So, too, the release from slavery is based on moral transformation which the Spirit effects, for once again γάρ links verses 14 and 15, and the reference to slavery recalls the impotence of the law to deliver one from sin (7:14, 23, 25). To sum up, the context decidedly emphasizes the new life believers live as a result of Christ's work on the cross and the presence of the Spirit. Thus, not only the particular wording of Romans 8:4, but also the near context suggests that Paul is speaking of Christians obeying the law.

If Paul speaks of believers obeying the law here, then what is the significance of the use of the singular "ordinance" (δικαίωμα, *dikaiōma*)? How could he be referring to obedience to the law as a whole and use the singular? Not all the explanations are mutually exclusive, and I shall explain three of them here. First, some understand the "ordinance of the law" to refer to the law of love.[12] This is attractive since elsewhere Paul sums up the law by citing the command to love one another (Rom. 13:8–10; Gal. 5:14). Second, Sanders claims Paul implicitly reduces the law here, eliminating those commands that distinguish Jews from Gentiles (such as circumcision, sabbath, and food laws),[13] while others say the singular refers to the law as a unity, focusing particularly on the moral

---

12. H. M. W. van de Sandt, "Research into Rom. 8,4a: The Legal Claim of the Law," and "An Explanation of Rom. 8,4a," *Bijdragen* 37 (1976): 252–69 and 361–78; Richard W. Thompson, "How Is the Law Fulfilled in Us? An Interpretation of Rom. 8:4," *LS* 11 (1986): 32–33.

13. E. P. Sanders, *Paul, the Law, and the Jewish People*, (Philadelphia: Fortress, 1983), 100, 102.

law.[14] J. A. Ziesler has shown in his careful study of the word δικαίωμα both in the New Testament and the Septuagint that the singular never clearly refers to the law as a whole.[15] But if Paul does not speak of the law as a whole, what single requirement does he denote? Ziesler suggests plausibly that the tenth commandment lies in Paul's mind.[16] He points out that in Romans 7:7 Paul explicitly cites the command against coveting to explain his view that the law provokes sin.[17] Moreover, Ziesler suggests that the prohibition against coveting fits well with the portrait of human inability to put the law in practice in 7:13–25. Paul cannot be thinking of other commandments in the decalogue, for it simply is not true that people generally cannot restrain themselves from stealing, committing adultery, murder, and the like. The tenth commandment blends ideally with Paul's discussion since it is the only commandment that specifically treats inward desires, not just outward actions. Thus, Ziesler posits in 8:4 that Paul has the tenth commandment in mind when he speaks of the law being fulfilled in believers.[18]

I believe Ziesler correctly states that Paul has the tenth commandment in view. Nevertheless, he fails to take advantage of his own view when he says that Paul uses a "faulty paradigm" since only the tenth commandment deals with internal desires, and thus Paul's comments about the law here do not apply to the other commandments.[19] Ziesler's point is technically correct, but he fails to appreciate why Paul selected the tenth commandment as his paradigm. The very selection of that commandment over others indicates that those scholars are not far off who see Paul as interpreting the law in the same way Jesus did in Matthew 5:21–48. One could keep the command not to steal, but the tenth commandment indicates that even coveting the possessions of another

14. Charles E. B. Cranfield, *A Critical and Exegetical Commentary on the Epistle to the Romans* (Edinburgh: T. and T. Clark, 1975, 1979), 2.384; G. Schrenk, "δικαίωμα," *TDNT*, 2:221.

15. J. A. Ziesler, "The Just Requirement of the Law (Romans 8.4)," *AusBR* 35 (1987): 78–79.

16. Ibid., 79.

17. Of course, what Paul has in mind when he speaks of ἐπιθυμία in Rom. 7:7 is itself disputed. The nomistic interpretation of Rudolf Bultmann ("Romans 7 and the Anthropology of Paul," *Existence and Faith* [New York: Meridian, 1960], 147–57) and Stanislaus Lyonnet ("'Tu ne convoiteras pas,'" *Neotestamentica et Patristica Festschrift for Oscar Cullmann* [Leiden: Brill, 1962], 157–65) has been decisively refuted by Heikki Räisänen ("Zum Gebrauch von ΕΠΙΘΥΜΙΑ und ΕΠΙΘΥΜΕΙΝ bei Paulus," *The Torah and Christ* [Helsinki: Finnish Exegetical Society, 1986], 148–67). Robert H. Gundry understands Paul to be referring to sexual lust ("The Moral Frustration of Paul before his Conversion: Sexual Lust in Romans 7:7–25," D. A. Hagner and M. J. Harris, eds., *Pauline Studies: Essays Presented to Professor F. F. Bruce on his Seventieth Birthday* [Grand Rapids: Eerdmans, 1980], 228–45), but J. A. Ziesler demonstrates that this view is not persuasive ("The Role of the Tenth Commandment in Romans 7," *JSNT* 33 [1988]: 43–46).

18. Ziesler, "The Tenth Commandment," 80.

19. Ziesler, "The Just Requirement," 79–80; see also idem, "The Tenth Commandment," 49, 51.

is sinful. One may not commit adultery, but the tenth commandment applies to the desire for the wife of another. Indeed, Paul linked coveting with idolatry in Ephesians 5:5 and Colossians 3:5, indicating that one who broke the tenth commandment also broke the first. The selection of the tenth commandment as paradigmatic, then, is not arbitrary but rooted in a profound and accurate understanding of the decalogue. The root sin in failure to obey all the commandments is idolatry, which delights in someone or something else more than God. If the tenth commandment does indeed encompass the other commands of the law, then even though Ziesler is correct in saying that the "ordinance" of the law in Romans 8:4 refers to only one commandment, Paul refers to this one command since it sums up the rest of the law. If a person does not covet then all the other commandments are being kept. Those scholars who see the whole law reflected in "ordinance" are substantially correct. Peter van der Osten-Sacken insightfully remarks that the love command is the exact correspondence to not coveting.[20] Nevertheless, Paul does not expect believers to obey the whole law because he clearly excludes circumcision, food laws, the offering of sacrifices, and the observance of days. Thus, Sanders is also on target in detecting an implicit reduction of the law here.

Romans 2 provides further evidence that Christians should obey the law. For example, 2:26 asks, "If then the uncircumcised person observes the ordinances of the law, shall not his uncircumcision be reckoned as circumcision?" Some scholars think that Paul is speaking hypothetically here, and thus this verse should not be used to urge Christians to keep the law. I will argue at more length in chapter 7 that the text refers to Gentile Christians who keep the law through the power of the Holy Spirit.

It is interesting to note that in 2:26, when Paul speaks of an uncircumcised person (obviously a Gentile) keeping "the ordinances of the law" he uses the same word *ordinance* (δικαίωμα, *dikaiōma*) used in Romans 8:4. The significant difference is that here Paul uses the plural rather than the singular. The plural suggests Paul gives a generalizing summary and so is viewing the law as a whole. One might conclude that Paul lands himself in a contradiction here, for he says elsewhere that Gentile Christians should not be circumcised (for example, Rom. 4:9–12; Gal. 5:2–6). And if Gentile Christians are not circumcised, then they cannot be keeping the entire law. Surely Paul was aware of this tension, for he specifically speaks of an *uncircumcised person* (ἀκροβυστία, *akrobystia*) as the one who "keeps the ordinances of the law," and notes that this

---

20. Osten-Sacken, *Die Heiligkeit der Tora*, 45.

person's obedience to the law constitutes circumcision in God's sight. Paul is suggesting that physical circumcision does not matter because the person who keeps the law is reckoned as spiritually circumcised. This point is absolutely crucial. Paul in the same verse can speak of an uncircumcised person as one who "keeps the ordinances of the law." How can an uncircumcised person keep the law without ever being physically circumcised, since circumcision was one of the commandments of the law? Paul reduces the law here, so that the command to be circumcised is fulfilled through spiritual circumcision. Then how can Paul expect believers to keep the law, and at the same time argue that the Mosaic covenant is abolished if certain commandments remain normative? Another verse referring to keeping the law needs to be examined so that we can answer this question.

First Corinthians 7:19 is strikingly similar to Romans 2:26. Once again, Paul speaks positively of believers keeping commandments and yet excludes circumcision. He declares, "Circumcision is nothing and uncircumcision is nothing, but keeping the commandments of God is everything." I have pointed out before that this is a shocking statement from a Jew, since circumcision was considered to be one of the divine commandments. We see the same tension here as in Romans 2:26. The keeping of divine commandments is imperative and required for believers, and yet Paul no longer considers physical circumcision one of the requisite commandments.

The exclusion of circumcision from the commandments shows that Paul works with a reduction of the law here. But does the word *commandments* (ἐντολῶν, *entolōn*) necessarily refer to the law here? The reference may be to the teaching of Jesus (compare 1 Cor. 7:10),[21] although the word *commandment* (ἐντολή, *entolē*) is not used in 1 Corinthians 7:10. Stephen Westerholm sees a reference to instruction from the Holy Spirit in 1 Corinthians 7:19. This is improbable since the word *commandments* designates some kind of external instruction.[22] *Commandment* designates Paul's own apostolic instructions in 1 Corinthians 14:37, and the plural is used of personal instructions given to the Colossians concerning Mark (Col. 4:10). Nevertheless, *commandment* most commonly in Paul refers to commandments from the law. The word occurs six times in Romans 7 (vv. 8, 9, 10, 11, 12, 13), referring, I have argued, to the tenth commandment. Even if the tenth commandment is not in view, scholars universally agree that Paul is referring to the Old Testament law. Romans 13:9 says "any other commandment" is

---

21. C. H. Dodd, "ΕΝΝΟΜΟΣ ΧΡΙΣΤΟΥ," *Studia Paulina in honorem J. De Zwaan* (Haarlem: Bohn, 1953), 96–110.
22. Westerholm, *Israel's Law*, 201 n. 11.

summed up in love. Paul has just finished citing other commandments from the Mosaic law, and thus the other commandments also certainly derive from the law. In Ephesians 6:2 Paul describes the injunction from the decalogue (Exod. 20:12) to honor one's father and mother as a "commandment." Moreover, Ephesians 2:15 asserts that Christ has abolished "in his flesh, the law of the commandments consisting of decrees." The conjunction of *commandments* with *law* (τὸν νόμον τῶν ἐντολῶν, *ton nomon tōn entolōn*) demonstrates that "commandments" refers to those from the law. Finally, Frank Thielman shows that the phrase "keeping commandments" would designate the law of Moses in Jewish literature.[23] For example, Sir 32:23 uses *keeping of commandments* (τήρησις ἐντολῶν, *tērēsis entolōn*) to refer to the commands in the Mosaic law (see also Matt. 19:17–19). Over forty times the Septuagint speaks of keeping the commandments of the Old Testament law, employing the verb (φυλάσσω, *phylassō*). *Commandments* in 1 Corinthians 7:19 may be wider than the law, including perhaps Paul's apostolic instructions and the teaching of Jesus. However, given Paul's use of the word, he likely has the Mosaic law in view when he exhorts the Corinthians to keep the commandments of God.[24] Since Paul excludes circumcision from the commandments in this verse, it is evident that the law he has in mind is a reduced law.

Paul's focus on the moral dimensions of the law is not totally surprising. Karl Wilhelm-Niebuhr, in his analysis of law and parenesis in early Judaism, has demonstrated that the focus was on the moral law.[25] Of course, early Jewish literature did not differentiate between moral and cultic law. Nor did it explicitly critique cultic law. The moral law received prominence, however, while the cultic law receded into the background. The emphasis on the moral law may have been due to contact with Hellenistic culture. To the extent that Jewish literature stresses the moral law, it serves as a forerunner to Paul's teaching that the moral law must be fulfilled. Of course, Paul goes beyond his Jewish

23. Frank Thielman, "The Coherence of Paul's View of the Law: The Evidence of First Corinthians," *NTS* 38 (1992): 138–39.

24. See Ulrich Wilckens, "Zur Entwicklung des paulinischen Gesetzesverständnisses," *NTS* 28 (1982): 159. G. Schrenk argues ("ἐντολή," *TDNT*, 2:550–53) that ἐντολή almost always refer to OT commandments in Paul, but, contra Schrenk, ἐντολή is almost surely the original reading of the text in 1 Cor. 14:37.

25. Karl-Wilhelm Niebuhr, *Gesetz und Paränese: Katechismusartige Weisungsreihen in der frühjüdischen Literatur* (Tübingen: J. C. B. Mohr, 1987), 7, 12–14, 26, 61–64, 160, 162, 233–34. Niebuhr focuses in his study on *Psuedo-Phocylides*, Josephus' *Against Apion*, Philo's *Hypothetica* 7:1–9, and the *Testament of the Twelve Patriarchs*. He includes a shorter discussion of *Sibylline Oracles*, *Slavonic Enoch*, *Testament of Abraham*, *Apocalypse of Abraham*, *Tobit*, *Jubilees*, *Wisdom of Solomon*, *4 Maccabees*, *Psalms of Solomon*, and *Dramatic Gnomologion*. See also the work of Reinmuth, *Geist und Gesetz*, 22–41.

predecessors by *criticizing* the practice of circumcision, sabbath, and food laws.

Cessation of the Law during the Messianic Age?

How do we explain the implicit reduction of the law in Paul?[26] Some scholars argue that Paul saw the teaching of Jesus as a new Torah, replacing the old.[27] This is often linked with the theory that rabbinic Judaism believed that when the Messianic age arrived the old Torah would cease.[28] But nowhere does the rabbinic literature clearly teach such a cessation. It merely infers that a few rather peripheral commandments might be changed, and that a fuller and more accurate understanding of Torah would be realized.[29]

Jesus' Words as a New Torah?

It is also unlikely that Paul understood the sayings and example of Jesus as a new law, the Torah of Christ. Of course, the words of Jesus certainly were authoritative for Paul (see 1 Cor. 7:10–11; 9:14). However, it does not necessarily follow that the words of Jesus constituted a new Torah, which superseded the old Torah. The fact that Paul explicitly appeals so seldom to the Jesus traditions demonstrates this, and it is particularly evident when one compares Paul's citations of the Old Testament with his citations of the words of Jesus. Paul cites the

26. For a survey of some of the possible answers to this question, with a particular emphasis on the views of C. H. Dodd, David Daube, and W. D. Davies see Stephen Westerholm, "Law and Christian Ethics," in Peter R. Richardson and Stephen Westerholm, eds., *Law in Religious Communities in the Roman Period* (Waterloo: Wilfrid Laurier University Press, 1991), 75–91. Westerholm concludes by presenting his own distinctive view with which we will interact later in the chapter.

27. Dodd, "ΕΝΝΟΜΟΣ ΧΡΙΣΤΟΥ," 96–110; W. D. Davies, *Paul and Rabbinic Judaism: Some Rabbinic Elements in Paul's Theology* (London: SPCK, 1948), 136–46, and *The Setting of the Sermon on the Mount* (Cambridge: Cambridge University Press, 1964), 352–64; Richard N. Longenecker, *Paul, Apostle of Liberty* (1964; repr., Grand Rapids: Baker, 1976), 126–32, 183–96; A. Feuillet, "Loi de Dieu, Loi du Christ, et Loi de l'Esprit d'aprés Les Epîtres Pauliniennes," *NovT* 22 (1980): 45–57.

28. See Albert Schweitzer, *The Mysticism of Paul the Apostle* (1931; repr., New York: Seabury, 1968), 187–92; Hans Joachim Schoeps, *Paul: The Theology of the Apostle in the Light of Jewish Religious History* (Philadelphia: Westminster, 1959), 171–75; Krister Stendahl, "The Apostle Paul and the Introspective Conscience of the West," *Paul Among Jews and Gentiles and Other Essays* (Philadelphia: Fortress, 1976), 84; Joseph A. Fitzmyer, "Paul and the Law," in M. J. Taylor, ed., *A Companion to Paul* (New York: Alba, 1975), 74–75.

29. For a careful sifting of the evidence see W. D. Davies, *Torah in the Messianic Age* (Philadelphia: SBL, 1952). Against the Messianic age doctrine see Peter Schäfer, "Die Torah der messianischen Zeit," *ZNW* 65 (1974): 27–42; Heikki Räisänen, *Paul and the Law* (Philadelphia: Fortress, 1983), 77–82; E. P. Sanders, *Paul and Palestinian Judaism: A Comparison of Patterns of Religion* (Philadelphia: Fortress, 1977), 479–80.

Old Testament often, but the indisputable quotations from the words of Jesus are in comparison remarkably few. Therefore, it seems unlikely that the words of Jesus constituted a new law. Second, the "law of Christ" in Galatians 6:2 does not refer to the teaching of Jesus.[30] Paul nowhere in the letter appeals directly to the words of Jesus. If the words of Jesus were a new law that displaced the Mosaic law, then Galatians would seem to be precisely the place where Paul would make this clear. He could have said the Sinai Torah is abolished and declared the words of Jesus a new law for the Christian. In the same way, the "law of Christ" in 1 Corinthians 9:21 does not refer clearly to the words of Jesus.[31] Instead, in 9:21 Paul avoids a misunderstanding by qualifying the declaration that he is "not under law" with the reservation that he is "subject to the law of Christ." Paul's qualifying statement demonstrates that freedom from the law does not dissolve all ethical norms for Christians.

What Paul means by the expression *law of Christ* should be explored more precisely. In 1 Corinthians 9:21 Paul does not want his readers to conclude that, because he is without law, he is an antinomian. The origin of the expression here is best explained rhetorically. Paul coins it in the course of his discussion to delineate his stance regarding the law. Moreover, the context suggests that when Paul says he is "not under the law" (9:20) and "without law" (9:21), he is specifically thinking of the law insofar as it creates a breach between Jews and Gentiles. Thus, specific laws such as circumcision, food laws, and sabbath are particularly in view. Paul adapts his lifestyle so that he lives as a Jew when with Jews ("under law") and as a Gentile when with Gentiles ("without law"), so he can proclaim the gospel to each. Nevertheless, he stresses that he is not "without the law of God but subject to the law of Christ." This probably means that Paul abides by the moral norms of the law, not considering his freedom a license to violate the moral norms of the law. The wider context of 1 Corinthians 8-10 supports this observation, for the issue under discussion is food offered to idols. Jews would consider such food unclean, while Gentiles would tend to view the eating of such foods as a matter of indifference.

Much discussion has been generated from the phrase *law of Christ* in Galatians 6:2. Contrary to Hans Dieter Betz it is hardly clear that the phrase is polemical,[32] especially since Paul uses it in the parenetical

---

30. So Furnish, *Ethics in Paul*, 51–65; Deidun, *New Covenant Morality*, 172–73; see also Räisänen, *Paul and the Law*, 77–82, 245–48.

31. Furnish (*Ethics in Paul*, 61) rightly points out that Paul's point here is simply to indicate that freedom from the law does not involve libertinism; see also Fee, *First Corinthians*, 430 n. 44.

32. Hans Dieter Betz, *Galatians* (Philadelphia: Fortress, 1979), 298–301.

section of the epistle without providing any substantial clue that the phrase should be understood as a response to opponents. Otfried Hofius provocatively interprets 6:2 in the light of the sin-bearing Servant in Isaiah,[33] but this probably reads too much into the call to bear one another's burdens. Richard Hays and Hans Schürmann argue that the verse focuses on the paradigmatic self-giving of Christ Jesus.[34] Although this is supported by other passages in the Pauline literature and even in the earlier chapters of Galatians, it is too far removed from the immediate context of chapter 6 to be credible.

Such a little-used phrase as *law of Christ*, is best interpreted in the immediate context, which begins with the parenesis that extends from 5:13–6:10.[35] Here Paul stresses life in the Spirit and calls believers to "walk in the Spirit" (5:16), "be led by the Spirit" (5:18), manifest "the fruit of the Spirit" (5:22–23), "live by the Spirit" (5:25), "keep in step with the Spirit" (5:25), and "sow to the Spirit" (6:8). This demonstrates that believers can fulfil the law of Christ only by the power of the Spirit. Indeed, this exhortation is addressed (6:1) to "the spiritual," who live in the Spirit's strength. The emphasis on the Spirit shows that the "law of Christ" cannot be described as legalistic or constraining. The other contextual links forged in the context are *law* (νόμος, *nomos*) and *fulfil* (ἀναπληρώσετε, *anaplērōsete*) which recall 5:14 where "the whole law" is fulfilled (πεπλήρωται, *peplērōtai*) in love. In 5:14 Paul clearly has in mind the Old Testament law when he specifically cites Leviticus 19:18. The connection between these two texts suggests that the one who fulfils the law of Christ also fulfils the Old Testament law, which is summed up in the law of love. In previous verses in Galatians (for example, 2:11–14; 4:10; 5:2–6) Paul proclaims that food laws, circumcision, and the observance of certain days are no longer binding upon believers. So, is the "law of Christ" limited to the law of love? Yes and no. Love is the heartbeat and center of the Pauline ethic. And yet, even in Galatians, Paul unfolds the true nature of love by delineating what is not loving (5:15, 19–21, 26) and what is loving (5:22–23; 6:1–2, 6–10). A comparison of 5:14 with Romans 13:8–10 shows that for Paul the moral norms of the law must be included when defining love.

---

33. Otfried Hofius, "Das Gesetz des Mose und das Gesetz Christi," *ZTK* 80 (1983): 262–86

34. Hans Schürmann, "'Das Gesetz des Christus' (Gal 6:2): Jesu Verhalten und Wort als letztgültige sittliche Norm nach Paulus," in J. G. Gnilka, ed., *Neues Testament und Kirche. Festschrift für R. Schnackenburg*; (Freiburg: Herder, 1974), 282–300; Richard B. Hays, "Christology and Ethics in Galatians: The Law of Christ," *CBQ* 49 (1987): 268–90.

35. For a similar interpretation of the expression *law of Christ* and a survey of scholarship see Reinmuth, *Geist und Gesetz*, 61–65. Reinmuth points out (63–64) that in Jewish thought there was an expectation that the law would be fulfilled in the end time. See *Sib. Or.* 5:414–31; *2 Apoc. Bar.* 7:2; 73:1–74:1; *1 Enoch* 39:6–7; *Pss. Sol.* 17:1–18:12.

Sinai Torah Versus Zion Torah?

Similar to the preceding view is the suggestion that Paul believed in the abolition of the Sinai Torah, while upholding the continuing validity of the Zion Torah.[36] The Zion Torah is distinct from the Sinai Torah in that it hails from Zion, is eschatological in character, applies to all people, and is connected with the thank offering. The Achilles' heel of this theory is that nothing in the Old Testament intimates that the new covenant (Jer. 31:31–34) would contain a different law from the old one.[37] When God says, "I will put my law within them, and on their heart I will write it" (Jer. 31:33), he does not refer to a new law. Rather, he alludes to the Mosaic law, which was previously broken (Jer. 31:32) but later will be kept. Nor is it clear that Paul understands the law proceeding from Zion (Isa. 2:1–4; Micah 4:1–4) as a new Torah that cancels the Mosaic Torah. It also cannot be demonstrated that when Paul speaks of fulfilling the law or the "law of Christ" that he has the Zion Torah in mind. For example, in Romans 13:8–10 the commandments that Paul says are fulfilled through love are found in the Mosaic law, and he does not imply that these commandments belong to a Zion Torah, which is to be distinguished from the Sinai Torah.

Mosaic Covenant as Abolished and Fulfilled

If the three theories presented above are not persuasive, then how do we understand Paul's claim that some of the commands of the law are normative, while at the same time he appears to teach the abolition of the Mosaic law? Paul's view of the Mosaic covenant was complex. In a sense the Mosaic covenant had passed away and in a sense it remained authoritative for the church of Christ.[38] The Mosaic covenant has passed away because Messiah has come. Nevertheless, this cessation of the Mosaic covenant does not constitute an abrogation of the law but a fulfillment and establishment of the law (Rom. 3:31). In other words, one cannot give an unqualified "yes" or "no" answer regarding the cessation

36. H. Gese, *Essays on Biblical Theology* (Minneapolis: Augsburg, 1981), 80–92; Peter Stuhlmacher, "The Law as a Topic of Biblical Theology," in *Reconciliation, Law, and Righteousness: Essays in Biblical Theology* (Philadelphia: Fortress, 1986), 110–33, especially 114–17.

37. For two devastating critiques see Martin Kalusche, "'Das Gesetz als Thema biblischer Theologie'? Anmerkungen zu einem Entwurf Peter Stuhlmachers," *ZNW* 77 (1986): 194–205; Heikki Räisänen, "Zionstora und Biblische Theologie: Zu einer Tübinger Theorie," *The Torah and Christ* (Helsinki: Finnish Exegetical Society, 1986), 337–65.

38. Donald A. Hagner ("Paul and Judaism: The Jewish Matrix of Early Christianity: Issues in the Current Debate" [Paper presented at a symposium, Institute for Biblical Research, San Francisco, November, 1992]) says that "Paul both does away with and upholds the law in different senses," and that "we must learn to tolerate the paradoxical both/and."

of the law in Paul. In one sense it has passed away, and in another sense it has been fulfilled. We shall proceed inductively so we can determine the precise sense in which the Mosaic covenant has been abrogated and the nature of its fulfillment.

Before we begin to explore the texts in Paul, I must note that the law itself anticipates a future fulfillment. The Pentateuch is an unfinished book because the promises given to Abraham have scarcely begun to be fulfilled. In Deuteronomy 30 Moses looks forward to the day when God would circumcise the heart of his people, resulting in their obedience to his law. The famous "new covenant" passage in Jeremiah 31:31–34 and the promise of the Spirit in Ezekiel 36:26–27 show that the promises given to Abraham had not yet reached their consummation. Israel was still looking forward to the fulfillment of all that God had promised. The anticipation of a future fulfillment, of course, is characteristic of the prophetic literature in the Old Testament. Paul claims that the fulfillment has now arrived in the person of Jesus the Messiah (Rom. 1:2–3). He interprets the Old Testament Scriptures in the light of this fulfillment, and we need to discern how he understood the ongoing validity of the Mosaic law in light of its fulfillment in Christ.

Paul believed that the sacrifices of the Old Testament cultus were superfluous now that Jesus as Messiah had died on the cross. Apparently this was not a controversial issue in Pauline communities, for nowhere in his letters does he respond to a contrary view. In fact, Paul makes no explicit statements that Old Testament sacrifices are defunct, but we logically draw this conclusion from what he says about the sacrifice of Jesus on the cross. For instance, Paul uses sacrificial language from the Old Testament to describe Jesus' work on the cross. The atoning significance of Christ's blood is clearly related to sacrifice (Rom. 3:25; 5:9; 1 Cor. 11:25; Eph. 1:7; 2:13; Col. 1:20). Paul describes Christ's death as a "sin offering" (περὶ ἁμαρτίας, *peri hamartias*, in Romans 8:3; compare Lev. 5:6–7 and 9:2 in the LXX).[39] Paul clearly implies that Christ's death has replaced Old Testament sacrifices when he says "if justification were through the law, then Christ died for nothing" (Gal. 2:21). Here *law* would include Old Testament sacrifices. If atonement and forgiveness were available through sacrifices, then obviously Christ's death would be completely unnecessary. The same kind of argument appears in Galatians 3:10–13 as I have mentioned. Those who do not obey the law perfectly are under the curse of the law (3:10). The Old Testament presupposes that people will sin and provides through the cultus a way of atonement and forgiveness. Paul sees only one way of

---

39. N. Thomas Wright, "The Meaning of ΠΕΡΙ ΑΜΑΡΤΙΑΣ in Romans 8.3," *The Climax of the Covenant: Christ and the Law in Pauline Theology* (Minneapolis: Fortress, 1991), 220–25.

being delivered from the curse of the law—the redemption that Christ provided by becoming a curse for us (see 2 Cor. 5:21). The Old Testament sacrifices did not actually remove the curse; only the death of Christ was a sufficient price.

A similar argument appears in Romans 3:21–26. In Romans 1:18–3:20 Paul established his thesis that no one is righteous, that all are sinful and guilty before God. Now if the animal sacrifices could really atone for sin, then Paul would merely point out that one should offer the prescribed sacrifices. Instead, he insists that justification comes only through the redemption that Jesus Christ accomplished (3:24). God's wrath was only propitiated through the blood of Christ, not through the blood of animals. Indeed, God "in his divine forbearance . . . passed over former sins" (3:25). This probably means that under the old covenant sacrifices did not atone for sins, but simply pointed to the sacrifice of Christ, which was the effective means of atonement.

We can conclude, therefore, that animal sacrifices are no longer to be practiced by believers. Paul does not disparage Old Testament sacrifices but simply observes that they pointed forward to the sacrifice of Christ, which fulfilled what the Old Testament sacrifices anticipated. The animal sacrifices were part of the interim period of the Mosaic covenant, and now that Christ has come believers should read these Old Testament passages with the fulfillment in mind. Paul's teaching on sacrifices provides a clue regarding his understanding of the Mosaic law. Believers are no longer "under the law," for Old Testament sacrifices are passé. On the other hand, it would be too simplistic to say sacrifices are abolished. To claim they were fulfilled in the sacrifice of Christ states it more accurately. The texts on Old Testament sacrifices still function as the authoritative word of God for Paul, but they must be interpreted in the light of what Christ has done on the cross.

A similar situation obtains with regard to Old Testament feasts. Does Paul think believers should observe the feasts of Passover, Unleavened Bread, Pentecost, and Tabernacles? He does not comment on all of these feasts, but his remarks on the Passover are paradigmatic on this issue. Offering a Passover lamb is not necessary because "Christ, our passover, was sacrificed" (1 Cor. 5:7). Christ is the fulfillment to which the Passover sacrifice pointed. So too, the requirement not to eat unleavened bread no longer applies in a literal way to believers. Paul asserts that believers are themselves "unleavened" (1 Cor. 5:7), and speaks of "the unleavened bread of sincerity and truth" (1 Cor. 5:8). Paul's understanding of Jesus as the passover lamb may have been transmitted to him in traditions about the Lord's supper (see 1 Cor.

11:23–26), so that such an understanding of the Passover is traceable to pre-Pauline Christianity.[40]

Of course, Paul does not mention every Old Testament feast, and a one-to-one New Testament correspondent for every Old Testament event could result in unrestrained allegorizing. It is not necessary, for instance, to conclude that leaven must be a symbol for evil. Paul's handling of Passover and Unleavened Bread, however, demonstrates that these feasts are no longer understood to be literally applicable to believers. They are understood in light of the fulfillment of salvation history—Jesus Christ. Presumably, the same conclusion could be drawn regarding the other festivals in Israel's history.

Paul clearly did not think believers should be required to adhere to food laws (see Rom. 14:1–23; 1 Cor. 8:1–13; 10:23–11:1; Gal. 2:11–14). The statement in Romans 14:14 that "nothing is common ["unclean," κοινόν, *koinon*] in itself" overturns the Old Testament law, which proscribed certain foods as unclean (Leviticus 11; Deuteronomy 14). Paul's conclusion on this issue may derive from Jesus himself (see Mark 7:14–23). But why does Paul no longer see such laws as normative? Any answer is speculative, but it may be that Paul views believers as "the temple" of the Spirit (1 Cor. 3:16; 6:19; 2 Cor. 6:16). In the Old Testament the purity laws and food laws were designed as a picture of the holiness required in order to enter God's presence in the tabernacle or temple. Now, however, the fulfillment of what the Old Testament pointed to has arrived. God dwells in his people, the church (see Lev. 26:11; 2 Cor. 6:16).

Paul concludes in 2 Corinthians 6:17 that since God dwells in his people, they should separate from those who are evil and "touch no unclean thing." The language of uncleanness is now used in an ethical sense, with reference to association and cooperation with unbelievers (2 Cor. 6:14–16). A person is no longer defiled because of eating unclean food, childbirth, leprosy, or involuntary bodily discharges (Leviticus 11–15). These merely affect a person outwardly and, with the advent of a new era in which Christians themselves are the temple of God, no longer render one "unclean." The author of Hebrews makes this much more explicit than Paul, claiming that food and drink regulations and washing requirements were temporary and yielded to a transcendent reality (Heb. 9:9–10).

Are the purity laws abolished? Yes, in the sense that believers are no longer bound to observe them literally. Nevertheless, the purity laws remain the word of God and have an ethical application to the Christian.

---

40. I. Howard Marshall (*Last Supper and Lord's Supper* [Grand Rapids: Eerdmans, 1980]) argues persuasively that the Last Supper was a Passover meal.

In Paul's theology Christ is the true sacrifice and Christians are the true temple, so the need for an Old Testament priesthood has ceased. Paul rarely discusses the priesthood language (see Rom. 15:16), but there is little question that the foundation of the priesthood is taken away by what he has said about sacrifices and the temple. If the early church understood that believers were the temple of God and Jesus offered the definitive sacrifice, then Peter's assertion that all believers are priests is fitting (1 Pet. 2:9). All believers have direct access to God through Jesus Christ. Paul does not develop the idea that Jesus is the high priest as the author of Hebrews did. We should not expect in occasional letters to churches the explication of everything found in the Old Testament. What we do see in Paul, however, gives us a paradigm by which we can understand his view of the Old Testament law.

Paul also recognizes the church as the new Israel (Gal. 6:16). Some scholars object to this designation, claiming it cannot be substantiated from the Pauline literature. I have argued elsewhere that when Paul describes the church as the true circumcision (Rom. 2:28–29; Phil. 3:3), he is in effect saying that the church is the new people of God, for the church now has the covenant sign by which one enters the people of God.[41] Genuine Jewishness and authentic circumcision are not "outward in the flesh" (Rom. 2:28). Rather, the true Jew is "one in secret," and genuine circumcision "is of the heart, in the Spirit, not the letter" (Rom. 2:29). Paul does not call the church "the true Israel" or "the new Israel" here. He implies this, however, when he says believers are Jews "in secret" and possess "circumcision of the heart." Membership in the people of God is not based on ethnic heritage but spiritual reality.

Paul makes a similar point in Philippians 3:2–3. Gentile believers were physically uncircumcised, but they possessed "the true circumcision" because they "worshipped in the Spirit of God and boasted in Christ Jesus and did not put confidence in the flesh" (v. 3). In these verses Paul responds to Judaizers, who insisted that Gentiles must be circumcised to be part of the people of God.[42] He insists that they need not be circumcised because they have the "true" circumcision.[43] Some of those who have the physical sign are not members of God's people. Those who have the Holy Spirit are circumcised in the true sense. The concept of church as the true circumcision suggests that it would be appropriate to also call

41. "The Church as the New Israel and the Future of Ethnic Israel in Paul," *Studia Biblica et Theologica* 13 (1983): 17–38.

42. See Peter T. O'Brien, *The Epistle to the Philippians* (Grand Rapids: Eerdmans, 1991), 26–35.

43. Phil. 3:3 does not actually use the word "true," but simply says ἡμεῖς γὰρ ἐσμεν ἡ περιτομή. Since this statement is in contrast to verse 2, the idea of the church being the "true" circumcision is present.

the church the "true" Israel. Even though Paul does not specifically call the church the "new Israel," he presents the idea that the church is the new people of God. Paul also calls believers "the sons of Abraham" (Gal. 3:7) and "the seed of Abraham" (Gal. 3:29). Being sons of Abraham and seed of Abraham is equivalent to being part of the people of God, the true Israel. Paul himself argued in Romans 9:6 that "not all those from Israel are Israel." The true children of Abraham are the "children of promise" (Romans 9:8). The church has inherited the promises given to Abraham through *the* "seed of Abraham," Jesus Christ (Gal. 3:16).

The status of the church as the true Israel should not be interpreted to say that ethnic Israel has no future (Romans 11). Nevertheless, ethnic Israel's salvation comes through faith in Christ, and when ethnic Israelites put their faith in Christ, they become part of the new people of God, comprised of Jews and Gentiles. For Paul the death of Christ has broken down the barriers between Jews and Gentiles, and they now compose one united body in Christ (Eph. 2:11–3:13). Once again the significance of this for Paul's understanding of the Old Testament is crucial. Israel in the Old Testament was both a religious and a political entity. It was religious as a nation formed to be solely devoted to Yahweh, and he graciously took the nation into covenant with himself as his people. But Israel was also a political entity, a nation with boundaries, rulers, courts, and laws. The civic and religious dimensions of life were interwoven, and one entered the community by circumcision. Paul's understanding of the church as composed of both Jews and Gentiles from all people groups sunders the religious from the national. The people of God are no longer confined to one nation, and Paul does not expect believers to establish a civil government. The government was largely staffed by unbelievers (Rom. 13:1–7), and believers lived under its jurisdiction.

Perhaps this gives us some insight as to why Paul believed that circumcision should be dissolved as the entrance rite into the people of God. We have already seen that he vigorously resisted imposing circumcision on Gentiles because he interpreted this as compromising the gospel of grace. But he could have required circumcision as a gracious response to God's work in Christ. Why, then, was it rejected? Probably because physical circumcision marked one as a Jew; it was both a religious and a political sign of entrance into the people of God. Thus, Paul sees the significance of the command to be circumcised in spiritual terms. Outward circumcision is insignificant; only inward circumcision counts, which is the result of the Holy Spirit's work in the heart (Rom. 2:28–29). Those who are truly circumcised "worship in the Spirit of God and boast in Christ Jesus" (Phil. 3:3). Paul does not want the new community of faith to be confused with the ethnic and political entity called Israel. Of course, he is not against circumcision; it is irrelevant (1 Cor. 7:19; Gal. 5:6; 6:15). Ethnic Jews may practice the rite, as long as they do not impose it upon Gentiles.

Recent scholarship correctly asserts that Paul rejected circumcision because it demanded that people become part of ethnic Israel to be members of the people of God. His basic objection against circumcision, however, lies not with nationalism. Circumcision is no longer in force because there has been a salvation-historical shift. God intended that Israel be both a political and religious entity during the time of the Mosaic covenant. With the coming of Christ the era in which the people of God are set apart both ethnically and religiously has ceased. The church is comprised of people who believe in Christ from every people group.

Is circumcision abolished? Yes and no. One no longer must observe the rite to be part of the people of God (compare Gen. 17:9–14). What physical circumcision pointed to has been fulfilled in Christ. The circumcision of the heart, to which Moses and Jeremiah referred (Deut. 10:16; 30:6; Jer. 4:4), has become a reality with the gift of the Holy Spirit (Rom. 2:28–29; Phil. 3:3). The fulfillment inaugurated by Jesus Christ means that the literal rite is left behind and what the rite pointed to is now embraced.

How does the difference between the church and Israel relate to the applicability of the Old Testament law? The implication is that the civil laws given to the Old Testament people of God are not in force today. Paul, for instance, never conceived of a situation in which the church would exercise political power over the state. In addition, if the civil law of the Old Testament was particularly designed for Israel as a political entity, then it would not be surprising that some of the laws related to Israel's particular cultural situation. For example, the Old Testament contains regulations relating to slavery (Exod. 21:1–11; Lev. 25:39–46; Deut. 15:12–18) which are directed to Israel's specific historical and cultural situation. Paul's comments on slavery should be understood as regulating an evil human institution; he never speaks approvingly of the practice. It is quite probable that some evils, such as slavery or polygamy, were tolerated and regulated by the Old Testament law. The cessation of the Mosaic covenant, as described in 2 Corinthians 3 and Galatians 3, implies that the civil law in Israel was part and parcel of what Paul sees as passing away. Paul's writings in the New Testament help us to understand more clearly where the Old Testament contains moral norms and where it regulates and tolerates existing evils.[44]

44. See the perceptive discussion of this issue in Murray, *Principles*, 14–19. Murray appeals to the progressive revelation to solve some of the difficulties. He suggests that there are intimations in the Old Testament itself that polygamy does not deserve moral approbation. For a similar approach see John Goldingay, *Theological Diversity and the Authority of the Old Testament* (Grand Rapids: Eerdmans, 1987), 155–57.

Now this does not mean that modern states should not be informed by some of the principles from the Mosaic law. The requirement that no one be condemned except upon the basis of two or three witnesses (Deut. 19:15) is a wise requirement for adjudicating charges against an accused person, for the principle calls for sufficient evidence to convict a person of a crime. Interestingly, Paul applies this principle to disputes within the church in 2 Corinthians 13:1 and 1 Timothy 5:19. Another interesting example is found in 1 Corinthians 5. Paul insists that the man committing incest should be removed from the church. Verse 13, using language from the Old Testament, enjoins the church to "remove the wicked man from among yourselves." In the Old Testament the injunction to remove the wicked person from the community meant the death penalty for idolaters (Deut. 13:5; 17:7), the rebellious (17:12; 21:21), and fornicators (Deut. 22:21). Paul does not think, however, that the man committing incest should be put to death. The language that signaled the death penalty in the Old Testament applies to expulsion from the church in the New Testament. The community, which God commands to remain pure, no longer functions as a political entity, for God will ultimately judge unbelievers (1 Cor. 5:13). Instead, the community that must remain undefiled is the church of God.

Certainly, many of the complex issues regarding the "civil law" need more attention.[45] Neither do we know how Paul would apply each Old Testament law to the life of the church. We do see, however, that laws originally applicable to Israel as a political entity are applied to the life of the church. In one sense these laws are abolished; adulterers are no longer to be put to death for their sin. On the other hand, they still function as an authoritative word. Those who commit the sin of adultery and fail to repent should be removed from the church.

This evidence persuades me that Christian reconstructionists are incorrect in thinking that the Old Testament law and Old Testament penalties should be enforced in civil states today. This is not to say that modern states will never prohibit an action the Old Testament proscribes, nor does it imply that the penalties will never be the same. But the Old Testament laws do not enjoy a binding authority over modern states merely by virtue of their origin. The laws given to the people of Israel were designed for that nation during a certain period of salvation-history, and the role of Israel as both a "church" and a state does not fall

---

45. An attempt to flesh out the current applicability of the OT law for the church today is provided in the provocative and thoughtful work by Vern S. Poythress, *The Shadow of Christ in the Law of Moses* (Brentwood, Tenn.: Wolgemuth and Hyatt, 1991). I am not endorsing all of Poythress' conclusions. He is closer to the Theonomist model for the OT law than I am, although there are still significant differences between him and Theonomists. Nonetheless, his paradigm for how the OT law relates to the church today is fruitful and should be seriously considered.

to any country today. The failure of Christian reconstructionists to perceive this salvation-historical shift is the most serious deficiency in their agenda.[46]

When we considered why Paul rejected circumcision as the church's rite of initiation I argued that circumcision signified entrance into both a political and religious entity. The church is not a political but a religious institution; therefore, a new initiatory rite—baptism—was inaugurated for a new stage of salvation history. Another reason Paul rejects circumcision is that he views circumcision and the cross as mutually exclusive. Entrance into the people of God is no longer based on circumcision but rather on the cross of Christ.[47] Galatians 5:2 illustrates the polarity between the cross and circumcision where Paul insists that Christ will be of no benefit to the Galatians if they receive circumcision. This statement materially parallels Galatians 2:21: "If righteousness comes through the law, then Christ died for nothing." Circumcision represents the decision to accept the whole law (Galatians 5:3), and if righteousness is gained through circumcision and the law, then Christ died to no purpose.

Galatians 5:11 and 6:12–14 reinforce the fact that circumcision and the cross are mutually exclusive ways of righteousness. Paul is persecuted because he no longer preaches circumcision (5:11), and this refusal to herald circumcision is the scandal of the cross, for the cross repudiates any human attempt to please God. Those who insist on circumcision detract from the cross, which provides the only means of entrance into the people of God, the only way to escape the curse of the law (Gal. 3:10, 13). In 6:12–14 circumcision and the cross are again contrasted. Those who are seeking to impose circumcision on others want to escape persecution and "boast in your flesh." But Paul boasts only in the cross, excluding any other avenue of access to God. It is an either-or decision: either one depends on Christ's cross for righteousness, or one depends upon circumcision and observance of the law.

Paul does not explicitly argue that the cross replaces circumcision, but he comes very close in Colossians 2:11. The circumcision of the believer is accomplished "without hands" in "the circumcision of Christ." The "circumcision of Christ" probably refers to his death, for the participial clause in verse 12 indicates that the circumcision Paul

---

46. For a helpful critique of Christian reconstructionism and the place of the law today see Walter C. Kaiser, Jr., "God's Promise Plan and His Gracious Law," *JETS* 33 (1990): 289–302.

47. See Peder Borgen, "Paul Preaches Circumcision and Pleases Men," in M. D. Hooker and S. G. Wilson, eds., *Paul and Paulinism: Essays in Honour of C. K. Barrett* (London: SPCK, 1982), 37–46; idem, "Observations on the Theme 'Paul and Philo': Paul's Preaching of Circumcision in Galatia (Gal. 5:11) and Debates on Circumcision in Philo," in S. Pederson, ed., *The Pauline Literature and Theology* (Göttingen: Vandenhoeck and Ruprecht, 1980), 85–102.

describes occurred when "we were buried together with him in baptism." Thus, the decisive circumcision for believers is the "cutting off" of Christ at the cross. Entrance into the church is based on Christ's work at the cross, not the acceptance of circumcision. Baptism was an appropriate rite for entrance into the church since it illustrates the cleansing work of Christ on the cross. In addition, circumcision only applies to men, whereas both men and women participate in Christian baptism.

So when we look at circumcision from another angle we see again that it is both abolished and yet fulfilled.[48] It is abolished in that the literal rite does not apply. It is spiritually fulfilled in what Christ accomplished for believers on the cross.

Does Paul's understanding of the law envision observance of the sabbath? This has been a matter of intense controversy in the church, and the brief treatment here cannot adequately treat all of the issues involved.[49] I do not believe Paul thought sabbath observance should be imposed upon Gentile believers. Galatians 4:10 hints at this by negatively referring to the Galatians' observance of "days and months and seasons and years." Presumably, the observance of days would include the sabbath since it was the day most commonly observed by Jews, and Galatians reflects a Judaizing heresy. Paul's stance on the sabbath would be similar to his view of circumcision. He would not object to those who desired to observe the sabbath, but he would not see it imposed on all people.

Romans 14:5–6 strengthens my understanding of Paul's view of the sabbath. The background to Romans 14:1–15:13 is disputed, but it probably relates to Jew-Gentile tensions in Rome.[50] Romans 14:14 and 14:20 support the theory that the weak ones were primarily Jewish. Here Paul refers to food that is "common" or "clean," and concern over the cleanliness of foods would be natural for Jews. Now if these chapters reflect Jew-Gentile tensions, then the disputes over the observance of days in verses 5 and 6 relate to the same question. Presumably Jews would be inclined to "judge one day above another" (v. 5), while Gentiles "would consider every day alike" (v. 5). Surely one of the days the Jews would consider to be above others would be the sabbath, while Gentiles would

---

48. See Osten-Sacken, *Die Heiligkeit der Tora*, 48.

49. For further study see W. Rordorf, *Sunday: The History of the Day of Rest and Worship in the Earliest Centuries of the Christian Church* (London: SCM, 1968); Paul K. Jewett, *The Lord's Day: A Theological Guide to the Christian Day of Worship* (Grand Rapids: Eerdmans, 1971); Samuele Bacchiocchi, *From Sabbath to Sunday: A Historical Investigation of the Rise of Sunday Observance in Early Christianity* (Rome: Pontifical Gregorian University, 1977); R. T. Beckwith and W. Stott, *This Is the Day: The Biblical Doctrine of the Christian Sunday in Its Jewish and Early Christian Setting* (London: Marshall, Morgan and Scott, 1978); D. A. Carson, ed., *From Sabbath to Lord's Day: A Biblical, Historical and Theological Investigation* (Grand Rapids: Zondervan, 1982).

50. So James D. G. Dunn, *Romans*, 2 vols. (Dallas: Word, 1988), 2:794–843.

not assign special significance to that day. Paul does not condemn Jews for thinking that some days are specially significant, nor Gentiles for concluding that all days are the same. "Each one should be fully convinced in his own mind" (v. 5). Paul does rule out imposing Jewish convictions on Gentiles. This suggests that Paul does not see the sabbath as normative for believers.

Colossians 2:16 also addresses the tension surrounding certain foods and particular days. Paul declares, "Let no one judge you with respect to food or drink or in the matter of a feast or new moon or sabbath." Even though the heresy in Colossae may have had some Hellenistic elements, the reference to sabbath demonstrates the Jewish dimensions of the Colossian heresy.[51] Presumably, the reference to foods refers to Old Testament restrictions as well. Here we have an explicit statement from Paul that believers should not be judged or condemned for their behavior on these matters. Colossians 2:21 makes it clear that Paul's opponents insisted that believers abstain from eating foods they considered defiled, and they required believers to observe certain days. For Paul the observance of feasts, new moons, and the sabbath are irrelevant because these things were only "a shadow of the coming things, and the body belongs to Christ" (Col. 2:17). The sabbath requirement has ended, so it should not be imposed on others. The sabbath had a salvation-historical function only during the period of history that ended with the coming of Christ.

How do Paul's comments on the sabbath relate to the theme of the abolition and fulfillment of the Mosaic law? Literal observance of the sabbath on Saturday is no longer required. Believers are not under the authority of the Mosaic covenant. Paul never says the sabbath has been fulfilled in Christ, but Christ's coming may have fulfilled some aspects of it. Since Paul wrote occasional letters, he could not expatiate on each issue connected with the Old Testament. He spoke against sabbath observance only because some were trying to mandate it. Interestingly, the author of Hebrews connects the sabbath to the eschatological rest already enjoyed by believers (Heb. 4:1–11). Christ's return will consummate this rest. The sabbath points to a rest now enjoyed by those who trust in Jesus as Messiah.[52]

We have seen that Paul argued that the Mosaic covenant had passed away, and that a number of its specific commandments, including sac-

---

51. For a defense of the Jewish character of the heresy see Peter T. O'Brien, *Colossians, Philemon* (Waco: Word, 1982), xxx–xxxviii; N. Thomas Wright, *The Epistles of Paul to the Colossians and to Philemon* (Grand Rapids: Eerdmans, 1986), 23–30.

52. I think it is probable that there is also a principle in the sabbath commandment that each person should rest one day out of seven. This is not specifically articulated by Paul or any other NT writer, however.

rifices, circumcision, purity laws, food laws, and sabbath, were not required of Christians. This does not mean, however, that these laws have no relevance to believers. They all point forward to Christ and are fulfilled in him in various ways.[53] On the other hand, we have also seen that Paul expects believers to obey other parts of the law, such as honoring parents (Eph. 6:2) and prohibitions against coveting, adultery, murdering, and stealing (Rom. 7:7; 13:9). Moreover, believers should love their neighbor as themselves (Rom. 13:9; Gal. 5:14), and abstain from idolatry (1 Cor. 10:14). Paul also commends Gentile Christians for keeping the law (Rom. 2:26), says that the purpose of Christ's death was that the law should be fulfilled (Rom. 8:4), and praises the keeping of God's commandments (1 Cor. 7:19).[54]

The most reasonable conclusion is that the moral norms or absolutes of the law still obligate Christians. When Paul speaks of "keeping God's commandments" (1 Cor. 7:19) or the "ordinances of the law" (Rom. 2:26), he thinks of the moral norms of the law, which believers are enabled to keep by the power of the Holy Spirit.[55] In the case of commandments that enshrine moral norms the fulfillment brought by Christ does not change the content of the commands at all. It simply provides the power to put them into effect.

On the other hand, Paul still insists that the Mosaic covenant has passed away, even though the moral norms or absolutes of that covenant remain in force. The Mosaic covenant was intended for an interim period in salvation history when distinctions between Jews and Gentiles were erected, probably to keep the people of God untainted by the pagan practices of the nations. But with the coming of Christ the promise to Abraham has begun to be fulfilled in all nations, so that the distinctions between Jews and Gentiles, including the laws enshrining those distinctions, are no longer observed literally. The Mosaic covenant also had a salvation historical function. Many of the laws contained in that covenant, such as sacrifices and circumcision, pointed

---

53. On the importance of fulfillment in Paul's theology see Osten-Sacken, *Die Heiligkeit der Tora*, 40–46.

54. Thielman ("Paul's View of the Law," 235–53) argues a case similar to mine from the evidence of 1 Corinthians.

55. For a similar distinction see George Eldon Ladd, *A Theology of the New Testament* (Grand Rapids: Eerdmans, 1974), 510; Cranfield, "St. Paul and the Law," 49–52, 66; Daniel P. Fuller, "Paul and the Works of the Law," *WTJ* 38 (1975): 38–39; C. F. D. Moule, "Obligation in the Ethic of Paul," in W. R. Farmer, C. F. D. Moule, and Reinhold R. Niebuhr, eds. *Christian History and Interpretation: Studies Presented to John Knox* (Cambridge: Cambridge University Press, 1967), 397; Robert H. Gundry, "Grace, Works and Staying Saved in Paul," *Bib* 66 (1985): 7; J. R. Hempel, "On the Problem of the Law in the Old and New Testaments," *ATR* 34 (1952): 229–31; C. Haufe, "Die Stellung des Paulus zum Gesetz," *TLZ* 91 (1966): 171–78; Kaiser, "His Gracious Law," 289–302; Osten-Sacken, *Die Heiligkeit der Tora*, 47.

forward to something greater, which was fulfilled in the coming of Christ. Now that the fulfillment has come, the shadow is no longer needed.

Some might object that Paul would never expect believers to keep the moral norms of the law, for the law condemns, provokes sin, increases sin, and brings death (Rom. 5:20; 7:1–25; 1 Cor. 15:56; 2 Cor. 3:7–11; Gal. 2:19; 3:10–13; 3:22). These texts imply that freedom from all the law is necessary since the law encourages and even increases sin's power. After all, Paul insisted so strongly that to be "under law" was to be "under sin."[56] He cannot bring the law in through the back door now! This suggests that the problem with the Mosaic law was not simply its cultural inclusivity, but the law possessed the intrinsic complication of producing more unrighteousness. One can see why Stephen Westerholm concludes that the law must be abolished altogether to counter sin.[57]

These objections can be answered. Doubtless, Paul sees a close relationship between the law and sin, but he never sees the problem with the law as such (Rom. 7:12, 14; Gal. 3:21). The problem lies with the flesh and with sin, which use the law to produce sin (Rom. 7:8, 11, 14, 17–18, 24). Thus, when Paul speaks of release from the law (Rom. 7:6), he does not imply that all external law is counterproductive for Christians. The point is that the flesh cannot obey God (Rom. 8:4–8), and obedience to the law is not possible apart from the Holy Spirit. The law apart from the Spirit kills. Believers need freedom from the law insofar as it enslaves people under sin. In the new age, the power of the Spirit makes obedience to the law possible (Rom. 8:4).[58] Thus, when Paul relates sin and the law, he thinks of the moral demands of the law and argues that the person in the flesh cannot obey the law and stands condemned (Gal. 3:10–13). His solution is not to do away with all external commands. He asserts that Christians, by the power of the Spirit, can now fulfil what the law demands.[59]

---

56. Douglas J. Moo ("The Law of Moses or the Law of Christ," in J. S. Feinberg, ed., *Continuity and Discontinuity: Perspectives on the Relationship between the Old and New Testaments. Essays in Honor of S. Lewis Johnson, Jr.* [Westchester, Ill.: Crossway, 1988], 211), for example, says, "The very question about whether one could sin with impunity because one was no longer under the law strongly suggests that not being under the law involves for Paul not being under its precepts."

57. See footnote 3 of this chapter.

58. So also Reinmuth, *Geist und Gesetz*, 48–74. Reinmuth (74–93) argues that the same conception that the law will be fulfilled through the agency of the Holy Spirit is also present in early Jewish literature.

59. See Brendan J. Byrne, "Living out the Righteousness of God: The Contribution of Rom. 6:1–8:13 to an Understanding of Paul's Ethical Presuppositions," *CBQ* 43 (1981): 557–81.

Now that the age of the Spirit has arrived, and Christ has broken the power of sin, the age of slavery to sin has ended. The Mosaic covenant had at least two functions. It had certain rites and practices that separated the Jews from the Gentile nations surrounding them, and it is also demonstrated that those living before the advent of the Spirit were powerless to keep the law. The liberation from the law does not mean that now the external commands of the law are irrelevant for the believer. Gerry Breshears, therefore, leaps over the evidence when he claims that Paul "rejects any sort of nomistic life style [*sic*], any sort of lifestyle which views the life of the godly person as regulated by the Torah, which serves as a touchstone of God's standard for life."[60] Instead, freedom from the law means that the Spirit now enables believers to obey the law (Rom. 8:4).

A qualification should be added here. Paul speaks about what is largely or generally true in the old and new eras.[61] The example of Abraham suggests Paul would not deny that the Spirit brought new life to some in the Old Testament, nor would he deny that by faith some obeyed the law. But, generally speaking, people failed to obey the law during the Old Testament era. Thus, the extent of obedience to the law is greater in the new covenant because the Spirit has been poured out upon people of all nations.

Another objection to a positive use of the law in the life of the Christian stems from 1 Timothy 1:8–11.[62]

> Now we know that the law is good, if anyone uses it lawfully, because we know this, namely, that the law is not appointed for a righteous person, but for the lawless and rebellious, for the ungodly and sinners, for the unholy and profane, for people who kill their fathers and mothers, for murderers, for the sexually immoral and homosexuals, for kidnappers, for liars, and those who swear falsely, and for whatever else opposes sound teaching, according to the glorious gospel of the blessed God, with which I have been entrusted.

60. Gerry Breshears, "The Place of Law in the Life of the Believer in Christ" (paper read at ETS, 1989). For another example of the radical disjunction he sees between the Spirit and law, see p. 8 where Breshears says, "Law-keeping and Spirit do not mix following the distinction between Old and New Covenants." On the contrary, now that the Spirit has come the law can be kept.

61. See Thomas E. Provence ("'Who Is Sufficient for These Things?' An Exegesis of 2 Corinthians ii 15–iii 18," *NovT* 24 [1982]: 68) who says, "The dispensation of the γράμμα had a propensity toward death (iii 7). Nevertheless, there were some during that age who, motivated by the Spirit were made alive." So also Daniel P. Fuller, *The Unity of the Bible* (Grand Rapids: Zondervan, 1992), 462.

62. See p. 86 n. 35, for my understanding of authorship in the Pastoral letters.

It has often been pointed out that the sins mentioned here may accord with the decalogue, especially the second table.[63] The text also agrees with Romans 7:12 and 16 in saying that the law is good. But the question this text raises for our purposes relates to the ongoing validity of the law. Some scholars argue that since Paul says here the law is not intended for a righteous person that it should have no role in the life of the Christian. The law still has a function for unbelievers, presumably to restrain sin. Righteous people, these scholars suggest, do not need the law. They are free from its commands.[64] It is not surprising that these verses have been used to defend complete freedom from the law. It is probably a mistake to draw such a comprehensive conclusion from this text. Donald Guthrie—despite disagreeing with my conclusion on these verses— remarks, "There is no necessity to suppose that this statement excludes every other function of the law."[65]

We should remember that Paul is responding to false teachers who were wrongly using the law (compare 1 Tim. 1:3–7). He reminds Timothy that the law is good, but it does not hold the key for Christian living. To say that the law has no function at all for a Christian would be to read more than is warranted by these verses. Of course, if Christians were morally perfect and completely righteous there would be no need for the law. Since Christians still battle against sin and are caught in the tension between the already and the not-yet, the law and moral norms still have a role to play in the life of the believer. Paul emphasizes in this text that the law should not be overestimated. It does not actually produce righteousness; it only restrains sin.[66] To think that the law alone possesses power to transform is a serious mistake. Unrighteous people (unbelievers) are particularly prone to seeing the dissemination of moral norms as all that is necessary to produce righteousness. Paul observes that righteous people actually do not need the law at all. Not that it plays no function in a believer's life, for we have seen elsewhere in this chapter that the law should be obeyed by the power of the Holy Spirit, but that the law does not hold the solution to the human dilemma.[67]

---

63. Gordon D. Fee, *1 and 2 Timothy, Titus* (Peabody: Hendrickson, 1988), 45–46; Martin Dibelius and Hans Conzelmann, *A Commentary on the Pastoral Epistles* (Philadelphia: Fortress, 1972), 23; J. N. D. Kelly, *A Commentary on the Pastoral Epistles* (reprint; Grand Rapids: Baker, 1981), 49–50; Donald Guthrie, *The Pastoral Epistles* (Grand Rapids: Eerdmans, 1957), 61. For a contrary opinion see A. T. Hanson, *The Pastoral Epistles* (Grand Rapids: Eerdmans, 1982), 59.

64. For this interpretation see Fee, *1 and 2 Timothy, Titus*, 45; Guthrie, *Pastoral Epistles*, 61; Kelly, *Pastoral Epistles*, 49–50.

65. *Pastoral Epistles*, 61.

66. How Paul can both say that the law provokes and restrains sin is explained in chapter 3.

67. Donald G. Bloesch's discussion on the role of the law today (*Freedom for Obedience: Evangelical Ethics in Contemporary Times* [San Francisco: Harper and Row, 1987], 126–49) is filled with wisdom and balance. I would not endorse all of his conclusions, but on the whole his perspective is quite similar to the one I suggest.

A distinctive view is suggested by David A. Dorsey.[68] He argues that none of the laws of the Old Testament are binding upon believers "legally," but all the laws are still binding in a "revelatory and pedagogical sense."[69] The latter statement is a helpful one, but the former one is somewhat misleading since the word *legally* has a negative connotation. Paul, at least, believed that the prohibitions regarding murder and adultery were still in force, and the reasoning he gives suggests that he does so because they are part of the law (Rom. 13:8–10). Dorsey rightly points out that some of the laws are not binding upon the church because they were intended for Israel as a separate people, and he correctly sees that the cultic system for Israel was fulfilled in Christ. Dorsey lists numerous laws that Christians could not obey today and uses this as an argument against the idea that the Old Testament law is legally binding. There is merit to this argument, but the danger is that Dorsey may fail to see that believers today have the same problem with the New Testament. The holy kiss, for instance, is not typically practiced in the United States, but it does not follow that this admonition is not authoritative for Christians in the United States. The intention in giving such an admonition is that there should be warm greetings among believers, but each culture shares such greetings in different ways. New Testament interpreters need to discern the principle that informs Paul's particular exhortation. Similarly, gleaning is irrelevant to our culture, but the principle that one should care for the poor is not.[70]

Dorsey also has a point when he says that every one of God's laws is moral.[71] I have argued in this chapter, though, that some of the commands given in the Old Testament, such as animal sacrifices, are no longer to be observed because they are fulfilled in Christ. So, too, laws given for a specific purpose to Israel as a nation have a revelatory function, but Dorsey correctly concludes that they are not binding upon the church. Nevertheless, some laws apply to the church directly. Prohibitions against adultery, murder, lying, homosexuality, and coveting all continue as a standard for the church today.

Dorsey thinks the church would never have adopted the moral laws as authoritative if they would have understood the cultural particularity of the commands given. The fifth commandment, for example, promises

68. David A. Dorsey, "The Law of Moses and the Christian: A Compromise," *JETS* 34 (1991): 321–34.

69. Ibid., 325.

70. Dorsey ("The Law of Moses," 330) says that the NT "speaks of the law in quite monolithic terms. Legal obligation to only a portion of the corpus is nowhere suggested." But if my exegesis as presented in this chapter is correct, then Dorsey's statement here is simply false. See 1 Cor. 7:19.

71. Ibid., 330–31.

long life in the land of Canaan if one honors one's father and mother. But if this is so culturally bound, why does Paul use this very commandment in his exhortation to the Ephesians (Eph. 6:2), even mentioning the Old Testament promise? Indeed, the examples Dorsey gives imply that if any cultural particularity can be found in a command, it cannot be a universal norm. Virtually all of the Pauline letters were written to specific situations and involve some cultural particularity, yet we extract principles from these letters for the church of today. Universal moral norms can be tucked into specific situations without suggesting that it only applies to that situation. And some of the specific case laws simply apply moral norms to practical situations. For example, the parapet law (Deut. 22:8) should not be practiced literally in the United States, but surely there is a principle supporting the idea of safety in housing and authorizing the establishment of housing codes. So too, we do not use an ox to tread out grain (Deut. 25:4), but the principle is that animals should be treated with compassion and deserve to be fed for their work.[72]

Paul speaks of the end of the Mosaic law, and this clearly involves a number of its specific commandments. But our inductive study of Paul shows that he also speaks of the fulfillment of the Mosaic law. Some of the laws from the Old Testament era are no longer literally practiced because they are fulfilled in Christ. Paul believes the moral norms of the law are still in force, and he thinks believers can carry them out by the power of the Holy Spirit.

Some object to any distinction between parts of the law that labels some laws as normative because Judaism offers no evidence supporting such divisions.[73] This is not a strong objection for two reasons. First, it has been pointed out that even within Judaism, particularly in the dispersion, there was a tendency to exalt the ethical over the ritual law.[74] Second, Paul's position differs from Judaism in that circumcision, food laws, and the observance of days are now canceled for theological reasons. We should not expect to find that Judaism parallels Paul's theology in every respect. What segment of Judaism would have agreed with Paul's stance on circumcision? The dawn of the new era and Paul's conversion caused him to rethink his whole understanding of Judaism in a way that departed significantly from many of his Jewish contemporaries.

---

72. Dorsey, "The Law of Moses," 331.

73. Bruce, "Paul and the Law," 266; Andrea van Dülmen, *Die Theologie des Gesetzes bei Paulus* (Stuttgart: Katholisches Bibelwerk, 1968), 130–31; Moo, "Works of Law," 84–85; Donald Guthrie, *New Testament Theology* (Downers Grove, Ill.: InterVarsity, 1981), 696.

74. See Niebuhr, *Gesetz und Paränese*, 7, 12–14, 26, 59, 61–64, 160, 162, 233–34; Martin Hengel, *Between Jesus and Paul: Studies in the Earliest History of Christianity* (Philadelphia: Fortress, 1983), 174 n. 50; John J. Collins, *Between Athens and Jerusalem: Jewish Identity in the Hellenistic Diaspora* (New York: Crossroad, 1983), 162–63.

Some also object that distinguishing between various parts of the law will lead to a complex casuistry which contradicts Paul's way of thinking. Sanders claims that distinguishing between the law's moral norms and ritual elements in the case of idolatry would be extremely difficult.[75] Surely there are some places of difficulty, for all generalizations obscure some areas of difficulty. The specific example Sanders gives, however, is not persuasive. If ritual elements are involved in idolatry, then such rituals are forbidden in idolatrous contexts. Behind the command, is the principle that forbids idolatry. Naturally, idolatry can be practiced in different ways and different contexts, so one must discern whether idolatry is occurring. We also need to recall that the distinction between moral norms and other commands in the law is not the heart of Pauline ethics,[76] though these distinctions are part of Paul's ethic. The difficulty in distinguishing between various parts of the law is often overplayed; in many cases it is clear what segments of the law are moral norms that relate to the church directly, and which areas of the law have been fulfilled in Christ and are no longer literally practiced. Most of those who resist the idea that the moral norms are still in force are convinced that such a stance would compromise the originality of Paul's gospel, or wonder why any Jews would oppose him if he had such a conservative stance toward the law. Paul's refusal to enforce food laws and circumcision would be enough to render him suspicious in Jewish eyes, not to mention his radical departure from Judaism in his estimate of human ability to keep the law. The newness of his gospel does not consist in the rejection of all law but in ability to keep the law through the mighty work of the Spirit.

Conclusion

Paul's understanding of the continuing validity of the law is complex. One cannot respond with a simple "yes" or "no" as to whether the law remains in force. Paul argues that the Mosaic covenant has ended in one

---

75. *Paul, the Law*, 101–2.

76. Lindemann ("Die biblischen Toragebote," 246–61) argues that since in 1 Corinthians Paul does not cite the moral law as authoritative, he therefore must not hold it as such. For a similar argument see Moo, "The Law of Moses or the Law of Christ," 216. But this argument only proves that the OT law was not the heart of Paul's ethic; it does not demonstrate that it was not part of his ethic. Lindemann underestimates the extent to which the law does inform Paul's instructions in 1 Corinthians, for example, in the prohibition against idolatry in 1 Corinthians 10. In addition, the "commandments" in view in 1 Cor. 7:19 probably include those of the OT law. See especially Thielman, "Paul's View of the Law," 235–53. P. J. Tomson (*Paul and the Jewish Law: Halakha in the Letters of the Apostle to the Gentiles* [Minneapolis: Fortress, 1990]) argues for a very positive estimation of the law and Jewish halakah by Paul, although his argument is weakened by overestimating the place of halakah in Paul.

sense. The promises made to Abraham have begun to be fulfilled with the coming of Christ. The Mosaic covenant was designed for the interim period until Christ arrived. The Mosaic covenant, however, has ceased because it is fulfilled in Christ. Sacrifices, circumcision, and food laws are not observed literally; they point to deeper realities that have found their fulfillment in Jesus Christ. The Old Testament commands to offer sacrifices, be circumcised, and keep the food laws still function as the word of God for the church but must be interpreted in light of the Christ event.

The moral absolutes of the Mosaic law, however, are also fulfilled in Christ. The fulfillment of these commands, however, does not necessitate a change in the content of the commands. What is new is that the gift of the Holy Spirit now provides the power to obey what the law enjoins. Such a conclusion does not mean that today's church should press nation states to adopt the civil laws of the Old Testament. We also observed that Paul takes laws related to Israel as a theocracy and applies them spiritually to the life of the church. The church is not a political and religious entity like Israel but a spiritual people called out from many people groups. Thus, only the principles of the laws relating to Israel as a political entity are applied to the church, the new people of God.

7

Did Paul Teach Justification by Works?

So far I have answered the question of whether Paul taught justification by works with an emphatic "no." Paul asserts that no one can be righteous by works of law because no one can do perfectly all the law requires (Rom. 3:19–20; Gal. 3:10). And if no one practices the whole law, then it follows that no one can be justified by works of law. However, we also saw in chapter 6 that Paul expected believers to obey the moral norms of the law by the power of the Holy Spirit. Moreover, some statements in Paul seem to maintain that people will be justified by works. For example, Romans 2:6 says God "will repay each person according to his works." The necessity of works for justification is sharpened further by Romans 2:13, "For it is not the hearers of the law who are justified before God, but the doers of the law will be justified." Romans 2:13 seems to say specifically that one who practices the law will be justified. One wonders how these statements (and others) regarding justification or "repayment" by works cohere with Paul's claim that no one can be justified by works of law (Rom. 3:20, 28; Gal. 2:16; 3:2, 5).

I approach this issue by exploring in more detail what Paul means in Romans 2 when he says that God "will repay each one according to his works," and "the doers of the law shall be justified" (Rom. 2:6, 13). Romans 2 stands out most prominently in saying justification will be according to works. Is Paul seriously contemplating the possibility that

some will be judged righteous by their works?[1] Or does another interpretation explain more adequately his statements in Romans 2?

Some Attempted Solutions to the Puzzle

Some scholars argue that in Romans 2 Paul's belief that Gentiles can
be justified by obeying the law contradicts his assertion elsewhere that
no one can keep the law.[2] E. P. Sanders thinks that in Romans 2 Paul uti-
lizes a synagogue sermon from diaspora Judaism that does not harmonize with his statements elsewhere and says that one would conclude
from Romans 2 alone that one should practice the law in order to be a
true Jew.[3] Both Sanders and Heikki Räisänen contend that Romans 2
makes some exaggerated statements about the Jews, for not all Jews were
guilty of stealing, adultery, and robbing temples![4] Räisänen suggests
that, since Paul's intent in Romans 2 is to attack the Jews, Paul implicitly
assumes that fulfilling the law is possible for unbelieving Gentiles.[5]
This contradicts what Paul says elsewhere and demonstrates that he is
not a consistent thinker.[6]

Sanders and Räisänen correctly perceive tensions between this text
and other Pauline statements. Their claim that Paul contradicts himself, however, is not valid.[7] Even if Paul does use a synagogue sermon
in Romans 2 (which is questionable), his use of tradition signals his

---

1. For a history of interpretation on Romans 2 see M. Lackmann, *Vom Geheimnis der Schöpfung: Die Geschichte der Exegese von Römer I,18–23, II,14–16 und Acta XIV,15–17, XVII,22–29
vom 2. Jahrhundert bis zum Beginn der Orthodoxie* (Stuttgart: Evangelisches Verlagswerk,
1952), 95–140 and 212–35. A brief survey of interpretation is found in J. Reidl's, "Die Auslegung
von R 2,14–16 in Vergangenheit und Gegenwart," *Studiorum Paulinorum Congressus Internationalis Catholicus 1961* (Rome: Pontifical Biblical Institute, 1963), 1.271–81. For a very full bibliography both of the history of interpretation and of modern exegesis see Klyne R. Snodgrass,
"Justification by Grace—To the Doers: An Analysis of the Place of Romans 2 in the Theology of
Paul," *NTS* 32 (1986): 87–93.

2. William Wrede, *Paulus*, 2d ed. (Tübingen: J. C. B. Mohr, 1907), 49; W. Joest, *Gesetz und
Freiheit: Das Problem des 'Tertius usus legis' bei Luther und die neutestamentliche Parainese*
2d ed. (Göttingen: Vandenhoeck and Ruprecht, 1956), 169–76; Heikki Räisänen, *Paul and the
Law* (Philadelphia: Fortress, 1983), 106–7; E. P. Sanders, *Paul, the Law, and the Jewish People*
(Philadelphia: Fortress, 1983), 123–35; Otto Pfleiderer, *Der Paulinismus. Ein Beitrag zur
Geschichte der urchristlichen Theologie*, 2d ed. (Leipzig: Reisland, 1890), 281–83.

3. Sanders, *Paul, the Law*, 123, 129.

4. Ibid., 124–25; Räisänen, *Paul and the Law*, 98–101.

5. Räisänen, *Paul and the Law*, 106.

6. Ibid., 106–8; Sanders, *Paul, the Law*, 124.

7. George P. Carras ("Romans 2,1–29: A Dialogue on Jewish Ideals," *Bib* 73 [1992]: 183–207)
defends the cogency of Paul's argument in Romans 2. He thinks that Paul uses a diatribal style
in order to refute the idea that Jewish privileges will spare them from judgment. The nature of
Paul's argument, Carras maintains, was thoroughly Jewish and would have been recognized for
its Jewish character. He concludes (206) that "Paul's rebuttal of the 'critic' is one from which few
pious Jews would have dissented."

agreement with it. Sanders objects that this passage provides an exception to Paul's normal use of tradition since there is nothing distinctively Christian about the passage, and nowhere else does Paul make salvation dependent upon the law.[8] But this argument fails, for even Sanders acknowledges that Paul uses traditions in vice and virtue lists that are not distinctively Christian. It is artificial to say that the tradition employed fits with Paul only if it has a Christian stamp, for Paul as a Christian was still deeply influenced by his Jewish heritage. The central issue, however, is whether it accords with Paul's thought to make salvation dependent upon obeying the law. I will argue shortly that such a position is no contradiction.

The claim that Paul makes exaggerated charges against the Jews which do not accord with reality is also incorrect.[9] It is simply not true that Paul charges *every* Jew with adultery, stealing, and robbing temples. These infractions are listed as *illustrations* of the principle that the Jews do not keep the law that they treasure and teach. Paul uses colorful examples to drive home his main point that the Jews fail to keep the law.[10] Sanders and Räisänen illegitimately conclude from his illustrations that he pronounces all Jews are guilty of the specific infractions mentioned. He simply demonstrates that all Jews stand condemned because they fail to perform perfectly all that the law requires. The problem with Sanders' and Räisänen's interpretation is that they fail to distinguish between the illustrations Paul uses and the main point that these illustrations support: that all Jews deserve judgment because they fail to observe the law perfectly. In Romans 3:9–20 Paul argues that no one is righteous by "works of law" because all sin. Thus, Paul does not introduce the illustrations to convict every Jew of these specific sins but to support the thesis that all Jews sin.

Romans 3:20 and 28 also cast doubt on the contention that Paul is inconsistent. Paul says no one can be righteous by works of law, and it is quite unlikely that he has forgotten what he has just written in Romans 2.[11] Indeed, Romans 3:19–20 functions as the concluding statement for all of 1:18–3:18, a section teaching that all people without

8. Sanders, *Paul, the Law*, 131–32.
9. Timo Laato, (*Paulus und das Judentum: Anthropologische Erwägungen* [Åbo: Åbo Academy Press, 1991], 98–119) in a careful analysis of Romans 2 argues that the Pauline argument is not exaggerated. Rather, Laato contends, Räisänen exaggerates the difficulty of this chapter.
10. Carras ("Romans 2,1–29," 199–202) rightly notes that Paul's argument is rhetorical in this section, concluding that he is not suggesting that every Jew is guilty of the particular sins mentioned in Romans 2.
11. Charles E. B. Cranfield ("Giving a Dog a Bad Name: A Note on Heikki Räisänen's Paul and the Law," *JSNT* 38 [1990]: 77–85) uses Romans 2 as his case study in subjecting Räisänen's study to scrutiny. Cranfield concludes that Räisänen opts too simplistically for contradiction in Paul's thought.

exception are sinners (see 3:9–18). The statements asserting that no one can keep the law and that some keep the law and are thereby justified occur in the same context. Possibly Paul did not perceive a contradiction between these two kinds of statements, but it is more probable that he was aware of the tension but did not see it as a contradiction.

Francis Watson has attempted to explain Romans 2 from a sociological perspective.[12] According to Watson, Paul wanted to convince believers in Rome to break with the Jewish community. Paul's ultimate goal was to transform the Roman community from a reform movement within Judaism into a sect which would break with Judaism. Therefore, Paul argues in Romans 2 that Gentile Christians are "true Jews" because they obey the law, while the Jews who possess the law do not obey it and delude themselves by thinking they will be saved by grace alone. The assertion in Romans 2 that one is justified by works does not contradict the statement (Romans 3:20) that justification cannot be obtained by "works of law," according to Watson, for in the latter passage Paul's point is that one does not need to follow the way of life of the Jewish people to be justified.[13] Paul's purpose is the same in both passages, says Watson: to show Roman Christians that they should separate from the Jewish community since they already possess the privileges claimed by the Jews.

Watson takes seriously the statements concerning Gentile obedience to the law in Romans 2, but his thesis as a whole has two problems.[14] First, he drives a wedge between sociology and theology, virtually forgetting the latter. Such an approach is too one-dimensional in its method of exegesis.[15] Second, he minimizes Paul's exhortations to Gentile Christians in Romans 11 and 14:1–15:13.[16] In 11:17–24 Paul warns the Gentiles not to be proud of their ingrafting onto the olive tree while the Jews have been cut off. Nothing indicates that his primary concern is separation from the Jewish community; rather, Paul seems concerned

---

12. *Paul, Judaism and the Gentiles: A Sociological Approach* (Cambridge: Cambridge University Press, 1986), 109–22.

13. Ibid., 129–30.

14. For other criticisms of Watson see Carras, "Romans 2,1–29," 188.

15. So John M. G. Barclay, *Obeying the Truth: A Study of Paul's Ethics in Galatians* (Edinburgh: T. and T. Clark, 1988), 238–39, 242; W. S. Campbell, "Did Paul Advocate Separation from the Synagogue? A Reaction to Francis Watson: *Paul, Judaism and the Gentiles: A Sociological Approach*," *SJT* 42 (1989): 461–62.

16. See Watson (*Sociological Approach*, 94–98, 168–173) for his discussion of these texts. Such exhortations have led some to say Paul primarily addresses Gentiles in Romans. So H. W. Bartsch, "The Historical Situation of Romans," *Encounter* 33 (1972): 329–38; W. S. Campbell, "Why Did Paul Write Romans?" *ExpT* 85 (1974): 264–69; idem, "Romans 3 as the Key to the Structure and Thought of the Letter," *NovT* 23 (1981): 22–40; idem, "The Freedom and Faithfulness of God in Relation to Israel," *JSNT* 13 (1981): 27–45.

that the Gentiles may think the Jews are cut off forever from the olive tree (11:23–32).[17] Romans 11 climaxes chapters 9–11, and thus the exhortations to the Gentiles are probably crucial to his argument.[18] Watson, however, argues that in the light of the rest of Romans, chapter 11 should be understood as directed mainly to the Jews.[19] Such a thesis runs aground on the fact that the specific exhortations in the text are directed to Gentiles. Watson's argument here seems to be an example of explaining away clear evidence to defend an a priori thesis.

Watson's explanation of Romans 14:1–15:13 is equally unconvincing. He stresses how much the Jewish Christians had to give up in order to be part of the Christian community. But this section plainly emphasizes the responsibility of Gentiles (14:1, 13–22; 15:1–4) to accept the Jewish Christians who were weak in faith.[20] By stressing the responsibility of the weak, Watson turns the emphasis of the text on its head. If the main concern in Romans was the desire for Christian congregations to separate from the Jewish community, one would expect Paul to encourage Gentiles to distance themselves from Jews who continued to adhere to Jewish cultural practices. This would effectively separate Christian congregations from Judaism. Since Paul focuses on the responsibility of Gentile believers toward Jews, Watson's analysis of the situation is called into question. It is also telling that Watson devotes over fifty pages to Romans 2–8, whereas only four pages are found on Romans 14:1–15:13. This suggests that his reconstruction fails to weigh appropriately the whole of Romans.[21] One can also query the wisdom of locating the sociological situation of Romans in chapters 2–8, especially since Watson forces Paul's specific exhortations to Gentiles in chapters 9, 14, and 15 into a procrustean bed to sustain the hypothesis derived from the earlier chapters.

A number of scholars argue that what Paul says here about obedience to the law is merely hypothetical; that is, only perfect obedience would

17. According to Campbell ("Separation from the Synagogue," 465), Watson's thesis only works "by dismissing the whole of Rom. 11." Campbell overemphasizes the point, though Watson surely underestimates the place of Romans 11.

18. Campbell ("Separation from the Synagogue," 465) notes that very few scholars are persuaded that Romans was addressed to "a Jewish Christian minority." Watson's thesis seems to depend upon this reconstruction in his understanding of Romans 9–11 and 14–15. The discussion of the situation that stimulated Romans is complex and disputed. For helpful inroads into the discussion see Karl P. Donfried, ed., *The Romans Debate*, rev. ed. (Peabody, Mass.: Hendrickson, 1991); A. J. M. Wedderburn, *The Reasons for Romans* (Edinburgh: T. and T. Clark, 1988).

19. Watson, *Sociological Approach*, 171.

20. I agree with Watson that the weaker Christians are primarily Jewish, while the strong are Gentile. For a good defense of this view see James D. G. Dunn's commentary on this section, *Romans*, 2 vols. (Dallas: Word, 1988), 2.794–853.

21. On Romans 2–8 see Watson, *Sociological Approach*, 106–59, while on Rom. 14:1–15:13, see 94–98.

gain righteousness but such obedience is not practically possible.[22] A complementary way of understanding the passage sees Paul as emphasizing that Gentiles possess their own standard of judgment (Rom. 2:12–16), and since they fail to meet that standard, or only obey the law occasionally, they will be judged.[23] Interpreters who support these views frequently point out that the purpose of Romans 1:18–3:20 is to show that all are under sin, not that some are righteous.

The theory that Paul is speaking hypothetically is a much more likely solution than the first two we have examined. Adherents of this view are correct in saying that Paul demanded perfect obedience for justification, and that he thought such perfect obedience was impossible. It is certainly possible, then, that the call to perform good works for justification simply acts as a rhetorical statement.[24] Paul could be saying that one must perform good works to be justified, but the flow of the argument reveals that he believes no one can do the necessary good works. Such an argument would fit nicely with my own emphasis in chapter 2 on the necessity of keeping the law perfectly in order to be saved. I argued there that no person could perform the requisite works. Nonetheless, even though this interpretation contains promise, the text decisively argues against both the hypothetical interpretation and the view that Paul only emphasizes the judgment of Jews and Gentiles.

First, 2:26–27 likely speaks of Gentiles who actually fulfil the law. Verses 28–29 supports this interpretation and provides the ground (γάρ,

22. Ulrich Wilckens, *Der Brief an die Römer* (Neukirchen-Vluyn: Neukirchener Verlag, 1978), 1.132–133, 145; Otto Kuss, *Der Römerbrief* (Regensburg: F. Pustet, 1957), 1.64–68, 90; Gunther Bornkamm, "Gesetz und Natur (Röm 2, 14–16)," in *Studien zu Antike und Urchristentum* (München: Chr. Kaiser, 1959), 2.110; Friedrich Kuhr, "Römer 2.14f. und die Verheissung bei Jeremia 31.31ff.," *ZNW* 55 (1964): 252–61; Andrea van Dülmen, *Die Theologie des Gesetzes bei Paulus*(Stuttgart: Katholisches Bibelwerk, 1968), 76–82; Frank Thielman, *From Plight to Solution: A Jewish Framework for Understanding Paul's View of the Law in Galatians and Romans* (Leiden: Brill, 1989), 94–96; J.-N. Aletti, "Rm 1,18–3,20: Incohérence ou cohérence de l'argumentation paulinienne?" *Bib* 69 (1988): 47–62; Douglas J. Moo, *Romans 1–8* (Chicago: Moody, 1991), 139–41, 166–68.

23. This category overlaps with the previous one, and thus some scholars can be found promulgating both views. Otto Kuss, "Die Heiden und die Werke des Gesetzes (nach Röm 2,14–16)," *MTZ* 5 (1954): 85–90, 95, 98; Kuhr, "Römer 2.14f," 255; Bornkamm, "Gesetz und Natur," 93–110; Lieselotte Mattern, *Das Verständnis des Gerichtes bei Paulus* (Zürich: Zwingli, 1966), 123, 130–33; Ernest Synofzik, *Die Gerichts und Vergeltungsaussagen bei Paulus: Eine traditionsgeschichtliche Untersuchung* (Göttingen: Vandenhoeck and Ruprecht, 1977), 80–83; Jouette M. Bassler, *Divine Impartiality: Paul's Letter to the Romans* (Chico, Calif.: Scholars, 1982), 141–45; Roger Mohrlang, *Matthew and Paul: A Comparison of Ethical Perspectives* (Cambridge: Cambridge University Press, 1984), 162–63 n. 57; J. C. Yates, "The Judgment of the Heathen: The Interpretation of Article XVIII and Romans 2:12–16," *Churchman* 100 (1986): 220–30; Walter Schmithals, *Der Römerbrief: Ein Kommentar* (Gütersloh: Gerd Mohn, 1988), 87–88, 91–93, 101; Rolf Walker, "Die Heiden und das Gericht: Zur Auslegung von Römer 2,12–16," *EvT* 20 (1960): 302–14.

24. Aletti especially ("Rm 1,18–3,20," 47–62) makes a good case for this view; see also Carras, "Romans 2,1–29," 196–98, 204.

gar) for verses 26–27. In particular, verse 29 reveals that the Spirit produces Gentile obedience. "But the true Jew is one in secret, and true circumcision is of the heart, by the Spirit, not the letter." By appealing to the work of the Holy Spirit, Paul shows that he is concerned with actual obedience, not a hypothetical argument.

Second, when Paul refers to repayment according to works (2:6), he is not thinking of the repayment of judgment only. The chiasmus in verses 7–10, which has both judgment and eternal life within its purview, makes this clear. "To those who by patient endurance in the good work are seeking glory and honor and immortality he will give eternal life" (2:7). "There will be glory and honor and peace to every one who does good, both to the Jew first and also to the Greek" (2:10). The promise of eternal life for those who do good works could possibly be hypothetical, but nothing in the text indicates that Paul speaks hypothetically. Thus, a better conclusion surmises that Paul believes some people do good works and thereby receive eternal life.

Third, judgment according to works plays an integral part in Paul's theology elsewhere.[25] For example, in Galatians 5:21 he states that those who practice the "works of the flesh" will be excluded from the kingdom of God.[26] He warns, "I am telling you in advance just what I told you before that those who practice such things will not inherit the kingdom of God." This verse from Galatians is illuminating since in that very letter Paul stresses that justification cannot be obtained by works of law (2:16; 3:2, 5, 10). Nevertheless, 5:21 makes it clear that he also believed that those who practiced the works of the flesh would not inherit the kingdom. Even though justification is not by works of law, works are necessary for a person to obtain eternal life. Those who do not practice good works are threatened with judgment.

A similar thought is found in Galatians 6:8. "The one who sows to his own flesh shall reap corruption from the flesh, but the one who sows to the Spirit will reap from the Spirit eternal life." The "corruption" (φθοράν, *phthoran*) spoken of here must refer to eternal judgment because it sets in antithesis to "eternal life" (ζωὴν αἰώνιον, *zōēn aiō-*

25. For some major studies on the place of works at the last judgment see Floyd V. Filson, *St. Paul's Concept of Recompense* (Leipzig: J. C. Hinrichs'sche Buchhandlung, 1931); Mattern, *Das Verständnis des Gerichtes*; Calvin J. Roetzel, *Judgement in the Community: A Study in the Relationship between Eschatology and Ecclesiology in Paul* (Leiden: Brill, 1972); Karl P. Donfried, "Justification and Last Judgment in Paul," *ZNW* 67 (1976): 90–110; Synofzik, *Gerichts und Vergeltungsaussagen bei Paulus*; Judy Gundry Volf, *Paul and Perseverance: Staying in and Falling Away* (Tübingen: J. C. B. Mohr, 1990). See also Nigel M. Watson, "Justified by Faith: Judged by Works —an Antinomy?" *NTS* 29 (1983): 209–21.

26. That the "kingdom of God" refers to eternal life or eschatological salvation is apparent in Col. 1:13. Those who are "rescued from the authority of darkness" are "transferred into the kingdom of his beloved son" (see also 1 Thess. 2:12).

nion). We can conclude that Paul threatens those who sow to the flesh with eternal judgment, and promises eternal life to those who sow to the Spirit. What does it mean to sow to the Spirit? The context provides some clues. Sowing to the Spirit involves material support for those who teach the word (6:6) and "doing good" to all people (6:9–10). "Doing good" here probably relates to financial support for those who are in need. Paul here may be generalizing the performance of good deeds, but this would not affect my major point. For in any case, the sowing to the Spirit involves the doing of good works, which are necessary for eternal life. Those who fail to do them will face judgment and destruction.

In 1 Corinthians 6:9–10 Paul threatens the "unrighteous" with the same judgment. "Or do you not know that the unrighteous will not inherit the kingdom of God. Do not be deceived; neither the sexually immoral, nor idolaters, nor adulterers, nor the effeminate, nor homosexuals, nor thieves, nor covetors, nor drunkards, nor revilers, nor robbers shall inherit the kingdom of God." Paul issues a warning to the believing community. The Corinthians were acting unrighteously by engaging in lawsuits (ὑμεῖς ἀδικεῖτε, *hymeis adikeite*, v. 8), and Paul links the action of the lawsuits with the subsequent threat to the "unrighteous" (ἄδικοι, *adikoi*, v. 9). Paul does not say that since justification is apart from works of law that the practice of sinful behavior is inconsequential. He argues that those who continue to engage in such behavior will be excluded from the kingdom. Entrance into the kingdom requires a transformed lifestyle.

Ephesians 5:5–6 also supports the notion that works will play a vital role on the day of judgment. "For you should know this, that no person who is sexually immoral, or unclean, or a covetor (who is an idolater), has an inheritance in the kingdom of Christ and God. Let no one deceive you with empty words. For on account of these things the wrath of God comes on the sons of disobedience" (see also Col. 3:5–6). Once again Paul threatens those who practice evil with eschatological wrath. Paul often uses *wrath* (ὀργή, *orgē*) to describe the anger with which God will inflict judgment upon unbelievers, while assuring believers that God will exempt them from his wrath on the last day (Rom. 2:5, 8; 5:9; 9:22; Eph. 2:3; Col. 3:6; 1 Thess. 1:10; 5:9). It should be noted that Paul writes this warning to a believing community. It accords with his assertion elsewhere that those who oppose the gospel will be judged on the last day according to their works (2 Cor. 11:15; 2 Tim. 4:14). Judgment according to works is not some relic from Paul's Jewish past, but a vital part of his theology. Those who claim to be part of the Christian community but persist in sin are threatened with exclusion from the kingdom of God. Apparently, Paul believed that works were necessary for eternal life.

In 1 Corinthians 9:24–27 Paul contends that one must run the race with discipline to win the prize. In fact, he emphasizes that he brings his body under subjection "lest somehow after preaching to others, I should be unapproved" (v. 27). The word "unapproved" (ἀδόκιμος, *adokimos*) here does not refer to a reward given above and beyond eternal life, for Paul always uses the word to refer to those who will not be "approved" or saved on the day of judgment (Rom. 1:28; 2 Cor. 13:5, 6, 7; 2 Tim. 3:8; Titus 1:16). Indeed, Paul exhorts the Corinthians to "test yourselves to see if you are in the faith; examine yourselves. Or, do you not know that Jesus Christ is in you, unless you are unapproved?" (2 Cor. 13:5). When Paul says "test yourselves to see if you are in the faith," he means examine yourselves so that you can discern whether or not you are really Christians. One indication that one is a Christian is if "Jesus Christ is in you." And if he is not, then one is "unapproved" (unsaved).

Paul's reference to bringing his body under subjection so that he will not be unapproved relates to his salvation at the eschatological judgment. Paul's point in 1 Corinthians 9:24–27 is strengthened by the pericope in 10:1–12, where the Corinthians are warned about presuming on God's grace. Even though God rescued Israel from Egypt, not all entered the land of promise. So, too, a mere profession of faith in Christ without perseverance will not avail on the day of judgment.

So even if one thinks the reference to good works in Romans 2 is hypothetical, Paul makes it unquestionably clear that works are necessary on the day of judgment for salvation. Likely Romans 2 makes the same point. Paul's statements in Romans 2 are not merely hypothetical; those who fail to do good works will face judgment, while those who practice good works will experience eternal life.

Finally, some scholars contend that in Romans 2 Paul considers pre-Christian Gentiles who observe the law and are justified by their obedience.[27] They claim this justification by works does not contradict Romans 3:20, for these Gentiles do not attempt to earn salvation by works, nor does Romans 2 speak of perfect obedience. What Paul has in mind are works stemming from the work of the Holy Spirit and faith.

This interpretation possesses a number of similarities with my view that Paul describes Christians who obey the law. Both views stress the necessity of obedience for salvation; that the Spirit, not self-effort, pro-

---

27. Snodgrass, "To the Doers," 72–93; J.-M. Cambier, "Le jugement de tous les hommes par Dieu seul, selon la vérité dans Rom 2.1–3.20," *ZNW* 67 (1976): 187–213; C. K. Barrett, *A Commentary on the Epistle to the Romans* (New York: Harper and Row, 1957), 45–52, 58–61; Glenn N. Davies, *Faith and Obedience in Romans: A Study in Romans 1–4* (Sheffield: JSOT, 1990), 53–70.

duces obedience, and that such obedience is not the earning of salvation by good works but the result of faith. The point of controversy concerns whether Paul is speaking of Christians or pre-Christians.

That he has pre-Christians in view seems less likely. First, Paul has just stressed in Romans 1:18–32 that Gentiles who have received a revelation of God through the created order have suppressed and distorted it. God reveals his wrath against "all ungodliness and unrighteousness of people who suppress the truth in unrighteousness" (v. 18). By observing the created order they understand that God exists and that he is powerful (vv. 19–20), but they spurn such a revelation, "so that they are without excuse" (v. 20). The knowledge they have of God through the created order does not save them. Instead, they "refused to glorify God and give him thanks" (v. 21). Their thinking was distorted so that they turned to idolatry instead of worshiping the one true God (vv. 22–25). Thus, Paul does not consider a positive response by unbelievers to natural revelation. Instead, the time previous to the reception of the gospel is one of sin and the forbearance of God (compare 3:25–26).[28] Paul argues specifically that people will not believe the gospel without hearing it, that they will not hear unless someone preaches it to them, and that one will not preach unless one is sent (10:14–17). Now if Paul believed that one had to hear the gospel to be saved, and that the revelation given through nature did not lead to salvation, then it is unlikely that he speaks of pre-Christian Gentiles in Romans 2.

Second, even though Klyne Snodgrass rightly says the Spirit worked effectively in some before the Christian era,[29] Paul emphasizes in his theology the remarkable increase of the Spirit's activity in the new covenant. Therefore, the greater glory of the new covenant eclipses the glory of the Mosaic covenant (2 Cor. 3:10). Indeed, Paul generally speaks of the old era in negative terms—a "ministry of death" (2 Cor. 3:7), a "ministry of condemnation" (2 Cor. 3:9)—and he equates being "under law" with being under the power of sin (Rom. 6:14–15; Gal. 3:21–22; 5:18) and refers to the era of law as one of infancy compared to the full inheritance now available (Gal. 3:23–4:7). Paul does not deny the Spirit's activity under the old covenant, nor does he claim that the Mosaic covenant teaches any form of legalism. He infers that the work of the Spirit was minimal in the old covenant in comparison to the new, and generally speaking the covenant with Moses ended in failure, while with the

---

28. So Moo, *Romans 1–8*, 121–24.

29. "To the Doers," 81. This admission does not damage the argument about the necessity of hearing the gospel for salvation. Paul argues that Abraham had the gospel preached to him before the coming of Christ (Gal. 3:8). Those who had access to such special revelation had the opportunity for salvation.

dawn of the new covenant, the law can now be obeyed by the power of the Spirit.[30]

It seems unlikely, therefore, that when Paul speaks of the work of the Spirit (Rom. 2:29) he would be thinking of obedience prior to the coming of the gospel. The thrust of his teaching (in accord with both the Old Testament and other Jewish literature of the Second Temple Period)[31] reveals that the work of the Spirit signifies the new age, while sin and failure highlighted the old era. In addition, since the Spirit-letter contrast elsewhere in Paul (Rom. 7:6; 2 Cor. 3:6) identifies the work of the Spirit in the new age, Romans 2 probably contains a similar idea.

Works and Judgment in Romans 2

It is, then, far more plausible that Paul in Romans 2 refers to those who have believed in the gospel, rather than pre-Christians. But this idea must be sustained by exegesis of the text. I shall argue that Paul has such Christian obedience in view in verses 7, 10, and 26–29. Many scholars agree that Paul describes Gentile Christians here, but what differentiates my view from theirs is that I think verses 14 and 15 depict non-believing Gentiles who will face condemnation.[32] This chapter is so difficult, then, because within it Paul describes both *believing and non-believing Gentiles.* Obviously, if Gentile Christians were being portrayed in verses 14–15, such a view would not affect my overall understanding of Paul's theology on this question since I see Gentile Christians in view in verses 7, 10 and 26–29. It is important, though, to distinguish verses 14 and 15 from verses 7, 10, 26–29. Many scholars think that, if they can show that Paul is describing nonbelievers in verses 14–15, then they have proved that Paul is not describing believers in verses 7, 10, and 26–29. Such an approach is flawed, for to show that non-believers are in view in verses 14–15 does not prove that unbelieving Gentiles are also in the purview of verses 7, 10, and 26–29. The text,

---

30. For support of this thesis in Galatians and Romans see Thielman, *From Plight to Solution*, 46–116.

31. Ibid., 28–45.

32. Most scholars who support the Gentile Christian interpretation also see Gentile Christians in view in Rom. 2:14–15. For this view see W. Mundle, "Zur Auslegung von Röm 2,13ff," *TBl* 13 (1934): 249–56; F. Flückiger, "Die Werke des Gesetzes bei den Heiden (nach Röm. 2,14ff.)," *TZ* 8 (1952): 17–42; Karl Barth, *A Shorter Commentary on Romans* (Richmond: John Knox, 1959), 36–39; J. B. Souček, "Zur Exegese von Röm. 2,14ff.," *Antwort, Festschrift for Karl Barth* (Zollikon-Zürich: Evangelischer Verlag, 1956), 99–113; A. König, "Gentiles or Gentile Christians? On the Meaning of Romans 2:12–16," *J Th So Africa* 15 (1976): 53–60; Charles E. B. Cranfield, *A Critical and Exegetical Commentary on the Epistle to the Romans*, 2 vols. (Edinburgh: T. and T. Clark, 1975, 1979), 1:152–62, 173–76.

however shows that verses 7, 10, and 26–29 illustrate Christian obedience, while non-believing Gentiles are described in verses 14 and 15.

Before examining the relevant texts in Romans 2 I must establish the general context of the section. The primary purpose of Romans 2 is to prove that the Jews are guilty before God, for they transgressed the revelation they received,[33] just as the Gentiles rejected the revelation they received (1:18–32).[34]

First, that Paul is speaking exclusively of Gentiles in 1:18–32 is supported by the fact that he refers only to natural revelation in these verses (see Rom. 1:19–21), and a condemnation of the Jews would probably refer also to their transgression of the Torah. In addition, homosexuality[35] (1:26–27) and overt idolatry (1:23–25) were not typical Jewish vices, and thus would be more fitting in describing the Gentile world.

Second, an indictment of Gentiles only in 1:18–32 receives support from the probability that Paul was drawing in these verses on Jewish tradition which was typically used to condemn the Gentile world.[36]

Third, Romans 2:1–5 most likely refers to the Jews because it is the Jews who would consider themselves morally superior due to possession of the law. They, as God's elect people, would reckon that God's kindness to them would make punishment unlikely (2:4).

Fourth, Romans 2:17 explicitly mentions the "Jew," and the theme of verses 17–29 is similar to 2:1–16, appearing in many respects—although not all—to be a repetition of verses 1–16. The doubling of this section suggests the Jews are in view in verses 1–16 as well as in verses 17–29.

33. Snodgrass ("To the Doers," 76) and Davies (*Faith and Obedience*, 80–104) question whether the primary purpose of this section is to show that all are sinners. But Moo (*Romans 1–8*, 87–218) convincingly shows that this is the main point of Rom. 1:18–3:20.

34. The view that Paul addresses Gentiles in Rom. 1:18–32 and Jews in 2:1–16 is found in most commentaries. For some representative examples see Kuss, *Römerbrief*, 1.30, 60–61; Wilckens, *Römer*, 1.93, 121; John Murray, *The Epistle to the Romans* (Grand Rapids: Eerdmans, 1959), 35, 54–56; Cranfield, *Romans*, 105–6, 138–39; Heinrich Schlier, *Der Römerbrief* (Freiburg: Herder, 1977), 48, 68, 77–79; Dunn, Romans, 78. Against the theory that Paul is speaking of Gentiles and Jews, respectively see F.-J. Leenhardt, *The Epistle to the Romans* (London: Lutterworth, 1961), 59, 73–74; Barrett, *Romans*, 43; Stanley K. Stowers, *The Diatribe and Paul's Letter to the Romans* (Chico, Calif.: Scholars, 1981), 112; Lloyd Gaston, *Paul and the Torah* (Vancouver: University of British Columbia Press, 1987), 119–20; Bassler, *Divine Impartiality*, 121–23; Davies, *Faith and Obedience*, 47–52.

35. Robin Scroggs (*The New Testament and Homosexuality: Contextual Background for Contemporary Debate* [Philadelphia: Fortress, 1983], 66–98) documents that in Jewish circles homosexuality was considered to be a Gentile vice. It should be noted, however, that Scroggs (110–11) still thinks that Rom. 1:18–32 is directed to both Jews and Gentiles.

36. See, for example, Wisd. of Sol. 13–15; *2 Apoc. Bar.* 54:17–19; *T. Naph.* 3:3; *As. Mos.* 1:13.

Romans 2:6–10

Now that I have established that Paul directs Romans 2 to the Jews, we are prepared to look more carefully at the text itself. Romans 2:6 is a crucial text for our discussion since Paul says here that God "repays each person according to his works." This verse must be investigated in its context if we hope to understand precisely how it should be interpreted. Verse 6 undergirds Paul's assertion in verse 5 that the Jews are "storing up wrath" for themselves in the day of God's eschatological judgment. Wrath is being stored up *because* God judges each person according to *works*, and verses 1–4 make it plain that the works of the Jews are evil. They have failed to live up to the very standards by which they evaluate the Gentile world.

Judgment according to works was a common theme in Jewish literature.[37] Paul's insistence upon works as a standard would, therefore, hardly be a matter of surprise or controversy. Indeed, verse 6 alludes to Psalm 62:12. We have already seen as well that such a theme is not even novel for Paul, for elsewhere in his teaching he acknowledges the importance of works.

Following on the heels of verse 5, verse 6 has a decidedly negative ring. Certainly nothing in the text thus far indicates that anyone will actually be justified on the last day by works. Paul has emphasized the judgment Jews will face for failing to practice the moral standards they proclaim. However, verses 7–10 further explain the proposition articulated in verse 6. The chiasmus in verses 7–10 alternates between the negative and positive. Verses 8–9 highlight the negative: Eschatological judgment awaits those who disobey the truth and practice evil. The use of *wrath* suggests that Paul speaks of eschatological judgment in verse 8. Verse 5 also uses *wrath* and clearly refers to eschatological judgment ("According to your hard and unrepentant heart you are storing up wrath for yourself in the day of judgment and the revelation of the righteous judgment of God"). Moreover, the antithesis to such punishment is the reception of "eternal life" (ζωὴν αἰώνιον, *zōēn aiōnion*) in verse 7. Verses 7–10 leave no doubt, then, that the repayment (ἀποδώσει, *apodōsei*) in verse 6 anticipates an eschatological repayment, whether the repayment is eternal life or fiery wrath.[38]

---

37. For example, Job 34:11; Ps. 28:4; Prov. 24:12; Jer. 17:10; 25:14; 32:19; 51:24; Ezek. 33:20; 1QS 10:16–18; 1QH 18:12–13; 1QpHab 8:1–2; 4 Ezra 6:19; 7:17, 33–44; *Pss. Sol.* 2:15–17, 33–35; 9:4–5; *2 Apoc. Bar.* 13:8; 44:4; 54:21; *Jub.* 5:12–19; 21:4; 33:18; *T. Levi* 3:2; 4:1; *T. Gad* 7:5; *T. Ben.* 10:7–9; *1 Enoch* 1:7–9; *As. Mos.* 12:10–11; *Sib. Or.* 4:183–85.

38. Actually, the eschatological character of the repayment in verse 6 was already evident before reading verses 7–10, since verse 6 provides the ground for verse 5, and the latter refers to eschatological judgment.

The negative judgment of verses 8–9 fits with judgment according to works, for those who are consumed by selfish-ambition and disobey the truth will face wrath (v. 8). Verse 9 complements verse 8: judgment will be meted out to those "who practice evil" (τοῦ κατεργαζομένου τὸ κακόν, *tou katergazomenou to kakon*).

It needs to be stressed, however, that Paul does not apply the eschatological repayment on the basis of works only to those who will experience wrath on the last day. Paul also speaks of "the one who does good" (τῷ ἐργαζομένῳ τὸ ἀγαθόν, *tō ergazomenō to agathon*, v. 10), and predicts that that person will receive an eschatological reward of "glory, and honor and peace" (δόξα δὲ καὶ τιμὴ καὶ εἰρήνη, *doxa de kai timē kai eirēnē*). Verse 7 describes such people as "seeking glory and honor and immortality by patient endurance in good work" (τοῖς μὲν καθ᾽ ὑπομονὴν ἔργου ἀγαθοῦ δόξαν καὶ τιμὴν καὶ ἀφθαρσίαν ζητοῦσιν, *tois men kath hypomonēn ergou agathou doxan kai timēn kai aphtharsian zētousin*).[39] It seems fair to conclude that eternal life will be granted to those who persevere in doing good works. Verses 7–10, then, undoubtedly constitute a fuller explanation of the traditional statement cited in verse 6.[40]

As I have noted, some argue that Paul describes hypothetical obedience or is speaking rhetorically. But the burden of proof lies with those who defend the hypothetical view since Paul apparently affirms with Judaism and the Old Testament that good works are necessary for eternal life. Indeed, many Pauline texts display concrete evidence, as noted above, that good works are necessary to inherit the kingdom of God. The course of Paul's argument possibly shows him to be speaking hypothetically, but I shall argue shortly that Romans 2:26–29 instead confirms that some obey the law and will be saved from the day of wrath.

Yet, calling these people *Christians* uses a word that Paul does not draw upon in 2:6–10. Are we smuggling it in from the outside?[41] Some interpreters unreasonably seem to demand that the whole of an author's message would be communicated in five verses. Every interpreter without exception must consider the larger context in order to sustain a coherent interpretation, and what the wider context teaches should be

---

39. Moo (*Romans 1–8*, 135) rightly says that ἔργου ἀγαθοῦ is an objective genitive to ὑπομονήν.

40. This text shows that the attempt to distinguish rigidly between ἔργα and ἔργον in Paul, the former being negative and the latter positive (so Mattern, *Das Verständnis Gerichtes*, 141–44; C. C. Crowther, "Works, Work and Good Works," *ExpT* 81 [1969–1970]: 169) cannot be sustained. The "works" in the plural that God recompenses (v. 6) can also be described in the singular in v. 7.

41. So Snodgrass, "To the Doers," 74–75. Watson (*Sociological Approach*, 118–19) complains that Cranfield can only see Christians in view by inserting "glosses" from Reformed theology.

considered in formulating an interpretive hypothesis. But is an appeal to the wider context justifiable here? I maintain that Paul does speak of Christians who do good works. In 2:26–29 Paul makes it clear that those who obey the law have been transformed by the Holy Spirit. The latter verses are not from a distant context but are close at hand, illuminating the previous statements in the chapter on repayment according to works.

An Aside on Romans 2:14–15

A summary of the entire structure of 2:6–12 will help us establish the context for a study of verses 14 and 15. Verse 6 serves as the thesis statement that God will repay each person according to works. Verses 7–10 explain this thesis through a chiasmus, showing that those who do good will receive eternal life (vv. 7, 10), while those who do evil will experience wrath and tribulation (vv. 8–9). Verse 11 grounds verses 6–10 (γάρ), explaining that since God is impartial he repays each person according to works (whether one is a Jew or a Gentile). The "for" (γάρ) in verse 12 supports the assertion of God's impartiality in verse 11.[42] Paul is saying that since God is impartial (v. 11) it follows (v. 12) that all those who sin without the law (Gentiles) will perish without the law, and all those who sin with the law (Jews) will be judged with the law (v. 12). God fairly judges each group according to the standard they possess. Verses 13–16 are tied to verse 12 and will be explained below.

I labeled the interpretation of Romans 2:14–15 "an aside" because it does not support (at least in my interpretation) the idea that some believers will be justified by works. Nonetheless, these verses need to be investigated since some interpreters, as noted previously, use them to demonstrate that unbelievers are under consideration throughout chapter 2. On the other hand, other scholars employ these same verses to say that Gentile Christians are in view. Neither conclusion persuades me. Contrary to the latter group, Gentile Christians are *not* described in verses 14–15. And contrary to the former, this does not prove that those described in verses 7, 10, and 26–29 are unbelievers.

In examining verses 12–16 it should be said at the outset that there is no intention here to fully exegete the text. I am only interested in ascertaining whether Paul is speaking of Gentile Christians in verses 14–15. I do not believe these verses speak of Gentile Christians. Paul describes unbelieving Gentiles who occasionally observe the law. This occasional obedience of the law does not merit justification but will result in judgment.

---

42. On the importance of God's impartiality in Romans see Bassler, *Divine Impartiality*, 121–70.

Verse 12 ("for as many as have sinned without the law shall also perish without the law, and as many as have sinned under the realm of the law, shall be judged through the law") restates the assertion that God will judge all people according to their works (see v. 6). The new feature introduced here is the law. Is the possession of the law any advantage to the Jew? Only if it is kept. He supports this statement in verse 13 (showing that his real concern in verse 12 is the situation of the Jew), saying "for it is not those who hear the law who are justified before God, but the doers of the law shall be justified." By stating that one who does the law will be justified, verse 13, like verses 6, 7, and 10, teaches that eternal life will be given on the basis of good works.

It is unlikely in this context, however, that Paul refers to Gentile Christians who are justified by their works. Verses 14–15 state, "For whenever Gentiles who do not have the law do by nature the things of the law, these not having the law are a law to themselves, who show forth the work of the law written on their hearts; their conscience bearing witness also and their thoughts alternately accuse or even defend them." Some scholars, contrary to my view, understanding the "for" (γάρ) in 2:14 to connect with 2:13b.[43] They claim the doers of the law in verse 13b are the Gentiles of verse 14. Such a connection between verses 13–14 is attractive in many ways but it seems more probable that the connection between verses 13–14 is found in connecting the main proposition of verse 14 to verse 13. The independent clause contains the central proposition of verse 14. It may be paraphrased: "These Gentiles, even though they do not have the Mosaic law, are a law to themselves." Paul wants to prove here that the Jews should not consider their possession of the Mosaic law as a sign of salvation; even the Gentiles who do not have the Mosaic law have "heard" the law. The Jews do not consider awareness of the law's moral norms sufficient for the Gentiles' salvation. Verses 13–14, then, do not emphasize that Gentiles *do* the law, and thus are justified. These verses show that the Gentiles, like the Jews, *have heard the law* in that it is written on their hearts, but such hearing of the law does not ensure justification.[44]

Paul does teach that one must do good works to be justified, but he does not bring up Gentiles in verses 14–15 to defend that thesis. Rather, in verses 14–15 he shows the Jews that the hearing of the law brings them no special favor in God's sight, for unbelieving Gentiles also, in a

43. So Mundle, "Auslegung von Röm 2,13ff," 251; Cranfield, *Romans*, 155; König, "Gentile Christians?" 56.
44. For a similar understanding of the connection between verses 13–14 see F. Godet, *Commentary on the Epistle to the Romans* (1889; reprint, Grand Rapids: Zondervan, 1956), 123.

sense, have heard the requirements of the law, without actually possessing it. Such hearing of the law does not guarantee justification.

The interpretation I have proposed for the relationship between verses 14–15 fits with my explanation of the connection between verses 12 and 13. In these verses Paul's main point is that the Jews' possession of the law grants them no advantage; it is not hearing the law but doing it that justifies. Paul's main purpose in bringing up the Gentiles' knowledge of the law in verses 12–16, then, demonstrates to the Jews that the possession of the law imparts to them no salvific advantage.

One could argue further against my interpretation by noting that in verse 14 the law's witness among Gentiles is confirmed by their *doing* (ποιῶσιν, *poiōsin*) of the law, and doing the law testifies that these Gentiles are Christians. Moreover, Paul's appeal to "the work of the law written in their hearts" (v. 15) alludes to Jeremiah 31:33 (38:33 LXX), confirming that these are Gentile Christians who are the recipients of new covenant blessing.[45]

Despite the strength of these arguments, two pieces of evidence weigh against the Gentile Christian interpretation. First, Paul does not seem to allude to the new covenant promise of Jeremiah 31:31–34. Jeremiah speaks of the law being written on the heart, while here Paul speaks of the "work of the law" (τὸ ἔργον τοῦ νόμου, *to ergon tou nomou*) written on the heart. That this "work of the law" (v. 15) is not the same as the new covenant promise of having God's law on one's heart seems to be confirmed by verse 14, which says Gentiles who do not have the law "are a law to themselves" (ἑαυτοῖς εἰσιν νόμος, *heautois eisin nomos*). To say that the Gentiles are a law to themselves would be an odd way to describe God's law written on the heart, but it fits nicely with the Greek conception of an unwritten law embedded on every person's heart.[46]

Second, verse 15b adds evidence against the Gentile Christian interpretation, for the work of the law in their hearts does not necessarily lead to salvation; rather it leads to accusing thoughts (τῶν λογισμῶν

45. For example, Cranfield, *Romans*, 158–59; König, "Gentile Christians?" 59–60; Souček, "Exegese von Röm 2,14ff," 102–3; Mundle, "Auslegung von Röm 2,13ff," 251.

46. So Kuhr, "Römer 2.14f," 259–60; Bornkamm, "Gesetz und Natur," 104–7; Ernst Käsemann, *Commentary on Romans* (Grand Rapids: Eerdmans, 1980), 64; Dunn, *Romans*, 100. If this interpretation is accepted, then Paul describes Gentiles who "do the law by nature" (φύσει τὰ τοῦ νόμου ποιῶσιν). In support of φύσει being linked with the verb ποιῶσιν see Dunn, *Romans*, 98; Moo, *Romans 1–8*, 146. On the other hand, König ("Gentile Christians?" 58) and Cranfield (*Romans*, 156–57) link φύσει to the participle ἔχοντα. If Paul means "doing the law by nature," as we suggest, he is not likely referring to Gentile Christians. So Kuhr, "Römer 2.14f," 255–56; Kuss, "Werke des Gesetzes," 90–91; Bornkamm, "Gesetz und Natur," 109, 111; contra Mundle, "Auslegung von Röm 2,13ff," 252; Flückiger, "Werke des Gesetzes," 29–33; Souček, "Exegese von Röm 2,14ff," 106–9.

κατηγορούντων, *tōn logismōn katēgorountōn*) on the day of judgment.[47] Such accusing thoughts indicate that the doing of the law described in verses 14–15 is not a saving obedience, but an occasional obedience to the law. Such occasional obedience explains why at times their conscience[48] defends their actions, though it usually condemns them.[49]

I conclude, then, that Paul does not refer to Gentile Christians in Romans 2:14–15. Instead, he describes non-Christian Gentiles who have written on their hearts the moral norms of the law. Occasionally they obey these moral norms, but usually they fail to keep the law, so their consciences will accuse them on the eschatological judgment day. Paul's main purpose in Romans 2:12–16 is to convince the Jews that their possession of the law avails them nothing for salvation. After all, Gentiles also are aware of the moral norms of the law and on occasion keep them, but that does not spare them from God's judgment. Obedience, not possession of the law, is necessary for justification.

Romans 2:26–29: Gentile Christians

The above excursus on Romans 2:14–15 prepares us for Romans 2:26–29. If the Gentiles described in verses 14–15 are unbelievers headed for eschatological judgment, does it follow that those described in verses 26–29 are unbelievers? I have argued throughout that verses 26–29 bring believing Gentiles into view in verses 7, 10, and 26–29. A brief summary of the flow of thought and the context should be provided before I defend this interpretation. In 2:17–24 Paul argues that the Jewish possession of, and pride in, the law are worthless without obedience. Jewish proclamation of the law without a corresponding submission to it only causes the Gentiles to revile God.

In verse 25 Paul anticipates a Jewish objection. God favors the Jews, not only in giving them the law, but also in confirming their elect status by circumcision. Thus, circumcision could be interpreted as a sign of protection from God's wrath.[50] Paul replies with the same logic as in verses 17–24. In verse 25 he declares: "For circumcision profits if you

---

47. Whether verse 16 is a gloss, and how it relates to verse 15 is debated. I accept the verse as authentic and understand the present tense of κρίνει to signify a future judgment in continuity with the present. For such a view see Dunn, *Romans*, 102–3; also Cranfield, *Romans*, 163–64, and Käsemann, *Romans*, 66–68. Bornkamm ("Gesetz und Natur," 107) sees verse 16 as a gloss. For the contrary view see Walker, "Die Heiden und das Gericht," 313–14.

48. Literature on the conscience in Paul is enormous. For an older bibliography see Kuss, "Werke des Gesetzes," 91–92 n. 46; idem, *Römerbrief*, 1.76–82. For bibliographies which include more recent work see Dunn, *Romans*, 93–94; Schmithals, *Römerbrief*, 93.

49. So Godet, *Romans*, 123; Dunn, *Romans*, 102; Moo, *Romans 1–8*, 149–50.

50. So Cranfield, *Romans*, 171; see Anders Nygren, *Commentary on Romans* (Philadelphia: Fortress, 1949), 132; Barrett, *Romans*, 58.

keep the law, but if you are a transgressor of the law, your circumcision has become uncircumcision." Circumcision only profits one who obeys the law. The Jew who does not obey the law has become uncircumcised in God's sight, and he is no longer considered a member of the covenant.

Conversely, verse 26 says "If then the uncircumcised person keeps the ordinances of the law, shall not his uncircumcision be reckoned as circumcision?" God considers the uncircumcised Gentile who obeys the law to be circumcised—a member of the people of God. Moreover, the one who is physically uncircumcised but keeps the law will judge the Jew who transgresses the law while possessing its covenantal privileges (v. 27).[51] Circumcision and Jewishness do not avail before God, for he is not impressed with physical descent or outward signs. "For the true Jew is not one outwardly, neither is true circumcision outward in the flesh, but the true Jew is one in secret, and true circumcision is of the heart, by the Spirit not the letter, whose praise shall not be from people but from God" (vv. 28–29). True Jewishness and circumcision are matters of the heart and are due to the work of the Spirit. God will reward those who are so transformed.

Much evidence in verses 26–27 suggests that Paul considers Gentile Christians. First, verse 26 says that the uncircumcised "keeps the ordinances of the law" (τὰ δικαιώματα τοῦ νόμου φυλάσσῃ, *ta dikaiōmata tou nomou phylassē*). This corresponds to Romans 8:4, which refers to "the ordinance of the law" (τὸ δικαίωμα τοῦ νόμου, *to dikaiōma tou nomou*) being fulfilled in believers who walk by the Spirit. The difference between the plural and singular of "ordinance" (δικαίωμα, *dikaiōma*) is not a material one;[52] in both texts Paul describes believers as observing what the law enjoins.

Second, verse 26b confirms that Paul focuses upon believers. There the uncircumcised Gentiles "are reckoned" (λογισθήσεται, *logisthēsetai*)[53] to be circumcised if they obey the law. To be reckoned as circumcised means that such Gentiles are considered to be members of the covenant since circumcision was the sign of the covenant between God and his people (see Gen. 17:9–14). Moreover, "reckon" (λογίζομαι, *logizomai*) is used twelve more times in Romans 3 and 4 (3:28; 4:3, 4, 5, 6, 8, 9, 10, 11, 22, 23, 24; see also 9:8; 2 Cor. 5:19; Gal. 3:6) of those reckoned as righteous before God. Such "reckoning" refers to one's actual status before God. Verse 26 in no way implies that such a reckoning is

---

51. Διά in verse 27 denotes attendant circumstances. So *BDF* ¶223 (3); Cranfield, *Romans,* 174; Käsemann, *Romans,* 74.

52. The focus in 8:4 is the unity of the diverse requirements of the law, while 2:26 emphasizes the diversity of the requirements. See on this point Cranfield, *Romans,* 384.

53. This word is a divine passive here. God does the reckoning.

merely hypothetical. The straightforward reading of this text suggests that Paul speaks of a genuine event.

Third, verse 27 does not support the hypothetical interpretation, for once again Paul speaks realistically of Gentiles keeping the law (τὸν νό-μον τελοῦσα, *ton nomon telousa*).[54] The reference to Gentiles judging Jews does not prove the hypothetical view, for it describes a real event in which Gentiles will function as a witness to the prosecution.[55]

Fourth, the "for" (γάρ, *gar*) introducing verses 28–29 is decisive for the Gentile Christian interpretation. The previous context has raised the question, how can Gentiles who obey the law be considered part of the people of God if they are not circumcised? Paul answers this in verses 28–29. True Jewishness and true circumcision are not outward matters. Instead, a Gentile who observes the law is considered to be a true Jew and circumcised. He is a Jew inwardly and circumcised in heart. Paul's explanation in verses 28–29 of how a Gentile can be a true Jew and be circumcised rules out any hypothetical interpretation of verses 26–27. The Gentiles are able to obey the law because God has circumcised their hearts.

Paul has moved beyond only criticizing the Jews. He now defends the possibility of such obedience among the Gentiles. Of course, the main function of this section still seeks to convict the Jews of sin. Paul's inclusion of Gentile Christians at this point in the argument does not represent a departure from his main theme. Paul focuses on Gentile obedience so the Jews would realize they have no advantage before God. They, too, must believe in order to be saved. Indeed, Romans 2 foreshadows Romans 11, where the inclusion of Gentiles is intended to provoke the Jews to jealousy and cause their repentance (11:11, 14; see also 10:19). There is no legitimacy, then, in the complaint that a reference to Gentile Christians veers away from Paul's intention to show that no one can be saved by doing the law. Paul's main point in this section is rather that no one can be saved and observe the law without the Holy Spirit. Those who have the Spirit are empowered to observe the law (8:4), but one only receives the Spirit by believing in Jesus, whom God has set forth as a propitiation for sin (3:21–26).

The primary reason we know that verses 26–27 speaks of Gentile Christians[56] is the phrase in verse 29: "by the Spirit not the letter" (ἐν

54. No significant distinctions should be drawn among the words πράσσειν (v. 25), φυλάσσειν (v. 26), and τελεῖν (v. 27).

55. So Cranfield, *Romans*, 174.

56. For a strong disagreement with this interpretation see Schmithals, *Römerbrief*, 100–1. It should also be noted that vv. 28–29 would include Jewish Christians as well, for surely Paul believed that some Jews were circumcised in heart, although his emphasis from verses 26–27 is to defend the inclusion of Gentiles into the people of God.

πνεύματι ού γράμματι, *en pneumati ou grammati*). "Spirit" (πνεῦμα, *pneuma*) is not a general reference to the spiritual reality of circumcision.[57] Paul refers, rather, to the Holy Spirit. The *letter-Spirit* antithesis elsewhere in Paul (Rom. 7:6; 2 Cor. 3:6) involves a polarity between the letter and the Holy Spirit.[58] Nothing indicates that Paul has anything different in mind in this text. Indeed, all three texts share a common theme, that mere possession of the law does not lead to obedience, but in fact, the law alone kills and produces sin (Rom. 7:5–6; 2 Cor. 3:6). These passages also explain that true fulfillment of God's will comes only through the power of the Holy Spirit. Once again we see that Paul does not say merely that no one can fulfil the law, but that those who do not have the Holy Spirit are unable to observe the law. The similar theme and wording of Romans 2, Romans 7, and 2 Corinthians 3 demonstrate that each passage contrasts the law as a letter and the work of the Holy Spirit.

Paul connects the genuineness of circumcision with the work of the Spirit in a parallel text in Philippians 3:3. "For we are the true circumcision, who worship in the Spirit of God" ('Ημεῖς γάρ ἐσμεν ἡ περιτομή, οἱ πνεύματι θεοῦ λατρεύοντες, *Hēmeis gar esmen hē peritomē hoi pneumati theou latreuontes*). In Philippians 3 Paul undoubtedly points to the work of the Holy Spirit, since he refers explicitly to the "Spirit of God" (πνεύματι θεοῦ, *pneumati theou*). The remarkable similarity between Philippians 3:3 and Romans 2:29 suggests that Paul depicts the Holy Spirit in both passages.

The antecedents in Jewish literature to the circumcision of the heart also point to the work of the Spirit.[59] In particular, Deuteronomy 30:6 looks forward to a future day when God will circumcise the hearts of his people.[60] Jeremiah reiterates the call to circumcise the heart (Jer. 4:4; compare Deut. 10:16)[61] and proclaims that the fulfillment of this com-

57. Contra M.-J. Lagrange, *Saint Paul Epître aux Romains* (Paris: Gabalda, 1950), 57; Barrett, *Romans*, 60; Paul Althaus, *Der Brief an die Römer* (Göttingen: Vandenhoeck and Ruprecht, 1978), 28.

58. For a survey of interpretation and an independent contribution on the letter-spirit dichotomy in Paul see Bernard Schneider, "The Meaning of St. Paul's Antithesis: 'The Letter and the Spirit,'" *CBQ* 15 (1953): 163–207.

59. For a survey of such antecedents see Stanislaus Lyonnet, "La circoncision du coeur, celle qui relève de l'Esprit et non de la lettre (Rom. 2:29)," in P. Bonnard, ed., *L'Evangile, hier et aujourd'hui* (Genève: Labor et Fides, 1968), 89–94; E. Schweizer, "'Der Jude im Verborgenen . . . , dessen Lob nicht von Menschen, sondern von Gott kommt' (Zu Röm 2, 28f und Mt 6, 1–18)," in J. Gnilka, ed., *Neues Testament und Kirche: Festschrift für R. Schnackenburg* (Freiburg: Herder, 1974), 118–19, 121–22.

60. Lev. 26:41 also looks ahead to a day when God would restore his people if they will humble their uncircumcised hearts.

61. That Jeremiah's teaching on the circumcision of the heart has its roots in Deuteronomy is defended by M. Weinfeld, "Jeremiah and the Spiritual Metamorphosis of Israel," *ZAW* 88 (1976): 34.

mand will be possible only when God writes his law on the heart in a new covenant (Jer. 31:31–34).[62] Ezekiel says that obedience will only be possible when God takes out the heart of stone and replaces it with the his Spirit (Ezek. 11:19–20; 36:26–27). The pseudepigraphical book *Jubilees* combines the themes of Jeremiah and Ezekiel, linking circumcision of the heart with the gift of the Holy Spirit (1:23). "But after this they shall return to me in all uprightness and with all of their heart and soul. And I shall cut off the foreskin of their heart and the foreskin of the heart of their descendants. And I shall create for them a holy spirit, and I shall purify them so that they will not turn away from following me and to all my commandments."[63] It is notable that the author of Jubilees cites Moses, who expects such a work of the Spirit in the future. Paul, like the author of *Jubilees* (or possibly with the book in mind) also saw the Old Testament passages of a circumcised heart as having eschatological fulfillment, but Paul saw these promises fulfilled in the gift of the Spirit to the new community.[64]

The parallels among Pauline texts and the Jewish antecedents to Romans 2:29 attest that Paul identifies the work of the Spirit here. Therefore, three implications should be pointed out: First, since Paul speak of the new covenant work of the Spirit, he thinks of genuine obedience, not hypothetical obedience. The new covenant promise involves obedience to God's law (see Jer. 31:31–34; Ezek. 36:26–27), not by human strength but by the renewing and transforming power of the Holy Spirit. Second, the Jewish antecedents point to a new age of the Spirit, in which hearts will be circumcised and God obeyed. According to Paul, this gift of the Spirit signals the new age. Thus, in verses 26–27 Paul probably specifies Gentile Christians who obey the law. He may have thought that a few Gentiles obeyed the law in the old era, but he emphasizes the domination of sin in the old age. Third, the obedience described in Romans 2:26–27 is rooted in, and dependent upon, the work of the Spirit, who has circumcised the heart (Rom. 2:28–29). The relationship between verses 26–27 and verses 28–29 (in which vv. 28–29 support vv. 26–27) clearly implies that the Spirit's work on the heart logically precedes the keeping of the law by the Gentiles. Paul does not

---

62. See J. A. Thompson, *The Book of Jeremiah* (Grand Rapids: Eerdmans, 1980), 216; Weinfeld, "Jeremiah," 34; H. S. Gehman, "An Insight and Realization: A Study of the New Covenant," *Int* 9 (1955): 284.

63. Translation of O. S. Wintermute in J. H. Charlesworth, ed., *The Old Testament Psuedepigrapha*, Vol. 2 (Garden City, N.J.: Doubleday, 1985).

64. For the idea that Paul had in mind the inbreaking of the new age in Rom. 2:28–29 see Käsemann, *Romans*, 74; Oscar Cullmann, *Salvation in History* (New York: Harper and Row, 1967), 261; Herman N. Ridderbos, *Paul: An Outline of His Theology* (Grand Rapids: Eerdmans, 1975), 334–35.

conceive of meriting salvation by keeping the law. The observance of the law signifies the work of the Spirit, the fruit of his power in one's life (see Gal. 5:22–23). Such a conception harmonizes with Jeremiah 31:31–34 and Ezekiel 36:26–27, where God's work logically precedes the keeping of the law.

The connection between keeping the law and obtaining a reward should also be noted. Romans 2:29 says that those who are true Jews and have experienced a circumcised heart will receive "praise" from God.[65] The *praise* (ἔπαινος, *epainos*) here is an eschatological reward from God (compare 1 Cor. 4:5; 1 Peter 1:7),[66] which Paul uses as a synonym for eternal life. Verse 26 infers that the reward is eternal life. There the uncircumcised person who keeps the law "is reckoned" as circumcised. I have already pointed out that to be reckoned as circumcised signifies inclusion in the covenant people. Verses 28–29 suggest the same thought: those who keep the law demonstrate that they are true Jews and truly circumcised. The praise which comes from God (v. 29), therefore, is God's acknowledgment of his people on the last day. The true Jews and the true circumcision may be hidden from the eyes of many until the last day, but then God will unveil those who are truly his own.

Verse 29's connection with 2:6–10 should also be highlighted. In verses 26–29 Paul says that those who keep the law have received a circumcision of the heart by the Spirit. And those who keep the law will receive an eschatological reward (ἔπαινος, *epainos*) on the day of judgment. The promise of eschatological reward for those who have obeyed the law is also found in verses 6–10, for there Paul says that those who do good works will receive eternal life. The reception of eternal life (vv. 6–10) describes the eschatological reward that God's people will receive (v. 29).

In Romans 2, verses 6–10 speak of doing good works to obtain eternal life, verses 26–29 of keeping the law to obtain an eschatological reward as a member of the covenant people, and verse 13 of justification through keeping the law. I conclude that those who observe the law are doing good works, which are necessary for justification and eternal life.

Conclusion: Objections and Responses

A possible objection to my overall interpretation is that it is too complicated. Christians are in view in 2:7, 10, and 26–29, but unbelieving

---

65. It is probable that ἔπαινος introduces a play on words here since there is a connection between *Judah* (יהודה) and *praise* (הודה) in Hebrew. So Cranfield, *Romans*, 175; Dunn, *Romans*, 123. Against this view see Käsemann, *Romans*, 77.

66. So Cranfield, *Romans*, 175–76; Käsemann, *Romans*, 77; Wilckens, *Römer*, 1:158.

Gentiles who will be condemned are described in 2:14–15. Such shift-
ing back and forth might show that either my exegesis or Paul's thought
is tortuous. I would respond that throughout my exegesis I sustain the
main thesis of Romans 2—that the Jews will escape judgment only if
they keep the law. Moreover, Paul argues that both Jews and Gentiles
who do not possess the Spirit are unable to keep the law, while Gentiles who have been transformed by the Spirit are empowered to
observe the law.

The three sections we have examined in this chapter advance this
same thesis in different ways. First, Romans 2:6–11 stresses God's
impartiality in judging according to works. In accord with the typical
Jewish view, Paul believes that some will be rewarded for good works,
and sinners who do evil will be judged. Here Paul uses the theme of
God's impartiality in judgment to counter any claim of Jewish privilege.
Any person who perseveres in doing good will receive eternal life,
whereas all who do evil, whether Jew or Gentile, will experience eschatological wrath.

Second, in Romans 2:12–16 Paul addresses a possible objection from
the Jews. Does not the possession of the Mosaic law show that God is
partial, that he favors the Jews? Paul argues that merely having the law
avails nothing. What counts is obeying it. Even unbelieving Gentiles are
conscious of moral norms, which they occasionally obey, but occasional
obedience will not spare them from eschatological judgment. Neither
will Jews who fail to keep the law escape God's wrath.

Third, in verses 25–29 Paul contends that circumcision does not warrant special favor for the Jews and is of no value apart from obedience to
the law. Indeed, the Old Testament rite of circumcision finds its true significance in the circumcision of the heart, which Christians, both Jew
and Gentile, experience through the work of the Holy Spirit. By stressing the inclusion of the Gentiles and the failure of the Jews to obey the
law, Paul implies that the Jews will never be able to obey the law as long
as they are separate from the Christian community. The work of the
Spirit among the Gentiles will, Paul hopes, provoke the Jews to jealousy
(Rom. 11:11, 14) and cause them to embrace his gospel. To sum up: Paul
answers possible Jewish objections in different ways, and in the course
of his argument shows that works are necessary for salvation and that
evil will be punished.

Finally, we must deal with the question of whether Paul's insistence
that people are justified by works contradicts his statement in Romans
3:20 that no one can be justified by doing the works of law. At first blush
there is a contradiction here, but it seems improbable that Paul would
embrace justification by works in one chapter and then deny it in the

next. Paul likely addresses two different situations in the two chapters. When he says that no one can be justified by works of law, he addresses those who think they can enter the new community by their obedience to the law. He tells them that perfect obedience is necessary to enter the kingdom. And since, according to Paul, perfect obedience is impossible ("All have sinned and are falling short of the glory of God" [Rom. 3:23]), sinners fool themselves by believing that they can put God in their debt by doing good works.[67]

The emphasis in 2:29 on the circumcision of the heart by the power of the Holy Spirit confirms this idea. Paul does not believe that Gentiles can obey the law sufficiently to be saved either. Before the law can be obeyed by anyone, Jew or Gentile, the Holy Spirit must enter the heart. Paul also teaches, however, that no one receives the Spirit simply by doing what the law demands (see Gal. 3:1–5). The Spirit is received by faith and is the mark that one belongs to the Christian church (Rom. 8:9). If the Spirit is received by faith *before* the law is obeyed, and if the presence of the Spirit identifies one as a believer, then it follows that no one enters the Christian church on the basis of good works. God gives his Spirit freely and graciously to all who put their faith in Jesus Christ. No one can be righteous before God by works of the law since no one can obey the law perfectly (Gal. 3:10). My point is that 2:29 clearly implies that the Spirit was given first and then the law was obeyed by Gentiles. Before Gentiles possessed the Spirit, they failed to keep the law. Thus, even in Romans 2 there is no conception of entering the kingdom (earning salvation) by obeying the law.[68]

On the other hand, even though Paul asserts that no one can attain salvation by good works, he also insists that no one can be saved without them, and that they are necessary to obtain an eschatological inheritance. The Spirit's work in a person produces obedience to the law (Rom. 2:26–29). The saving work of Jesus Christ radically changes people so that they can now obey the law they previously disobeyed (see Rom. 8:1–4). The works that are necessary for salvation, therefore, *do not constitute an earning of salvation but are evidence of a salvation already given.*[69] The transforming work of the Spirit accompanies and cannot be

---

67. For a defense of this interpretation on works of law see my "'Works of Law' in Paul," *NovT* 33 (1991): 217–44.

68. Laato (*Paulus und das Judentum*, 197–204) explains this point clearly and shows that Paul differs from Judaism here because the latter conceived of works as the contribution a person makes by exercising his or her free will. In Paul faith is a gift, and God produces all good works in believers.

69. C. F. D. Moule ("Jesus, Judaism, and Paul," in G. F. Hawthorne and Otto Betz, eds., *Tradition and Interpretation in the New Testament: Essays in Honor of E. Earle Ellis* [Grand Rapids: Eerdmans, 1987], 49) contrasts Paul's view with that of Palestinian Judaism, for in the latter good works are "the means of 'staying in'," while for Paul "they are a symptom of 'staying in.'"

separated from,[70] the justifying work of God.[71] Such good works manifest the work of the Holy Spirit in the believer's life. We should also
stress that Paul is not demanding perfect obedience, but obedience that
is significant, substantial, and observable. Even though the Spirit has
been given, Paul's theology still contains a "not yet." The day of full
redemption is still in the future (Rom. 8:10, 23). Thus, there is some
ambiguity in the Christian communities. Some who appear to be believers will be shown not to have received the saving gift of righteousness.
They will fail to pass the test on the last day, for their works will be lacking. Such a failure will prove that they were never truly part of the new
community.[72]

70. So Peter Stuhlmacher, *Gerechtigkeit Gottes bei Paulus*, 2d ed. (Göttingen: Vandenhoeck
and Ruprecht, 1966), 228–31. Stuhlmacher rightly rejects the theory of double justification,
which seems to suggest two different ways of salvation. For such a theory see Godet, *Romans*,
118; Joachim Jeremias, "Paul and James," *ExpT* 66 (1954–1955): 370. I am not saying that righteousness in Paul is a transformative gift. My point is that even if righteousness in Paul is only
forensic, salvation in Paul consists of more than this.
    71. So Sam K. Williams, "Justification and the Spirit in Galatians," *JSNT* 29 (1987): 91–100.
    72. For such a view see the recent study by Gundry Volf, *Paul and Perseverance*.

8

Soundings from the Rest of the New Testament

How does Paul's theology of law compare with what other New Testament writers have to say on the subject? Of course, the theology of the law in the rest of the New Testament provokes significant debate, and in one chapter I can hardly do justice to the exegetical issues, let alone the vast secondary literature available on these texts. "*Soundings* from the Rest of the New Testament" implies that a full and adequate analysis of the relevant texts cannot be undertaken here. Despite these obstacles, it will nonetheless be instructive to compare Paul's view of the law with that of other New Testament writers, particularly to see if other writers confirm some of the conclusions I have drawn from Paul's writings.[1]

Naturally, other New Testament authors have various emphases and concerns that differ from Paul's. I am not attempting to investigate here the distinctive contribution of each New Testament author regarding the law. Rather, this chapter seeks to discern how these authors correspond to the Pauline theology of law. A full-fledged study of each author in his own right would be methodologically preferable, but this would be the subject of quite a few other books. The approach of this chapter also will

---

1. For an attempt to discern precursors to the Pauline view after the death and resurrection of Jesus see Martin Hengel, *Between Jesus and Paul: Studies in the Earliest History of Christianity* (Philadelphia: Fortress, 1983), 1–29, 54–58. Interestingly, Hengel thinks (56) that the Hellenists "questioned the cultic and ritual parts of the law, but not its ethical side."

be quite eclectic; sometimes investigating a particular motif found in several authors and at other points examining the contribution of a particular author.

Faith and Works

Perhaps we should begin with the issue explored in chapter 7. Do other New Testament authors discuss whether works are necessary for justification? Immediately the famous verses in James 2:14–26 come to mind. James teaches that faith without works is "dead" and "useless" (2:17, 20, 26), and that a person "is justified by works and not by faith only" (2:24; see 2:21, 25).[2] Now if my conclusions about Paul in the preceding chapter are correct, then they go a long way in resolving the apparent contradiction between the teaching of Paul and James, for I argued that Paul thought that works are necessary for justification as well. It is simply false to conclude that Paul thought people would be justified if they did not do good works. Nevertheless, Paul and James still seem to contradict each other because James asserts that justification is "not by faith only" (2:24), while Paul says a person "is justified by faith apart from the works of the law" (Rom. 3:28).

The apparent contradiction is only verbal, however, because James and Paul use the word *faith* in different ways. James criticizes a faith that verbally subscribes to certain teachings but lacks heart-transforming reliance upon, or delight in, God.[3] James chastises faith that is only intellectual (v.19): "You believe that God is one, you do well. The demons also believe and tremble." Intellectual affirmation of central doctrines is not saving faith, for saving faith involves the transformation of the heart so that those who believe will, for example, help the poor when they are in need (2:15–16).[4] Paul's understanding of saving faith is actually remarkably similar. The faith that saved Abraham was not merely verbal assent to the doctrine that God was faithful. Abraham's

2. For an example of the view that sees James and Paul as contradictory see Martin Hengel, "Der Jakobusbrief als antipaulinische Polemik," in G. F. Hawthorne and Otto Betz, eds., *Tradition and Interpretation in the New Testament: Essays in Honour of E. Earle Ellis* (Grand Rapids: Eerdmans, 1987), 248–65. For a stronger solution to this text see Ralph P. Martin, *James* (Waco: Word, 1988), 75–101.

3. Peter H. Davids (*The Epistle of James* [Grand Rapids: Eerdmans, 1982], 50–51) also argues that James uses the word "faith" with a different meaning from Paul. His claim that the words "works" and "justify" also bear a different meaning is not as convincing. For further discussion on James 2:14–26 see, for example, C. Burchard, "Zu Jakobus 2,14–26," *ZNW* 71 (1980): 27–45; Joachim Jeremias, "Paul and James," *ExpT* 66 (1954–1955): 368–71.

4. Contra Earl D. Radmacher ("Faith according to the Apostle James by John F. MacArthur, Jr.," *JETS* 33 [1990]: 39–40) who argues that James is not referring to *saving* faith at all, but faith that is necessary to preserve one's life and inherit a reward beyond salvation.

assurance of God's faithfulness to his promises led him to stake his whole life on God's promises, even though reality seemingly contradicted those promises (Rom. 4:19, 21). In addition, both Paul and James understand saving faith to be the result of God's previous work in one's life, for James traces the beginning of Christian existence to God's gracious will (James 1:18; compare Rom. 8:28–39).

Other New Testament writers do not explicitly say that works are necessary for justification. But these writers display a remarkable unanimity in the belief that works are necessary to avert God's wrath on the day of judgment. I will cite just a few representative verses from various New Testament documents to support this statement. First John says, "By this we know that we have come to know him, if we keep his commandments. The one who says, 'I have come to know him,' and does not keep his commandments is a liar, and the truth is not in him" (1 John 2:3–4). When John speaks of "coming to know him," he refers to those who claim to be members of the church because of their knowledge of God. But he clearly says that those who do not keep God's commandments are not really Christians at all. They reveal their true allegiance by their disobedience. This is a major theme throughout the first letter of John (see also 1 John 1:6; 2:9; 4:20; 5:2).

Second Peter asserts that believers "confirm their calling and election" (1:10) by practicing the character qualities in 1:5–7. These good works do not constitute an earning of salvation, but good works confirm that one really belongs to the elect community. Those who turn back to "the corruptions of the world" (2:20) and do not follow Jesus Christ to the end will not experience salvation but judgment (2:20–22). Similarly, the author of Hebrews exhorts believers not to apostatize from the faith, for those who fall away will receive worse punishment than those who sinned under the covenant made with Moses (2:1–4; 5:11–6:8; 10:26–31; 12:25–29). Some scholars claim that the author of Hebrews merely speaks of losing rewards or some other temporal punishment. This exegesis, however, reflects special pleading.[5] The author of Hebrews insists that those who experience eternal life will persevere in the faith until the end (see 3:14).

The author of Revelation drives home the same point. Those who "overcome" will experience the life of the age to come (2:7, 11, 17, 26; 3:5, 12, 21). But those who submit to the will of the beast will experience

---

5. For an example of this exegesis see Zane C. Hodges, *Absolutely Free* (Grand Rapids: Zondervan, 1989), 82–83. For the view that the author of Hebrews is speaking of final judgment in his warnings see Philip E. Hughes, *A Commentary on the Epistle to the Hebrews* (Grand Rapids: Eerdmans, 1977), 215–18; F. F. Bruce, *The Epistle to the Hebrews* (Grand Rapids: Eerdmans, 1964), 258–59; Donald A. Hagner, *Hebrews* (New York: Harper and Row, 1983), 72–73.

"the wrath of God" (14:10), and eternal punishment (14:11). Therefore, believers are called to "endurance" and the "keeping of God's commandments" (14:12). A prior profession of faith will not save those who apostatize. Only those who persist despite persecution will experience eternal life.

Matthew also stresses that only those who live a life of righteousness will enter the kingdom of heaven.[6] Only those whose righteousness exceeds that of the scribes and Pharisees will enter the kingdom (5:20). Anger (5:21–22) and lust (5:27–30) put one in danger of future judgment. Entrance into the kingdom of heaven is not gained by saying "Lord, Lord" (7:21), or by prophesying, casting out demons, and performing miracles (7:22). Only those "who do the will of my Father in heaven" (7:21) will enter the kingdom. "Those who practice lawlessness" (7:23) will be commanded to depart from Jesus. "The one who endures to the end will be saved" (24:13).

Luke emphasizes the need for perseverance and obedience. True discipleship involves total commitment to Jesus (9:57–62; 14:25–33). The rich ruler cannot be saved and enter the kingdom unless he is willing to give up all that he has (18:18–30). A proper use of possessions indicates whether one belongs to the kingdom of God (see 16:1–31).

This all too brief sketch of New Testament writers reveals that they considered obedience and good works essential for entrance into the kingdom. In fact, other New Testament writers stress this point even more than Paul. Do these other New Testament authors, however, share Paul's belief that entrance into the kingdom is not earned by good works? A more in-depth analysis of this issue is needed, but there are indications that other authors agree with Paul on this question as well.

Legalism and Inability to Obey the Law

We have already indicated that James' statements on faith and works do not contradict the Pauline formulation. Here I shall briefly examine the contributions of John, Luke, and Matthew. Perhaps one reason the community in 1 John struggled with antinomianism is that the Gospel of John strongly emphasizes that eternal life is based on belief.[7] John

---

6. It is almost universally accepted that Matthew uses the word *righteousness* in an ethical sense. See Benno Przybylski, *Righteousness in Matthew and His World of Thought* (Cambridge: Cambridge University Press, 1980).

7. I am assuming that both the gospel of John and 1 John were written by the same author. For the view that they were written by different authors see Raymond E. Brown, *The Epistles of John* (Garden City, N.J.: Doubleday, 1982), 19–30. In defense of common authorship see D. A. Carson, Douglas J. Moo, and Leon Morris, *An Introduction to the New Testament* (Grand Rapids: Zondervan, 1992), 445–50.

uses the verb *believe* (πιστεύω, *pisteuō*)) ninety-eight times in the Gospel.[8] Thereby John underscores that entrance into the church is not predicated on doing but believing. The fundamental "work" for people is to "believe in him [Jesus] whom he [God] has sent" (6:29). Faith means that one comes to Jesus for the satisfaction of one's hunger and thirst because he is "the bread of life" (6:35). Of course, John warns that not all belief is genuine (2:23–25; 8:31–59). False belief manifests its true colors by doing the works of the devil (John 8:41). Nonetheless, the root problem is failure to put one's faith in Jesus and come to him for life (8:42, 45). Those who believe in the Son (John 3:18) come to the light because their works have been performed "in God" (3:21). John, like Paul, viewed *unbelief* as the fundamental issue in a person's relationship to God. Genuine belief produces good works, while unbelief and hatred of the light result in evil works.

The Lukan and Matthean emphasis on obedience may lead one to think that good works are necessary to merit entrance into the kingdom. Other texts in these Gospels, however, divulge that the performance of works does not constitute a claim on God and that entrance into the kingdom is still by grace. The clearest indication of this grace in Luke is the parable of the Pharisee and tax collector. The tax collector is "justified" in God's sight (18:14), even though his life is characterized by evil (18:11). He has no works with which to impress God; all he can do is plead to God for mercy (18:13). Entrance into the kingdom is not based on working for God, but on the recognition that nothing one does can earn God's favor. Being right with God is dependent on his mercy, not human works.[9] The story of the prodigal son sounds a similar theme (15:11–32). Here, the father graciously welcomes the repentant son into his house, despite the evil the son has done. Another notable example is the thief on the cross (23:40–43). The thief's life was characterized by evil, but his repentance and faith in Jesus on the cross assured him a place in paradise.

The theme of God's grace is also present in Matthew in the faith of the centurion (8:10), the calling of tax collectors and sinners (9:9–13), and the recognition that the poor in Spirit possess the kingdom of heaven (5:3).[10] Matthew and Luke highlight good works. Indeed, as we have seen, they emphasize such works as crucial. That emphasis, however,

---

8. According to Leon Morris, *The Gospel According to John* (Grand Rapids: Eerdmans, 1971), 335.

9. See Joachim Jeremias, *The Parables of Jesus*, rev. ed. (New York: Scribner's, 1972), 139–44.

10. For more detailed evidence of a theology of grace in Matthew, and the claim that the difference between Matthew and Paul is one of emphasis see Roger Mohrlang, *Matthew and Paul: A Comparison of Ethical Perspectives* (Cambridge: Cambridge University Press, 1984), 78–81, 91–92.

must be maintained alongside an equal emphasis on the grace of God in Matthean and Lukan theology. Their approach to this matter differs from Paul's in that they place the accent on the behavior necessary for entrance into the kingdom. Yet this shows no ultimate difference in theology; Matthew and Luke maintain that saving faith inevitably leads to a radical change of life, to utter commitment to Jesus. If such a change is lacking, it calls into question the reality of one's faith.

Do other New Testament documents support the contention that Jewish legalism troubled the church? While a full investigation of this issue lies outside the scope of this book, a few texts will sample the evidence. The parable of the Pharisee and tax collector (Luke 18:9–14) seems to show one such response.[11] The parable was effective precisely because Pharisees were respected and honored by the people during the time of Jesus. The Pharisees were the object of Jesus' critique not because they were the most notorious hypocrites of Jesus' day but because they were the highest example of religious piety.[12] If Pharisees fell short of God's requirements, then it followed that all others did so.[13] The Pharisee in the parable represents a self-righteous person (v. 9) who bases his righteousness on his own goodness,[14] for he fasts twice a week and gives a tithe of all his possessions (v. 12). That the root problem in his life was pride in his good works is supported by verse 14. Luke informs the reader that "everyone who exalts himself will be humbled." Indeed, verse 14 even uses the verb *justify* (δεδικαιωμένος, *dedikaiōmenos*). The tax collector who humbled himself before God was "justified." The Pharisee was condemned because his religion was

11. For an instructive interpretation of the parable which supports the interpretation presented here see Kenneth E. Bailey, *Through Peasant Eyes: A Literary-Cultural Approach to the Parables in Luke* (Grand Rapids: Eerdmans, 1983), 142–56.

12. The literature on and debate about the Pharisees is beyond the scope of my purpose here. For the most significant recent work see Jacob Neusner, *The Rabbinic Traditions about the Pharisees before 70*, 3 vols. (Leiden: Brill, 1971). See also Martin Hengel, *The Pre-Christian Paul* (Philadelphia: Trinity, 1991), 40–53; Ellis Rivkin, *A Hidden Revolution* (Nashville: Abingdon, 1968). Neusner's views have had a great influence on NT scholarship, but for a different emphasis see E. P. Sanders, *Jewish Law from Jesus to the Mishnah* (Philadelphia: Trinity Press International, 1990), 97–254; idem, *Judaism: Practice and Belief. 63 BCE–66 CE* (Philadelphia: Trinity Press International, 1992), 380–451. For Neusner's response to Sanders see his "Mr. Sanders' Pharisees and Mine: A Response to E. P. Sanders, *Jewish Law from Jesus to the Mishnah*," *SJT* 44 (1991): 73–95. James D. G. Dunn (*Jesus, Paul, and the Law: Studies in Mark and Galatians* [Louisville: Westminster, 1990], 61–88) argues that Mark 2 and 7 accurately portray the conflict between Jesus and the Pharisees. Jesus wanted to extend the "boundaries" of purity beyond what was acceptable to the Pharisees.

13. For a balanced perspective on the Pharisees see Moisés Silva, "The Place of Historical Reconstruction in New Testament Criticism," in D. A. Carson and J. D. Woodbridge, eds., *Hermeneutics, Authority, and Canon* (Grand Rapids: Zondervan, 1986), 112–20.

14. So Joseph A. Fitzmyer, *The Gospel According to Luke*, 2 vols. (Garden City, N.J.: Doubleday, 1981, 1985), 1185.

a front for self-exaltation. I. Howard Marshall rightly comments, "Jesus' lesson is precisely that the attitude of the heart is ultimately what matters, and justification depends on the mercy of God to the penitent rather than upon works which might be thought to earn God's favour."[15]

This Lukan account does not claim that all Pharisees were legalists.[16] The inclusion of the parable, however, indicates that—at least according to Luke—some Jews were guilty of legalism and used their law observance as a means of self-adulation. Luke presumably included this account because he felt it spoke powerfully to the human tendency to justify ourselves before God on the basis of works. The reader does not expect God to justify the tax collector who has lived a blatantly immoral life. Thus, the parable exhibits God's graciousness to all who repent of their sin. It is not surprising that Joachim Jeremias concluded from this parable that "the Pauline doctrine of justification has its roots in the teaching of Jesus."[17] In any case, the problem of legalism does not merely reside in Pharisees or Jews. Joseph A. Fitzmyer remarks that "there remains in everyone more than a little of the Pharisee."[18]

Aside from Paul's Epistles, few New Testament documents specifically attack the idea that one could do good works to earn salvation. The sabbath controversies in the Gospels, however, reveal a preoccupation with minor points in the law or oral tradition (Matt. 12:1–14; Mark 2:23–3:6; Luke 6:1–11; 13:10–17; 14:1–6; John 5:1–18; 7:22–24; 9:13–17). The Gospels often portray the religious leaders in Judaism as more concerned with technicalities of law than with human need. Excessive attention to the minutiae of the law easily leads to legalism. All four Gospels record a number of sabbath controversies, showing that the early church felt that there was a significant division with the Jewish community on this issue. It seems fair to assume that the early church believed that the Jews' devotion to the fine points of the law prevented them from showing mercy to those in need.

Other controversy stories describe tensions between Jesus and the religious leaders (see Mark 2:1–22). The accounts regarding tax collectors (Mark 2:13–17) and fasting (Mark 2:18–22) show a perception of significant difference between followers of Christ and Christ's Jewish opponents. The Jewish concern with cleanness and religious observance prevented them from being part of the new work being inaugurated with

15. I. Howard Marshall, *The Gospel of Luke* (Grand Rapids: Eerdmans, 1978), 681.

16. The idea that not all Pharisees were alike is supported by rabbinic literature in the account of the seven different types of Pharisees. See Claude G. Montefiore and H. Loewe, *A Rabbinic Anthology* (New York: Schocken, 1974), 487–89.

17. Jeremias, *Parables*, 141. For some qualifications on this point see Fitzmyer, *Luke*, 1185.

18. Fitzmyer, *Luke*, 1185.

Jesus.[19] Similarly, in Mark 7:1–23 the Pharisees and scribes overlook the fundamental and abiding commandment to honor one's parents. Their oversight is rooted in an excessive devotion to traditions that actually conflict with the commands of God.

The strictures against the scribes and Pharisees in Matthew 23 (see also Luke 11:37–52) similarly reflect this tension. Matthew portrays the religious leaders as consumed with getting praise from people (vv. 1–12), making casuistic distinctions to justify breaking oaths (vv. 16–22), centering on tithing instead of justice and mercy (vv. 23–24), and focusing on what is on the outside instead of the inside (vv. 27–28). It is interesting to debate the historical accuracy of such criticisms or the extent to which they reflect the words of the historical Jesus. Such considerations are not the issue presently before us; rather, the question is whether the early church perceived Judaism as focusing on trivial legal issues. Allegiance to picayune matters of the law does not necessarily constitute legalism, but this kind of veneration is at least well down the road to it.

A passion for obedience to specific requirements is not necessarily legalistic. Some people view any call to obedience and righteousness as legalistic. The Gospel writers do not criticize the religious leaders of Judaism for their concern with keeping the law in the particular areas of everyday life. They rebuke them because relatively minor matters take on more significance than do major issues. In addition, the religious leaders demanded obedience to laws not contained in the Scriptures but in their traditions.

Even though the Gospels do seem to critique a kind of legalism, their crushing indictment is that the religious leaders do not keep the law themselves.[20] Heikki Räisänen misses the significance of this point when he argues that, apart from Paul, no evidence exists that the law could not be fulfilled.[21] On the contrary, ample evidence shows that other New Testament writers concurred with Paul that the law could not be kept sufficiently.

Matthew, for example, quotes Jesus when he insists that the righteousness of the scribes and Pharisees is not sufficient to enter the kingdom of heaven (5:20), that their sin disqualifies them. The Baptist warns the Pharisees and Sadducees that genealogical descendance from Abraham is not adequate (3:7–10). They need to produce "fruit worthy of

---

19. Dunn (*Jesus, Paul, and the Law*, 10–36) argues that these controversies are rooted in the life of the historical Jesus.

20. Silva ("Historical Reconstruction," 119–21) uses Mark 7:1–23 and Matthew 5 to support this thesis.

21. Heikki Räisänen, *Paul and the Law* (Philadelphia: Fortress, 1983), 119–20.

repentance" (v. 8). In Matthew 23 Jesus implies that their lives are unrighteous, fatally flawed because they do not practice what they preach. "Do not do according to their works. For they say what to do, and do not practice it themselves" (v. 3).[22] Jesus does not condemn their tithing of mint, dill, and cummin, but he reproves them for their lack of "mercy and faithfulness" (v. 23). To be clean on the outside is commendable (vv. 25–26). To be clean on the outside and "full of robbery and self-indulgence" on the inside (v. 25) is lamentable. Jesus here speaks of hypocritical legalism, not the inability of religious leaders to keep the law. But if the religious leaders who are most devoted to the law cannot keep it, then no one can.[23]

In Mark 7:1–23 (see also Matt. 15:1–20) the exaltation of tradition is so pernicious because it leads to the setting aside of a "commandment of God" (v. 8). Indeed, they end up "rejecting" (ἀθετεῖτε, *atheteite*, v. 9) God's commandment to honor one's father and mother and thereby "invalidate" (ἀκυροῦντες, *akyrountes*, v. 13) the word of God. Devotion to tradition leads to disobedience to God's commandment.

Similarly, some probably excused anger because it did not constitute murder (vv. 21–26). Jesus shows that anger is the root of murder. Others may have defended lustful fantasies since they were not literally adultery (vv. 27–30). Jesus counters that even lust is adulterous. Some Jews employed technicalities to justify divorce (vv. 31–32; see Matt. 19:3–12; Mark 10:2–12). Jesus contends that divorce contravenes God's will, and that divorce and remarriage constitutes adultery. The Jews invented a clever casuistry to justify their failure to keep oaths (vv. 33–37), but Jesus protests that this casuistry only hides lies and swerves from God's demand to be truthful. Old Testament texts were used to justify personal vengeance (vv. 38–42) and hating one's enemies (vv. 43–48). Jesus rebuts such exegesis, contending for the way of nonretaliation and love for enemies. Matthew is probably implying here that some Pharisees and scribes used scriptural practices to rationalize their behavior. Their righteousness fails because they did not really keep the law (vv. 20–48).

The Lukan portrait is similar. Luke 11:37–52 parallels Matthew 23, which was considered above. The same indictments against religious leaders are found. The parable of the Good Samaritan is given in response to a lawyer who "desired to justify himself" (10:29), presumably because he failed to love his neighbor. Jesus did not trim the

22. For a thorough analysis of Matthew 23 see David E. Garland, *The Intention of Matthew 23* (Leiden: Brill, 1979).

23. This does not minimize Matthew's insistence that one must be righteous to enter the kingdom of heaven. In Matthew's theology those who recognize that they are poor in spirit (5:3), and experience the power of the kingdom are enabled to keep God's commandments.

command but sharpened it, revealing the lawyer's failure to love. The Pharisees' love for money (16:13–15) caused them to mock Jesus' claim that one cannot be devoted to God and mammon. Jesus replies by analyzing their motives. Their mocking was due to self-justification because in their hearts they treasured what was abominable toward God. In Acts 6:11–14 Stephen is charged with speaking against the temple and the law. In his defense Stephen indicts his accusers for being the real law breakers. "You received the law by the ordinance of angels, but you did not keep it" (Acts 7:53).

Finally, an interesting verse in John makes the same point. In 7:19 Jesus asks the religious leaders, "Did not Moses give you the law? And not one of you practices the law. Why are you seeking to kill me?" The connection of "not one of you practices the law" with "why are you seeking to kill me?" suggests that the violation of the law is revealed in their desire to kill an innocent man (Jesus).[24] The religious leaders prided themselves on their observance of the law of Moses, but their attitude toward Jesus showed that they did not actually observe it. It should not be concluded that disobedience of the law was only a problem with the religious leaders. We shall see that Peter argues that all people fail to obey the law sufficiently (Acts 15:10–11). Such a conclusion coheres with Paul's theology.

The Continuing Validity of the Law

A comparison of Paul with other New Testament writers also raises the question of the continuing validity of the law. What function does the law have in the life of the believer according to the rest of the New Testament? Is it still in force, abolished, or is there the same emphasis we saw in Paul regarding fulfillment and abolition? Once again brief soundings will be taken of various New Testament authors to gain some insight into this issue.

The letter to the Hebrews suggests that the law of Moses is no longer in force. The author states, "For when the priesthood is changed, of necessity there takes place a change of law also" (7:12). That the priesthood of the old covenant was not intended to last forever is apparent for at least two reasons, according to the author. First, it was prophesied that another priest would arise according to the order of Melchizedek (7:11; see also Ps. 110:4). If the Aaronic priesthood were intended to last forever there would have been no prediction of a priesthood of

---

24. So C. K. Barrett, *The Gospel According to St. John*, 2d ed. (Philadelphia: Westminster, 1978), 319; Barnabas Lindars, *The Gospel of John* (Grand Rapids: Eerdmans, 1972), 289; George R. Beasley-Murray, *John* (Waco: Word, 1987), 109.

another order. Second, the prediction of a different priesthood, a Melchizedekean one, proves that the Aaronic priesthood was inferior and did not bring "perfection" (7:11). The author describes the Aaronic priesthood as weak and useless (7:18), since those priests died and could not exercise their priesthood permanently, while Jesus, by virtue of his resurrection, has a permanent priesthood (7:23–24). Thus the salvation he offers is effective. Indeed, the Aaronic priests showed the weakness of their office by having to make sacrifices for their own sins, while the Son, who was without sin and is exalted above all, needed to make only one definitive sacrifice for the sin of all (7:26–28). In addition, the sacrifice of animals could not really cleanse people from sin, for these sacrifices were brute beasts and not willing victims (9:11–13; 10:4). The need called for the sacrifice of a perfect human being who willingly offered himself (9:14; 10:5–10) and displayed further the ineffectiveness of the priesthood. The repetition of the sacrifices proved they could not really take away sins (9:25; 10:1, 11). By repeating the sacrifices the worshiper is reminded that his or her sins are not actually removed (10:2–3). The offering of Christ was far superior, because one offering removed sin forever (9:23–28; 10:11–18). The failure of the Aaronic priesthood demonstrates the superiority of the new covenant over the old (10:16).

The author of Hebrews anticipates an objection in 8:1–9:28. If the Aaronic priesthood was so defective, why did God institute it at all?[25] The answer is that it functioned as a pattern, model, or type of the heavenly priesthood and the supreme high priest who would offer the superior, definitive sacrifice. Furthermore, the Scriptures themselves predicted that there would be a new, far more effective covenant (8:7–13). Now that this new covenant has arrived, the old covenant is no longer necessary.

The author of Hebrews views the Aaronic priesthood and the old covenant as obsolete. This does not mean that the Old Testament texts no longer function as Scripture, but the texts referring to the Aaronic priesthood function as the pattern for the priesthood of Christ. The new covenant gloriously fulfils all which the old foretold. Thus, we should not be surprised that the author intertwines the change of priesthood with a change of law (7:12): "For, on the one hand, there is a setting aside of the former commandment because of its weakness and uselessness (for the law made nothing perfect), and on the other hand there is a bringing in of a better hope, through which we draw near to God" (7:18–19). If the law made nothing perfect, if a change of law has occurred, if the Aaronic

---

25. Räisänen (*Paul and the Law*, 210) thinks Hebrews does not adequately explain why the law was given at all since it was so ineffectual.

priesthood has ended, and if the new covenant has replaced the old, then the Mosaic law is, according to Hebrews, no longer in force. Clearly, believers should not live under the Mosaic covenant, which required animal sacrifices, and priests appointed from among the descendants of Aaron.

The stance of the author of Hebrews corresponds to Paul's in some respects.[26] Believers are not bound by the Mosaic covenant. The realization of the new covenant cancels many of the provisions of the Mosaic one. Paul also taught concerning the passing away of the old covenant, the termination of the Aaronic priesthood, and the fulfillment of the animal sacrifices. Only on such a basis could one explain why circumcision and food laws are no longer valid. In addition, as we pointed out, Paul's claim that Christ's sacrifice atones for sin presupposes that animal sacrifices and the law are not sufficient for the forgiveness of sins (Rom. 3:21–26; Gal. 2:21; 3:10–13). Therefore, certain Old Testament teachings and practices are no longer valid because their reason for existing has been fulfilled. The author of Hebrews uses a similar argument regarding animal sacrifices and the Aaronic priesthood.

The emphases of the Epistle to the Hebrews can best be explained if it was directed against certain Christians who desired to return to Judaism. Would the author agree with Paul that, while the law is fulfilled, its moral norms still apply to believers? Unfortunately, there is not much evidence to answer this question. Perhaps the author's positive citation of the new covenant prophecy of Jeremiah 31:31–34 provides a clue. Jeremiah said that one day the law would be written on the heart (see Heb. 8:10; 10:16).[27] If the moral norms of the old covenant are fulfilled in the new, the law of the old covenant might be said to have been written on the heart of the believer. This expression would be remarkably similar to Paul's claim that the believer, by the agency of the Holy Spirit, now is able to fulfill the law (see Rom. 8:4; 2 Corinthians 3).

It has often been remarked that the letter of James stems from conservative Jewish Christian circles. It is not surprising, then, that James describes the law as "the perfect law of liberty" (1:25), "the royal law" (2:8), and "the law of liberty" (2:12).[28] James urges the believer to practice the law or "word" in the everyday life (1:21–23, 25; 2:8–12; 4:11–12; see also 2:14–26; 3:1–18). James nowhere commands believers to keep

26. Harold W. Attridge (*The Epistle to the Hebrews* [Philadelphia: Fortress, 1989], 204) says Paul concludes that the law cannot give life, while the author of Hebrews says that the law does not give perfection.

27. The word νόμος is in the plural as in the LXX of Jer. 38:33.

28. For a brief analysis of νόμος in James see H. Frankemölle, "Gesetz im Jakobusbrief. Zur Tradition, kontextuellen Verwendung und Rezeption eines belasteten Begriffes," in K. Kertelge, ed., *Das Gesetz im Neuen Testament* (Freiburg: Herder, 1986), 200–2.

any part of the ceremonial law. He mentions not a word about circumcision, food laws, or sabbath.[29] The failure to address these matters is even more remarkable when it is recognized that James 2:14–26 probably corrects a false understanding of Paul's teaching on justification by faith.[30] Presumably, then, James knew that Paul taught that circumcision was unnecessary.[31] If so it is significant that James nowhere demands that circumcision be practiced. Apparently he did not think that Paul's teaching on circumcision was harmful since he does not even mention it. Moreover, Acts 15:13–21 and Galatians 2:1–10 confirm that James did not think circumcision should be imposed on Gentile converts.[32] Thus, it would be a mistake to think that in writing, "For whoever keeps the whole law, but stumbles in one matter, has become guilty of all" James demands adherence to the whole Old Testament law, including the ritual law.

What does James have in mind, then, when he refers to the law? James 2:8–12 is the most helpful passage for answering this question. There "the royal law" is seen to be in accord with the Old Testament command to love one's neighbor as oneself (James 2:8; compare Lev. 19:18).[33] *Law* obviously refers to the Old Testament law. James 2:11 specifically cites the commandments prohibiting murder and adultery (Exod. 20:13–14; Deut. 5:17–18). When James thinks of certain commands of the Mosaic law as obligatory for Christians, he thinks of moral norms from the

29. On this point see Davids, *Commentary on James*, 47; Martin Dibelius, *A Commentary on the Epistle of James*, revised by H. Greeven (Philadelphia: Fortress, 1975), 18, 146.

30. See Sophie Laws, *A Commentary on the Epistle of James* (New York: Harper and Row, 1980), 15–18, 131–32; Douglas J. Moo, *The Letter of James* (Grand Rapids: Eerdmans, 1985), 27–28. For a contrary opinion see Davids, *Commentary on James*, 20–21.

31. Much depends, of course, on when precisely James was written. If James was written early, then 2:14–26 may reflect a response to a distortion of the Pauline gospel before James had met Paul and understood his gospel (the position of Moo, who dates the letter A.D. 45–47 [*James*, 33–34]). If the letter is later, James could still be responding to a distortion of Pauline teaching on justification. Hengel ("Jakobusbrief," 248–56) thinks the letter was written between A.D. 58–62 by James the brother of the Lord, although he also thinks that the letter is an anti-Pauline polemic. There is firm evidence in Galatians (2:1–10) that James did not require circumcision for Gentile converts. My discussion here is based on the assumption that James was written by the Lord's brother (so Moo, *James*, 19–30; J. B. Adamson, *James: The Man and His Message* [Grand Rapids: Eerdmans, 1989], 3–52). Davids (*Commentary on James*, 2–22) argues that the letter was written in two stages. The first stage was composed by James the brother of the Lord, but the final redaction was made by another author between A.D. 55–65 or 75–85. For a similar view see Martin, *James*, lxxv–lxxvii. Dibelius-Greeven (*James*, 11–21) argue that the book is pseudonymous and composed between A.D. 80–130.

32. Of course, the historical veracity of the Acts account is disputed. See note 62 below.

33. Thus, Adamson (*The Man and His Message*, 200–3) and Laws (*James*, 109–10) understand the law to refer to the law of love. Against this interpretation see Dibelius and Greeven, *James*, 142. The latter argue that the argument in James 2:10–11 is only intelligible if the law comprises more than one commandment. Therefore, "the law of love" is not being exalted as the chief commandment in this passage.

Mosaic law, not circumcision or sabbath.[34] Martin Hengel remarks, "Perhaps the puzzling νόμος (τῆς) ἐλευθερίας in James 1:25; 2:12 is also to be understood as the pure moral law 'free' from the ritual law, which culminates in the 'royal' commandment to love (2:8) and which must be observed as a whole."[35]

We should also observe how James' argument in 2:8–12 correlates to Paul's teaching. The assertion that "whoever keeps the whole law, but stumbles in one matter, has become guilty of all" (2:10) reminds us of Paul's claim that one can only escape the curse of the law by doing everything the law demands (Rom. 3:19–20; Gal. 3:10).[36] Of course, James uses a similar kind of argument in a different context, where the issue of justification is not central. Selective obedience of God's commandments will not do, says James; partiality is just as sinful as murder or adultery.

I have not exhausted James' understanding of law by saying that he refers to the Mosaic law in using the word *law* (νόμος). James clearly made a connection between the law (1:25) and the word (λόγος, *logos*, 1:21, 22–23).[37] The readers are exhorted to "receive the implanted word which is able to save your souls" (1:21), and to be "doers of the word" and not just hearers of it (1:22–23). James also describes the doing of the word as "abiding by the perfect law of liberty" (1:25). We can conclude, then, that the "doing of the word" and the practice of the law are virtually synonymous for James. *Word* for James refers to the gospel since James says it is an "implanted word which is able to save your souls" (1:21). There is a suggestion, then, that the law of which James speaks is to be interpreted in light of the "word." This helps explain why James includes no requirement to be circumcised or practice purity laws. Indeed, it has often been noted that the letter of James has many parallels with the teaching of Jesus, particularly the Sermon on the Mount.[38] I shall argue below that Jesus taught that the law should be interpreted in light of his fulfillment of the Scriptures. If James depends on the teaching

34. See O. F. J. Seitz, "James and the Law," *SE* 2 (1964): 485; Moo, *James*, 48–49. Dibelius and Greeven (*James*, 120) say that James conceives of the law as the "perfect moral law."

35. Hengel, *Between Jesus and Paul*, 174 n. 52. One reason the ritual law is not prominent, says Hengel ("Jakobusbrief," 252–53) is that the issue was not acute between A.D. 58–62 when the letter was written.

36. Martin (*James*, 69) misreads the intent of James 2:10 in concluding that one may fail in keeping one commandment of the law, and yet still keep the whole law through observing the law of love.

37. So Moo, *James*, 49–50; Frankemölle, "Gesetz im Jakobusbrief," 204–5.

38. For the relationship between James and the teaching of Jesus see Adamson, *The Man and His Message*, 169–94; W. D. Davies, *The Setting of the Sermon on the Mount* (Cambridge: Cambridge University Press, 1964), 402–5; Davids, *Commentary on James*, 47–48. Dibelius-Greeven (*James*, 28–29) concur that James was influenced by the traditions about Jesus.

of Jesus, as seems likely, and if Jesus interpreted the law in light of his coming, then we find further evidence that James did the same.[39]

What does it mean to say that James interpreted the law in light of the fulfillment of Old Testament promises? When James speaks of the "implanted word," he likely is thinking of Jeremiah's promise that the law will be written on the heart (Jer. 31:31–34).[40] Thus, James does not encourage believers to obey the word or law in their own strength.[41] The "royal" law from the king is a "law of liberty" (1:25; 2:12) because it is now written on the heart, meaning God has provided the ability to keep it. Keeping the law is not a burdensome duty imposed from without, but the delight and joy of every heart that has the implanted word. Consequently, the gospel does not abolish the prohibitions against adultery or murder (2:11), nor the command regarding love for neighbor (2:8); rather, it enables believers to practice this law, because the word has been implanted deep within their hearts, and they have been brought to life by the "word of truth" (1:18).

The Johannine writings are notable for their insistence that believers keep the commandments.[42] In the fourth Gospel Jesus says those who love him will keep his commandments (14:15, 21; 15:10, 12), and the letters of John stress keeping the commandments of the Father (1 John 2:3, 4; 3:22, 23, 24; 4:21; 5:2–3; 2 John 6). The distinction between the commandments of Jesus and those of the Father should not be pressed too far, since the Gospel of John emphasizes repeatedly that Jesus' teaching comes from the Father (for example, 3:34; 7:16; 12:49; 14:24). The command of Jesus, indeed his new command, requires that believers love one another (John 13:34; 15:12; 1 John 3:23; 4:21; 2 John 5).

First John 2:7–11 points out that this "new" command is not really new; it is a command the community had "from the beginning" (2:7). John says the "old command is the word which you have heard" (2:7). He likely refers here to the Old Testament command to love one's neighbor (Lev. 19:18). This could also be understood as a summary of the "ten

39. This is not the same as saying that the teachings of Jesus comprise the new law for James (so Davids, *Commentary on James*, 100; Davies, *Sermon on the Mount*, 402–5). The flaw in this theory is that James specifically cites commands from the OT law in James 2:11. This suggests that it is too simple to conclude that the teachings of Jesus displace the OT law, although it is certainly true that the traditions from Jesus influenced James' view of the OT law. On this latter point see Martin, *James*, 67–68, 71.

40. So C. Leslie Mitton, *The Epistle of James* (Grand Rapids: Eerdmans, 1966), 72.

41. See Frankemölle, "Gesetz im Jakobusbrief," 204–5.

42. What John emphasizes is that the OT scriptures predicted what has now been fulfilled in the life and death of Jesus of Nazareth. See S. Pancaro, *The Law in the Fourth Gospel* (Leiden: Brill, 1975), especially 492–546; D. A. Carson, "John and the Johannine Epistles," in D. A. Carson and H. G. M. Williamson, eds., *It is Written: Scripture Citing Scripture. Essays in Honour of Barnabas Lindars* (Cambridge: Cambridge University Press, 1988), 245–64.

words" of the Old Testament. "Moses wrote upon the stone tablets the words of the covenant, the ten words" (Exod. 34:28). Raymond Brown argues that the oscillation in some Johannine passages between *word* (λόγος, *logos*) and *commandment* (ἐντολή, *entolē*) indicates that the terms are virtually synonymous.[43]

John 14:21–24 also displays the connection between commandments and word. The one who keeps Jesus' commandments is the one who loves him (14:21). In verse 23 Jesus says "if anyone loves me, he will keep my word," and in verse 24 he makes the negative distinction that "the one who does not love me does not keep my words."[44] The same connection between word and commandments appears in 1 John 2:3–6. Those who know God "keep his commandments" (v. 3), but those who do not know him "do not keep his commandments" (v. 4). In the next verse John speaks of "keeping his word" (v. 5).

In 1 John 2:7–11, the command to love is not new, for this command was present in the Old Testament from the very beginning. The newness of the command lies in its fulfillment through Jesus Christ. It is "true in him and in you" (v. 8), for the old age of darkness is passing away and the true light is now shining. Thus, the one who hates a brother or a sister (vv. 9–11) abides not in the light at all but lives and walks in the darkness of the old age, for Satan has blinded that person's eyes. *Newness* lies in the new ability to obey the commandments, which is a gift of the new area inaugurated by Jesus.

John can summarize the keeping of the commandments under love because love accurately describes what the commandments intend. The connection of *commandments* with *word* suggests that this love is not separate from the ten commandments but fulfils them. Believers manifest their observance of commandments in particular by loving their brothers and sisters. No one can claim to keep God's word, and harbor hatred against fellow believers.

John insists, however, that to fulfil the commandments one must believe that Jesus Christ is the Messiah. God's commandment is "that we believe in the name of his Son, Jesus Christ" (1 John 3:23). Those who deny that Jesus is the Messiah who has come in the flesh are antichrists (1 John 2:22–23; 4:3; 2 John 7). John recognizes an indissoluble connection between keeping the commandments, loving brothers and sisters, and believing in Jesus as the Messiah (1 John 5:1–2). These things are possible only for those who "have been born of God" (1 John 5:1).

43. Brown, *Epistles of John*, 252, 254, 265.
44. The switch to the plural λόγους indicates that no significance should be attached to the fact that λόγος was singular earlier.

Perhaps this brief discussion will help us understand the pregnant saying in John 1:17. "Because the law was given through Moses, grace and truth have come about through Jesus Christ." The *because* (ὅτι, *hoti*) connects verse 17 with verse 16. Verse 16 has its own difficulties, for it is unclear what John means by "grace instead of grace" (χάριν ἀντὶ χάρι-τος, *charin anti charitos*).[45] Nevertheless, the main thrust of verse 16 is clear. Grace has been lavishly poured out upon believers through the fullness of Jesus Christ. Verse 17 probably relates to verse 16 by empha-sizing that the outpoured grace has been made available at this period of salvation history through the ministry of Jesus Christ. Some scholars argue that John does not criticize Moses (as representative of the law) here but claims instead that both Moses and Jesus Christ dispersed grace.[46] Such an interpretation seems improbable since a greater dis-tinction between Moses and Christ seems evident. It is crucial, however, to understand precisely the point of the contrast.[47] John does not say that the Old Testament was intrinsically flawed, nor that grace was unavailable under Moses. Rather, the one to whom Moses pointed has come. Jesus Christ fulfils all that Moses wrote about (John 1:45; 3:14; 5:45–47). Thus, with the coming of Jesus Christ grace has been poured out to a greater extent than was the case under Moses. The Spirit was present at times under the old covenant. God withheld the full outpour-ing of the Spirit, however, until Jesus was glorified (John 7:37–39). The contrast of Moses and Jesus, then, does not infer that the law of Moses is flawed. John simply points out that those who believe in Jesus Christ have received grace that was never given during the Mosaic era.

The outpouring of grace through Jesus Christ explains why John does not emphasize keeping Old Testament commandments. Instead, John's Gospel focuses on keeping the commandments of Jesus (13:34; 14:15, 21; 15:10, 12; compare 15:14, 17), and 1 John on keeping the command-ments of God (2:3, 4; 3:22, 23, 24; 4:21; 5:2, 3). We see the same emphasis regarding *word*. Those who believe in Jesus and keep his word will receive eternal life (John 5:24; 8:31, 51; 14:23–24), while 1 John 2:5 says God's love has been perfected in those who keep the word of the Father. The word of the Father and that of Jesus cannot be separated from one another, since Jesus derives his words from the Father (John 17:6, 14).

45. See especially Ruth B. Edwards, "Χάρις ἀντὶ χάριτος (John 1:16): Grace and the Law in the Johannine Prologue," *JSNT* 32 (1988): 3–15; see also D. A. Carson, *The Gospel According to John* (Grand Rapids: Eerdmans, 1991), 131–33. For an interpretation of John 1:17 in light of Exo-dus 34 see William J. Dumbrell, "Law and Grace: The Nature of the Contrast in John 1:17," *EvQ* 58 (1986): 25–37.
46. See Raymond E. Brown, *The Gospel According to John*, 2 vols. (Garden City, N.J.: Dou-bleday, 1966, 1970), 16.
47. Pancaro (*Law in the Fourth Gospel*, 539–40) overemphasizes the nature of the contrast.

The spotlight is no longer on the Mosaic law but on Jesus, who fulfils that law.[48] The Mosaic law is not incompatible with the message of Jesus, but the law pales in comparison to its fulfillment.

We turn now to the question of whether Jesus, by word or example, taught that the sabbath was no longer in force. Relevant texts include Matthew 12:1–14; Mark 2:23–3:6; Luke 6:1–11; 13:10–17; 14:1–6, and John 5:1–18; 7:22–24, and 9:13–17. The ongoing validity of the sabbath is a very complex issue, and I do not intend to examine it in depth here.[49] My understanding, however, is that Jesus nowhere violates the sabbath nor teaches that its observance is unnecessary. Rather, he insists that some of the Jewish regulations regarding the sabbath are inappropriate, for it is a day on which it is fitting to do such good works as healing.[50] Most sabbath controversies, however, focus on Christology rather than continued sabbath observance.[51] Jesus, as the Son of man, proclaims his sovereign authority to interpret the sabbath (Mark 2:28), and his right to work since his Father is working (John 5:17). Even if Jesus did teach that the sabbath is no longer obligatory for his disciples, that would not greatly affect the thesis of this book. Paul certainly did not believe sabbath observance to be binding upon the church (Rom. 14:5–6; Gal. 4:10; Col. 2:16), and the author of Hebrews sees the Old Testament sabbath fulfilled in the eschatological rest provided for the people of God. It is possible that the Gospels teach that the purpose of the Sabbath has been fulfilled now that Jesus has come. But if the view proposed here, that Jesus did not teach the dissolution of the sabbath, is true, does this mean that Paul contradicts the teaching of Jesus? Probably not. The shift in salvation history explains the divergence. Nor do the Gospels intend to chronicle in detail what practices in the Old Testament would be valid after his ministry.[52] For instance, Jesus did not speak of the validity of circumcision, an issue of great consequence for the early church. Jesus' intention in the sabbath controversies, then, was not to explain his view on the validity of the sab-

48. For a full discussion of the themes examined in this paragraph see Pancaro, *Law in the Fourth Gospel*, 403–51.

49. See D. A. Carson, "Jesus and the Sabbath in the Four Gospels," in D. A. Carson, ed., *From Sabbath to Lord's Day* (Grand Rapids: Zondervan, 1982), 57–97; see also in the same volume, Max M. B. Turner, "The Sabbath, Sunday, and the Law in Luke/Acts," 100–57.

50. So Mohrlang, *Matthew and Paul*, 10–11; Joseph A. Fitzmyer, *Luke the Theologian: Aspects of His Teaching* (New York: Paulist, 1989), 184–85; Sanders, *Jewish Law*, 23.

51. So S. G. Wilson, *Luke and the Law* (Cambridge: Cambridge University Press, 1983), 31–39; R. Banks, *Jesus and the Law in the Synoptic Tradition* (Cambridge: Cambridge University Press, 1975), 113–31; Douglas J. Moo, "Jesus and the Authority of the Mosaic Law," *JSNT* 20 (1984): 16–17.

52. Sanders (*Jewish Law*, 1–96) labors to prove that Jesus observed the law, and the areas in which his behavior was questionable were minor. Sanders' main point may be granted, but he lessens the extent to which Jesus differed from Judaism over the law, particularly by questioning the authenticity of Mark 7:15.

bath but to confront his hearers with his authority as the Son of Man, and to fulfil the Father's mission. The question of the validity of the sabbath is dealt with after Jesus' death and resurrection, when Gentiles were streaming into the church. The validity of the sabbath was assumed during Jesus' ministry to the Jews, and Jesus himself did not question this, for he lived in the era before the message went out to the gentiles. To question the legitimacy of the sabbath itself would have obscured the real issue during Jesus' ministry. The question was not, "Should the sabbath be observed?" but "What do you think of the Son of Man?"

On the other hand, Jesus' teaching on food laws leads to the conclusion that they are no longer binding. This is particularly clear in the Markan account (7:1–23).[53] The controversy begins over the failure of Jesus' disciples to wash their hands and to observe other oral traditions. Jesus rebukes the Pharisees for nullifying "the command of God" because of their tradition (7:8–9, 13). The command he has in mind is the fifth commandment which enjoins children to "honor their father and mother" (Exod. 20:12; Deut. 5:16; see also Exod. 21:17; Lev. 20:9).[54] Pharisaic tradition held that one could refuse to help needy parents because of what one has promised to God. By failing to help one's parents, therefore, one fails to obey the fifth commandment. Jesus says in an unmistakable way that "the command of God" (7:8–9) or "the word of God" (7:13) is authoritative, and the Jewish traditions are merely "commandments of men" (7:7).

If the account ended here, it would be a powerful indictment of Pharisaic tradition, but Jesus proceeds to teach that nothing entering into a person can defile; only that which comes out of the heart defiles someone (Mark 7:15, 18–23). This pronouncement by Jesus infers the abolition of purity laws and food laws.[55] Indeed, Mark adds an editorial comment that thus Jesus "cleansed all foods" (7:19). Perhaps the import of what Jesus said on this occasion was not clear to all immediately. Since

53. Dunn (*Jesus, Paul, and the Law*, 37–60) investigates what original saying lay behind Mark 7:15, concluding that the wording of Matt. 15:11 is closest to Jesus' original words. What is important for our purposes is the final redaction of the saying as it is now present in Mark. Dunn agrees (38) that Mark 7:15, as it stands, indicates that purity laws are no longer obligatory. Sanders (*Jewish Law*, 28) concurs that the final redaction of Mark says that food laws are no longer in force. He thinks that this saying is too radical to be attributed to the historical Jesus.

54. It is interesting to note that Mark (7:8–9, 13) has the same linkage between *command* (ἐν-τολή) and *word* (λόγος) we saw in John.

55. Barnabas Lindars ("All Foods Clean: Thoughts on Jesus and the Law," in Barnabas Lindars, ed., *Law and Religion*, [Cambridge: James Clarke, 1988], 61–71) accepts the saying as authentic but argues that Jesus did not intend to abolish the law. Jesus' parabolic statement only superficially seemed to abolish the law. The most natural meaning of the parabolic statement, however, is that it does constitute an abolition of the law. In any case, this is Mark's understanding of the incident.

he often spoke parabolically and cryptically, undoubtedly some were confused over the implications of his statement. But as Mark and the church reflected on this teaching of Jesus, they were surely correct to deduce that the food laws were being done away with.[56]

Now we are prepared for the great surprise in this passage. The passage begins as Jesus rebukes the Pharisees for abrogating one of God's commandments, and concludes with Jesus abolishing the command of God related to food laws. How can Jesus criticize the Pharisees for nullifying commandments when he does the same thing? It seems to me that Jesus here does something very similar to what we have already seen Paul do.[57] The command to honor one's father and mother is a moral absolute and continues in force despite the change in redemptive history. The fulfillment of the old covenant leads to the keeping of this commandment. It is not a moral norm because it is included in the Mosaic covenant; it is in the Mosaic covenant because it is a moral norm. The prohibitions against certain foods, however, are not universal moral norms. They were intended to be in force for only a certain period of salvation history. With the fulfillment of God's promises, purity laws are no longer binding. They instead point to the truth that true uncleanness is internal. Paul makes similar distinctions in writing that certain commands continue to be obligatory after the inauguration of the new covenant, while other laws, such as circumcision and the food laws are no longer binding (Rom. 13:8–10).

Now we come to the Lukan view of the law.[58] The Lukan understanding of the law has been a matter of great controversy ever since Jacob Jervell's essay arguing that "Luke has the most conservative outlook within the New Testament."[59] A quick glance at Luke indicates why Jervell argues the position he does. The first two chapters of Luke emphasize the fulfillment of the law. Jesus is circumcised according to

56. Rightly Moo, "Jesus and the Mosaic Law," 14–15. Banks (*Jesus and the Law*, 144–45) wrongly sees the Markan account as relating to eating foods involved in the worship of idols, thereby minimizing the abrogation of the OT food laws in the Markan account.

57. See Klaus Berger, *Die Gesetzauslegung Jesu: Ihr historischer Hintergrund im Judentum und im Alten Testament (Teil I: Markus und Parallelen)* (Neukirchen-Vluyn: Neukirchener Verlag, 1972), 171–73; Robert H. Stein, *The Method and Message of Jesus' Teachings* (Philadelphia: Westminster, 1978), 102–4; David Wenham, "Jesus and the Law: An Exegesis of Matthew 5:17–20," *Themelios* 4 (1979): 93.

58. For a survey of recent work on the Lukan view of the law see K. Salo, *Luke's Treatment of the Law: A Redaction-Critical Investigation* (Helsinki: Annales Academiae Scientiarum Fennicae, 1991), 13–23.

59. Jacob Jervell, *Luke and the People of God: A New Look at Luke-Acts* (Minneapolis: Augsburg, 1972), 141. He continues to espouse this position in his most recent essay, "Retrospect and Prospect in Luke-Acts Interpretation," in E. H. Lovering, Jr., ed., *Society of Biblical Literature 1991 Seminar Papers* (Atlanta: Scholars, 1991), 383–404, especially 395–402. For similar view see Fitzmyer, *Luke the Theologian*, 175–202.

the law (2:21), and purification rites are carried out "according to the law of Moses" (2:22–24). Joseph and Mary leave Jerusalem only after "they had performed everything according to the law of the Lord" (2:39). In addition, Luke emphasizes the fulfillment of prophecy and God's covenant with his people (1:32–33, 54–55, 68–79; 2:29–32). The fulfillment of the Old Testament and the law permeates these chapters. The fulfillment of prophecy is also found in many other place in Luke-Acts (for example, Luke 4:18–19; 7:18–27; 24:25–27, 44–49; Acts 2:16–36; 3:11–26; 4:11; 8:32–35; 13:16–41; 15:13–21; 24:13–14; 26:22–23, 27).[60] Luke stresses that the law is eternally valid (Luke 16:17), and thereby sets the context in which Jesus' teaching on divorce should be understood (16:18). The sabbath accounts do not abrogate the law, but fulfil what was intended for the sabbath (Luke 6:1–11; 13:10–17; 14:1–6).

The early church in Acts observed the law by worshiping in the temple (3:1–10). The charge that Stephen does not keep the law is false (Acts 6:11–14); instead, Stephen thinks the law contains "living words" (7:38; see also 7:53). In Acts Luke depicts Paul as one who observes the law. He accepts the apostolic decree (15:22–29), circumcises Timothy (16:3), and takes a Nazirite vow (21:21–26; see also 18:18). He insists against all opponents that he has not violated the law in any respect (24:14–16; 25:8; 28:17).

Nevertheless, the evidence Jervell presents should be interpreted another way.[61] The basic issue is actually how one reads Luke-Acts. Jervell reads it from the perspective of redaction criticism, and thus perceives every incident related to the law in Luke-Acts to be theologically motivated. I agree that Luke is a theologian, and that redaction criticism can be very helpful in uncovering Lukan theology. But it should also be remembered that Luke writes as a historian, including material because it accords with the traditions passed on to him.[62]

60. See Turner, "The Law in Luke/Acts," 111.

61. For a critique of Jervell see Turner, "The Law in Luke/Acts," 116–23; Mark A. Seifrid, "Jesus and the Law in Acts," *JSNT* 30 (1987): 39–57. S. G. Wilson (*Luke and the Law*) thinks Luke adopts a fundamentally Hellenistic attitude toward the law, and in fact, Luke's perspective on the law is ambiguous because he is indifferent to the issue. I do not find Wilson's view convincing either but mention it to show how the evidence from Luke-Acts can be read in a different way. P. F. Esler (*Community and Gospel in Luke-Acts* [Cambridge: Cambridge University Press, 1987], 110–30) thinks Luke had a conservative agenda with regard to the law because of the community to which he wrote, although finally he could not conceal the fact that a genuine liberation from the norms of the law had occurred. For a view similar to Esler's see Salo, *Luke's Treatment of the Law*.

62. It is an accepted datum in some circles that Acts is not historically reliable. For the history of research see Ward W. Gasque, *A History of Criticism of the Acts of the Apostles* (Grand Rapids: Eerdmans, 1975). For a recent thorough defense of the historicity of Acts see Colin J. Hemer, *The Book of Acts in the Setting of Hellenistic History* (Tübingen: J. C. B. Mohr, 1989); see also Martin Hengel, *Acts and the History of Earliest Christianity* (Philadelphia: Fortress, 1979).

Craig L. Blomberg also emphasizes the significance of taking salvation history into account in reading Luke-Acts.[63] Luke stresses that Joseph and Mary did everything in accord with the law of Moses when Jesus was born, including circumcision and purification rites (Luke 1–2).[64] But why does Luke include these accounts? I am skeptical that Luke is exhorting the church to observe circumcision and purity rites. We know he does not require these from the accounts of Cornelius (Acts 10:1–11:18) and the Jerusalem Council (Acts 15:1–29). Instead, Luke most likely demonstrates that Jesus, who fulfilled all to which the law pointed, observed the law himself. This also explains why Jesus observed the sabbath, since his intent was not to abrogate the law during his ministry. With the descent of the Spirit on Pentecost, a new era of salvation history arrived. Furthermore, it is not surprising that the early church participated in temple worship, and that Paul continually defends himself by saying that he observed the law (Acts 21–28). The Jewish Christian community did not disavow all law observance. It was expected that when they were with other Jews they would observe the law in order to maintain social intercourse. This explains Paul's observance of the law in Acts 21–28. Nonetheless, what Paul emphasizes in these chapters is the fulfillment of all that the law and prophets predicted would occur (Acts 24:14–15; 26:6–7, 22–23, 27; see also 28:20). The resurrection of Jesus is the consummation of salvation history. Why, Paul asks, do Jews harass him for proclaiming the fulfillment of what the Jews have believed Scripture to promise? Paul circumcises Timothy for the sake of mission (16:3) and observes a vow to satisfy the sensibilities of other Jews (Acts 21:21–26). Luke does not have an agenda, though, for a complete fulfillment of the law. He simply reflects on what Paul and the early church did to accommodate Jewish concerns in this area. This is quite similar to Paul's own stance, according to 1 Corinthians 9:19–23. Thus, it is a mistake to read Luke as having the most conservative theology of law observance in the New Testament, and amounts to a fundamental misreading of the Lukan purpose. Luke's purpose relates much more to the fulfillment of prophecy than it does to detailed fulfillment of the law.

Acts 13:38–39, in fact, reveals a remarkable affinity between the Lukan and Pauline understanding of the law. Paul says, "Therefore, let it be known to you, men and brothers, that through this one [Jesus] forgiveness of sins is proclaimed to you, even from all things from which you were not able to be justified by the law of Moses. Everyone who

---

63. Craig L. Blomberg, "The Law in Luke-Acts," *JSNT* 22 (1984): 53–80; see also Seifrid, "Jesus and the Law," 39–57.

64. For Lukan terminology on law see Wilson, *Luke and the Law*, 1–11.

believes in this one is justified." Philip Vielhauer thinks Luke argues here that the law of Moses pardons some sins, and belief in Christ pardons those which could not be pardoned under Moses.[65] But this view is now almost universally rejected.[66] The idea that Luke portrays the law as a burden here is also incorrect.[67] Matthias Klinghardt is on the right track in contending that the Jewish covenant and law are not sufficient for salvation,[68] although he does not draw the correct implication from this. Luke's purpose here corresponds to what we found in Paul and Hebrews. Ultimately, the Mosaic covenant and the law do not save. Forgiveness of sins is only available through belief in Jesus. The law pointed to Jesus, and thus those who fail to believe in him reveal that they were not really trusting in the God of the Old Testament. Justification comes through believing in Jesus, not observing the law. This verse does not explain why justification does not come through the law. Nothing is said about inability to obey the law, for instance.

Acts 15:10–11 closely relates to 13:38–39. Peter says, "Now, therefore, why do you test God by laying a yoke upon the neck of the disciples that neither our fathers nor we were able to bear? But through the grace of the Lord Jesus we believe in order to be saved in the same manner as the rest [Gentiles]" (Acts 15:10–11). This verse has also been interpreted to say that the law was an oppressive burden on the Jews.[69] John Nolland, on the other hand, carefully argues that this is not the point of this text.[70] The intent here is to show, as in Acts 13:38–39, that the law does not bring salvation. The weakness of Jervell's scheme becomes apparent here, for Luke thinks the law is defective in a most important way![71] When Luke says that the disciples were not able to bear the yoke of the law, he probably means that they were not able to keep it. It is interesting

65. Philip Vielhauer, "On the 'Paulinism' of Acts," in L. E. Keck and J. L. Martyn, eds., *Studies in Luke-Acts* (Philadelphia: Fortress, 1980), 42.

66. For example, Ernst Haenchen, *The Acts of the Apostles: A Commentary* (Philadelphia: Westminster, 1971), 412; I. Howard Marshall, *The Acts of the Apostles* (Grand Rapids: Eerdmans, 1980), 228; Wilson, *Luke and the Law*, 59; Blomberg, "The Law in Luke-Acts," 65; Hans Conzelmann, *Acts of the Apostles* (Philadelphia: Fortress, 1987), 106; Richard N. Longenecker, *The Acts of the Apostles*, EBC (Grand Rapids: Zondervan, 1981), 9:426–27.

67. Contra Conzelmann, *Acts*, 106.

68. Matthias Klinghardt, *Gesetz und Volk Gottes* (Tübingen: J. C. B. Mohr, 1988), 108. See also Salo (*Luke's Treatment of the Law*, 221–22) for a view quite similar to Klinghardt's.

69. Haenchen, *Acts*, 446, 459; Conzelmann, *Acts*, 117.

70. John Nolland, "A Fresh Look at Acts 15.10," *NTS* 27 (1980): 105–15.

71. Jervell (*Luke and the People of God*, 146) reveals the weakness of his own position by assigning Acts 13:39–39 and 15:10–11 to tradition rather than Lukan redaction. This fails to answer the question why Luke included it in the tradition and constitutes special pleading. He still maintains his view in his most recent article ("Retrospect and Prospect," 397 n. 80). K. Salo (*Luke's Treatment of the Law*, 241) thinks this verse does not harmonize with the rest of the Lukan view, and that it probably stems from radical Pauline circles. More likely, these verses indicate the weakness of the interpretations proposed by Jervell and Salo.

to see how recent writers have misread Nolland on this point.[72] Nolland argues against the idea that the law was a burden, but he still thinks the verse says that no one is able to keep the law.[73] Thus, the main thrust of the verse seems to be that both Jews and Gentiles are saved the same way, not by keeping the law, but instead through the grace of Jesus Christ. Salvation does not come via the law because no one "can bear" the "yoke" of the law, which means that no one is able to keep it. This verse, then, makes the same point which Paul argued for so vigorously. Salvation does not come through observing the law because no one can obey the law perfectly. Thus, salvation is not finally due to human effort but the grace of God in Jesus Christ.

Acts 10:1–11:18 is also a significant passage for understanding the Lukan view of the law.[74] Peter has a vision in which God commands him to eat unclean foods (10:9–16). He puzzles (10:17) over this vision because the command contradicts what the Old Testament law says (see Leviticus 11). God said that Peter should "no longer call common what God has cleansed" (10:15). The import of this vision is soon revealed to Peter, for three men appear at his door inviting him to bring the gospel to a Gentile named Cornelius. The relationship between the vision that commanded Peter to eat unclean foods and his visit to Cornelius' house follows. Cornelius as a Gentile, even though he was a god-fearer, was considered to be unclean. Peter as a Jew could not sit down with a Gentile like Cornelius and enjoy table fellowship because Cornelius did not observe kosher food laws. The vision showed Peter that the food laws were no longer required. The Jews should fellowship with Gentiles and receive them into the kingdom without imposing on them food laws and circumcision. The full meaning of the Cornelius event did not dawn on Peter right away. In fact, he does not seem to grasp all the implications of his encounter with Cornelius until the Jerusalem Council (Acts 15:7–11). The point of the story, however, is that the food laws that erected barriers between Jews and Gentiles were no longer obligatory. Any Gen-

---

72. Jervell ("Retrospect and Prospect," 397–98 n. 81) thinks Luke is merely saying that the law has not been kept, not that it cannot be kept. See also Salo, *Luke's Treatment of the Law*, 240–41.

73. Nolland says ("Acts 15.10," 110), "The Jewish national history demonstrates that there was a characteristic human inability to come up to the law's expectations, since their history embodied the ambivalence of commitment but failure to keep it." And (111), "We can then speak of 'failure to carry the yoke', without speaking of 'oppressive burdens.'" He adds in a footnote (111 n. 23), "Obligations are not shown to be oppressive simply because they happen to fail to be met. The resistance of our human failings to our own highest aspirations seems to be a universal experience." He goes on to say (112) v. 10's "thought is far better served by a reference here to failure than by a reference to oppression." Finally, it (112) is "a yoke they had not the strength to carry."

74. See here Seifrid, "Jesus and the Law," 41–44.

tiles who believed in Jesus Christ and received the Holy Spirit were considered part of the church, without circumcision or observing the food laws.

Here again Luke indicates that he is not the New Testament's most conservative theologian regarding the law. The Cornelius account clearly implies that Jews do not need to include food laws when they preach the gospel to Gentiles.[75] Acts 11:2–3 informs us that some Jews criticized Peter because he ate a meal with uncircumcised Gentiles. There would be no problem for Peter to eat with Gentiles if he himself observed kosher food laws, and thus the point of the verse is that Peter has himself violated purity laws in eating with Gentiles. Luke demonstrates that Peter successfully defends himself, convincing his detractors that he obeyed what God himself commanded (Acts 11:4–18). It is important to note that Luke favorably portrays a Jew as violating the law. The Old Testament itself makes no exception for Jews who want to proselytize Gentiles. Instead, Peter receives a special vision from God to justify his eating unclean foods. Undoubtedly, then, Luke characterizes Peter positively when he disregards part of the Old Testament law.

Acts 15:1–29 is another crucial passage for the Lukan view of the law. Certain Pharisaic believers demanded that Gentiles observe circumcision and the rest of the law of Moses for salvation (vv. 1, 5). A council meets in Jerusalem to discuss this matter, concluding that circumcision is not necessary for Gentiles to be members in the church. Peter's recollection of the Cornelius event plays a major role in the council (vv. 7–11), for if God gave the Holy Spirit to Cornelius and his friends without requiring circumcision, then how can the church demand something that God himself did not? James concurs with Peter, pointing out that the Old Testament prophets envisioned a day when Gentiles would enter the community without the law being imposed on them (vv. 13–18). It is important to understand carefully the Lukan account. Nothing in the Old Testament itself teaches, contrary to Jervell,[76] that Gentiles become part of the people of God without circumcision.[77] Peter, after all, was surprised when God gave Cornelius the gift of the Spirit without circumcision. James argues that the prophets predicted this would happen, indicating that a new era of salvation history has commenced. But if a new era of salvation history has arrived, then the law has diminished. The Old Testament itself com-

---

75. So Turner, "The Law in Luke/Acts," 116.

76. Jervell, "The Law in Luke-Acts," 143–44; see also Fitzmyer, *Luke the Theologian*, 193–95.

77. Turner ("The Law in Luke/Acts," 117) says about Jervell's interpretation that "Acts 15 must surely be the Achilles' heel of such a construct." See also Seifrid, "Jesus and the Law," 44–47.

mands that males must be circumcised among all those who want to be part of the covenant community of Israel (Gen. 17:9–14). Luke, however, proclaims the dawning of a new day. Gentiles need not be troubled with circumcision (v. 19). It is unnecessary (v. 28). This is surely the burden of the Lukan story line, for when the Gentiles read the apostolic letter they rejoice (v. 31).

Once again we should note that Luke considers a significant part of the Old Testament law to be nullified. Jewish Christians may keep food laws and circumcision to mollify Jewish sensibilities (Acts 16:3), but they are not required for Gentiles who desire to join the church. Luke has no problem with Jews practicing these customs for the sake of cultural continuity, but the imposition of such laws upon the Gentiles is forbidden.

If Luke is teaching liberation from the law, then why is the decree of the apostolic council passed (Acts 15:20–21, 28–29)? The council leaders seem to say initially that Gentiles are free from the law, since circumcision is not required, but then they demand that Gentiles observe four other laws. I am persuaded that the decree stems from Jewish regulations found in Leviticus 17–18. I also think the Western text type incorrectly omits *strangled things* (πνικτοῦ, *pniktou*, 15:20, 29).[78] These regulations separate Jews from Gentiles, which makes the demand that they be practiced all the more curious since circumcision also separates Jews from Gentiles. Why observe some practices from the law and not others? The Western text type, by omitting *strangled things* understands the decree in a moral sense. Thus, the apostles were forbidding sexual immorality, murder, and idolatry. This is a neat solution, but it runs contrary to the best textual evidence. Moreover, why include instructions about only murder, sexual immorality, and idolatry? Are these the only matters Gentiles need to observe? More probably, Gentiles are being asked to concede to some Jewish scruples covered in Leviticus 17–18.[79] Jews would not eat the meat from animals that were strangled improperly or from which blood was not drained. The leaders request that Gentiles accede to this custom. Jews also considered food offered to idols to be unclean and defiled, so a similar request was made in this area. Finally, πορνεία (*porneia*) probably refers to marriages of

78. So Fitzmyer, *Luke the Theologian*, 194, 202 n. 45; Richard N. Longenecker, *Paul: Apostle of Liberty* (1964; repr. ed., Grand Rapids: Baker, 1976), 254–60; F. F. Bruce, *Commentary on the Book of Acts* (Grand Rapids: Eerdmans, 1954), 311–12, 315–16; Marshall, *Acts*, 246–47, 253. For a sustained argument against this interpretation see Wilson, *Luke and the Law*, 76–102.

79. See Turner, "The Law in Luke/Acts," 117–18. Seifrid ("The Law in Luke-Acts" 47–51) questions whether the decree stems from Leviticus 17–18, and also disputes whether the decree refers to ritual law. He may be correct on this latter point, but he does agree that the purpose of the decree was to facilitate fellowship between Jews and Gentiles.

near kin forbidden in Leviticus 18. Gentiles were not as strict as the Jews on this matter.

Does the passing of the decree contradict what Luke says elsewhere? There is a fundamental distinction between the circumcision issue and the decree. Circumcision was being required of the Gentiles for their salvation. On this matter Luke stands firm. Circumcision is not necessary for salvation, and it cannot be imposed on them. The items in the apostolic decree, however, were not required for salvation. They were suggested as a means of facilitating fellowship between Jews and Gentiles. Gentiles did not have to observe the decree to be saved, but their acceptance of the decree would make relationships between Jews and Gentiles smoother. Luke, then, maintains that obedience to the law is not necessary for salvation; his concern over the decree relates to fellowship.

Another question, though, asks how the decree relates to the Cornelius event, where Luke implies that Gentiles are not required to observe the food laws. The decree seems to reintroduce these laws through the back door. The differences between the two accounts need to be carefully observed. In the Cornelius account Jews proclaim the gospel to Gentiles. Here the Jews learn they should adapt to the Gentiles and not impose Jewish customs as a condition when meeting. The apostles' decree wrote to encourage Gentile believers to adapt to Jewish customs when they fellowship together. The earlier story in Acts 10–11 indicates that believing Jews also should be flexible when they fellowship with Gentiles.[80]

Overall, Luke seems to agree with Paul on a number of points. Acts 13:38–39 and 15:10–11 together say that no one is able to obey the law sufficiently to gain salvation. Perfect obedience is required. Salvation comes only through grace, by believing in the Lord Jesus. In addition, Luke agrees with Paul that circumcision and food laws are not mandatory for Gentiles. They cannot be imposed on them as requirements for salvation. On the other hand, Luke does not clearly speak of believers as fulfilling the law by the power of the Holy Spirit. It is not surprising that Acts lacks this emphasis. Luke did not intend to explain comprehensively his view of the law but to document the expansion of the church through the power of the Holy Spirit. The issue of the law appears only insofar as it relates to that theme.

The last author to explore is Matthew. The Matthean teaching on the law long has been debated and is the subject of numerous monographs

---

80. For further discussion on how this relates to Paul's own consistency on these matters see David A. (sic, D. A.) Carson, "Pauline Inconsistency: Reflections on 1 Corinthians 9.19–23 and Galatians 2.11–14," *Churchman* 100 (1986): 6–45.

and articles.[81] It will be helpful to note that Matthew (22:34–40), Mark (12:28–34), and Luke (10:25–28) all include accounts in which Jesus identifies the great commandment of the law—to love God with all one's strength (Deut. 6:4–9) and to love one's neighbor as oneself (Lev. 19:18).[82] When Paul sums up the law he also includes the command for neighbor love (Rom. 13:8–10; Gal. 5:14; compare with James 2:8), though we will not explore the lines of tradition between Jesus and Paul. The centrality of love in Matthew, Mark, and Luke shows that the particular commands of the Old Testament law are misunderstood if they are separated from love.[83] The commandments are to be fulfilled in a response of love to God and neighbor. Mechanical or external obedience to the law is not what the Synoptics have in mind when they speak of fulfilling the law. Loving God is the first and greatest commandment because it fulfils the first commandment to worship no other god. The fulfillment of the law cannot be calculated by keeping external requirements, for one can keep external requirements and not love God (Mark 10:17–27). The call to love God with all one's strength uncovers the depth of God's demand.[84]

Does love for God and neighbor sufficiently describe what the law demands? The Synoptic writers do not think so, for the Gospels contain numerous other commands that flesh out the nature of love. The priority of love is the key for rightly understanding the place of all the commandments.[85] Indeed, the supreme test of whether one loves God with one's whole heart is the willingness to be a disciple of Jesus. The account of the rich young ruler (Matt. 19:16–30; Mark 10:17–31; Luke 18:18–30) is instructive in this regard. Jesus does not ask the ruler if he has loved God with all his heart, but whether he has kept some of the commandments

81. See, for example R. S. McConnell, *Law and Prophecy in Matthew's Gospel: The Authority and Use of the Old Testament in the Gospel of St. Matthew* (Basel: Friedrich Reinhardt, 1969); Klyne R. Snodgrass, "Matthew and the Law," in David J. Lull, ed., *Society of Biblical Literature 1988 Seminar Papers* (Atlanta: Scholars, 1988), 536–54; John P. Meier, *Law and History in Matthew's Gospel: A Redactional Study of Matthew 5:17–48* (Rome: Biblical Institute Press, 1976); Banks, *Jesus and the Law*, passim; Hans Hübner, *Das Gesetz in der synoptischen Tradition* (Witten: Luther-Verlag, 1973), passim; G. Bornkamm, G. Barth, and J. H. Held, "Matthew's Understanding of the Law," *Tradition and Interpretation in Matthew* (Philadelphia: Westminster, 1963), 58–164; M. J. Suggs, *Wisdom, Christology, and Law in Matthew's Gospel* (Cambridge: Harvard University Press, 1970), 99–127; I. Broer, "Anmerkungen zum Gesetzesverständnis des Matthäus," in K. Kertelge, ed., *Das Gesetz im Neuen Testament* (Freiburg: Herder, 1986), 128–45.

82. A cursory reading of the Synoptics reveals significant differences between the accounts. It is not our purpose to investigate this matter here since on the matter I am interested in the accounts agree.

83. See Moo, "Jesus and the Mosaic Law," 11.

84. For some insightful comments on why love goes beyond written commandments see W. D. Davies and Dale C. Allison, Jr., *A Critical and Exegetical Commentary on the Gospel According to Saint Matthew*, 3 vols. projected (Edinburgh: T. and T. Clark, 1988–), 1:508–9.

85. So Mohrlang, *Matthew and Paul*, 21.

from the decalogue, all from the second table. Only Matthew includes the command "you shall love your neighbor as yourself" (19:19) as a summary of what the second table demands. When the ruler says that he has kept all these commands, Jesus' response that he should go and sell all that he has should not be interpreted as an extra command above and beyond the intention of the law.[86] Nor should this command be taken as a two-tier ethic implying that true disciples give up their possessions.[87] Rather, by asking the man to follow him in radical discipleship, Jesus probes this man's whole-hearted love for God and self-giving love for neighbor. If one is not willing to follow Jesus in radical discipleship, then one does not love God with all one's heart, mind, soul, and strength. The willingness to follow Jesus indicates where the heart is, and tests one's true treasure (see Matt. 19:21). Therefore, the rich ruler may have kept the law in that he never murdered or committed adultery. But Jesus reveals to him that such obedience is not in itself a product of love for God or love for the neighbor. Genuine love for God involves a willingness to follow Jesus.

One could appeal to this account and claim that a person could keep the whole law perfectly, yet still fall short of the kingdom. It seems more probable that Jesus' demand that the man sell all his possessions (v. 21) was designed to show him that he had not kept all the commandments perfectly.[88] He violated the first commandment because he worshiped another god more than the one true God. Charles E. B. Cranfield rightly says, "Jesus is not, as Lohmeyer has suggested, inviting him to take a step beyond the Commandments to something higher than their requirements: the one thing lacking is the all-important thing, a single-hearted devotion to God, obedience to the first of the Ten Commandments."[89] He also violated the tenth commandment because he desired money more than he desired God. The account, on this interpretation, does not support the idea that one can obey the entire law. Instead, Jesus punctures the illusion that he kept the law perfectly.

This account also implies that no one can claim to love God and their neighbor and commit adultery, murder, steal, bear false witness, or fail to honor one's father and mother. Love cannot be separated from specific commandments, which help define what love looks like in practice. Nevertheless, one may keep these commandments in an external sense without having love. It is a serious mistake to define love simply

---

86. Contra Banks, *Jesus and the Law*, 163; Wilson, *Luke and the Law*, 28; Turner, "The Law in Luke/Acts," 111; Moo, "Jesus and the Mosaic Law," 13.

87. Barth, "Matthew's Understanding," 96–97.

88. Rightly Charles E. B. Cranfield, *The Gospel According to Saint Mark* (Cambridge: Cambridge University Press, 1959), 328 30.

89. Ibid., 330.

in terms of obedience to moral norms. Love has its root in the heart, and thus true love for God and neighbor displays its true colors in one's response to Jesus' call to radical discipleship.

The more difficult question in Matthew concerns the ongoing validity of the law.[90] Jesus says, "Do not think that I came to abolish the law and the prophets; I did not come to abolish them but to fulfil them. For truly I say to you, until heaven and earth pass away, not one iota or hook will ever pass away from the law, until all things come to pass. Whoever then relaxes one of the least of these commands and teaches people to do thus, he will be called least in the kingdom of heaven, but whoever does and teaches them, this one shall be called great in the kingdom of heaven. For I say to you that unless your righteousness exceeds that of the scribes and Pharisees, you will never enter into the kingdom of heaven" (Matt. 5:17–20). The meaning of this passage continues to be debated. There is especially sharp discussion over the meaning of the word fulfil (πληρῶσαι, *plērōsai*, v. 17).[91] Methodologically, the context of Matthew 5:17–48 should determine the meaning of the word. The contrasting term, καταλῦσαι (*katalysai*), means "abolish" or "annul," and thus Jesus certainly emphasizes that his purpose was not to abolish the law or the prophets. Verse 18 underlines the thesis of verse 17 in hyperbolic language. Even the tiniest part of the law remains valid "until heaven and earth pass away," or "until all things come to pass." Some have interpreted this latter line as suggesting that the law is in force until all things are accomplished in Jesus' ministry.[92] It is unlikely, however, that this is Matthew's intention, for this would contradict the previous statement that the whole law will remain in force "until heaven and earth pass away."[93]

90. Räisänen (*Paul and the Law*, 86–90) thinks Matthew is not very clear, although he inclines to the view that there is no criticism of the law in Matthew, only of misinterpretation of the law.

91. Meier (*Law in Matthew's Gospel*, 80) sees an emphasis on the predictive function of the law. Banks (*Jesus and the Law*, 210) thinks the text refers to the fulfillment and transcendence of the law in the teachings of Jesus. Barth ("Abiding Validity," 68–69) opts for "establish," while Mohrlang (*Matthew and Paul*, 8) contends that Jesus is explaining the deeper meaning of the law. Moo ("Jesus and the Mosaic Law," 24–25) and D. A. Carson (*Matthew*, EBC [Grand Rapids: Zondervan, 1984], 142–44) follow Banks in seeing an eschatological fulfillment in the ministry of Jesus. Davies and Allison (*Matthew*, 485–87) conclude that the law is eschatological in that it points to Jesus, and that Jesus introduces a new law. Not all of these answers are mutually exclusive, although Snodgrass ("Matthew and the Law," 547) is probably correct in seeing the "accomplishment" of the law as intended. Jesus does not refer only to the fulfillment of prophecy. He also seeks concrete obedience in the lives of disciples. See the detailed discussion in McConnell (*Law and Prophecy*, 14–29).

92. For example, Banks, *Jesus and the Law*, 216. Rightly Mohrlang, *Matthew and Paul*, 9; Davies and Allison, *Matthew*, 494–95.

93. See Wenham, "Jesus and the Law," 93; Moo, "Jesus and the Mosaic Law," 26–27.

The saying about heaven and earth passing away refers to the passing of this age, as the parallel text in Matthew 24:35 shows. The phrase "until all things come to pass" parallels "until heaven and earth pass away," but Matthew inserts it to stress the fulfillment of all the prophets predicted.[94] The law and prophets will be in force until everything they predicted comes to pass. Verse 19 draws an inference from verses 17 and 18: If Jesus did not come to abolish the law but to fulfil every part of it, then those who intimate that any part of the law is not to be practiced and taught will be excluded from the kingdom of heaven.[95] The context does not infer that the commandments in verse 19 refer to those given by Jesus.[96] This is surely special pleading. The inferential *therefore* (οὖν, *oun*) links verse 19 to the previous verses, and the similar subject matter in the verses prove that the commandments of the law are still in view.

Matthew's understanding of fulfillment in 5:17 needs to be compared with the use of *fulfil* (πληρόω, *plēroō*) in the rest of the Gospel. Matthew employs a *fulfillment formula* on a number of occasions to emphasize that Jesus brings to fruition what the Old Testament pointed to (1:22; 2:15, 17, 23; 4:14; 8:17; 12:17; 13:35; 21:4; 27:9; see also 3:15; 26:54, 56). Indeed, the fulfillment specified in some of these texts (for example, 2:15) is only understood retrospectively in light of Jesus' coming. This implies that the fulfillment of the Old Testament in Matthew is christologically focused. The fulfillment brought about by Jesus, then, does not necessarily mean that the Mosaic covenant will apply in precisely the same way it did before. The Mosaic covenant needs to be interpreted in light of its fulfillment in Jesus Christ.

An initial reading of Matthew 5:17–20, however, might suggest the Old Testament law should be obeyed in every detail. Indeed, he does not say that any commandment of the law is passé, including circumcision. For this reason, some scholars have set the Matthean view of the law in contradiction to Paul's. They say Matthew represents a conservative Jewish Christian movement insisting on full adherence to the Old Testament law.[97] Such an understanding of Matthew, however, fails to account for the evidence of the entire Gospel. The antitheses, following 5:21–48, do not yield such a clean solution to the matter (more on this

---

94. So Carson, *Matthew*, 145–46; Davies and Allison, *Matthew*, 495.

95. "Being least in the kingdom of heaven" is another way of referring to those who will not enter the kingdom. For another possibility see Davies and Allison, *Matthew*, 497.

96. See Banks, *Jesus and the Law*, 222; Davies and Allison, *Matthew*, 496. Snodgrass ("Matthew and the Law," 545) notes numerous ways scholars have tried to evade the text by minimizing the validity of the OT law. He is correct in saying that these attempts have been singularly unsuccessful. See also Wenham, "Jesus and the Law," 93.

97. So Mohrlang, *Matthew and Paul*, 42–43.

below). Moreover, Matthew includes the saying in which Jesus asserts that that which enters the mouth does not defile a person (15:1–20). He does not add the Markan statement (Mark 7:19) that Jesus thereby declared all foods clean. But since Matthew was familiar with the Jewish law, he was well aware that the dissolution of the food laws was the implication of Jesus' statement.[98] It would seem fair to conclude that Matthew's understanding of the law's fulfillment does not require the observance of all that is found in the Old Testament.[99] But then how can Matthew speak of every jot and tittle of the law being fulfilled by Jesus?

What we have said about fulfillment provides part of the answer to this question. The life and ministry of Jesus fulfil what the law pointed to. Every part of the Old Testament must be interpreted in light of its fulfillment in Jesus Christ.

The antitheses in Matthew 5:21–48 also help us to understand the strong statement on the ongoing validity of the law in verses 17–20. For instance, verses 21–26 relate anger to the prohibition against murder. Jesus does not abrogate the prohibition against murder. He authoritatively interprets ("But I say to you . . .") what the commandment against murder involves (v. 22). The command intended, not merely to prevent murder, but to prohibit all selfish anger. Genuine fulfillment of the law goes beyond what the Pharisees demanded (v. 20).

In a similar way, the prohibition against adultery remains active (Matt. 5:27–30). Matthew wants his readers to realize, however, that the kind of obedience that pleases God comes from the heart, indicating a delight in God more than anything else (see Matt. 5:8). Thus, even lustful thoughts and fantasies are worthy of judgment since they are the root of which adultery is the fruit.

Jesus' words on divorce (Matt. 5:31–32; compare with Matt. 19:3–12) are more difficult. The account in Matthew 19 suggests the dissolution of the law in Deuteronomy 24:1–4. Formally, Matthew seems to be abrogating an Old Testament law. We need to be very careful, though, in explaining this situation. What Jesus says regarding divorce is better described as fulfilling the purpose of the law. The words of Genesis 1–2 are introduced so that Deuteronomy 24:1–4 will be interpreted correctly. The words from creation signify God's intention—that one man be married to one woman. Indeed, Deuteronomy 24:1–4 does not command divorce at all[100] but only permits and regulates it.[101] Nevertheless, here

---

98. So Carson, *Matthew*, 350.

99. Davies and Allison (*Matthew*, 490) comment that Matthew never mentions circumcision because he views it as unnecessary.

100. See Snodgrass, "Matthew and the Law," 552; Moo, "Jesus and the Mosaic Law," 19–21.

101. Mohrlang (*Matthew and Paul*, 12) says the Mosaic word should be viewed "as concession and not as legislation." Contra McConnell, *Law and Prophecy*, 51, 62.

is a clear example of an Old Testament law that allows divorce. Jesus now presents a proper interpretation of a law given to Israel in the course of its history.[102] This law should not have been used to justify divorce; rather, it was a concession to the hardness of human hearts. What Deuteronomy regulated, in essence, was adultery. Jesus explains that adultery is always wrong, even if there are concessions and regulations to mitigate an existing evil. Jesus uses the creation words of Genesis 1–2 to show the true intention in the Old Testament regarding marriage. Matthew seems to suggest that the Pharisees should have understood the evil of divorce from the Old Testament itself. [103]

The prohibition of all oaths also seems to abolish an Old Testament law (Matt. 5:33–37). As with Jesus' teaching on divorce, it is important to discern the intention. Old Testament laws regarding oaths were given to enshrine the importance of truthfulness. It seems apparent from both Matthew 5:33–37 and 23:16–22 that some oaths were not considered binding by the Pharisees. For example, if one swore by the temple or altar, then the oath was apparently considered to be nonbinding (Matt. 23:16–22). Such casuistry skated past the very reason these laws were given. Thus, Matthew probably does not intend to forbid all oath taking or to rescind the commands regarding oaths. Jesus' language is hyperbolic, and should not be pressed.[104] He reminds people of the original intention of the law.[105] This does not constitute an abolishment of the Old Testament law, but a strong reminder of the central purpose of the law.[106]

Many see an abrogation of the law in Matthew 5:38–42 since Jesus seems to reject the principle of "an eye for an eye and a tooth for a tooth," and instead calls on his hearers to not take revenge for evil.[107] This very

102. The Lukan account (Luke 16:17–18) should also not be read as a dissolution of the Mosaic law, contra Wilson, *Luke and the Law*, 43–51. Rightly Fitzmyer, *Luke the Theologian*, 180. Salo (*Luke's Treatment of the Law*, 144–49) thinks Luke undermines the law here but wants to conceal that fact.

103. For an insightful analysis of Matthean divorce teaching, see Craig L. Blomberg, "Marriage, Divorce, Remarriage, and Celibacy: An Exegesis of Matthew 19:3–12," *TrinJ* 11 (1990): 161–96.

104. For the presence of hyperbole in Jesus' teaching see Stein, *Method and Message of Jesus' Teachings*, 11–12. See Davies and Allison (*Matthew*, 535–36) who conclude that hyperbole is present here and Jesus is not forbidding all oath taking.

105. Rightly Snodgrass, "Matthew and the Law," 551. Against Banks, *Jesus and the Law*, 194; McConnell, *Law and Prophecy*, 63–65.

106. Moo ("Jesus and the Mosaic Law," 21) seems to conclude here that Jesus does cancel the Mosaic law; so also Carson, *Matthew*, 154.

107. Meier, *Law and History*, 157. Barth ("The Abiding Validity of the Law," 94) rightly sees that most of the antitheses counter the Pharisaic misinterpretation of the law, but he fails to see this in Matt 5:38–42, concluding that here there is a "complete abolition of an Old Testament commandment."

popular interpretation is probably mistaken.[108] Jesus counters here a misinterpretation of the command to exact an eye for an eye and a tooth for a tooth. An examination of the Old Testament shows that the *lex talionis*, in which the punishment is proportional to the offense, is found in civil contexts (Exod. 21:22–25; Lev. 24:17–22; Deut. 19:21). It has often been pointed out that this was a humane law, since it prevented people from unwarranted severity. Punishment had to fit the nature of the crime, and it could not be excessive simply because the person injured was enraged or had higher social standing than the accused. The words "an eye for an eye and a tooth for a tooth," then, are simply a way of saying that the punishment should fit the crime. Jesus does not suggest that governments cease using this principle of justice, for it is the only basis upon which punishment can be meted out righteously. Arbitrary punishments for crimes undercut society's moral standard.

What Jesus condemns, then, is the arrogation of this command into the personal sphere. Apparently some applied this teaching to their personal life, so that they felt justified in getting revenge upon anyone who personally wounded them. W. D. Davies and Dale Allison rightly remark that, "While in the Pentateuch the *lex talionis* belongs to the judiciary process, this is not the sphere of application in Matthew. Jesus, to repeat, does not overthrow the principle of equivalent compensation on an institutional level—that question is just not addressed—but declares it illegitimate for his followers to apply it to their private disputes."[109] Jesus states that personalization of the principle blatantly misinterprets this law, which was designed for a civil context, not everyday interaction with people. The disciple's heart should be full of forgiveness and mercy, not revenge or hatred. Indeed, one could externally obey the command to turn the other cheek and burn with hatred within toward the person who inflicted the injury. Jesus demands a righteousness that goes beyond external behavior.[110]

Romans 12:17–13:7 confirms this understanding. In 12:17–21 Paul, probably in dependence upon the teaching of Jesus, exhorts the Romans not to pay back evil for evil, to be at peace with all people, and to leave vengeance to God. The similarity to Jesus' words is unmistakable. Paul

---

108. See Moo, "Jesus and the Mosaic Law," 22.

109. *Matthew*, 542. They also note (542) that the examples given by Jesus are hyperbolic.

110. Carson (*Matthew*, 155) misunderstands this interpretation when he contends that if this is what Jesus was teaching, then he would go on to explain that the state has the function to repay evil. But the intention for giving this word was to prevent people from using the OT law as a pretext for revenge. Carson correctly suggests that the disciple of Jesus may refuse to use civil procedures in order to get his or her due, forgiving the damage altogether. Nevertheless, Jesus' concern here is personal unrighteousness in the heart, not how unrighteousness is resolved in society. It does not follow that he has no interest in justice being enforced by the state, or that this OT law has been abolished.

goes on to say in 13:1–7 that God has ordained the state to punish evildoers, insisting that it does not bear the sword in vain. Believers are not to take vengeance into their own hands, but the state rightly "is an avenger for wrath to the one practicing evil" (13:4). The state can take vengeance on those who do evil because it has a God-appointed ministry to do so. What Paul says in Romans is consistent with our understanding of Matthew 5:38–42. Believers' hearts are to be full of love and forgiveness toward those who have wronged them, but for the sake of justice God has appointed the state to punish those who commit crimes.

Matthew 5:43–48 should be interpreted similarly. No Old Testament command encourages people to love their neighbors and hate their enemies. Jesus responds here to a distortion by some (probably the Pharisees) of what the Old Testament says.[111] The true meaning of Leviticus 19:18 is that believers should love all people—friends and enemies— and by so doing they reveal that they are children of a God who loves all people and blesses them with many good gifts.

Matthew, then, exhorts disciples to practice the law and depicts Jesus as the true interpreter of the meaning of the law.[112] The fulfillment of the law by Jesus relegates the law to a lesser status. Jesus' statement in Matthew 15:1–20 clearly exemplifies the abrogation of the law regarding foods.[113] This incident, along with the words about divorce and oaths, are the most help in understanding the Matthean perspective on the law. Jesus came to fulfil the law, and he explains the role of the law in light of his ministry. In most Matthean texts Jesus does not abolish any law but simply clarifies the true intention of the law. Nevertheless, he does seem to abolish the purity laws, even if Matthew lacks Mark's clarifying

---

111. Davies and Allison (*Matthew*, 506) insist that Matt. 5:21–48 deals not with a misinterpretation of the law but with what the law really says. But the OT does not clearly teach that one must hate one's enemies (see Carson, *Matthew*, 157), so Jesus is probably responding to a misinterpretation in vv. 43–48.

112. Snodgrass ("Matthew and the Law," 541–42) and Barth ("The Abiding Validity of the Law," 104) point out that the fulfillment of the law in Matthew should be understood from a perspective in which the love command is central.

113. Note how Jesus ignored cleanliness regulations in touching a leper (Matt. 8:1–4) and a dead girl (9:25), although it is not clear if this would be viewed as a violation of the law, since Jesus may have followed the law's prescriptions regarding uncleanness subsequently. See Banks (*Jesus and the Law*, 105) on this latter point. Banks also (92) argues that it cannot be clearly established that Jesus' attitude with regard to the temple tax (Matt. 17:24–27) violated the OT law. Snodgrass ("Matthew and the Law," 552–53), Barth ("The Abiding Validity of the Law," 89–91), and Mohrlang (*Matthew and Paul*, 11–12) fail to see an abrogation of the law in Matthew 15. For a more satisfactory view see Carson, *Matthew*, 351–52. Matthew does seem to have a positive view of Rabbinic traditions on occasion (23:2–3, 23), but in light of the Matthew 15 criticisms, 23:2–3a should probably be interpreted as ironical (for this view see Carson, *Matthew*, 472–74). Mohrlang argues that scribal tradition remains authoritative for Matthew and thus concludes that Paul's view of the law is "more fully thought-out and consistent" than Matthew's (*Matthew and Paul*, 12–14, 47).

statement (Mark 7:19). In addition, the concession for divorce also is ruled out or rightly interpreted. Thus, the fulfillment Jesus speaks of in Matthew 5:17 does not mean that the church must practice every law of the Old Testament. Matthew's point is probably that the ministry of Jesus fulfils the true intention in giving the law, and one cannot understand the Old Testament without identifying the one to whom it pointed. Moreover, the moral norms of the law, now clarified, remain in force for the church.

Conclusion

New Testament writers emphasize different themes in a theology of law. Nevertheless, they affirm the same theology. The early church generally agreed that good works are needed to enter the kingdom or obtain eternal life, but these good works do not merit entrance into the kingdom or salvation. Instead, they understood good works to be the effect of God's grace in a person's life. Paul stressed that, since no one could do them perfectly, good works did not merit entrance into the kingdom. He also warned against a legalistic mindset, which believed that a person could earn eternal life through good works. Other New Testament authors, however, do not emphasize these two themes to the extent that Paul did. However, these two themes are present through the New Testament documents, so Paul was not alone in saying that the law could not be obeyed and in warning against legalism.

Other New Testament writers also reveal the same tension found in Paul regarding the ongoing validity of the Mosaic law. They universally agreed that the coming of Jesus Christ fulfilled prophecy and all of the law. Thus, the author of Hebrews argues that the covenant with Moses is no longer operative, and that the Aaronic priesthood and animal sacrifices are passé. No New Testament writer requires circumcision. The silence of Matthew and the letter of James on this score particularly telling, while Luke explicitly informs the reader that circumcision was not required for Gentile converts. The status of the sabbath is somewhat ambiguous in the Gospels, which is not surprising since a salvation-historical shift separates the events of the Gospels and the Pauline writings. Matthew, Mark, and Luke all agree, however, that purity laws are no longer in force. We see a remarkable agreement with Paul, therefore, that the fulfillment of the law by Jesus means that believers are not bound by the law in the same way Old Testament saints were. Although some ambiguity remains, various New Testament writers seem to agree that believers should obey the moral norms of the law in this age of fulfillment. This obedience is now possible because Jesus has been exalted, the Spirit has been given, and the new covenant has been inaugurated.

Conclusion

In drawing this book to a close I shall chronicle the significance of some of the conclusions made during this study. First, a word will be said about the last chapter of the book. That Paul's theology of the law is the most developed in the New Testament is hardly surprising, given his Pharisaic background and training. Chapter 8's brief glance at the rest of the New Testament, however, shows that other New Testament writers present most of the same themes. New Testament scholarship often exaggerates the distance between Paul and other New Testament writers. I do not deny the distinctive element in Pauline theology, nor minimize the different emphases found through the rest of the New Testament. These differences in emphasis should not blind us to areas of common ground between Paul and the rest of the writers (see 1 Cor. 15:11).

The use of the term *law* (νόμος, *nomos*) in Paul usually refers to the Mosaic law and in particular to the commandments of the law. Some doubt this conclusion, but most Pauline scholars accept it. However, in some texts Paul probably uses the *law* in a figurative way. Such creative uses should not surprise us since Paul was an artful writer.

The reason Paul excludes righteousness by *works of law* is, of course, more controversial. I have defended the view that works of law do not save because no one can obey the law perfectly. Paul does not base his polemic against works of law on the assumption that the very attempt to keep the law is sin. Neither is it Paul's primary consideration that works of law are legalistic. Paul believes people would be saved if they could keep the law in its entirety. Since this is impossible, right-standing with God comes only through Jesus Christ. To say Paul excludes works of law because they focus on those ethnic laws that separate Jews from Gentiles is also inadequate. He vigorously resisted any attempt to impose circumcision, food laws, and the observance of days upon Gentiles. He was passionately committed to Gentiles being included as the seed of

241

Abraham. Nonetheless, his use of the term *works of law* cannot be forced to focus on only part of the law. It refers to the whole law. Those who do not keep the whole law are cursed (Gal. 3:10). Paul does not reason that nationalism or exclusion of Gentiles causes the Jews to be accursed. He fundamentally criticized the Jews because they did not observe the law sufficiently.

Some scholars, notably E. P. Sanders, have asserted that Paul argues from solution to plight. Since salvation comes only through Christ, the law does not save. Paul excludes the law as a way of salvation for salvation-historical reasons. Sanders has identified an important truth here. One reason the law does not save is that a salvation-historical shift has occurred. Old Testament sacrifices atoned for sins, but now that Jesus Christ has come, only his sacrifice is effective. A salvation-historical answer, though, is not comprehensive enough. Paul at the same time relentlessly argues that the problem under the old covenant was human sin. Israel failed to keep the law. Paul drew here on Old Testament theology, for the Old Testament itself testifies again and again that Israel failed to keep the law. Paul did not only argue from solution to plight; he also argued from plight to solution.

That the law was given to increase sin is one of the most surprising Pauline theology assertions. Chapter 3 sifted his writings for this theme. He does not conclude from this that the law is flawed. Part of the exceeding sinfulness of sin lies in its degradation of something good for evil ends. Some scholars say that Paul's God must be rather cynical or unjust if he gave a law that people could not keep and that only increased their sin. Paul, of course, perceived the situation quite differently. Human beings are justly condemned because in sinning they simply follow the desires of their hearts (see Eph. 2:1-3). Why did God give a law that people could not keep in their own power? Paul answers that the triumph of grace over sin shines brighter when the full depth of human sin is realized (Rom. 5:20-21). Human beings do not realize the extent and gravity of their corruption until they measure themselves against the standard of the law. They reveal the intensity of their rebellion when they try to obey the law and discover they cannot. Their fundamental sin is the failure to glorify God as God and give him thanks and praise (Rom. 1:21). They are committed to worshiping and serving the creature rather than the creator (Rom. 1:23, 25). Sin has the power to use the law to increase rebellion, but the power of grace rises to that challenge and conquers sin. Thus, people praise and thank God for their marvelous deliverance.

The revolution in Pauline studies is best known for its claim that Judaism was not legalistic and that Paul was not opposing any form of

Jewish legalism. Sanders' work *Paul and Palestinian Judaism* sent shock waves through New Testament studies by contending that the picture of Judaism in New Testament scholarship was seriously flawed. Sanders' study is beneficial because he critiques Bible students' tendency to caricature New Testament Judaism. We should continually refine our view of Judaism by analyzing extant sources. Moreover, scholarship is not conducted in a vacuum. Anti-Semitism has played a role in the interpretation of Judaism. Chapter 4, however, showed that these interpretations fail to prove that Paul was countering something other than legalism. Careful exegesis of a number of relevant texts clearly shows that Paul sees the problem as a works-righteousness mindset. Could Paul have been wrong and distorted Judaism? We should be cautious about making such a claim. Paul was trained as a Pharisee and knew Judaism extremely well. In addition, contemporary scholarship is faced with the problem of trying to interpret Judaism on the basis of extant sources, while Paul actually lived in the first century.

I find some good arguments for the existence of legalism in Sanders' own depiction of Palestinian Judaism. To see the Judaism of Paul's day as legalistic is not anti-Semitism. That charge could only stick if one said that legalism was only a problem for the Jews. But the attempt to gain right-standing before God on the basis of good works is a fundamental human problem. Human beings often think they deserve eternal life because they are fundamentally good, or at least good enough to deserve entrance into the kingdom. The root problem in legalism is pride. Pride and egocentricity are characteristic of all peoples and racial groups. Consequently the Reformers correctly understood that Paul opposed legalism. Their exegesis more accurately interprets the Pauline letters than that of many scholars today. However, we must scrutinize the exegesis of our forebears because traditional opinions are not always valid. On the other hand, modern scholars have a tendency to accept new hypotheses with enthusiasm. We should be open to a new reading of the evidence and to the possibility that an older interpretation is correct. I believe the Reformers were profoundly correct in insisting that Paul's gospel is supremely a gospel of grace that was framed in the context of a legalistic soteriology with roots in Judaism.

Probably the most difficult area in constructing a Pauline theology of the law is the tension between the abolition and the fulfillment of the law. Both emphases are clearly present in his writings. Therefore, the solutions run from a radical discontinuity between law and gospel to a continuity that scarcely sees any differences between the old covenant and the new. Marcion (c. 85–160) espoused an extreme discontinuity. He renounced the Old Testament as revelation, positing a radical disjunction between the God of the Old Testament and the God of the New Testament. The church repudiated his drastic solution. A similar emphasis on discontinuity—though not to the extent of Marcion's—lives today in Lutheran scholarship (for example, the work of Rudolf Bultmann) and in some forms of dispensational theology. Conversely, an example of radical continuity is present in the theonomist movement which applies the Old Testament law and penalties to the context of modern states. Reformed theology presents a more moderate form of continuity, seeing the two covenants as basically continuous in principle but recognizing the differences in salvation history.

According to Paul, the Mosaic covenant has reached its fulfillment in Jesus Christ. This fulfillment means that the Mosaic covenant no longer is in force. The age of consummation and the era of the new covenant have arrived. The commandments in the Mosaic law are still part of the Word of God, but they no longer function in the same way now that the fulfillment of what the Old Testament promised has come. For example, physical circumcision pointed to the spiritual circumcision of the heart, and the reality of the latter displaces the need for the former. Old Testament sacrifices pointed to the sacrifice of Christ, which definitively accomplishes what Old Testament sacrifices merely anticipated. Neither are the purity laws incumbent on the church, since they signaled the need for holiness that is now a reality through the work of Jesus Christ.

The covenantal shift also explains why Paul and the rest of the New Testament writers had no interest in applying the Old Testament law to the church or the state of Rome. The church is not a civil entity, however. It consists of people called from many different ethnic groups. God uniquely established Israel as a religious people and a nation. One should not transpose Old Testament laws to modern states simply because those laws hail from the Old Testament. Yet that does not mean modern civil states should not consider Old Testament law. For example, the principle that punishment should fit the crime is found in the statement that there should be an "eye for an eye." The principle of just compensation is the basis of law in any just society. Insisting that the Old Testament law is normative for modern states, however, is a massive hermeneutical error, rooted in a failure to see the covenantal shift between the Testaments and the unique role of Israel in salvation history.

Nevertheless, Paul still viewed the laws given to govern the state of Israel as the Word of God. The fulfillment introduced by Christ led him to creatively apply the law to the life of the church. For example, the Old Testament required that one who committed idolatry or adultery must be executed (Deut. 17:7; 22:21, 22). Paul borrows the language used in the Septuagint for the purging of evil from Israel and applies it to the person committing incest in Corinth (1 Cor. 5:13). Such a person must be expelled from the church. The fulfillment of the law in Christ indicates that the state no longer has the function of punishing idolatry or adultery with the death penalty. The church as God's new community, however, is God's new *holy* community. Those who do not repent of sin are to be removed from the community. I do not claim a "spiritual" application for every law in the Old Testament. I do think more detailed work needs to be done, though, regarding how Paul applied the Old Testament to the life of the church. The situation is much more complex than simply opting for discontinuity or total continuity.

How does the fulfillment of the Mosaic law in Christ relate to the moral law? Many scholars misunderstand Paul's theology of freedom and argue that the moral norms of the law no longer play any role in the Christian life. But the fulfillment of the law in Christ means that the Spirit enables believers to keep the moral norms of the law. When Paul says that the law kills and does not give life, he does not mean that the presence of moral norms or ethical absolutes dampens life in the Spirit. If Paul believed this, then he blatantly contradicted his own theology. His ethical parenesis is full of "oughts" and "shoulds." Freedom from law for Paul does not mean freedom from "ought." It means freedom from the power of sin which uses the law to produce death. Death and sin are the result when the law confronts an unregenerate person. In other words, the law without the Spirit leads to death. But those who have the Holy Spirit have the power to keep the law. The new covenant prophesied by Jeremiah and Ezekiel is fulfilled when the Spirit comes and the law is written on the heart. The moral norms of the law can now be kept because of the internal working of the Spirit of God. The law is no longer just an external standard; it is also an inward delight.

To put it another way, love comprises the heart and soul of Paul's ethic. Those who have the Spirit of God are filled with love, which is the fulfillment of the law. The centrality of love in Paul is crucial because he recognized that no law could adequately describe the kind of righteousness demanded for believers. Love goes beyond what can be specified and calculated by law. It delves into motivation, which law seldom touches. People can keep the law in an external sense and still not be motivated by love. Nonetheless, even though love resides at the center of Paul's ethic, this does not mean that love and law are polar opposites. The law is a partial description of how love expresses itself. The law guards us from sentimentality and vagueness in a society that knows all too well how to justify almost any course of action by an appeal to love.

Seeing the moral norms of the law as fulfilled in the life of the Christian does not contradict the newness of Paul's theology. It rather testifies to the newness of his theology that believers now keep the law. That believers can obey the law also shows the grace of God since Paul emphatically states that such obedience is only possible through the Holy Spirit. The charismatic and Spirit-saturated Paul do not oppose the law-abiding Paul! John Calvin was, after all, a remarkably faithful expositor of the Pauline theology of the law with regard to the "third use of the law."

The necessity of keeping the moral norms of the law naturally raises the issue of justification by works. Paul insisted that believers could not enter the kingdom by good works. No one can earn salvation, for all fall short of God's righteousness. Faith establishes the only pathway to salvation. Nonetheless, those who are saved will not be justified without good works. Good works are the evidence and result that salvation actually occurred. The dynamic work of the Spirit makes a difference in the way a person lives. If good works are lacking, a person's membership in the people of God is questionable. According to Paul, the work of the Spirit makes a profound difference in a person's life. Those who have received the Spirit will never be the same. By the power of the Spirit they will fulfil the law. Of course, since the fulfillment of the new covenant contains an "already" and a "not yet," believers will not keep the law perfectly, but the Spirit will produce observable and significant fruit in one's life.

Appendix

Mark Karlberg's View of the Mosaic Law

Mark W. Karlberg, in his erudite and learned articles, represents a person who advocates a return to the Reformation understanding of the law, an understanding with which, in large part, I am in agreement.[1] I want to focus on the distinctive and more controversial aspects of Karlberg's thesis. Karlberg, in conscious dependence upon Calvinistic predecessors, thinks that the Mosaic covenant has a double character. Under the Mosaic covenant justification in the spiritual sphere was by faith alone and not by works. But the Mosaic covenant functioned in a different way in the earthly sphere; in time and space the covenant was based on "works-inheritance," so that obedience brought blessing but disobedience punishment.[2] The Judaizers made the mistake of applying the works principle from the earthly sphere to the spiritual sphere, with the result that they made salvation dependent upon works.[3] Karlberg contends that the Mosaic covenant is a covenant of works at the earthly and temporal level. But this covenant of works should not be applied to the spiritual and eternal arena, for even in the Mosaic covenant salvation was by faith alone in the spiritual sphere. Blessing for obedience

---

1. For some of Mark W. Karlberg's contributions see "Reformed Interpretation of the Mosaic Covenant," *WTJ* 43 (1980): 1–57; "Justification in Redemptive History," *WTJ* 43 (1981): 213–46; "Legitimate Discontinuities Between the Testaments," *JETS* 28 (1985): 9–20; "Reformation Politics: The Relevance of OT Ethics in Calvinist Political Theory," *JETS* 29 (1986): 179–91; "The Original State of Adam: Tensions within Reformed Theology," *EvQ* 87 (1987): 291–309; "Moses and Christ: The Place of Law in Seventeenth Century Puritanism," *TrinJ* 10 (1989): 11–32.

2. "Reformed Interpretation," 15–16, 28, 30, 55; "Legitimate Discontinuities," 14; "Reformation Politics," 181–82.

3. "Reformed Interpretation," 56.

and punishment for disobedience apply only to the earthly sphere of the covenant.

Karlberg grapples with an explanation of how the Mosaic covenant is continuous and discontinuous with the new covenant. His solution sees a principle of works at one level of the Mosaic covenant, but he does not deny that the covenant still teaches that salvation is by grace alone. This principle of works explains why Paul can make such negative statements about the law in Galatians and Romans (for example, Rom. 10:5; Gal. 3:12). Paradoxically, Karlberg himself adopts the view that Paul's negative comments on the law were directed against those who, through a "misunderstanding," applied what was said about the law in the earthly sphere to the eternal sphere. This is a provocative admission; elsewhere he criticizes those who have argued that the Mosaic covenant is wholly gracious and who say that Paul is only responding to those who, through misinterpretation, have distorted the originally gracious nature of the Mosaic covenant.[4] Apparently, Karlberg also affirms that a problem with the Judaizers arose because of a misunderstanding of how to apply the Mosaic law. The Judaizers made the interpretative mistake, according to Karlberg, of applying the temporal meaning of the Mosaic covenant to the eternal sphere.

But if Karlberg's thesis is correct, then one wonders why it was so blameworthy to understand the Mosaic covenant as one of works, especially since the earthly sphere was dominant in the Old Testament.[5] At the very least one would have to make a very nuanced hermeneutical distinction to see that the works-principle of the Mosaic covenant applied only to the earthly sphere. This would be particularly difficult for Israelites in the old covenant since the earthly sphere was so intimately wedded to the eternal one. The close relationship between the earthly and spiritual arenas is illustrated in the case of Old Testament sacrifices, which were offered to maintain a relationship with God but pointed to a deeper reality, the sacrifice of Christ.

Meredith G. Kline[6] like Karlberg, defends the notion of a covenant of works in the typological sphere through his interpretation of Rom. 5:13–14. He argues that the interval "from Adam until Moses" does not focus on all people who lived between the time of Adam and Moses. Instead, Paul is referring only to those who were part of the covenant community of God who lived between the era of Adam and Moses. Kline sees support for this interpretation in the words "sin is not reckoned while there is no law" (v. 13).

4. Ibid., 21, 29–33, 37, 41–43, 48–56.
5. See the comments of Calvin cited by Karlberg, "Reformed Interpretation," 15.
6. "Gospel until the Law: Rom. 5:13–14 and the Old Covenant," *JETS* 34 (1991): 433–46.

Kline argues that this is not true of all people who lived in the interval between Adam and Moses; it is only true of those who lived under grace—those who were part of the Abrahamic covenant. He contends that this passage constitutes significant support for distinguishing the covenant of works in the Adamic and Mosaic covenants from the covenant of grace found in the Abrahamic covenant. Kline provides a creative and ingenious defense for traditional covenant theology in his interpretation of Rom. 5:13–14. Nonetheless, there is paltry evidence in vv. 13–14 to support the idea that Paul is restricting his focus to the covenant community. Nowhere does he even mention the Abrahamic covenant. The interval is broadly designated as that between Adam and Moses (v. 13). The covenant of grace figures large in Kline's interpretation, but one looks in vain for any reference to such a covenant in the text. Also, it is hardly clear that Paul focuses upon those who received grace when he speaks of those to whom sin is not reckoned (v. 13). In fact, Paul does not emphasize that these people received grace; he says that they died (v. 14). Death is the consequence of sin (Rom. 6:23). Thus, the fact that sin was not reckoned does not mean these people experienced grace. Finally, the most natural way to understand the time interval is to see a reference to all people who lived between Adam and Moses. Most commentators understand these verses to refer to all people of this era. Since the era is designated generally, more specific evidence is needed to prove that Paul was restricting himself to the covenant community.

It seems to me that Daniel P. Fuller and John Murray correctly see a fundamental problem here with typical Reformed theology.[7] It seems more reasonable to see the covenant with Moses as wholly gracious and to conclude that Paul responds, at least in part, to a misinterpretation of the nature of the Mosaic covenant. This is not to say that the answers of Murray and Fuller are themselves completely satisfactory,[8] but Karlberg's solution to the relationship between the testaments differs from Fuller's because he thinks the misunderstanding consists in applying the works principle of the Mosaic covenant to the sphere of salvation. The Mosaic covenant does teach works in the earthly sphere. Against Karlberg, it seems hard to condemn people for misunderstanding the Mosaic covenant as one of works in the realm of salvation if a works

7. See Daniel P. Fuller, *Gospel and Law: Contrast or Continuum?* (Grand Rapids: Eerdmans, 1980); John Murray, "Covenant Theology," in Philip E. Hughes, ed., *The Encyclopedia of Christianity*, (Marshalltown, Iowa: National Foundation for Christian Education, 1972), 3.199–216. The latter reference is from Karlberg, "Reformed Interpretation," 48.

8. For a penetrating analysis of Fuller's view the reader should consult Douglas J. Moo, "Review of D. P. Fuller. *Gospel and Law. Contrast or Continuum? The Hermeneutics of Dispensationalism and Covenant Theology,*" *TrinJ* 3 (1982): 99–103.

principle were central to that covenant in the earthly realm. Despite some of the weaknesses of Fuller's work which we have mentioned elsewhere, he is fundamentally right on this point in his criticism of the typical Reformed view.

I have endeavored to prove throughout this book that a salvation-historical shift occurred with the coming of Jesus, which accounts for Paul's setting aside of the Mosaic law. Another defect of the Mosaic law was that it did not provide power for obedience. The giving of the law was not coterminous with the gift of the Holy Spirit. Paul does not criticize the content of the law. The problem is that the law without the Spirit does not grant life. In addition, there seems to be an element of truth in the view of Fuller and Murray that the Judaizers distorted the Mosaic law by interpreting it in a legalistic way. Paul counters the Judaizers by presenting a more satisfactory understanding of the Mosaic law.

Old Testament scholarship today generally agrees that the Mosaic covenant was gracious, which identifies an even more serious weakness in Karlberg's view. Yahweh redeemed his people from Egypt before giving them the law (Exod. 19:3–6; 20:1–17). He did not give the law as a way to earn salvation, but obedience to the law was an expression of gratefulness for the salvation effected by Yahweh. Of course, Karlberg agrees that salvation was by grace even under the Mosaic covenant. But the Old Testament does not exegetically warrant seeing the Mosaic covenant as double-sided—gracious at one level and based on works at another.

Some Lutheran scholars go even farther astray than Karlberg on this question, for they essentially argue that the law presents a different way of salvation based on works. This interpretation has a long history, and one can see from some of Paul's statements that distinguish faith from law why such a view has been promulgated. Such an interpretation should be rejected, though, because the Mosaic covenant was fundamentally gracious. Yahweh gave his people the law after he chose and liberated them from Egypt and set his electing love upon them.

My comments here should not be interpreted to mean that there is no discontinuity between the Mosaic covenant and the new covenant. Some of the discontinuities and continuities have been outlined in this book. The issue here is Karlberg's claim that the Mosaic covenant was actually intended to be based on works at the earthly level. It was not.

Karlberg makes a valid point that Adam would have been rewarded with eternal life if he had obeyed the law perfectly. Karlberg and the Reformed tradition rightly grasp the parallel between Adam and Christ in this regard. If one denies that Adam would have gained eternal life through his obedience, then one wonders how Christ could function as the substitute for human sin because of his obedience. Perhaps Fuller and Karlberg have more in common than one might suspect with regard to Adam. If I read Fuller correctly, he wants to maintain that Adam's obedience to the law would only be true obedience if it was based on faith. Fuller seems to oppose the idea that obedience to the law apart from faith leads to a reward. If Fuller suggests this, then his view is not that far apart from Karlberg's. Presumably, if Adam exercised faith in God at every moment and in this way lived in obedience he would obtain eternal life. Jesus' obedience, according to the Gospel of John, was due to dependence on the Father (see John 5:19, 30). Fuller seems correct in suggesting that all obedience is rooted in trust in God's promises; this would be true even for Adam and Jesus. He seems to read covenant theology as saying that if Adam had obeyed the law perfectly, then such obedience would not have been rooted in faith. I am not sure this accurately depicts Reformed theology. Perhaps I am missing something here, but I think we can maintain what both Karlberg and Fuller want to guard. Regarding Fuller, Scripture offers no reason to deny that any obedience Adam rendered was based on faith. And Karlberg is correct in concluding that, if Adam obeyed the law perfectly, he would obtain eternal life.

Bibliography

Adamson, J. B. *James: The Man and His Message*. Grand Rapids: Eerdmans, 1989.

Aletti, J.–N. "Rm 1,18–3,20: Incohérence ou cohérence de l'argumentation paulinienne?" *Bib* 69 (1988): 47–62.

Althaus, Paul. *Der Brief an die Römer*. Göttingen: Vandenhoeck and Ruprecht, 1978.

———. *The Divine Command*. Philadelphia: Fortress, 1966.

Attridge, Harold W. *The Epistle to the Hebrews*. Philadelphia: Fortress, 1989.

Augustine. *Saint Augustine: Anti-Pelagian Writings*. Philip Schaff, ed. *Nicene and Post-Nicene Fathers of the Christian Church*, Vol. 5. Repr. ed., Grand Rapids: Eerdmans, 1987.

Avis, P. D. L. "Moses and the Magistrate: A Study in the Rise of Protestant Legalism." *JEH* 26 (1975): 149–72.

Bacchiocchi, Samuele. *From Sabbath to Sunday: A Historical Investigation of the Rise of Sunday Observance in Early Christianity*. Rome: Pontifical Gregorian University, 1977.

Badenas, Robert. *Christ the End of the Law: Romans 10:4 in Pauline Perspective*. Sheffield: JSOT, 1985.

Bahnsen, Greg L. *Theonomy in Christian Ethics*. Nutley, N.J.: Craig, 1977.

Bailey, Kenneth E. *Through Peasant Eyes: A Literary-Cultural Approach to the Parables in Luke*. Grand Rapids: Eerdmans, 1983.

Bammel, Ernst. "Νόμος Χριστοῦ." In F. L. Cross, ed. *Studia Evangelica Vol. 3: The New Testament Message*. Berlin: Akademie-Verlag, 1964, 120–28.

Bandstra, Andrew J. "Paul and The Law: Some Recent Developments and An Extraordinary Book." *Calvin Theological Journal* 25 (1990): 249–61.

Banks, Robert. *Jesus and the Law in the Synoptic Tradition*. Cambridge: Cambridge University Press, 1975.

Barclay, John M. G. *Obeying the Truth: A Study of Paul's Ethics in Galatians*. Edinburgh: T. and T. Clark, 1988.

———. "Paul and the Law: Observations on Some Recent Debates." *Themelios* 12 (1986): 5–15.

Barker, William S. and W. R. Godfrey, eds. *Theonomy: A Reformed Critique*. Grand Rapids: Zondervan, 1990.

Barrett, C. K. *A Commentary on the Epistle to the Romans*. New York: Harper and Row, 1957.

————. *A Commentary on the First Epistle to the Corinthians.* New York: Harper and Row, 1968.

————. *The Gospel According to St. John,* 2d ed. Philadelphia: Westminster, 1978.

Barth, G. "Matthew's Understanding of the Law." In G. Bornkamm, G. Barth, and J. H. Held, *Tradition and Interpretation in Matthew.* Philadelphia: Westminster, 1963, 58–164.

Barth, Karl. *A Shorter Commentary on Romans.* Richmond: John Knox, 1959.

————. *Church Dogmatics.* Edinburgh: T. and T. Clark, 1956, I.2.

Barth, Markus. "Die Stellung des Paulus Gesetz und Ordnung." *EvT* 33 (1973): 496–526.

Bartsch, Hans W. "The Historical Situation of Romans." *Encounter* 33 (1972): 329–39.

Bassler, Jouette M. "Divine Impartiality in Paul's Letter to the Romans." *NovT* 26 (1984): 43–58.

————. *Divine Impartiality: Paul and a Theological Axiom.* Chico, Calif.: Scholars, 1982.

Bauer, Walter, W. F. Arndt, and F. W. Gingrich. *A Greek–English Lexicon of the New Testament and Other Early Christian Literature,* 2d ed., revised by F. W. Gingrich and F. W. Danker. Chicago: University of Chicago Press, 1979.

Beasley–Murray, George R. *John.* Waco: Word, 1987.

Beckwith, R. T., and W. Stott. *This is the Day: The Biblical Doctrine of the Christian Sunday in Its Jewish and Early Christian Setting.* London: Marshall, Morgan and Scott, 1978.

Beker, J. Christiaan. "Romans 9–11 in the Context of the Early Church." *Princeton Seminary Bulletin Supp* (1990): 40–55.

Belleville, Linda L. *Reflections of Glory: Paul's Polemical Use of the Moses-Doxa Tradition in 2 Corinthians 3.1–18.* Sheffield: JSOT, 1991.

————. "'Under Law': Structural Analysis and the Pauline Concept of Law in Galatians 3.21–4.11." *JSNT* 26 (1986): 53–78.

Berger, Klaus. *Die Gesetzauslegung Jesu: Ihr historischer Hintergrund im Judentum und im Alten Testament (Teil I: Markus und Parallelen).* Neukirchen–Vluyn: Neukirchener Verlag, 1972.

Best, T. F. "The Apostle Paul and E. P. Sanders: The Significance of Paul and Palestinian Judaism." *ResQ* 25 (1982): 65–74.

Bertram, Georg. "Παιδαγωγός." *Theological Dictionary of the New Testament,* ed. G. Friedrich. Grand Rapids: Eerdmans, 1967, 5:596–625.

Betz, Hans Dieter. *Galatians.* Philadelphia: Fortress, 1979.

————. "Spirit, Freedom, and Law: Paul's Message to the Galatian Churches." *SEÅ* 39 (1974): 145–60.

Blank, J. "Warum sagt Paulus: Aus Werken des Gesetzes wird niemand gerecht'?" *Rechtfertigung als Freiheit: Paulusstudien.* Neukirchen: Neukirchener Verlag, 1974, 79–95.

Bläser, Peter. *Das Gesetz bei Paulus.* Münster: Aschendorff, 1941.

Blass, F. and A. DeBrunner. *A Greek Grammar of the New Testament and Other Early Christian Literature.* Trans. and rev. by R. W. Funk. Chicago: University of Chicago Press, 1961.

Bloesch, Donald G. *Freedom for Obedience: Evangelical Ethics in Contemporary Times.* San Francisco: Harper and Row, 1987.

Blomberg, Craig L. "The Law in Luke-Acts." *JSNT* 22 (1984): 53–80.

———. "Marriage, Divorce, Remarriage, and Celibacy: An Exegesis of Matthew 19:3–12," *TrinJ* 11 (1990): 161–96.

Boers, Hendrikus. "'We Who Are by Inheritance Jews; Not from the Gentile Sinners.'" *JBL* 111 (1992): 273–81.

Borgen, Peder. "Observations on the Theme 'Paul and Philo': Paul's Preaching of Circumcision in Galatia (Gal 5:11): and Debates on Circumcision in Philo." In S. Pederson, ed. *The Pauline Literature and Theology.* Göttingen: Vandenhoeck and Ruprecht, 1980, 85–102.

———. "Paul Preaches Circumcision and Pleases Men." In M. D. Hooker and S. G. Wilson, eds. *Paul and Paulinism: Essays in Honour of C. K. Barrett.* London: SPCK, 1982, 37–46.

Bornkamm, Gunther. *Studien zu Antike und Urchristentum.* München: Chr. Kaiser, 1959.

Bornkamm, Heinrich. *Luther and the Old Testament.* Trans. E. W. Gritsch and R. C. Gritsch; edited by V. I. Gruhn. Philadelphia: Fortress, 1969.

Braswell, J. P. "'The Blessing of Abraham' versus 'The Curse of the Law': Another Look at Gal 3:10–13." *WTJ* 53 (1991): 73–91.

Breshears, Gerry. "The Place of Law in the Life of the Believer in Christ." Paper read at ETS, 1989.

Bring, Ragnar. "Paul and the Old Testament: A Study of the Ideas of Election, Faith and Law in Paul, with Special Reference to Romans 9:30–10:30." *ST* 25 (1971): 21–60.

———. "Preaching the Law." *SJT* 13 (1960): 1–32.

Broer, I. "Anmerkungen zum Gesetzesverständnis des Matthäus." In K. Kertelge, ed. *Das Gesetz im Neuen Testament.* Freiburg: Herder, 1986, 128–236.

Brown, Raymond E. *The Epistles of John.* Garden City, N.J.: Doubleday, 1982.

———. *The Gospel According to John.* 2 vols. Garden City, N.J.: Doubleday, 1966, 1970.

Bruce, F. F. *Commentary on the Book of Acts.* Grand Rapids: Eerdmans, 1954.

———. *The Epistle to the Galatians.* Grand Rapids: Eerdmans, 1982.

———. *The Epistle to the Hebrews.* Grand Rapids: Eerdmans, 1964.

———. *The Letter of Paul to the Romans,* 2d ed. Grand Rapids: Eerdmans, 1985.

———. "Paul and the Law in Recent Research." In Barnabas Lindars, ed. *Law and Religion.* Cambridge: James Clarke, 1988, 115–25.

———. "Paul and the Law of Moses." *BJRL* 57 (1975): 259–79.

Bugge, C. A. "Das Gesetz und Christus: nach der Anschauung der ältesten Christengemeinde." *ZNW* 4 (1903): 89–110.

Bultmann, Rudolf. "Christ the End of the Law." *Essays Philosophical and Theological.* London: SCM, 1955, 36–66.

———. "Romans 7 and the Anthropology of Paul." *Existence and Faith.* New York: Meridian, 1960, 147–57.

———. *Theology of the New Testament.* 2 vols. New York: Scribner's, 1951, 1955.

Burchard, C. "Zu Jakobus 2,14–26." *ZNW* 71 (1980): 27–45.

Burton, Ernest. DeW. *A Critical and Exegetical Commentary on the Epistle to the Galatians.* Edinburgh: T. and T. Clark, 1921.

Byrne, Brendan. J. "Living out the Righteousness of God: The Contribution of Rom 6:1–8:13 to an Understanding of Paul's Ethical Presuppositions." *CBQ* 43 (1981): 557–81.

Caird, G. B. "Review of E. P. Sanders. *Paul and Palestinian Judaism: A Comparison of Patterns of Religion.*" *JTS* 29 (1978): 538–43.

Callan, T. "Pauline Midrash: The Exegetical Background of Gal 3:19b." *JBL* 99 (1980): 549–67.

Calvin, John. *Calvin's Commentaries*, vols., 8 and 11, ed. D. W. Torrance and T. F. Torrance. Grand Rapids: Eerdmans, 1961.

———. *Institutes of the Christian Religion.* 2 vols., edited by John T. McNeill. Philadelphia: Westminster, 1960.

Cambier, J.–M. "Le jugement de tous les hommes par Dieu seul, selon la vérité, dâns Rom 2 1–3 20." *ZNW* 67 (1976): 187–213.

Campbell, William S. "Christ the End of the Law: Romans 10:4." *StudBib* 3 (1978): 73–81.

———. "Did Paul Advocate Separation from the Synagogue? A Reaction to Francis Watson: *Paul, Judaism and the Gentiles: A Sociological Approach.*" *SJT* 42 (1989): 457–67.

———. "The Freedom and Faithfulness of God in Relation to Israel." *JSNT* 13 (1981): 27–45.

———. "Romans 3 as the Key to the Structure and Thought of the Letter." *NovT* 23 (1981): 22–40.

———. "Why Did Paul Write Romans?" *ExpT* 85 (1974): 264–69.

Carras, George P. "Romans 2,1–29: A Dialogue on Jewish Ideals." *Bib* 73 (1992): 183–207.

Carson, D. A., Douglas J. Moo and Leon Morris. *An Introduction to the New Testament.* Grand Rapids: Zondervan, 1992.

Carson, D. A. *Divine Sovereignty and Human Responsibility: Biblical Perspectives in Tension.* Atlanta: John Knox, 1981.

———. *Exegetical Fallacies.* Grand Rapids: Baker, 1984.

———. *The Gospel According to John.* Grand Rapids: Eerdmans, 1991.

———. "Jesus and the Sabbath in the Four Gospels." In D. A. Carson, ed. *From Sabbath to Lord's Day: A Biblical, Historical and Theological Investigation.* Grand Rapids: Zondervan, 1982, 57–97.

———. "John and the Johannine Epistles." In D. A. Carson and H. G. M. Wilson, eds. *It is Written: Scripture Citing Scripture. Essays in Honour of Barnabas Lindars.* Cambridge: Cambridge University Press, 1988, 245–64.

———. *Matthew* in *The Expositor's Bible Commentary*, ed. F. E. Gaebelein. Grand Rapids: Zondervan, 1984, 8:1–599.

———. "'Silent in the Churches': On the Role of Women in 1 Corinthians 14:33b–36." In J. Piper and W. Grudem, eds. *Recovering Biblical Manhood and Womanhood.* Wheaton: Crossway, 1991: 140–53.

Carson, David (sic: D. A.). "Pauline Inconsistency: Reflections on I Corinthians 9.19–23 and Galatians 2.11–14." *Churchman* 100 (1986): 6–45.

Charlesworth, J. H. *The Old Testament Pseudepigrapha*, 2 vols. Garden City, N.J.: Doubleday, 1985.

Cohn-Sherbok, D. "Some Reflections on James Dunn's: 'The Incident at Antioch (Gal. 2.11–18).'" *JSNT* 18 (1983): 68–74.

Collins, John J. *Between Athens and Jerusalem: Jewish Identity in the Hellenistic Diaspora.* New York: Crossroad, 1983.

Conzelmann, Hans. *Acts of the Apostles.* Philadelphia: Fortress, 1987.

Cooper, K. T. "Paul and Rabbinic Soteriology: A Review Article." *WTJ* 44 (1982): 123–39.

Cosgrove, Charles H. "Arguing Like a Mere Human Being: Galatians 3.15–18 in Rhetorical Perspective." *NTS* 34 (1988): 536–49.

———. *The Cross and the Spirit: A Study in the Argument and Theology of Galatians.* Macon: Mercer, 1988.

———. "The Law has Given Sarah No Children (Gal. 4:21–30)." *NovT* 29 (1987): 219–35.

———. "The Mosaic Law Preaches Faith: A Study in Galatians 3." *WTJ* 41 (1978): 146–64.

———. "What If Some Have Not Believed? The Occasion and Thrust of Romans 3:1–8." *ZNW* 78 (1987): 90–105.

Cranfield, Charles E. B. *A Critical and Exegetical Commentary on the Epistle to the Romans,* 2 vols. Edinburgh: T. and T. Clark, 1975, 1979.

———. "Giving a Dog a Bad Name: A Note on H. Räisänen's *Paul and the Law.*" *JSNT* 38 (1990): 77–85.

———. *The Gospel According to Saint Mark.* Cambridge: Cambridge University Press, 1959.

———. "Romans 9:30–10:4." *Int* 34 (1980): 70–74.

———. "St. Paul and the Law." *SJT* 17 (1964): 43–68.

———. "'The Works of the Law' in the Epistle to the Romans." *JSNT* 43 (1991): 89–101.

Crowther, C. "Works, Work and Good Works." *ExpT* 81 (1969–1970): 166–71.

Cullmann, Oscar. *Salvation in History.* New York: Harper and Row, 1967.

Davids, Peter H. *The Epistle of James.* Grand Rapids: Eerdmans, 1982.

Davies, Glenn N. *Faith and Obedience in Romans: A Study of Romans 1–4.* Sheffield: JSOT, 1990.

Davies, W. D. and Dale C. Allison, Jr. *A Critical and Exegetical Commentary on the Gospel According to Saint Matthew.* 3 vols. projected. Edinburgh: T. and T. Clark, 1988.

Davies, W. D. "Law in the New Testament." *Jewish and Pauline Studies.* Philadelphia: Fortress, 1984, 227–42.

———. *Paul and Rabbinic Judaism: Some Rabbinic Elements in Paul's Theology.* London: SPCK, 1948.

———. "Paul and the Law: Reflections on Pitfalls in Interpretation." *Jewish and Pauline Studies.* Philadelphia: Fortress, 1984, 91–122.

———. *The Setting of the Sermon on the Mount.* Cambridge: Cambridge University Press, 1964.

———. *Torah in the Messianic Age.* Philadelphia: Society of Biblical Literature, 1952.

Deidun, Thomas J. *New Covenant Morality in Paul.* Rome: Biblical Institute Press, 1981.

Dibelius, Martin. *A Commentary on the Epistle of James.* Rev. by H. Greeven. Philadelphia: Fortress, 1975.

Dibelius, Martin. and Hans Conzelmann. *A Commentary on the Pastoral Epistles.* Philadelphia: Fortress, 1972.

Dodd, C. H. "ΕΝΝΟΜΟΣ ΧΡΙΣΤΟΥ." *Studia Paulina in honorem J. de Zwaan.* Haarlem: Bohn, 1953, 96–110.

Donaldson, T. L. "The 'Curse of the Law' and the Inclusion of the Gentiles: Galatians 3.13–14." *NTS* 32 (1986): 94–112.

———. "Zealot and Convert: The Origin of Paul's Christ–Torah Antithesis." *CBQ* 51 (1989): 655–82.

Donfried, Karl P. "Justification and Last Judgment in Paul." *ZNW* 67 (1976): 90–110.

———, ed. *The Romans Debate*. Rev. ed. Peabody: Hendrickson, 1991.

Dorsey, David A. "The Law of Moses and the Christian: A Compromise." *JETS* 34 (1991): 321–34.

Drane, John W. *Paul, Libertine or Legalist? A Study of the Theology of the Major Pauline Epistles*. London: SPCK, 1975.

———. "Tradition, Law and Ethics in Pauline Theology." *NovT* 16 (1974): 167–78.

Dülmen, Andrea van. *Die Theologie des Gesetzes bei Paulus*. Stuttgart: Katholisches Bibelwerk, 1968.

Dumbrell, William J. "Law and Grace: The Nature of the Contrast in John 1:17." *EvQ* 58 (1986): 25–37.

Dunn, James D. G. "The Incident at Antioch (Gal. 2:11–18)." *JSNT* 18 (1983): 3–57.

———. *Jesus, Paul, and the Law: Studies in Mark and Galatians*. Louisville: Westminster, 1990.

———. "The Justice of God: A Renewed Perspective on Justification by Faith." *JTS* 43 (1992): 1–22.

———. "The New Perspective on Paul." *BJRL* 65 (1983): 95–122.

———. *Romans*, 2 vols. Dallas: Word, 1988.

———. "Works of the Law and the Curse of the Law (Galatians 3.10–14)." *NTS* 31 (1985): 523–42.

———. "Yet Once More—'The Works of the Law': A Response." *JSNT* 46 (1992): 99–117.

Ebeling, Gerhard. "On the Doctrine of the *Triplex usus Legis* in the Theology of the Reformation." *Word and Faith*. Philadelphia: Fortress, 1963, 62–78.

Edwards, Ruth B. "Χάρις ἀντὶ χάριτος (John 1:16): Grace and the Law in the Johannine Prologue." *JSNT* 32 (1988): 3–15.

Elert, W. *Law and Gospel*. Philadelphia: Fortress, 1967.

Elliott, J. K. "In Favour of καυθήσωμαι at I Corinthians 13:3." *ZNW* 62 (1971): 297–98.

Elliott, Neil. *The Rhetoric of Romans: Argumentative Constraint and the Strategy of Paul's Dialogue with Judaism*. Sheffield: JSOT, 1990.

Esler, P. F. *Community and Gospel in Luke-Acts*. Cambridge: Cambridge University Press, 1987.

Espy, John M. "Paul's 'Robust Conscience' Re-examined." *NTS* 31 (1985): 161–88.

Fee, Gordon D. *1 and 2 Timothy, Titus*. Peabody: Hendrickson, 1988.

———. *The First Epistle to the Corinthians*. Grand Rapids: Eerdmans, 1987.

Feuillet, A. "Loi de Dieu, Loi du Christ, et Loi de L'Esprit d'après Les Epîtres Pauliniennes." *NovT* 22 (1980): 29–65.

Filson, Floyd V. *St. Paul's Concept of Recompense*. Leipzig: J. C. Hinrichs'sche Buchhandlung, 1931.

Fischer, J. "Paul in His Jewish Context." *EvQ* 57 (1985): 211–36.

Fitzmyer, Joseph A. *The Gospel According to Luke*. 2 vols. Garden City, N. J. : Doubleday, 1981, 1985.

———. *Luke the Theologian: Aspects of His Teaching*. New York: Paulist, 1989.

———. "Paul and the Law." *A Companion to Paul*, ed. M. J. Taylor. New York: Alba, 1975, 73–87.

Flückiger, F. "Christus, des Gesetzes τέλος." *TZ* 11 (1955): 153–57.

———. "Die Werke des Gesetzes bei den Heiden (nach Röm. 2, 14ff.)." *TZ* 8 (1952): 17–42.

Forde, G. O. "Law and Gospel in Luther's Hermeneutic." *Int* 37 (1983): 240–52.

Frankemölle, H. "Gesetz im Jakobusbrief. Zur Tradition, kontextuellen Verwendung und Rezeption eines belaseten Begriffes." In K. Kertelge, ed. *Das Gesetz im Neuen Testament.* Herder: Freiburg, 1986, 175–221.

Friedrich, Gerhard. "Das Gesetz des Glaubens Röm. 3,27." *TZ* 10 (1954): 401–17.

Fryer, N. S. L. "The Meaning and Translation of *Hilastērion* in Romans 3:25." *EvQ* 59 (1987): 99–116.

Fuller, Daniel P. *Gospel and Law: Contrast or Continuum?* Grand Rapids: Eerdmans, 1980.

———. "Paul and 'The Works of the Law'." *WTJ* 38 (1975): 28–42.

———. *The Unity of the Bible.* Grand Rapids: Zondervan, 1992.

Fung, Ronald Y. K. *The Epistle to the Galatians.* Grand Rapids: Eerdmans, 1988.

Furnish, Victor Paul. *Theology and Ethics in Paul.* Nashville: Abingdon, 1968.

Gager, John G. *The Origins of Anti–Semitism: Attitudes Toward Judaism in Pagan and Christian Antiquity.* New York: Oxford University Press, 1983.

Garland, David E. *The Intention of Matthew 23.* Leiden: Brill, 1979.

Garlington, D. B. "The Obedience of Faith in the Letter to the Romans; Part I: The Meaning of ὑπακοὴν πίστεως (Rom 1:5; 16:26)." *WJT* 52 (1990): 201–24.

———. "The Obedience of Faith in the Letter to the Romans Part II: The Obedience of Faith and Judgment by Works." *WTJ* 53 (1991): 47–72.

Gasque, Ward W. *A History of Criticism of the Acts of the Apostles.* Grand Rapids: Eerdmans, 1975.

Gaston, Lloyd. *Paul and the Torah.* Vancouver: University of British Columbia Press, 1987.

Geer, T. C. "Paul and the Law in Recent Discussion." *ResQ* 31 (1989): 93–107.

Gehman, H. S. "An Insight and Realization: A Study of the New Covenant." *Int* 9 (1955): 279–93.

Gese, H. *Essays on Biblical Theology.* Minneapolis: Augsburg, 1981.

Gessert, R. A. "The Integrity of Faith: An Inquiry Into the Meaning of Law in the Thought of John Calvin." *SJT* 13 (1960): 247–61.

Getty, M. A. "Paul and the Salvation of Israel: A Perspective on Romans 9–11." *CBQ* 50 (1988): 456–69.

Godet, F. *Commentary on the Epistle to the Romans.* 1889; repr. ed., Grand Rapids: Zondervan, 1956.

Godfrey, W. R. "Calvin and Theonomy." In William S. Barker and W. B. Godfrey, eds. *Theonomy: A Reformed Critique.* Grand Rapids: Zondervan, 1990, 299–312.

Goldingay, John. *Theological Diversity and the Authority of the Old Testament.* Grand Rapids: Eerdmans, 1984.

Gordon, T. David. "A Note on ΠΑΙΔΑΓΩΓΟΣ in Galatians 3.24–25." *NTS* 35 (1989): 150–54.

———. "The Problem at Galatia." *Int* 41 (1987): 32–43.

———. "Why Israel did not Obtain Torah-Righteousness: A Translation Note on Rom 9:32." *WTJ* 54 (1992): 163–66.

Grafe, E. *Die paulinische Lehre vom Gesetz nach vier Hauptbriefen.* Tübingen: J. C. B. Mohr, 1884.

Gundry, Robert H. "Grace, Works, and Staying Saved in Paul." *Bib* 66 (1985): 1–38.

———. "The Moral Frustration of Paul Before His Conversion: Sexual Lust in Romans 7:7–25." In Donald A. Hagner and M. J. Harris, eds. *Pauline Studies: Essays Presented to Professor F. F. Bruce on His Seventieth Birthday.* Grand Rapids: Eerdmans, 1980, 228–45.

Gutbrod, W. "Νόμος." *Theological Dictionary of the New Testament*, ed. Gerhard Kittel. Grand Rapids: Eerdmans, 1967, 4:1036–91.

Guthrie, Donald. *Galatians.* Grand Rapids: Eerdmans, 1973.

———. *New Testament Introduction*, rev. ed. Downers Grove, Ill.: InterVarsity, 1990.

———. *New Testament Theology.* Downers Grove, Ill.: InterVarsity, 1981.

———. *The Pastoral Epistles.* Grand Rapids: Eerdmans, 1957.

Haenchen, Ernst. *The Acts of the Apostles: A Commentary.* Philadelphia: Westminster, 1971.

Hafemann, Scott J. "Entering and Remaining: E. P. Sanders' View of Palestinian Judaism." *Studia Biblica et Theologica* 11 (1981): 139–49.

———. "The Glory and Veil of Moses in 2 Cor 3:7–14: An Example of Paul's Contextual Exegesis of the OT—A Proposal." *HBT* 14 (1992): 31–49.

———. *Paul and Moses, The Letter/Spirit Contrast and Argument from Scripture in 2 Cor. 3* (tentative title). Tübingen: J. C. B. Mohr, forthcoming.

———. "'Self-Commendation' and Apostolic Legitimacy in 2 Corinthians: A Pauline Dialectic?" *NTS* 36 (1990): 66–88.

Hagner, Donald A. *Hebrews.* New York: Harper and Row, 1983.

———. "Paul and Judaism: The Jewish Matrix of Early Christianity: Issues in the Current Debate." Paper presented at a symposium, Institute for Biblical Research, San Francisco, November, 1992.

———. "Paul in Modern Jewish Thought." In Donald A. Hagner and M. J. Harris, eds. *Pauline Studies: Essays Presented to F. F. Bruce on His Seventieth Birthday.* Grand Rapids: Eerdmans, 1980, 143–65.

Hahn, F. "Das Gesetzesverständnis im Römer—und Galaterbrief." *ZNW* 67 (1976): 29–63.

Hall, Jerome. "Paul, the Lawyer, on Law." *Journal of Law and Religion* 3 (1985): 331–79.

Hamerton–Kelly, Robert G. "Sacred Violence and the Curse of the Law (Galatians 3.13): The Death of Christ as a Sacrificial Travesty." *NTS* 36 (1990): 98–118.

———. "Sacred Violence and 'Works of Law.' 'Is Christ Then an Agent of Sin?' (Galatians 2:17)." *CBQ* 52 (1990): 55–75.

Hanson, A. T. *The Pastoral Epistles.* Grand Rapids: Eerdmans, 1982.

Harrisville, R. A. *Romans.* Minneapolis: Augsburg, 1980.

Haufe, C. "Die Stellung des Paulus zum Gesetz." *TLZ* 91 (1966): 171–78.

Hays, Richard B. "Christology and Ethics in Galatians: The Law of Christ." *CBQ* 49 (1987): 268–90.

———. *Echoes of Scripture in the Letters of Paul.* New Haven: Yale University Press, 1989.

———. "Recent Books on New Testament Ethics." *Quarterly Review* 6 (1986): 13–30.

Heiligenthal, R. "Soziologische Implikationen der paulinischen Rechtfertigungslehre im Galaterbrief am Beispiel der 'Werke des Gesetzes.'" *Kairos* 26 (1984): 38–53.

Hemer, Colin J. *The Book of Acts in the Setting of Hellenistic History.* Tübingen: J. C. B. Mohr, 1989.

Hempel, J. R. "On the Problem of the Law in the Old and New Testaments." *ATR* 34 (1952): 227–32.

Hengel, Martin. *Acts and the History of Earliest Christianity*. Philadelphia: Fortress, 1979.

———. *Between Jesus and Paul: Studies in the Earliest History of Christianity*. Philadelphia: Fortress, 1983.

———. "Der Jakobusbrief als antipaulinische Polemik." In G. F. Hawthorne and Otto Betz, eds. *Tradition and Interpretation in the New Testament: Essays in Honor of E. Earle Ellis*. Grand Rapids: Eerdmans, 1987, 248–78.

———. *Judaism and Hellenism: Studies in Their Encounter in Palestine during the Early Hellenistic Period*, 2 vols. Philadelphia: Fortress, 1974.

———. *The Pre-Christian Paul*. Philadelphia: Trinity, 1991.

Hill, David. "Salvation Proclaimed IV. Galatians 3:10–14: Freedom and Acceptance." *ExpT* 93 (1982): 196–200.

Hodges, Zane C. *Absolutely Free*. Grand Rapids: Zondervan, 1989.

Hofius, Otfried. "Das Gesetz des Mose und das Gesetz Christi." *ZTK* 80 (1983): 262–86.

———. "Gesetz und Evangelium nach 2. Korinther 3." *Paulusstudien*. Tübingen: J. C. B. Mohr, 1989, 75–120.

Hooker, Morna D. "Paul and 'Covenantal Nomism.'" In Morna D. Hooker and S. G. Wilson, eds. *Paul and Paulinism: Essays in Honour of C. K. Barrett*. London: SPCK, 1982, 47–56.

Houlden, J. L. "A Response to James D. G. Dunn." *JSNT* (1983): 58–67.

Howard, George E. "Christ the End of the Law: The Meaning of Romans 10:4ff." *JBL* 88 (1969): 331–37.

———. *Paul: Crisis in Galatia. A Study in Early Christian Theology*. Cambridge: Cambridge University Press, 1979.

Hübner, Hans. *Das Gesetz in der synoptischen Tradition*. Witten: Luther-Verlag, 1973.

———. *Law in Paul's Thought*. Edinburgh: T. and T. Clark, 1984.

———. "Pauli Theologiae Proprium." *NTS* 26 (1980): 445–73.

———. "Was heisst bei Paulus 'Werke des Gesetzes'?" In E. Gräßer and O. Merk, eds. *Glaube und Eschatologie: Festschrift für Werner Georg Kümmel zum 80. Geburtstag*. Tübingen: J. C. B. Mohr, 1985, 123–33.

Hughes, J. J. "Hebrews IX 15ff. and Galatians III 15ff.: A Study in Covenant Practice and Procedure." *NovT* 21 (1979): 26–96.

Hughes, Philip E. *A Commentary on the Epistle to the Hebrews*. Grand Rapids: Eerdmans, 1977.

Jeremias, Joachim. *The Parables of Jesus*, rev. ed. New York: Scribner's, 1972.

———. "Paul and James." *ExpT* 66 (1954–1955): 368–71.

Jervell, Jacob. *Luke and the People of God: A New Look at Luke-Acts*. Minneapolis: Augsburg, 1972.

———. "Retrospect and Prospect in Luke-Acts Interpretation." In E. H. Lovering, Jr., ed. *Society of Biblical Literature 1991 Seminar Papers*. Atlanta: Scholars, 1991, 383–404.

Jewett, Paul K. *The Lord's Day: A Theological Guide to the Christian Day of Worship*. Grand Rapids: Eerdmans, 1971.

Jewett, Robert. "The Law and the Coexistence of Jews and Gentiles in Romans." *Int* 39 (1985): 341–56.

Joest, W. *Gesetz und Freiheit. Das Problem des 'Tertius usus Legis' bei Luther und die neutestamentliche Parainese*, 3d ed. Göttingen: Vandenhoeck and Ruprecht, 1961.

Jüngel, E. "Das Gesetz zwischen Adam und Christus: Eine theologische Studie zu Röm 5, 12–21." *ZTK* 60 (1963): 42–74.

Kaiser, Walter C., Jr. "God's Promise Plan and His Gracious Law." *JETS* 33 (1990): 289–302.

———. "Leviticus 18:5 and Paul: Do This and You Shall Live (Eternally?)." *JETS* 14 (1971): 19–28.

———. *Toward an Exegetical Theology.* Grand Rapids: Baker, 1981.

———. "The Weightier and Lighter Matters of the Law: Moses, Jesus and Paul." In G. F. Hawthorne, ed. *Current Issues in Biblical and Patristic Interpretation: Studies in Honor of Merrill C. Tenney.* Grand Rapids: Eerdmans, 1975: 176–92.

Kalusche, Martin. "'Das Gesetz als Thema biblischer Theologie?': Anmerkungen zu einem Entwurf Peter Stuhlmachers." *ZNW* 77 (1986): 194–205.

Karlberg, Mark W. "Covenant Theology and the Westminster Tradition." *WTJ* 54 (1992): 135–52.

———. "Justification in Redemptive History." *WTJ* 43 (1981): 213–46.

———. "Legitimate Discontinuities Between the Testaments." *JETS* 28 (1985): 9–20.

———. "Moses and Christ: The Place of Law in Seventeenth Century Puritanism." *TrinJ* 10 (1989): 11–32.

———. "The Original State of Adam: Tensions within Reformed Theology." *EvQ* 87 (1987): 291–309.

———. "Reformation Politics: The Relevance of OT Ethics in Calvinist Political Theory." *JETS* 29 (1986): 179–91.

———. "Reformed Interpretation of the Mosaic Covenant." *WTJ* 43 (1980): 1–57.

Käsemann, Ernst. *Commentary on Romans.* Grand Rapids: Eerdmans, 1980.

Keck, Leander E. "The Law and 'The Law of Sin and Death' (Rom 8:1–4): Reflections on the Spirit and Ethics in Paul." In J. L. Crenshaw and S. Sandmel, eds. *The Divine Helmsman: Studies on God's Control of Human Events, Presented to Lou H. Silberman.* New York: Ktav, 1980, 41–57.

Kee, Howard Clark. "The Ethical Dimensions of the Testaments of the XII as a Clue to Provenance." *NTS* 24 (1977–1978): 259–70.

Kelly, J. N. D. *A Commentary on the Pastoral Epistles*, repr. ed. Grand Rapids: Baker, 1981.

Kertelge, Karl. "Gesetz und Freiheit im Galaterbrief." *NTS* 30 (1984): 382–94.

King, D. H. "Paul and the Tannaim: A Study in Galatians." *WTJ* 45 (1983): 340–70.

Klein, Günter. "Heil und Geschichte nach Römer IV." *NTS* 13 (1966): 43–47.

———. "Eine Sturmzentrum der Paulusforschung." *Verkündigung und Forschung* 33 (1988): 40–56.

———. "Sündenverständnis und theologia crucis bei Paulus." In C. Andresen and Günter Klein, eds. *Theologia Crucis—Signum Crucis: Festschrift für Erich Dinkler.* Tübingen: J. C. B. Mohr, 1979, 249–82.

Klein, Meredith G. "Gospel until the Law: Rom 5:13–14 and the Old Covenant." *JETS* 34 (1991): 433–46.

Klinghardt, Matthias. *Gesetz und Volk Gottes.* Tübingen: J. C. B. Mohr, 1988.

Knox, John. *Romans.* In *The Interpreter's Bible*, vol. 9, ed. G. A. Buttrick. New York: Abingdon, 1954.

König, A. "Gentiles or Gentile Christians? On the Meaning of Romans 2:12–16." *J Th So Africa* 15 (1976): 53–60.

Kuhr, Fredrich. "Römer 2:14f. und die Verheissung bei Jeremia 31:31ff." *ZNW* 55 (1964): 252–61.

Kuss, Otto. "Die Heiden und die Werke des Gesetzes (nach Röm 2, 14–16)." *MTZ* 5 (1954): 77–98.

———. "Nomos bei Paulus." *MTZ* 17 (1966): 173–227.

———. *Der Römerbrief.* 3 vols. Regensburg: F. Pustet, 1959, 1963, 1978.

Laato, Timo. *Paulus und das Judentum: Anthropologische Erwägungen.* Åbo: Åbo Academy Press, 1991.

Lackmann, M. *Vom Geheimnis der Schöpfung: Die Geschichte der Exegese von Römer I,18–23, II,14–16 und Acta XIV,15–17, XVII,22–29 vom 2. Jahrhundret bis zum Beginn der Orthodoxie.* Stuttgart: Evangelisches Verlagswerk, 1952.

Ladd, George Eldon. *A Theology of the New Testament.* Grand Rapids: Eerdmans, 1974.

Lagrange, M.-J. *Saint Paul Epître aux Romains.* Paris: Gabalda, 1950.

Lambrecht, Jan. "Gesetzesverständnis bei Paulus." In K. Kertelge, ed. *Das Gesetz im Neuen Testament.* Freiburg: Herder, 1986, 88–127.

———. "The Line of Thought in Gal. 2.14b–21." *NTS* 24 (1978): 484–95.

———. "Transgressor by Nullifying God's Grace. A Study of Gal 2,18–21." *Bib* 72 (1991): 217–36.

———. "Why is Boasting Excluded? A Note on Rom 3,27 and 4,2." *ETL* 61 (1985): 365–69.

Lang, F. "Gesetz und Bund bei Paulus." In J. Friedrich, W. Pöhlmann, and P. Stuhlmacher, eds. *Rechtfertigung: Festschrift für Ernst Käsemann zum 70. Geburtstag.* Tübingen: J. C. B. Mohr, 1976, 305–20.

Larsson, E. "Paul: Law and Salvation." *NTS* 31 (1985): 425–36.

Laws, Sophie. *A Commentary on the Epistle of James.* New York: Harper and Row, 1980.

Leenhardt, F.-J. *The Epistle to the Romans.* London: Lutterworth, 1961.

Lichtenberger, Hermann. "Paulus und das Gesetz." In Martin Hengel and U. Heckel, eds. *Paulus und das antike Judentum.* Tübingen: J. C. B. Mohr, 1991, 361–78.

Liebers, Reinhold. *Das Gesetz als Evangelium: Untersuchungen zur Gesetzeskritik des Paulus.* Zürich: Theologischer Verlag, 1989.

Lietzmann, Hans. *An die Römer.* Tübingen: J. C. B. Mohr, 1928.

Lightfoot, J. B. *The Epistle of St. Paul to the Galatians.* 1865; repr. ed., Grand Rapids: Zondervan, 1957.

Lightstone, J. N. "Torah Is *Nomos*—Except When it is Not: Prolegomena to the Study of the Law in Late Antique Judaism." *SR* 13 (1984): 29–37.

Lindars, Barnabas. "All Foods Clean: Thoughts on Jesus and the Law." In Barnabas Lindars, ed. *Law and Religion.* Cambridge: James Clarke, 1988, 61–71.

———. *The Gospel of John.* Grand Rapids: Eerdmans, 1972.

Lindemann, Andreas. "Die biblischen Toragebote und die paulinische Ethik." In W. Schrage, ed. *Studien zum Text und zur Ethik des Neuen Testaments.* Berlin: de Gruyter, 1986, 242–65.

———. "Die Gerechtigkeit aus dem Gesetz Erwägungen zur Auslegung und zur Textgeschichte von Römer 10:5." *ZNW* 73 (1982): 231–50.

Linss, W. C. "Exegesis of telos in Romans 10:4." *BR* 33 (1988): 5–12.

Loader, B. "Paul and Judaism—Is He Fighting Strawmen?" *Colloquium: The Australia and New Zealand Theological Review* 16 (1984): 11–20.

Logan, Samuel T., Jr. "New England Puritans and the State." In William S. Barker and W. R. Godfrey, eds. *Theonomy: A Reformed Critique*. Grand Rapids: Zondervan, 1990, 353–84.

Lohmeyer, Ernest. "Probleme paulinischer Theologie. II. 'Gesetzeswerke.'" *ZNW* 28 (1929): 177–207.

Longenecker, Richard N. "The Acts of the Apostles." In Frederick E. Gaebelein, ed. *The Expositor's Bible Commentary*. Grand Rapids: Zondervan, 1981, 9:207–573.

———. *Galatians*. Dallas: Word, 1990.

———. *Paul: Apostle of Liberty*. 1964; repr. ed., Grand Rapids: Baker, 1976.

———. "The Pedagogical Nature of The Law in Galatians 3:19–4:7." *JETS* 25 (1982): 53–61.

———. "Three Ways of Understanding Relations between the Testaments: Historically and Today." In G. F. Hawthorne and Otto Betz, eds. *Tradition and Interpretation in the New Testament: Essays in Honor of E. Earle Ellis*. Grand Rapids: Eerdmans, 1987, 22–32.

Longman, Tremper, III. "God's Law and Mosaic Punishments Today." In William S. Barker and W. R. Godfrey, eds. *Theonomy: A Reformed Critique*. Grand Rapids: Zondervan, 1990, 41–54.

Lowe, J. "An Examination of Attempts to Detect Developments in St. Paul's Theology." *JTS* 42 (1941): 129–42.

Lührmann, Dieter. "Paul and the Pharisaic Tradition." *JSNT* 36 (1989): 75–94.

Lull, David J. "'The Law Was Our Pedagogue': A Study in Galatians 3:19–25." *JBL* 105 (1986): 481–98.

Luther, Martin. *Luther's Works*, 55 vols. Edited by J. Pelikan (vols. 1–30) and H. T. Lehmann (vols. 31–55). Philadelphia: Fortress, 1957.

Lyonnet, Stanislaus. "La circoncision du coeur, celle qui relève de l'Esprit et non de la lettre: (Rom 2:29)." In P. Bonnard, ed. *L'Évangile, hier et aujourd'hui: Mélanges offerts au Franz J. Leenhardt*. Genève: Labor et Fides, 1968, 87–97.

———. "Paul's Gospel of Freedom." In M. J. Taylor, ed. *A Companion to Paul*. New York: Alba House, 1975, 89–99.

———. "'Tu ne Convoiteras pas.'" In *Neotestamentica et Patristica. Festschrift for O. Cullmann*. Leiden: Brill, 1962, 157–65.

Mani, A. "Love and Law According to St Paul." *Indian Theological Studies* 23 (1986): 5–21.

Marshall, I. Howard. *The Acts of the Apostles*. Grand Rapids: Eerdmans, 1980.

———. *The Gospel of Luke*. Grand Rapids: Eerdmans, 1978.

———. *Last Supper and Lord's Supper*. Grand Rapids: Eerdmans, 1980.

Martens, Elmer A. "Embracing the Law: A Biblical Theological Perspective." *BBR* 2 (1992): 1–28.

Martin, Brice L. *Christ and the Law in Paul*. Leiden: Brill, 1989.

———. "Paul on Christ and the Law." *JETS* 26 (1983): 271–82.

Martin, Ralph P. *James*. Waco: Word, 1988.

Martyn, J. Louis. "Apocalyptic Antinomies in Paul's Letter to the Galatians." *NTS* 31 (1985): 410–24.

———. "A Law-Observant Mission to Gentiles: The Background of Galatians." *SJT* 38 (1985): 307–24.

Mattern, Lieselotte. *Das Verständnis des Gerichtes bei Paulus*. Zürich: Zwingli, 1966.

McConnell, R. S. *Law and Prophecy in Matthew's Gospel: The Authority and Use of the Old Testament in the Gospel of St. Matthew.* Basel: Friedrich Reinhardt, 1969.

McEleney, Neil J. "Conversion, Circumcision and the Law." *NTS* 20 (1974): 319–41.

McGrath, Alister E. *Iustitita Dei: A History of the Christian Doctrine of Justification,* 2 vols. Cambridge: Cambridge University Press, 1986.

McKnight, Scot. "Review of E. P. Sanders, Jesus and Judaism." *TrinJ* 6 (1985): 219–25.

Meier, John P. *Law and History in Matthew's Gospel: A Redactional Study of Matthew 5:17–48.* Rome: Biblical Institute Press, 1976.

Meyer, Paul W. "Romans 10:4 and the 'End' of the Law." In J. L. Crenshaw and S. Sandmel, eds. *The Divine Helmsman: Studies on God's Control of Human Events, Presented to Lou H. Silberman.* New York: Ktav, 1980, 59–78.

Michel, Otto. *Der Brief an die Römer.* Göttingen: Vandenhoeck and Ruprecht, 1966.

Mitton, C. Leslie. *The Epistle of James.* Grand Rapids: Eerdmans, 1966.

Mohrlang, Roger. *Matthew and Paul: A Comparison of Ethical Perspectives.* Cambridge: Cambridge University Press, 1984.

Montefiore, Claude G. *Judaism and St. Paul.* London: Max Goschen, 1914.

Montefiore, Claude G. and H. Loewe. *A Rabbinic Anthology.* New York: Schocken, 1974.

Moo, Douglas J. "Jesus and the Authority of the Mosaic Law." *JSNT* 20 (1984): 3–49.

———. "The Law of Moses or the Law of Christ." In J. S. Feinberg, ed. *Continuity and Discontinuity: Perspectives on the Relationship between the Old and New Testaments. Essays in Honor of S. Lewis Johnson, Jr.* Westchester: Crossway, 1988, 203–18.

———. "'Law,' 'Works of the Law,' and Legalism in Paul." *WTJ* 45 (1983): 73–100.

———. *The Letter of James.* Grand Rapids: Eerdmans, 1985.

———. "Paul and The Law in the Last Ten Years." *SJT* 40 (1987): 287–307.

———. "Review of D. P. Fuller. Gospel and Law: Contrast or Continuum? The Hermeneutics of Dispensationalism and Covenant Theology." *TrinJ* 3 (1982): 99–102.

———. Reviews of Heikki Räisänen. *Paul and the Law* and E. P. Sanders. *Paul, the Law and the Jewish People. TrinJ* 5 (1984): 92–99.

———. *Romans 1–8.* Chicago: Moody, 1991.

Moore, George Foote. "Christian Writers on Judaism." *HTR* 14 (1921): 197–254.

Morris, Leon. *The Epistle to the Romans.* Grand Rapids: Eerdmans, 1988.

———. *The Gospel According to John.* Grand Rapids: Eerdmans, 1971.

Morris, T. F. "Law and the Cause of Sin in the Epistle to the Romans." *HeyJ* 28 (1987): 285–91.

Moule, C. F. D. "A Christian Understanding of Law and Grace." *Christian Jewish Relations* 14 (1981): 52–61.

———. "Jesus, Judaism, and Paul." In G. F. Hawthorne and O. Betz, eds. *Tradition and Interpretation in the New Testament: Essays in Honor of E. Earle Ellis.* Grand Rapids: Eerdmans, 1987, 43–52.

———. "Obligation in the Ethic of Paul." In W. R. Farmer, C. F. D. Moule, and Reinhold R. Niebuhr, eds. *Christian History and Interpretation: Studies Presented to John Knox.* Cambridge: Cambridge University Press, 1967, 389–406.

Müller, G. "Der Dekalog im Neuen Testament: Vor–Erwägungen zu einer unerledigten Aufgabe." *TZ* 38 (1982): 79–97.

Müller, K. "Gesetz und Gesetzeserfüllung im Frühjudentum." In K. Kertelge, ed. *Das Gesetz im Neuen Testament.* Freiburg: Herder, 1986, 11–45.

Mundle, W. "Zur Auslegung von Röm 2,13ff." *TBl* 13 (1934): 249–56.

Murphy-O'Connor, Jerome. "Review of Sanders. Paul and Palestinian Judaism." *RB* 85 (1978): 122–26.

Murray, John. "Covenant Theology." in Philip E. Hughes, ed. *The Encyclopedia of Christianity.* Vol. 3. Marshallton: National Foundation for Christian Education, 1972, 199–216.

———. *The Epistle to the Romans.* Grand Rapids: Eerdmans, 1959, 1965.

———. *The Imputation of Adam's Sin.* Grand Rapids: Eerdmans, 1959.

———. *Principles of Conduct: Aspects of Biblical Ethics.* Grand Rapids: Eerdmans, 1957.

Mussner, F. "Christus (ist): des Gesetzes Ende zur Gerechtigkeit für jeden, der glaubt (Röm 10,4)." *Paulus—Apostat oder Apostel? Judische und christliche Antworten.* Regensburg: Friedrich Pustet, 1977, 31–44.

———. "Gesetz-Abraham-Israel." *Kairos* 25 (1983): 200–22.

Neusner, Jacob. "Comparing Judaisms: A Review of Paul and Palestinian Judaism." *HR* 18 (1978): 177–191.

———. "Mr. Sanders' Pharisees and Mine: A Response to E. P. Sanders, *Jewish Law from Jesus to the Mishnah.*" *SJT* 44 (1991): 73–95.

———. *The Rabbinic Traditions about the Pharisees before 70,* 3 vols. Leiden: Brill, 1971.

———. "The Use of the Later Rabbinic Evidence for the Study of Paul." In W. S. Green, ed. *Approaches to Ancient Judaism: Essays in Religion and History,* 2.9. Chico, Calif.: Scholars, 1980, 43–63.

Niebuhr, Karl-Wilhelm. *Gesetz und Paränese: Katechismusartige Weisungsreihen in der frühjüdischen Literatur.* Tübingen: J. C. B. Mohr, 1987.

Nolland, John. "A Fresh Look at Acts 15.10." *NTS* 27 (1980): 105–15.

———. "Uncircumcised Proselytes?" *JSJ* 12 (1981): 173–94.

Nygren, Anders. *Commentary on Romans.* Philadelphia: Fortress, 1949.

O'Brien, Peter T. *Colossians, Philemon.* Dallas: Word, 1982.

———. *The Epistle to the Philippians.* Grand Rapids: Eerdmans, 1991.

O'Neill, J. C. *Paul's Letter to the Romans.* Harmondsworth, England: Penguin, 1975.

Osten-Sacken, Peter von der. *Die Heiligkeit der Tora: Studien zum Gesetz bei Paulus.* München: Kaiser, 1989.

———. "Das paulinische Verständnis des Gesetzes im Spannungsfeld von Eschatologie und Geschichte: Erläuterungen zum Evangelium als Faktor von theologischem Antijudaismus." *EvT* 37 (1977): 549–87.

———. *Romer 8 als Beispiel paulinischer Soteriologie.* Göttingen: Vandenhoeck and Ruprecht, 1975.

Pancaro, S. *The Law in the Fourth Gospel.* Leiden: Brill, 1975.

Pentecost, J. Dwight. "The Purpose of the Law." *BSac* 128 (1971): 227–33.

Pfleiderer, Otto. *Der Paulinismus. Ein Beitrag zur Geschichte der urchristlichen Theologie,* 2d ed. Leipzig: Reisland, 1890.

Piper, John. *The Justification of God.* Grand Rapids: Baker, 1983.

Poythress, Vern S. *The Shadow of Christ in the Law of Moses.* Brentwood, Tenn.: Wolgemuth and Hyatt, 1991.

Pregeant, R. "Grace and Recompense: Reflections on a Pauline Paradox." *JAAR* 47 (1979): 73–96.

Provence, Thomas E. "'Who is Sufficient for These Things?' An Exegesis of 2 Corinthians ii 15 –iii 18." *NovT* 24 (1982): 54–81.

Przybylski, Benno. *Righteousness in Matthew and His World of Thought*. Cambridge: Cambridge University Press, 1980.

Radmacher, Earl D. "'Faith according to the Apostle James' by John F. MacArthur, Jr." *JETS* 33 (1990): 35–41.

Räisänen, Heikki "Galatians 2.16 and Paul's Break With Judaism." *NTS* 31 (1985): 543–53.

———. "Das 'Gesetz des Glaubens' (Rom. 3:27): und das 'Gesetz des Geistes' (Rom. 8:2)." *NTS* 26 (1980): 101–17.

———. "Legalism and Salvation by the Law: Paul's Portrayal of the Jewish Religion as a Historical and Theological Problem." In S. Pedersen, ed. *The Pauline Literature and Theology*. Göttingen: Vandenhoeck and Ruprecht, 1980, 63–83.

———. *Paul and the Law*. Philadelphia: Fortress, 1983.

———. "Paul's Conversion and the Development of His View of the Law." *NTS* 33 (1987): 404–19.

———. "Paul's Theological Difficulties with the Law." *Studia Biblica* 1978; E. A. Livingston, ed. *Papers on Paul and Other New Testament Authors*. Sheffield: JSOT, 1980, 301–20.

———. *The Torah and Christ*. Helsinki: Finnish Exegetical Society, 1986.

Refoulé, F. "Note Sur Romains IX, 30–33." *RB* 92 (1985): 161–86.

———. "Romains, X, 4. Encore une fois." *RB* 91 (1984): 321–50.

Reicke, B. "Paulus über das Gesetz." *TZ* 41 (1985): 237–57.

Reid, Daniel G. "The Misunderstood Apostle." *CT* 34 (1990): 25–27.

Reinmuth, Eckart. *Geist und Gesetz: Studien zu Voraussetzungen und Inhalt der paulinischen Paränese*. Berlin: Evangelische Verlagsanstalt, 1985.

Rhyne, C. T. *Faith Establishes the Law*. Chico, Calif.: Scholars, 1981.

———. "*Nomos Dikaiosynēs* and the Meaning of Romans 10:4." *CBQ* 47 (1985): 486–99.

Richardson, Peter R. "Spirit and Letter: A Foundation for Hermeneutics." *EvQ* 45 (1973): 208–18.

Ridderbos, Herman N. *Paul: An Outline of His Theology*. Grand Rapids: Eerdmans, 1975.

Riedl, J. "Die Auslegung von R 2, 14–16 in Vergangenheit und Gegenwart." In *Studiorum Paulinorum Congressus Internationalis Catholicus 1961*. Rome: Pontifical Biblical Institute, 1963, 1:271–81.

———. "Salus paganorum secundum Rom 2." *VD* 42 (1964): 61–70.

Rivkin, Ellis. *A Hidden Revolution*. Nashville: Abingdon, 1968.

Roetzel, Calvin J. *Judgement in the Community: A Study of the Relationship between Eschatology and Ecclesiology in Paul*. Leiden: Brill, 1972.

Rordorf, W. *Sunday: The History of the Day of Rest and Worship in the Earliest Centuries of the Christian Church*. London: SCM, 1968.

Ruether, Rosemary R. *Faith and Fratricide: The Theological Roots of Anti-Semitism*. New York: Seabury, 1974.

Rushdoony, Rousas J. *Institutes of Biblical Law*. Nutley, N.J.: Craig, 1973.

Sailhamer, John H. "The Mosaic Law and the Theology of the Pentateuch." *WTJ* 53 (1991): 241–61.

Salo, K. *Luke's Treatment of the Law: A Redaction-Critical Investigation*. Helsinki: Annales Academiae Scientiarum Fennicae, 1991.

Sanday, William, and A. C. Headlam. *The Epistle to the Romans*. New York: Scribner's, 1910.

Sanders, E. P. *Jesus and Judaism*. Philadelphia: Fortress, 1985.

———. *Jewish Law from Jesus to the Mishnah*. Philadelphia: Trinity, 1990.

———. "Judaism and the Grand 'Christian' Abstractions: Love, Mercy, and Grace." *Int* 39 (1985): 357–72.

———. *Judaism: Practice and Belief. 63 BCE–66 CE*. Philadelphia: Trinity, 1992.

———. *Paul and Palestinian Judaism: A Comparison of Patterns of Religion*. Philadelphia: Fortress, 1977.

———. *Paul, the Law, and the Jewish People*. Philadelphia: Fortress, 1983.

———. "Puzzling Out Rabbinic Judaism." In W. S. Green, ed. *Approaches to Ancient Judaism: Essays in Religion and History*, 2.9. Chico, Calif.: Scholars, 1980, 65–79.

Sanders, J. A. "Torah and Christ." *Int* 29 (1975): 372–90.

———. "Torah and Paul." In J. Jervell and W. Meeks, eds. *God's Christ and His People: Studies in Honor of Nils Alstrup Dahl*. Oslo: Universitetsforlaget, 1977, 132–40.

Sandt, H. M. W van de. "An Explanation of Rom. 8,4a." *Bijdragen* 37 (1976): 361–78.

———. "Research into Rom 8,4a: The Legal Claim of the Law." *Bijdragen* 37 (1976): 252–69.

Schäfer, Peter. "Die Torah der messianischen Zeit." *ZNW* 65 (1974): 27–42.

Schiffman, L. H. "The Temple Scroll and the Systems of Jewish Law of the Second Temple Period." In G. J. Brooke, ed. *Temple Scroll Studies*. Sheffield: JSOT, 1989.

Schlier, Heinrich. *Der Brief an die Galater*. Göttingen: Vandenhoeck and Ruprecht, 1965.

———. *Der Römerbrief*. Freiburg: Herder, 1977.

Schmithals, Walter. *Der Römerbrief: Ein Kommentar*. Gütersloh: Gerd Mohn, 1988.

———. *Paul and the Gnostics*. Nashville: Abingdon, 1972.

Schnabel, Eckhard J. *Law and Wisdom from Ben Sira to Paul: A Tradition Historical Enquiry into the Relation of Law, Wisdom, and Ethics*. Tübingen: J. C. B. Mohr, 1985.

Schneider, Bernardin. "The Meaning of St Paul's Antithesis 'The Letter and the Spirit'." *CBQ* 15 (1953): 163–207.

Schneider, E. E. "Finis legis Christus: Röm 10, 4." *TZ* 20 (1964): 410–22.

Schoeps, Hans Joachim. *Paul: The Theology of the Apostle in the Light of Jewish Religious History*. Philadelphia: Westminster, 1959.

Schrage, W. *Die konkreten Einzelgebote in paulinischen Paränese*. Gütersloh: Gerd Mohn, 1961.

Schreiner, Thomas R. "The Abolition and Fulfillment of the Law in Paul." *JSNT* 35 (1989): 47–74.

———. "The Church as the New Israel and the Future of Ethnic Israel in Paul." *Studia Biblica et Theologica* 13 (1983): 17–38.

———. "Circumcision." In G. F. Hawthorne and Ralph P. Martin, eds. *Interpreting Paul and His Letters*. Downers Grove, Ill.: InterVarsity, forthcoming.

———. "Does Romans 9 Teach Individual Election Unto Salvation? Some Exegetical and Theological Reflections." *JETS*, forthcoming.

———. "Is Perfect Obedience to the Law Possible? A Re–examination of Galatians 3:10." *JETS* 27 (1984): 151–60.

———. "Israel's Failure to Attain Righteousness in Romans 9:30–10:3." *TrinJ* 12 (1991): 209–20.

———. "Paul and Perfect Obedience to the Law: An Evaluation of the View of E. P. Sanders." *WTJ* 47 (1985): 245–78.

————. "Paul's View of the Law in Romans 10:4–5." *WTJ*, forthcoming.

————. "'Works of Law' in Paul." *NovT* 33 (1991): 217–44.

Schrenk, G. "Δικαίωμα." *Theological Dictionary of the New Testament*, ed. Gerhard Kittel. Grand Rapids: Eerdmans, 1967, 2:178–225.

————. "Ἐντολή." *Theological Dictionary of the New Testament*, ed. Gerhard Kittel. Grand Rapids: Eerdmans, 1967, 2:544–56.

Schürmann, H. "'Das Gesetz des Christus' (Gal 6,2): Jesu Verhalten und wort als letztgültige sittliche Norm nach Paulus." In J. Gnilka, ed. *Neues Testament und Kirche. Festschrift für R. Schnackenburg.* Freiburg: Herder, 1974, 282–300.

Schweitzer, Albert. *The Mysticism of Paul the Apostle.* 1931; repr. ed., New York: Seabury, 1968.

Schweizer, E. "'Der Jude im Verborgenen . . . , dessen Lob nicht von Menschen, sondern von Gott kommt': (Zu Röm 2,28f und Mt 6,1–18)." In J. Gnilka, ed. *Neues Testament und Kirche. Festschrift für Rudolf Schnackenburg.* Freiburg: Herder, 1974, 115–24.

Scroggs, Robin. *The New Testament and Homosexuality: Contextual Background for Contemporary Debate.* Philadelphia: Fortress, 1983.

Segal, A. F. "Torah and *nomos* in Recent Scholary Discussion." *SR* 13 (1984): 19–27.

Seifrid, Mark A. "Jesus and the Law in Acts." *JSNT* 30 (1987): 39–57.

————. "Paul's Approach to the Old Testament in Romans 10:6–8." *TrinJ* 6 (1985): 3–37.

Seitz, O. F. J. "James and the Law." *SE* 2 (1964): 472–86.

Silva, Moisés. *Biblical Words and Their Meaning: An Introduction to Lexical Semantics.* Grand Rapids: Zondervan, 1983.

————. "Is the Law Against the Promises? The Significance of Galatians 3:21 for Covenant Continuity." In William S. Barker and W. R. Godfrey, eds. *Theonomy: A Reformed Critique.* Grand Rapids: Zondervan, 1990, 153–66.

————. "The Law and Christianity: Dunn's New Synthesis." WTJ 53 (1991): 339–53.

————. *Philippians.* Grand Rapids: Baker, 1992.

————. "The Place of Historical Reconstruction in New Testament Criticism." In D. A. Carson and J. D. Woodbridge, eds. *Hermeneutics, Authority, and Canon.* Grand Rapids: Zondervan, 1986, 109–33.

Slaten, A. W. "The Qualitative Use of νόμος in the Pauline Epistles." *AJT* 23 (1919): 213–18.

Sloan, Robert B. "Paul and the Law: Why the Law Cannot Save." *NovT* 33 (1991): 35–60.

Snodgrass, Klyne R. "Justification by Grace—To the Doers: An Analysis of the Place of Romans 2 in the Theology of Paul." *NTS* 32 (1986): 72–93.

————. "Matthew and the Law." In Daniel J. Lull, ed. *Society of Biblical Literature 1988 Seminar Papers.* Atlanta: Scholars, 1988, 536–54.

————. "Spheres of Influence: A Possible Solution to the Problem of Paul and the Law." *JSNT* 32 (1988): 93–113.

Söding, Thomas von. "'Die Kraft der Sünde is das Gesetz' (I Kor 15,56): Anmerkungen zum Hintergrund und zur Pointe einer gesetzeskritischen Sentenz des Apostels Paulus." *ZNW* 83 (1992): 74–84.

Souček, J. B. "Zur Exegese von Röm. 2.14ff." *Antwort: Karl Barth zum Siebzigsten Geburtstag am 10. Mai 1956.* Zollikon-Zürich: Evangelischer Verlag, 1956, 99–113.

Stanley, Christopher D. "'Under A Curse': A Fresh Reading of Galatians 3:10–14." *NTS* 36 (1990): 481–511.

Stegemann, E. W. "Die umgekehrte Tora: Zum Gesetzesverständnis des Paulus." *Judaica* 43 (1987): 4–20.

Stendahl, Krister. *Paul Among Jews and Gentiles and Other Essays.* Philadelphia: Fortress, 1976.

Stein, Robert H. *The Method and Message of Jesus' Teachings.* Philadelphia: Westminster, 1978.

Stern, Menahem. *Greek and Latin Authors on Jews and Judaism*, 2 vols. Jerusalem: Israel Academy of Sciences and Humanities, 1976, 1980.

Stockhausen, Carol K. *Moses' Veil and the Glory of the New Covenant: The Exegetical Substructure of II Cor. 3,1–4,6.* Rome: Pontifical Biblical Institute, 1989.

Stowers, Stanley K. *The Diatribe and Paul's Letter to the Romans.* Chico, Calif.: Scholars, 1981.

———. "Paul's Dialogue with a Fellow Jew in Romans 3:1–9." *CBQ* 46 (1984): 707–22.

Stuhlmacher, Peter. "The Law as a Topic of Biblical Theology." *Reconciliation, Law, and Righteousness: Essays in Biblical Theology.* Philadelphia: Fortress, 1986, 110–33.

———. *Gerechtigkeit Gottes bei Paulus*, 2d ed. Göttingen: Vandenhoeck and Ruprecht, 1966.

———. "Paul's Understanding of the Law in the Letter to the Romans." *SEÅ* 80 (1985): 87–104.

Suggs, M. J. *Wisdom, Christology, and Law in Matthew's Gospel.* Cambridge: Harvard University Press, 1970.

Synofzik, Ernest. *Die Gerichts und Vergeltungsaussagen bei Paulus: Eine traditionsgeschichtliche Untersuchung.* Göttingen: Vandenhoeck and Ruprecht, 1977.

Syreeni, K. "Matthew, Luke, and the Law: A Study in Hermeneutical Exegisis." In Timo Veijola, ed. *The Law in the Bible and its Environment.* Helsinki: The Finnish Exegetical Society, 1990, 127–55.

Thielman, Frank. "The Coherence of Paul's View of the Law: The Evidence of First Corinthians." *NTS* 38 (1992): 235–53.

———. *From Plight to Solution: A Jewish Framework for Understanding Paul's View of the Law in Galatians and Romans.* Leiden: Brill, 1989.

Thompson, J. A. *The Book of Jeremiah.* Grand Rapids: Eerdmans, 1980.

Thompson, Richard W. "How is the Law Fulfilled in Us? An Interpretation of Rom. 8:4." *LS* 11 (1986): 31–40.

———. "The Inclusion of the Gentiles in Rom 3,27–30." *Bib* 69 (1988): 543–46.

———. "Paul's Double Critique of Jewish Boasting: A Study of Rom 3:27 in its Context." *Bib* 67 (1986): 520–31.

Tomson, P. J. *Paul and the Jewish Law: Halakha in the Letters of the Apostle to the Gentiles.* Minneapolis: Fortress, 1990.

Turner, Max M. B. "The Sabbath, Sunday, and the Law in Luke/Acts." In D. A. Carson, ed. *From Sabbath to Lord's Day: A Biblical, Historical, and Theological Investigation.* Zondervan, 1982, 100–57.

Tyson, J. B. "'Works of Law' in Galatians." *JBL* 92 (1973): 423–31.

Vielhauer, Philip. "On the 'Paulinism' of Acts." In Leander E. Keck and J. L. Martyn, eds. *Studies in Luke-Acts.* Philadelphia: Fortress, 1980, 33–50.

Volf, Judy Gundry. *Paul and Perseverance: Staying in and Falling Away*. Tübingen: J. C. B. Mohr, 1990.

Vollenweider, S. "Zeit und Gesetz: Erwägungen zur Bedeutung apokalyptischer Denkformen bei Paulus." *TZ* 44 (1988): 97–116.

Walker, Rolf. "Die Heiden und das Gericht: Zur Auslegung von Römer 2, 12–16." *EvT* 20 (1960): 302–14.

Wallace Daniel B. "Galatians 3:19–20: A *Crux Interpretum* for Paul's View of the Law." *WJT* 52 (1990): 225–45.

Wallis, G. "Torah und Nomos: Zur Frage nach Gesetz und Heil." *TLZ* 105 (1980): 321–32.

Walvoord, John F. "Law in the Epistle to the Romans." *BSac* 93 (1937): 15–30.

Watson, Francis. Paul, *Judaism and the Gentiles: A Sociological Approach*. Cambridge: Cambridge University Press, 1986.

Watson, Nigel M. "Justified by Faith: Judged by Works—an Antimony?" *NTS* 29 (1983): 202–21.

Wedderburn, A. J. M. "Paul and the Law." *SJT* 38 (1985): 613–22.

———. *The Reasons for Romans*. Edinburgh: T. and T. Clark, 1988.

Weder, Hans. "Einsicht in Gesetzlichkeit: Paulus als verständnisvoller Ausleger des menschlichen Lebens." *Judaica* 43 (1987): 21–29.

———. "Gesetz und Sünde Gedanken zu einem Qualitativen Sprung im Denken des Paulus." *NTS* 31 (1985): 357–76.

Weima, Jeffrey A. D. "The Function of the Law in Relation to Sin: An Evaluation of the View of H. Räisänen." *NovT* 32 (1990): 219–35.

Weinfeld, M. "Jeremiah and the Spiritual Metamorphosis of Israel." *ZAW* 88 (1976): 15–56.

Wenham, David. "Jesus and the Law: An Exegesis on Matthew 5:17–20." *Themelios* 4 (1979): 92–96.

Westerholm, Stephen. *Israel's Law and the Church's Faith: Paul and His Recent Interpreters*. Grand Rapids: Eerdmans, 1988.

———. "Law and Christian Ethics." In Peter Richardson and Stephen Westerholm, eds. *Law in Religious Communities in the Roman Period*. Waterloo, Iowa: Wilfrid Laurier University Press, 1991, 75–91.

———. "Law, Grace and the 'Soteriology' of Judaism." In Peter Richardson and Stephen Westerholm, eds. *Law in Religious Communities in the Roman Period*. Waterloo, Iowa: Wilfrid Laurier University Press, 1991, 57–74.

———. "Letter and Spirit: The Foundation of Pauline Ethics." *NTS* 30 (1984): 229–48.

———. "On Fulfilling the Whole Law (Gal. 5:14)." *SEÅ* 51–52 (1986–87): 229–37.

———. "The Law and the 'Just Man' (1 Tim 1,3–11)." *ST* 36 (1982): 79–95.

———. "*Torah, nomos*, and Law: A Question of 'meaning.'" *SR* 15 (1986): 327–36.

———. "Whence 'The Torah' of Second Temple Judaism." In Peter Richardson and Stephen Westerholm, eds. *Law in Religious Communities in the Roman Period*. Waterloo: Wilfrid Laurier University Press, 1991, 19–43.

Wilckens, Ulrich. *Der Brief an die Römer*, 3 vols. Neukirchen: Neukirchener Verlag, 1978, 1980, 1982.

———. "Was heisst Paulus: 'Aus Werken des Gesetzes wird kein Mensch gerecht'?" *Rechtfertigung als Freiheit: Paulusstudien*. Neukirchen: Neukirchener Verlag, 1974, 77–109.

———. "Zur Entwicklung des paulinischen Gesetzesverständnisses." *NTS* 28 (1982): 154–90.

Williams, Sam K. "Justification and the Spirit in Galatians." *JSNT* 29 (1987): 91–100.

———. "The 'Righteousness of God' in Romans." *JBL* 99 (1980): 241–290.

Wilson, R. McLaren. "*Nomos*: The Biblical Significance of Law." *SJT* 5 (1952): 36–48.

Wilson, S. G. *Luke and the Law*. Cambridge: Cambridge University Press, 1983.

Winger, Michael. *By What Law? The Meaning of* Νόμος *in the Letters of Paul*. Atlanta: Scholars, 1992.

Wischmeyer, O. "Das Gebot der Nächstenliebe bei Paulus: Eine traditionsgeschictliche Untersuchung." *BZ* 30 (1986): 161–87.

Wrede, William. *Paulus*, 2d ed. Tübingen: J. C. B. Mohr, 1907.

Wright, Christopher J. H. "The Ethical Authority of the Old Testament: A Survey of Approaches. Part I." *TynBul* 43 (1992): 101–20.

———. "The Ethical Authority of the Old Testament: A Survey of Approaches. Part II." *TynBul* 43 (1992): 203–31.

Wright, D. F. "The Ethical Use of the Old Testament in Luther and Calvin: A Comparison." *SJT* 36 (1983): 463–85.

Wright, N. Thomas. *Christian Origins and the People of God*. Vol. 1: *The New Testament and the People of God*. Minneapolis: Fortress, 1992.

———. *The Climax of the Covenant: Christ and the Law in Pauline Theology*. Minneapolis: Fortress, 1991.

———. *The Epistles of Paul to the Colossians and to Philemon*. Grand Rapids: Eerdmans, 1986.

———. "The Paul of History and the Apostle of Faith." *TynB* 29 (1978): 61–88.

———. "Putting Paul Together Again: Towards a Synthesis of Pauline Theology." In J. M. Bassler, ed. *Pauline Theology*. Vol. 1. Philadelphia: Fortress, 1991, 183–211.

———. "Romans and the Theology of Paul." In E. H. Lovering, Jr., ed. *The Society of Biblical Literature 1992 Seminar Papers*. Atlanta: Scholar's, 1992, 184–213.

Yates, J. C. "The Judgment of the Heathen: The Interpretation of Article XVIII and Romans 2:12–16." *Churchman* 100 (1986): 220–30.

Yates, R. "Saint Paul and the Law in Galatians." *ITQ* 51 (1985): 105–24.

Young, Norman H. "Paidagogos: The Social Setting of a Pauline Metaphor." *NovT* 29 (1987): 150–76.

Zeller, Dieter. "Zur neueren Diskussion über das Gesetz bei Paulus." *TP* 62 (1987): 481–99.

———. "Der Zusammenhang von Gesetz und Sünde im Römerbrief: Kritischer Nachvollzug der Auslegung von Ulrich Wilckens." *TZ* 38 (1982): 193–212.

Ziesler, J. A. "The Just Requirement of the Law (Romans 8.4)." *AusBR* 35 (1987): 77–82.

———. *Paul's Letter to the Romans*. Philadelphia: Trinity Press International, 1989.

———. "The Role of the Tenth Commandment in Romans 7." *JSNT* 33 (1988): 41–56.

Ancient Writings Index

Author Index

Subject Index

Aaron, 216
Aaronic priesthood, 164, 214–16, 240
Ability to keep law. *See* Inability, human.
Abolition of law, 18, 26–27, 30, 31, 82,
    123–43, 145, 156, 160–61, 162, 164,
    169, 214–40, 243–44, 250
Abraham, 24–25, 96–97, 98, 101, 117, 160,
    165, 173, 188n, 206, 242
Abrahamic covenant, 30, 39, 45, 57, 62, 79,
    124–29, 140, 142, 145, 161, 165, 171,
    178, 197, 249
Accountability before God, 23, 65–66, 70
Acts, 225–31
Adam, 70n, 85, 89–90, 248–49, 250–51
Adiaphora, 148, 158
Adultery, 55, 68, 141, 143, 147, 149, 153,
    154, 167, 171, 175, 180, 181, 186, 213,
    217, 218, 219, 233, 236, 237, 244
Against Apion (Josephus), 156n
Angels, 22, 71, 214
Anger, 53, 208, 213, 236
Animals, care for, 176
"Another" law, 152
Anthropology, Pauline, 29, 70n, 74
Anti-Semitism, 25, 120–21, 243
Antichrist, spirit of, 220
Apocalypse of Abraham, 156n
Assyria, 48
Atonement, 15, 44–71, 73, 95, 107, 113,
    145, 151–52, 161, 162, 164, 168–69,
    198, 215–16, 226–27, 228, 242, 244,
    248, 250, 251
Augustine. *See* Reformation consensus.
Authority. of Christ, 222–23; of law, 23,
    215, 244–45
Authorship, 14n, 52n, 86n, 208n, 217n

Babylonian conquest, 48
Baptism, 24, 139–40, 168, 169
Beast of the Revelation, 207–8
Belief. *See* Faith.
Believe, term, 208–9
Blameless, term, 70
Blasphemy, 53
Blessings, covenant. *See* Covenant.
Blindness of sin, 220
Boasting, 64–65, 95–98, 100, 112–14, 118,
    120, 164, 165, 212
Bondage to law/sin, 23, 25, 64n, 76, 77–81,
    85, 90, 94, 123n, 124, 127–28, 166,
    172–73, 227–28
Bread of life, 208
Bridle, law as, 78
Brother love, 220
Bultmann school, 16–17, 42, 60, 120, 244

Calvin, John. 17, 28, 29, 50; *See also* Refor-
    mation consensus.
Causative function of law, 65
Centurion, faith of, 209
Ceremonial law, 15, 18, 40, 140, 141, 142,
    216–17
Christ. *See* Jesus Christ.
Christian reconstruction. *See* Theonomy.
Christian. ethics, 16, 27, 29; law and,
    145–73, 174, 214–40; observance of
    Sabbath, 169–71; weaker brother and,
    183
Christian Reconstruction. *See* Theonomy.
Church. as "true" circumcision, 163–68,
    178, 197–201; early, 70, 222, 225, 231;
    law and, 148, 160, 168–72, 173, 175–78,

152, 172, 241, 242; systematic theology
and, 29–31; term, 33–40, 75, 218, 241;
"under," 77–81, 188; validity of,
145–73, 214–40; whole, 51n, 64n, 65,
73, 153, 159, 168, 179, 217, 218,
154–55, 242; works of, 94, 96, 104–12,
179–204, 241, 242; written on hearts,
194–95, 216, 219, 244, 245. See also
Legalism; Moral Law; Mosaic Cove-
nant/law; *Nomos*; Obedience to law.
Lawlessness, 208, 220
Lawsuits, 186
Legalism. 15, 18, 20, 21–23, 24–25, 27, 28,
30, 40, 43, 51, 58, 59, 86, 93–121, 130,
134–36, 138–41, 188, 210–14, 240, 241,
242, 243, 247, 250
Letter-spirit, contrast, 81n, 82, 164
Lex talionis, 237–38, 244
Liberation. from Egypt, 93n, 131; from law,
28, 137, 158n, 172, 173, 174, 225n,
229–30, 240, 245; from sin, 77, 79, 80,
124, 151–52; from world, 17; through
Holy Spirit, 131
Libertinism, 27, 138, 158n
Liberty, law of , 216
Life, eternal, 185; in the Spirit, 151–52,
158, 159; new, 36; source of, 60–61,
109, 124, 130, 127, 209, 216n, 250
Light, 220
Literature, Jewish. See Judaism.
Logos, 220, 221
Lord's Supper, 24, 162–63
Love. brother, 220; enemy, 213, 239; failure
to, 66–67; fulfillment of law, 145–49,
156, 159; Holy Spirit and, 149; law of,
145–57, 159, 218, 219–20, 232–34,
245–46; neighbor, 137, 145–49, 171,
213–14, 217, 218, 219, 232–34, 238,
239; obedience and, 147–49; toward
God, 25, 131, 154, 221, 232–34, 238;
toward Jesus, 220
Luke, Gospel of, 208, 209–10, 211, 213–14,
224–32, 240
Lust, 208, 213, 236
Luther, Martin, 17, 27–28, 50, 118, 119,
120. *See also* Reformation consensus.
Lying, 53, 175, 213

Maccabees, books of, 156n
Malice, 53
Mammon, love for, 213, 214, 233

Manager. *See* Pedagogue.
Marcion, 243–44
Mark, Gospel of, 213, 223–24, 232, 239, 240
Marriage of near kin, 230–31
Masoretic text, 45
Matthew, Gospel of, 208, 209–10, 212–13,
231–40, 232, 239, 240
Meat offered to idols, 148
Mediator, covenant, 127
Melchizedek, priesthood of, 214
Mercy of God, 88, 108–9, 209, 221, 238
Merit. *See* Legalism; Righteousness.
Messiah. law and, 145, 157, 160, 161, 164;
Jesus as, 24, 26, 63, 220, 221
Metaphorical use of *law*, 35–36
Ministry. of condemnation, 129, 130, 188;
of death, 82–83, 129, 130, 188; of Spirit,
82–83
Miracles, 208
Mishnah, 19, 115–17
Model. *See* Type.
Monergistic soteriology, 29
Moral law. Christian and, 16, 18, 21, 27–29,
30–31, 171–78, 179, 216, 217–18; fulfillment of law and, 245; love and,
146–57, 159, 232–34, 238, 240; Mosaic
law and, 36, 40, 51–56, 58–59, 143,
166–67, 224; Sin and, 74, 143, 146–57,
159, 166–67, 171, 172, 175, 176, 177,
178, 179, 194, 208n, 216, 217–18, 224,
230, 233–34, 238, 240, 245. *See also*
Reduction of law.
Mosaic covenant/law. 93n, 96n; abolition
of, 18, 20, 26–27, 28, 30, 31, 43–46, 60,
64, 82, 93–121, 103, 123–43, 145, 150,
156, 160–78, 213–16, 219, 222, 223n,
224, 230, 237–38, 243–44, 250; ceremonial, 15, 18, 40, 53n, 140, 141, 142, 156,
175, 216–17; continuing norms of,
141–43, 145, 147–48, 149–57, 167, 174,
219–40; curse of, 25, 29, 41, 42, 43,
44–45, 46, 47–51, 57–64, 76, 77, 95,
130, 131, 161–62, 168, 190, 191, 242,
247–48; double character of, 247, 248;
Gentiles and, 21, 23, 24–26, 44, 45–46,
51, 56, 57, 62, 64–65, 102–3, 106, 124,
125–26, 139–40, 142, 171, 173, 183,
197, 228–31, 241–42; glory of, 130, 132,
215, 222; Israel in, 19–20, 25, 43–44, 51,
78, 102, 105, 108–9, 112, 113, 117, 126,
142, 165, 173, 175, 178, 190, 194–95,